The Village Baker's Wife

The Village Baker's Wife

THE DESSERTS AND PASTRIES
THAT MADE GAYLE'S FAMOUS

Gayle and Joe Ortiz
with Louisa Beers

TEN SPEED PRESS
BERKELEY, CALIFORNIA

Ten Speed Press
Box 7123
Berkeley, California 94707

Distributed in Australia by E. J. Dwyer Pty. Ltd., in Canada by Publishers Group West, in New Zealand by Tandem Press, in South Africa by Real Books, in Singapore and Malaysia by Berkeley Books, and in the United Kingdom and Europe by Airlift Books.

Cover and text design by Nancy Austin.
Photography by Jonathan Chester, Extreme Images, Berkeley, California.
Illustrations by Ann Miya, Santa Cruz, California.
Gayle's postage stamps designed by Joe Ortiz.

Adaptation of Candied Orange Peel on page 111, Cobbler Crust on page 269, and Clay's Puff Pastry on page 85 from *Chez Panisse Desserts*, by Lindsey Remolif Shere. Copyright © 1985 by Lindsey Remolif Shere. Reprinted with permission of Random House, Inc. and Lescher & Lescher, Ltd. Adaptation of Mission Fig Crostata on page 272, from *Cucina Simpatica* by Johanne Killeen and George Germon. Copyright © 1991 by Johanne Killeen and George Germon. Reprinted by permission of HarperCollins Publishers, Inc. Adaptation of Chocolate Macaroons on page 139, from *Maida Heatter's Book of Great Chocolate Desserts*, by Maida Heatter. Copyright © 1995. Reprinted with permission. Adaptation of Cindy Mushet's Chocolate Pot de Creme on page 274, which appeared in the *Baking with the American Harvest* newsletter, reprinted with permission. Profile of Pierre Hermé on page 279 excerpted from an article originally published in *Food & Wine* in November 1995.

Library of Congress Cataloging-in-Publication Data

Ortiz, Gayle.
    Village baker's wife : the desserts and pastries that made Gayle's famous / Gayle Ortiz and Joe Ortiz, with Louisa Beers.
        p.   cm.
    Includes index.
    ISBN 0-89815-869-9 (alk. paper)
    1. Desserts.   I. Ortiz, Joe, 1946-   .   II. Beers, Louisa.
III. Gayle's (Bakery)   IV. Title.
TX773.078   1997
641.8'6--dc21   96-40240
                                                                        CIP

Printed in the United States
First printing, 1997

1 2 3 4 5 6 7 8 9 10 — 01 00 99 98 97

This book is dedicated to the memory of my mom, Fern Tomlinson,
who taught me that creativity is as easy as apple pie.
And to my father, Jack Tomlinson, whom we have to thank for
the bakery's success. We wouldn't have gotten so far without his help.
He's always there for us.

CONTENTS

Acknowledgments

BAKERS: Linda Younger, Dan Zimmer, Marcos Chavez, Christopher Love, Chris Rominger, Sergio Sumano, and Steve Powell.

PAST BAKERS: Kelly Porter, Bonny Berry, Judith Swift, Kat Peters, Robyn Johnson, Debra Lynn, and all others whose imprint on Gayle's is indelible.

BAKER FRIENDS: Lindsey Shere, for giving me my first chance to bake professionally; Johanne Killeen, Hildy Marshall, Alice Medrich, David Morris, Tom King, Flo Braker, Norman Love, Jean-Claude and Pierrette Poilpre, the late Cornelus Van Peski, Nick Malgieri, and Marion Cunningham, for their relentless inspiration and help.

FRIENDS AND FAMILY: Our publisher Kirsty Melville and editor Lorena Jones, who know how to make bakers sound like writers; agent Martha Casselman; Louisa's husband, Brian Beers, head of dough production, who helped prepare the manuscript; designer Nancy Austin; photographer Jonathan Chester; artist Ann Miya, for her patience and ability to draw our hands in action; my sister, Joellen Alward; Goldie Hirsch and Robert and Gretchen Beers; helpers from the start, Jay Leite and Gretchen Collins; Christie Carlson, for her constant creative inspiration; purchaser and assistant Lisa Hindley, for technical help; Gayle's staff, past and present, for making it happen on a daily basis (without you, Gayle's would not be the place it is); and Charles Shere. Special thanks also to all of our wonderful customers, who have been with us since the beginning.

RECIPE TESTERS: Jodi Alward, Roxanne Areias, Sybil Breitwieser, Kristin Brookins, Joan Carl, Barbara Castro, Jonathan Collins, Tracey Comin, Mary Cowley, Betty Deodiuc, Nancy Edgerly, Kathy Getty, Diana Giacomaro, Cathy Holdaway, Audrey Hull, Margaret Lietz, Laurie E. Liss, Sue Lundquist, Kate Hartzell, Kerry Hosley, Carol Jaques, Pat Lamson, Debra Lynn, Carol Marini, Pat McClellan, Ann Miya, Sue Porter, Judy Primavera, Barbara Rider, Kelly Roberts, Jean Shanahan, Carol Sida, Robin Sirakides, Allen Smith, Jim Spaulding, Melinda Tao (special thanks), Vi Thall, Shannon Tullius, Sara Van Artsdalen (thanks so much for testing more than your fair share of recipes, especially the hardest ones), Tamara Walters, Lucille Ward, Ann Wasserman, Rachel Wedeen, Margot Wells, and Marge Zott.

Introduction

This book is an entire pastry shop between two covers. It contains over 150 recipes from the cases of Gayle's, our bustling bakery in the seaside town of Capitola, which is about ninety miles south of San Francisco on the California coast. *The Village Baker's Wife* also tells the story of the bakery and of the baking life, including how we got started, how we do what we do, and why it's so important to us. We hope that our recipes and stories will inspire and help you bake for your family and friends the way Gayle's bakers bake for our community—in the spirit of generations of village bakers.

When my husband Joe first suggested we call this book *The Village Baker's Wife,* I was appalled. After all, I was the first baker in the family, even though Joe has been a bread baker for fifteen years and wrote *The Village Baker.* But I came to see the humor in the title and decided it was the perfect name for the sequel to Joe's book and a tribute to the wonderful Marcel Pagnol movie, *La Femme du Boulanger.* So please don't take our title too seriously—it's just a playful nod to the times when a village baker's wife brought a smile to her customers' faces.

Because Joe was the one who encouraged (okay, needled) me to write this book, I've asked him to tell our story. I hope you will enjoy the book and that it will inspire you to bake more at home.

Back in 1976, Gayle decided she wanted to open a bakery. It took years of research and study and many people had their doubts at the beginning, but Gayle's continues to thrive and is still growing nearly twenty years later. Since the bakery's modest birth on Valentine's Day in 1978, Gayle's has grown from an 800-square-foot shop to a 10,000-square-foot food emporium. In that time, Gayle's has served over 25 million cakes, pastries, and desserts to over 5 million adoring customers. Each month we transform raw ingredients into 20,000 Danish pastries, 15,000 assorted croissant goodies, 6,500 muffins, and 22,000 cookies, to mention just a few. In a month's time we use 2.5 tons of butter, 32,000 eggs, 32,500 pounds of flour, and 990 pounds of chocolate. Our accountant, Jay Leite, calls it an inventory mill. We still call it a village bakery.

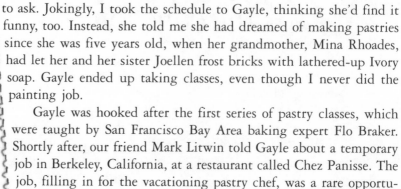

The Gayle's bakery story actually began in 1976 when I was a housepainter and did an estimate for Jack Lirio's cooking school in San Francisco. When I delivered the bid, Jack handed me a schedule of classes and proposed that we do a trade. I shook my head in disbelief, thinking it a little bold of him even to ask. Jokingly, I took the schedule to Gayle, thinking she'd find it funny, too. Instead, she told me she had dreamed of making pastries since she was five years old, when her grandmother, Mina Rhoades, had let her and her sister Joellen frost bricks with lathered-up Ivory soap. Gayle ended up taking classes, even though I never did the painting job.

Gayle was hooked after the first series of pastry classes, which were taught by San Francisco Bay Area baking expert Flo Braker. Shortly after, our friend Mark Litwin told Gayle about a temporary job in Berkeley, California, at a restaurant called Chez Panisse. The job, filling in for the vacationing pastry chef, was a rare opportunity for a novice baker, but the folks at Chez Panisse knew that it would be easier to instill a unique approach in a green baker with lots of energy than it would to teach an experienced baker a new way of looking at desserts.

After an inspiring two-month apprenticeship at the restaurant, Gayle spent the next several years visiting Bay Area restaurants and bakeries with determination in her eyes and a notebook in hand. She recorded every piece of information she could gather about all aspects of baking. She cajoled the bakers she met into giving her recipes, equipment suggestions, and the names of food purveyors. She met a lot of nice people along the way, including David Morris of the Bread Garden, Hildegard Marshall of Fat Albert's, Tom King of Cabrillo College, and Alice Medrich of Cocolat. She visited two of our favorite San Francisco bakeries—Just Desserts and Tassajara Bakery—just to soak up the ambience. Everywhere she went she gathered inspiration as well as information. While at Chez Panisse, she met Lily Lecocq, a lunch chef. When Lily opened a bakery, she asked Gayle to help. Gayle worked at La Farine for several months, which helped her realize she really wanted to run her own bakery.

Finally, in 1978, Gayle found the location she had been looking for, a former real estate office in Capitola. (Years later, local realtors would use the sales pitch "within walking distance of Gayle's" in their advertisements for property listings.) It took us one month to remodel the new bakery, which was to be called Gayle's Fine Pastries and Bread. We made lists and lists of possible names, from Croissant Lady to Village Bakery to CroisSantaCruz. Eventually, "Gayle's" stuck.

Our practice run was the day before Valentine's Day, and we brought in close to fifty dollars. We had only one employee, our friend Gretchen Friewald, for the first few months. The first products we made were challah, baguettes (just twenty-four of them), beer rye, croissants, chocolatines, a cake or two, and lemon tarts. (The third day, when no one bought lemon tarts and we had a case of lemons to get rid of, we thumbed through a few books and found a recipe for lemon bread. We've been making our own version ever since.) Today we make over 200 different baked goods each day.

The early years were busy for both of us. I was still painting houses as well as baking. Gayle and I would arrive at the bakery at 2 A.M. and work all morning. At 10 A.M., my painting partner would pick me up and I would go off to my painting job. Gayle would stay at the bakery doing prep for the next day and some sales work, talking to customers, and paying bills. When I got back to the bakery at 5 or 6 P.M., we'd both clean up. We would go home sometime around 7 P.M., have a light dinner, and fall into bed. The next morning at 2 A.M. we'd start all over again.

Two years after the bakery opened, Gayle and I started making trips to Europe to see how the bakers there do their jobs. It was inspiring to see bread and pastries made and enjoyed the European way. Back then, Europeans were definitely more passionate about their food than most Americans; it was an elemental part of their lives. We went to Europe every year after that to stock up on rest, a few good meals, and more inspiration.

All the European bakers we met shared their insights into how the methods, work schedules, and techniques they used were as important as the ingredients. We learned not to waste anything, to appreciate the integrity and ecology of baking. We saw how valuable it was for customers to be able to talk with their bakers (if they were still awake) and find out what ingredients went into each baked good. We learned that baking is not only a craft performed from day to day, but that it is also an art. The beauty of the products themselves and the tastefulness of the displays in bakeries, open-air markets, butcher shops, and charcuteries all became inspiration we carried back to Capitola.

The European experience also reaffirmed what Gayle knew all along and I eventually figured out: that a village bakery is an integral part of a community. At Gayle's we know many of our customers by name because we see them daily, and sometimes even more often. In today's rushed, impersonal world, we have the uncommon pleasure of providing a place—our village bakery—that draws the community together to sip coffee and nibble fresh-baked goodies or to exchange greetings and news as they meet in front of the case. One of the other ways Gayle's participates in the community is by using recycled paper products whenever possible and maintaining an ambitious recycling campaign. It helps us do our part to conserve in an industry that uses a lot of packaging.

People often ask us to open a bakery in their community. It's the nicest compliment we could get and tells us we must be doing our jobs so well that the whole business looks easy enough to replicate. But, of course, running the bakery does take a lot of effort: in addition to our general manager and partner, Louisa, who oversees every detail of the business, there's a bookkeeper, a purchaser, an office manager, three sales managers, thirteen dishwashers, four department heads, fourteen bakers, three drivers, four floor supervisors, eleven cooks, and forty-one sales people—an ever-fluctuating staff of nearly one hundred people working together to make the finest baked goods possible. With this in mind, we hope you'll understand why you won't see a Gayle's in your neighborhood anytime soon. We simply have too much to learn and do right here in Capitola. However, we hope you'll visit us and, when you can't drop in to pick up fresh-baked goodies, that you'll turn to the following pages and try baking our recipes at home.

PART ONE

Before You Start Baking

We know it's tempting to roll up your sleeves and get right to the recipes, but we recommend you hold off just long enough to read the following chapters on baking ingredients, equipment, and basic techniques. Each of these chapters contains core information you need to know to make the recipes successfully. Whether you're an experienced baker or a beginner, reading up on the basics will spare you the embarrassment I suffered when I began baking. I remember one time in particular, when I was making one of my first batches of croissants. I didn't know it then, but I didn't have the dough and butter at the proper temperature and I hadn't done the roll-in correctly. These two seemingly little mistakes caused most of the butter to melt out of the dough while it was in the oven, sending smoke billowing out our windows. It was not a scene to inspire confidence in an aspiring village baker.

If you read the following chapters carefully and refer to them whenever your skills get a little rusty, you'll find that baking is a piece of cake...so to speak!

About Ingredients

All good baking starts with good ingredients—the best you can find. In 1976, when I was first researching the techniques, recipes, and equipment for Gayle's, the concept of using the best ingredients was almost a novelty. While restaurants back then were already starting to experiment with fresh, regional, and seasonal ingredients, most bakeries were still stuck in the 1950s mode of using inexpensive, labor-saving ingredients such as margarine, shortening, frozen eggs, and processed jellies and jams. Donuts ruled. Cakes and breads were made from mixes. The prevailing belief was that bakery customers didn't know or care whether a baked good had subtle flavor nuances as long as it was sweet and affordable.

It's true that several San Francisco bakeries, notably Just Desserts and Tassajara, two of our first role models, were already using first-rate ingredients in the early 1970s. My hope was that Santa Cruz, an area with a reputation for loving natural foods, would be an ideal place to make and sell pastries using fresh, real ingredients. As it turned out, I only got resistance from suppliers who said we couldn't afford to use real butter or real eggs because our customers wouldn't pay the higher price for baked goods made with quality ingredients. But time proved them wrong. We persisted, and now using good ingredients is an accepted practice in bakeries throughout the United States.

Home bakers, too, should use only the best-quality ingredients. Why go to the trouble of baking for family or friends unless your desserts and pastries are going to taste as good as possible? You don't have to use exotic or overly expensive ingredients to make good cakes and pastries; most of the recipes in the book call for easily obtainable ingredients. Like every village baker, you should be able to find exceptional, affordable ingredients right in your own backyard. You don't have to seek out vanilla from Madagascar or rose water from Ceylon to give your desserts an exotic flair. Simple, pure ingredients are now sold in regular supermarkets throughout the country and, if they don't have what you need, grocers will usually special order items for you. We also recommend exploring health food stores, local farmers' markets, and roadside produce stands, where you'll find some of the freshest, most wholesome ingredients available.

For the occasional special ingredient, we've included a list of some of our favorite suppliers in the back of the book (see page 317). But remember, at Gayle's we've selected ingredients by trying them and seeing how they taste in the finished products. There's no mystery to the process. Just use the ingredients that make your baked goods turn out the way you like them. Many times, it's just a matter of personal taste.

Here's a list of the essential ingredients we use and a few words about what we mean when we call for them in the recipes:

Baking Soda and Baking Powder

Both are used as leavening agents. Baking soda works when combined with an acidic ingredient like buttermilk. Baking powder leavens from a reaction between acid and alkali. It is critical that these two ingredients be very fresh. After one year, throw them away and replace with new ones.

Butter

We use two kinds of butter in this book: salted and unsalted or "sweet" butter. Many bakers will tell you that the only butter to use is unsalted. We know that most home bakers don't keep unsalted butter on hand, so when we call for butter, we are referring to salted butter. However, you may substitute unsalted butter in any recipe, if you prefer. Just add a pinch or two of salt more than the recipe calls for. Some recipes, such as some of the cake recipes, require unsalted butter because its sweetness is essential to achieving the right flavor. Few of the imported European butters are worth the price. We suggest finding a locally made, quality butter that you like. Sweet butter can be tightly wrapped and stored in the freezer for up to 1 month.

Pay close attention to the temperature of the butter called for in the recipes. This will help you make the best pastry possible. Using soft butter, for example, helps achieve a smooth texture when creamed with sugar; using cold butter gives pastries such as pie dough their flakiness.

Chocolate

For the purposes of this book, semisweet and bittersweet chocolate are interchangeable. Some will say that this is a travesty, but we believe that most of us have an opinion about the type of chocolate we like. Some like their chocolate very bitter, and for them, bittersweet is the best. For others, semisweet is the perfect balance between bitter and sweet. The only caution we give is to buy the best chocolate you can find. We like Ghirardelli, Guittard, and Lindt. Never use chocolate candy bars for baking.

Unsweetened or bitter chocolate has a lot of flavor but no sugar. We use it to add depth of flavor to a few of the recipes that already have enough sugar to compensate for its bitterness.

Chocolate chips can only be used when they are specifically called for and cannot be substituted for other types of chocolate. Chocolate chips contain more fat (to help them keep their shape when baked) and, as a result, are not good for most other uses.

Unsweetened cocoa powder is used when the addition of solid chocolate would not work in a pastry. However, we find that cocoa powder does not give the best chocolate flavor when it is the only type used in a pastry, so we combine it with a little semisweet chocolate to achieve a more complex chocolate flavor.

Eggs

We use grade AA large eggs in this book. Eggs should always be used at room temperature. For more about this, see "Bringing Ingredients to the Ideal Temperature," page 19.

Flour

You'll need five types of flour for the recipes in this book: bread flour, cake flour, pastry flour, unbleached all-purpose flour, and whole-wheat flour. Each is made from hard wheat, soft wheat, or a blend of both and produces a different texture.

BREAD FLOUR

Bread flour, usually made from hard winter wheat, is a strong flour with about 12 percent gluten. It is used to give breads good loft and a crumb of consistent texture.

CAKE FLOUR

Cake flour is milled into finer particles than all-purpose flour. We have used Softasilk brand cake flour for this book because it is most readily available. It is bleached.

PASTRY FLOUR

Sometimes it is necessary to use a flour that has a little less gluten than unbleached all-purpose flour. When we want to make a more tender pastry, we use pastry flour, which has 8 to 9 percent gluten. However, pastry flour has a higher protein content than cake flour, which results in more elastic doughs, like pie and tart doughs. In this book, we have used pastry flour in several cakes. It is available in health food stores, specialty food markets, and through the mail from baking supply catalogs (see page 317).

UNBLEACHED ALL-PURPOSE FLOUR

This flour contains about 10 percent gluten and is available in most supermarkets. We use it almost exclusively in the recipes in this book.

WHOLE-WHEAT FLOUR

This flour is not milled as finely as white flour, nor is it sifted as much during milling. It therefore contains much of the bran and wheat germ, making it darker, slightly coarser, and a little more nutritious than white flour.

Milk

Except for one of our croissant doughs and a few other items, we use only whole milk at Gayle's. In this book, we use whole milk exclusively. You may substitute lowfat milk for the whole milk in any of the recipes, but the results will not be as rich. We use milk powder when we want the flavor of milk but don't need all the moisture of whole milk.

Nuts

Make sure you always use fresh nuts. A rancid nut is the worst thing that can happen to a pastry. Be sure to buy your nuts from a reliable vendor with a high turnover and use only unsalted raw nuts. Store nuts in the freezer in an airtight container for up to 3 months. Many recipes call for toasted nuts (see page 23 for instructions) because they have a better flavor.

Pure Vanilla Extract

Always use the best vanilla you can find. Experiment by going to gourmet shops and trying different kinds. We like Nielsen-Massey vanillas (available from King Arthur Flour, see page 317 for ordering information). Their Mexican vanilla is very different and good. Try it sometime in custards.

Sweeteners

Sweeteners come in various forms, all of which are useful for different types of recipes and cannot be substituted for one another. When we call for "sugar" in the recipes, we are referring to granulated sugar unless otherwise specified.

BROWN SUGAR

Always pack brown sugar firmly into the measuring cup or spoon. Whether you use light or dark brown sugar is strictly a matter of taste. Dark brown sugar is drier and less sweet than light brown sugar. Experiment to see if you like the slightly stronger flavor of dark brown sugar.

CONFECTIONERS' SUGAR

Unless specifically instructed, do not sift confectioners' sugar. For more about measuring confectioners' sugar properly, see "Measuring Dry Ingredients," page 21. For home baking, we recommend using a good brand like C & H.

CORN SYRUP

We recommend light corn syrup for these recipes. Before measuring corn syrup, lightly butter the liquid measuring cup so the syrup will pour out easily.

GRANULATED SUGAR

Granulated sugar is made from sugarcane and is a complex sugar, which means it contains fructose and glucose. Buy a good brand like C & H; there is a difference.

HONEY

Honey lends a specific flavor and baking quality to pastries. Use it only when called for in a recipe. Do not substitue honey for other sweetners as it may change the texture of baked goods.

MOLASSES

Whether you use light or dark molasses depends on your preferences. Experiment to see if you like the stronger flavor of dark molasses. As with corn syrup, lightly butter the liquid measuring cup before measuring molasses.

Whipping Cream

Always use whipping cream that is very cold. Try to find a whipping cream that is not labeled "ultra-pasteurized," which means it has been boiled and contains preservatives to extend its shelf life. The only recipe for which we recommend using ultra-pasteurized whipping cream is Chocolate Ganache (page 262). (It makes a smoother ganache with fewer air bubbles than the non-pasteurized variety.) Look for the words "heavy whipping cream" or "whipping cream" on the carton. Searching out a good whipping cream in a gourmet market is worth the effort—you'll taste the difference.

Yeast

For easy handling, we use active dry yeast. Don't substitute quick-acting yeast. We indicate the amount of yeast by packages. Each package weighs .25 ounce. Pay close attention to the expiration date and keep the packages tightly closed after opening.

Essential Equipment

You don't need a lot of fancy equipment to bake wonderful desserts and pastries in a home kitchen. Although we've purchased and tested hundreds of items, from old standbys to the newest gadgets, we wouldn't be without the following equipment. It is by no means a complete list of the equipment available; it's simply an inventory of our most-used baking tools.

Bowls

We like to use stainless-steel bowls because they are unbreakable and lightweight. You can heat or freeze foods in them and they take up very little storage room because they nest inside each other.

Cooling Racks

These are used for cooling all sorts of baked goods. Buy sturdy racks that are welded well; the cheap variety wears out quickly. We recommend owning three or four large (17 x 11-inch) ones, so you've always got room to cool items at the optimum time.

Double Boilers

Double boilers are used to slowly heat ingredients and mixtures, such as chocolate and custards. If you do not have a double boiler, one can be rigged up very easily using the pans and bowls you have on hand. Just use a saucepan for the bottom and a heat-proof bowl for the top. The bowl should rest snugly in the opening of the saucepan, suspended at least $1^{1}/_{2}$ inches over the bottom of the saucepan. It's okay if the sides of the bowl extend several inches above the rim of the saucepan. When using a double boiler to melt chocolate, be sure there is no gap between the outer sides of the top bowl and the pan it rests in. If there is a gap, steam can escape and come into contact with the melting chocolate, causing it to harden immediately. This is called "seizing." Sometimes it's actually better to use a bowl nested in a saucepan instead of a double boiler. When this is the case, we have stated so in the recipe.

Dough Scraper or Bench Scraper

These tools usually have a wooden handle and metal blade. They are very useful in cleaning your work surface after making pie dough, croissants, and Danish.

Handheld Mixers and Whisks

For whipping cream and mixing cookie dough and pastries for 5 minutes or less, a handheld electric mixer is sufficient. For mixing muffin batter, we recommend using a handheld whisk because it will not overmix the ingredients.

Measuring Cups

Dry measuring cups are usually nested inside each other and are used to measure only the amount stated on the cup. They are the appropriate measuring tool for ingredients such as flour, sugar, and nuts. Wet measures are usually glass or Pyrex containers with a muglike handle and a little extra space above the last measurement. They are used to measure ingredients such as milk, water, corn syrup, and molasses. The two types are not interchangeable.

Measuring Spoons

Stainless-steel measuring spoons are best. Some dry ingredients tend to stick to plastic measuring spoons. They can also acquire an oily film that is difficult to clean off completely.

Mixers

We tend to use heavy-duty tabletop mixers more than just about anything in our kitchen. We believe if you only have one piece of high-quality equipment, it should be a heavy-duty mixer. They come with three attachments: a whip for beating eggs and cream, a flat beater for mixing cookie doughs and the like, and a dough hook for kneading bread doughs. An extra mixing bowl also comes in handy.

For some of the recipes that have very long mixing times (5 minutes or longer) it is almost mandatory that you use a tabletop mixer. It frees your hands for tricky ingredient additions and prep work.

Ovens

Ovens vary a lot! If you want to bake successfully, we can't overemphasize the importance of knowing your oven and its idiosyncrasies. Some of the newer electric "baking ovens" are very good, and convection ovens work well, too. At home, we use professional model gas ovens because they hold more items at one time. For more about irregular ovens, see "Adjusting Oven Temperatures and Baking Times," page 18.

Oven Thermometers

Don't waste your money on a spring-loaded oven thermometer; they don't work, even when new. Instead, buy a professional-quality thermometer. You can order one through the serviceperson who calibrates your oven. They cost about three times as much as the spring-loaded models, but last a lifetime if well cared for.

Pans

While it's fun to have a menagerie of pans, you only need about seven basic shapes and styles. Here's what works for us and why:

FOR PIES

We recommend glass pie plates, which bake more evenly than metal because they are heavier. Plus, glass pie plates let you see the bottom of the pie so you can check to see how the crust is browning as the pie bakes. To make it easier to move pies from one rack to another, and to catch any filling that may bubble over, we always set our pies on pizza pans to bake. We prefer to use round pizza pans because they are just the right size for pies and allow heat to flow more freely within the oven.

FOR BAR COOKIES

Use a 10 x 15 x 2-inch glass lasagna pan. This is a little larger than most recipes call for, but we think that you should always bake enough to share with friends and neighbors.

FOR CAKES

If possible, use heavy-duty aluminum pans. They are available from baking-supply catalogues (see page 317) and you only need five: two 9-inch-diameter x 2-inch-deep cake pans, one 9-inch-diameter x 3-inch-deep springform or removable-bottom pan, one 15 x 10 x 1-inch jelly-roll pan, and one 10 x 4 x 3-inch tube pan with a removable bottom.

FOR MUFFINS

Use nonstick pans, and butter them. If you don't have nonstick pans, butter the pans very well. If you prefer, paper muffin-cup liners can be used instead. They actually hold in moisture and extend muffins' shelf life.

Parchment Paper

This is one of the little things that makes baking a lot easier. When baking sheets are lined with parchment paper, they do not have to be buttered. Cakes baked in pans lined with parchment paper are easier to depan. Pre-cut parchment paper circles for round pans are available at gourmet kitchenware stores and from baking-supply catalogs (see page 317). Or, you can make your own by tracing around the bottom of the pan and cutting out the circle. Parchment paper can be found at most grocery stores.

Pastry Bags and Tips

For large decorating jobs, we prefer to use nylon pastry bags because they are easily cleaned and lightweight, which makes them easier to handle. For smaller jobs, pastry bags made out of parchment paper are more practical (for more about this, see "Making and Filling a Paper Pastry Bag," page 208).

Tips come in standard sizes and are available at gourmet kitchenware stores and from baking-supply catalogues (see page 317). Having a good assortment to work with can make the difference between a homemade-looking pastry and a professional-looking one. For more about the most useful tips to buy, see page 188.

Pastry Brushes

These essential items are most often used for applying glazes, melted butter, and soaking solutions. Use pastry brushes with natural, not nylon, bristles because natural bristles have a finer texture and don't curl after repeated use. Ideally, you should have two or three sizes: one 1-inch-wide brush, one 2 inches wide, and one 3 inches wide. Never use them for any other purpose, especially for basting meats, because it is hard to get strong flavors such as garlic out of them. (Hide them from the person who barbecues in your house!) Be sure to wash new brushes with warm, soapy water, pulling on the bristles to remove any that are loose, before you use them the first time.

Rolling Pins

You can get by with a standard rolling pin, but we recommend two types: For cookies and pie doughs, handleless rolling pins, which look like large dowels, are best because they let you feel the dough under the pin. Buy one that is just long enough for the largest job you are likely to use it for. (A good size is about 14 inches long.) A pin that is too long is hard to handle. For croissant, puff pastry, and Danish doughs, rolling pins with handles and ball bearings are best because you can apply the necessary pressure to the pin and the rolling action of the ball bearings makes it easier to roll out these firm doughs. Make sure to get a good-quality pin. The cheaper ones wear out too fast.

Rubber Spatulas and Plastic Bowl Scrapers

Both have their place in the baker's kitchen. A rubber spatula is handy because it has a handle that enables you to get into tight spots (like inside jars). It's also the best utensil for folding delicate ingredients into batters, doughs, and frostings.

A bowl scraper is a thin, half-circle-shaped utensil made of flexible plastic that is invaluable for scraping the last bit of ingredients out of a bowl. It's also great for cleaning off flour that's caked on a bowl after you've made a dough and for spreading batter in pans. If you don't have one, get one.

Professional Bakers' Tips and Techniques

Following the tips and techniques in this chapter will make everything you bake better. In addition, you'll find more specific tips and techniques scattered throughout the book. A list of the applicable tips and techniques, called "Baker's Basics to Review," and the pages on which they appear are given at the beginning of the recipes whenever we think it would be helpful for you to re-read these instructions before you start baking.

Adding Eggs

Unless otherwise directed, always add eggs one at a time, thoroughly incorporating each one before adding the next. This technique improves the appearance and texture of the end product. When the eggs are added all at once, they cannot be incorporated well enough without overbeating the ingredients. The batter may also separate if eggs are not added one at a time.

Adjusting Oven Temperatures and Baking Times

Because all ovens vary, you may need to adjust the temperatures and baking times given for the recipes in this book (or any other book, for that matter). You can still bake successfully with an oven that is 25 to 50 degrees off, as long as you know how far off it is. When possible (as with cookies), bake a small batch at the given temperature to see how the item bakes in your oven, then adjust the time and temperature accordingly. If you're baking a multiple-serving dessert or pastry, you may have to make it several times before you know how your oven behaves. If pastries are done before the indicated time or are too dark, your oven is too hot. If pastries take longer than the indicated time to bake, your oven is too cool.

You must bake a pastry at the temperature the recipe gives before knowing whether your oven needs adjusting. If it does, decrease or increase the temperature by 25 degrees. Even if you know your oven heats accurately, set the timer for a few minutes less than the baking time. If the total baking time is less than 20 minutes, check the pastries 5 minutes early and then every 5 minutes thereafter. If the baking time is longer than 20 minutes, check the pastries 10 minutes early, then every 5 minutes after that. Write any temperature and time adjustments in the cookbook so you can refer to them the next time you bake the pastry.

Hot spots in ovens can be a problem, too. Learn where your oven's hot spots are and turn your baking pans and sheets midway through baking to avoid burning certain areas. If your oven tends to burn baked goods on the bottom, always use the center or upper oven racks, or put a baking sheet under the sheet or pan you are baking on to diffuse some of the heat, or do both. If your baked goods always burn on the top, bake them on the center or lower racks, or cover loosely with aluminum foil while they bake, or do both. If your oven is not large enough to accommodate two baking sheets or pans side by side on the center rack with 2 inches of space around all sides, switch the top and bottom pans midway through baking.

If you are an avid baker, have your oven calibrated every two years and periodically check its accuracy with a professional oven thermometer (for more about oven thermometers, see page 15). And remember, there's no substitute for experience—the more you bake, the better you'll know your oven.

Bringing Ingredients to the Ideal Temperature

Ingredients are easier to incorporate when they are at room temperature rather than cold. Plus, adding a cold ingredient to a room-temperature mixture can change the structure of the batter or dough. For example, cold eggs can harden butter. So, unless otherwise stated, all ingredients should be brought to room temperature before they are used. Allow at least 1 hour for butter, eggs, and other refrigerated ingredients to come to room temperature after they are removed from the refrigerator. It is possible to bring eggs to room temperature more quickly by placing them in a glass of warm water. Butter will warm to room temperature faster if it is cut it into small pieces. Milk can be gently warmed over very low heat on the stove.

Similarly, some warm or hot ingredients can adversely alter a recipe if not properly cooled to room temperature before they are added to the primary mixture. For example, adding chocolate immediately after it has melted can melt the butter in a batter and make it too thin.

When it is especially crucial to bring the ingredients to room temperature, we have reminded you. However, cold ingredients are sometimes specified because they create certain textures or keep a mixture, such as pie dough, cool or firm, or both.

Creaming

Creaming is called for when butter, cream cheese, or other types of fat are mixed with sugar or another sweetener to create a smooth, creamy mixture. Sometimes the recipe will call for the mixture to cream 5 minutes or longer, which produces a fluffier texture.

To cream ingredients, use the flat beater of a heavy-duty electric mixer, a handheld electric mixer, or wooden spoon. Beat the butter or cream cheese first until it is a smooth consistency (or "creamed"). Scrape down the sides of the bowl and beaters, then add the sweetener, and beat vigorously until well incorporated.

Filling and Using a Nylon Pastry Bag

Place the desired tip inside the pastry bag. It should fit snugly and just barely protrude from the end of the bag. (If it doesn't, snip off the very end of the bag.) Hold one hand as if you had a glass of water in it. Grip the lower portion of the pastry bag as you would hold a glass and, with your other hand, turn down the top of the pastry bag (it should roll down far enough to cover the hand that's holding it and so that you can see the pastry tip inside). With a rubber spatula, begin to fill the bag with the batter, dough, frosting, icing, or other mixture, lifting the sides of the bag. Press the mixture down with the spatula after each addition. It is important to keep air pockets from forming because they can cause the mixture to spatter as it is piped out of the bag. When the bag is two-thirds full, close it by twisting the end very tightly and holding the twisted end in the groove between your right thumb and forefinger (or between your left thumb and forefinger if you are left-handed). Various mixtures require different amounts of pressure to be piped well. To determine the right amount, apply slight pressure at first, then increase or decrease as necessary. As with any skill, practice makes perfect.

Folding

This technique is used when it is important to maintain volume in a mixture, such as one that has a beaten-egg or whipped-cream base. Place the lighter mixture on top of the heavier mixture. Use a rubber spatula or, as professional bakers do, use your hand to do the folding. Insert the spatula into the center of the bowl at the farthest point away from you. With the spatula perpendicular to the work surface, drag it down through the mixture toward you, gently scraping the bottom of the bowl at all times and lifting the mixture on the bottom to the top. With your other hand, continually rotate the bowl one-quarter turn counterclockwise as you fold. Repeat this motion several times, or until the ingredients are fully combined.

Measuring

Measuring accurately is critical to successful baking. Take the time to do it right and always measure out all of the ingredients before beginning a recipe. It is important to use the appropriate measuring tool for the ingredient you are measuring. Using a wet measuring cup for dry ingredients will not give an accurate measure because it is impossible to level off the top of the ingredient. Dry measuring cups cannot be used for wet ingredients because it is difficult to measure right to the top without spilling.

MEASURING DRY INGREDIENTS

Measure dry ingredients over waxed paper or parchment paper to make clean-up easier. Do not measure over the mixing bowl; if you do, some of the excess will invariably end up in the mixture. Measure dry ingredients by fluffing them up with a large spoon, then spooning them into a dry measuring cup one spoonful at a time. Using a flat knife, remove any excess by leveling the top. Unless specified (as for brown sugar and, occasionally, other ingredients), do not tamp down or shake the measuring cup during this process. When a recipe calls for "1 cup sifted flour," for example, the ingredient should be sifted before it is measured. On the other hand, when a recipe calls for "1 cup confectioners' sugar, sifted," for example, the ingredient should be measured first and then sifted.

MEASURING WET INGREDIENTS

When measuring wet ingredients, place the container on the counter and pour the ingredient into the container to the level desired. Stooping so that your eyes are at counter level, check the accuracy of the measurement.

Melting Chocolate

Melting chocolate is easy. There are just a couple of principles you must follow:

- Always use a double boiler. (For more about double boilers, see page 13.)

- Make sure that the top bowl is completely dry and fits snugly in the bottom pan. If it doesn't, steam may escape and ruin the texture of the melting chocolate. Small amounts of moisture make chocolate seize or harden immediately. Once this has happened, the chocolate must be discarded and the process repeated; there is no way to re-melt seized chocolate.

- Always use a low heat; the water in the bottom of the double boiler should be barely simmering. When chocolate is melted over too high a heat, it will have a burnt smell and taste and may seize or separate.

Prepping Pans

Generally, the recipes will tell how to prepare the pans. As a rule, the more butter a recipe has in it, the less butter is needed to coat the pan. For example, many cookies do not need to be placed on a buttered baking sheet and can be baked on a parchment paper–lined sheet instead.

Scraping Down the Bowl and Beater(s)

Scraping the sides of the bowl while mixing is very important. Never continue mixing when there are unincorporated ingredients clinging to the sides of the bowl or the beater(s). Turn off the mixer and, using a rubber spatula, scrape the unmixed ingredients into the primary mixture, then resume mixing. Stop and scrape several times, if necessary.

Separating Eggs

Being able to separate eggs quickly and expertly is an essential skill. Professional bakers do it one of two ways—using the hand method or the shell method. To separate eggs using the hand method, crack open the egg while holding it over a mixing bowl and gently slide the whole egg into one hand. Separate your fingers slightly to allow the egg white to seep through into the bowl below. Pour the yolk and remaining egg white into your other hand and repeat the process. Alternate between both hands, until all of the white is in the bowl, working quickly yet gently so as not to break the yolk. To separate eggs using the shell method, crack the eggshell in half while holding the egg over a mixing bowl and lift off the top half of the shell, keeping all of the egg in the bottom half. Gently pour the egg into the top half of the shell, letting the white fall into a bowl below. Repeat this process until all of the white is in the bowl, working quickly yet gently so as not to break the yolk.

Egg whites can be separated and frozen for 2 weeks. To thaw, place them in the refrigerator overnight. When separating egg whites for whipping, be sure to keep all particles of broken yolk separate from the whites. The fat in the yolks will prevent the whites from developing as much loft as possible when whipped.

Storing Desserts and Pastries

When asked if a particular product will freeze, Joe says, "Anything will freeze—just put it in the freezer and it'll freeze right up!" But we actually recommend showing a little more restraint. Most everything will store for a few days in the refrigerator or for several weeks in the freezer if it is well wrapped. Double-wrap baked goods by sealing them in plastic wrap and then putting them in a plastic bag or in two plastic bags. Plastic produce bags or resealable plastic bags work well. Airtight metal or plastic containers are good for storing goods on the counter for a day or two. When appropriate, we tell you which desserts and pastries store particularly well.

Danish pastries are best hot from the oven the day they are made, but they do store fairly well. After the glaze has set, store them in double airtight plastic bags in the refrigerator for up to 3 days or in the freezer for up to 2 weeks. To serve, defrost the pastries in the plastic bags at room temperature, then remove them and warm in a 325° oven just until hot and slightly crispy. Warming times will vary according to the shape and volume of the pastry; start checking the smallest pastries after they have warmed for 7 minutes. Overwarming dries them out, so watch them carefully.

At the bakery we're sticklers for freshness. We bake our cakes every 2 or 3 days and freeze them before we ice them. We never freeze a finished product. With the exception of a couple of cookies, which are actually better after a few days, we sell all of our pastries the same day they are made. We do not recommend lengthy storage whether at room temperature, in the refrigerator, or in the freezer. The pastries simply deteriorate as the days go by. Try to get into the habit of eating things when they are fresh and giving any extra to neighbors and friends (they'll love you).

Testing for Doneness

There are many ways to test for doneness and they all work to some degree. The key is to know what you are looking for. By baking a pastry over and over you will learn exactly what it looks like when perfectly baked. In most recipes, we give one or more ways to test for doneness and offer as much information as possible about what the pastry or dessert should look like.

Toasting Nuts

Toasting nuts enhances and intensifies their flavors, often adding depth and richness to the recipes they're used in. The process is easy; just keep an eye on them as they toast because overtoasted nuts have a strong, almost bitter flavor.

PECANS, ALMONDS, AND WALNUTS

To toast pecans, almonds, and walnuts, spread nuts evenly on a dry baking sheet and place in a preheated 350° oven. Toast just until they start to color and become aromatic, about 5 to 7 minutes. Let cool completely, then chop or grind as directed.

HAZELNUTS

To toast hazelnuts, spread nuts evenly on a dry baking sheet and place in a preheated 350° oven. Toast just until slightly brown and aromatic, about 15 minutes. Remove the nuts from the oven and immediately wrap them in a kitchen towel. Set aside to cool. When cool, rub the nuts vigorously between your palms (still wrapped in the towel) to remove the slightly bitter skins. It is not necessary to remove all of the skins, but remove as many as possible. Use as directed.

Whipping

Whipping ingredients incorporates air into them and increases their volume. This can be achieved with either a handheld whisk, a handheld electric mixer, or a tabletop mixer. When whipped ingredients are added to a recipe, they are usually folded in (for more about this, see "Folding," page 20). Whipping is a different technique than whisking and produces a different result; it is important to know the difference.

Whisking

Whisking means to beat ingredients with a handheld wire whisk until they are mixed thoroughly. To keep the bowl stationary on the counter while whisking, roll a kitchen towel into a donut shape and place it around the base of the bowl.

Zesting Citrus

Using a fine grater, gently scrape the outer layer of peel off of the citrus. Be careful not to grate the bitter white interior. Always zest citrus just before the zest will be used. When citrus zest sits out for even 30 minutes, it loses some of its moisture and oils.

Above: What a selection! With over 200 items for sale each day it's hard to choose.

Left: Brushing croissants with egg glaze before they go into the oven.

Left: Rolling Downtowners in granulated sugar.

Below: A thousand (literally!) Danish pastries all lined up. On a busy Sunday we'll make well over one hundred dozen of them.

Above: Cutting Christopher's Buns, Schnecken, or Downtowners and...

Right:...transferring them to a tray to refrigerate until the next morning when they're placed on pans or in muffin tins to bake.

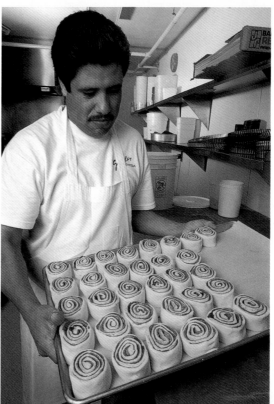

Left: The baker sheets a piece of Danish dough after the butter has been inserted...

Right:...and gives it a three-fold turn.

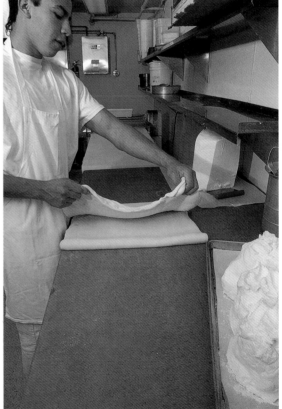

Above: While the first square of Danish dough is given its first turn, the other eleven pieces of softened butter wait to be rolled-in to separate pieces of dough.

Left: Tartlet shells being filled with pastry cream.

Below: The final glazing with a transparent jelly coating.

Opposite: Tartlets ready to be to placed in the showcase.

Above and right: Chocolate Ganache glaze being poured over our Rich Chocolate cakes. At the bakery we make twenty at a time to meet the demand on busy Saturdays.

At right: Piping whipped cream rosettes on Fresh Berry Genoise cakes.

Below: Fresh Berry Genoise ready for sale.

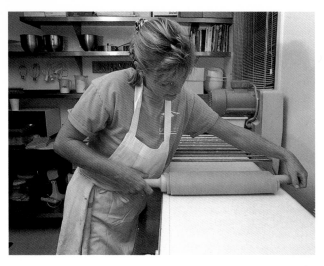

At left: Sheeting marzipan on the sheeter and rolling it onto a rolling pin for easy handling.

Right: Draping the marzipan over the cake. Note: A mound of whipped cream (not shown) creates the dome.

Below: Making a perfect edge by scraping off any whipped cream that peeks out from under the marzipan.

Above: About half the amount of Princess Cakes we typically make for a busy Saturday morning.

A Rosa Salva Venetian Party Sandwich—all filled, cut into 64 tea sandwiches, stacked and wrapped—is ready for a catering order.

The Recipes

The key to making good pastries is being precise. We initially learned this from Lindsey Shere, Flo Braker, and Cornelus Van Peski (for more about these bakers, see pages 83, 265, and 40, respectively), and we relearn it every time we visit a village bakery in Europe and watch Old World pastry chefs at work. All of these master bakers are meticulous about measuring ingredients; they've been doing it so long it's ingrained in their work habits.

When baking bread or cooking, one can often make minor adjustments to the ingredient proportions and still have success with a recipe. In dessert and pastry making, the formula should be considered sacrosanct. Did you ever wonder how your grandmother or mother made great pie dough without measuring? It's not that she guessed at the amounts every time. Instead, like any well-trained European pastry chef, after having prepared the recipe a hundred times she had memorized the ingredient proportions; she knew the right amounts by the look and feel of the ingredients in the bowl.

The lesson here is that until you've prepared a recipe so many times that you can make it in your sleep, you should adhere to the recipe proportions given. Find two or three recipes you like and make them over and over until you've perfected them. It's a great way to learn to bake. After you've made the recipes that many times, you'll start to know them the same way your grandma knew her pie dough recipe. Eventually, the recipes will truly become your own.

Technique also plays an important role in successful baking. There are many different ways to achieve a similar result, but the secret is being consistent. A baker gains an unconscious familiarity with a recipe through repeated action. If you mix a certain cookie in an electric mixer one day and by hand the next, chances are you'll get slightly different results. Try to prepare a recipe the same way every time. Your reward will be that your technique and end product will improve each time. Experience always shows us how the ingredients behave during their transformation.

We've made an effort to keep the descriptions of techniques brief and simple in the recipes, giving a list of tips and techniques you should review before beginning each recipe. Some recipes are straightforward enough so you won't need to review anything before making them. Some give two ways to complete a step (such as mixing the dough by hand or with an electric mixer). Drawing on our nearly twenty years of experience as well as our bakers' knowledge, we've streamlined all the recipes as much as possible while still maintaining their intrinsic qualities and characteristics. We've learned from experience that when you make close to 30,000 Danish pastries a month, the techniques have to be simple and foolproof. However, you should plan on preparing the more challenging building blocks and recipes (like croissant dough, puff pastry, and some cakes) several times before you can expect to achieve the ultimate look, taste, and texture.

Keeping it simple is all-important. No one wants to jump through hoops to make a dessert. Very often, the most useful baking secrets are in the simple turn of a hand or flick of the wrist—all you really need is the confidence to tackle the project.

The Building Blocks (Or How We Build Pastries in a Professional Bakery)

The first pastry shop Joe and I visited was in Paris. It was our first night there, and at 5 A.M. we couldn't sleep. We knew the bakers were up too, so off we went. The pastry shop we happened upon was called Moule a Gateaux. The shop had been open only a few days. So when the pastry chef kept saying, *"Huit jours en avance"* (eight days in advance) as he showed us around, we thought it had something to do with their recent opening. As we would soon learn, it meant much more than that.

The pastry chef led us down the arched stone stairway, its only hint of modernity being a hydraulic elevator attached to a railing. (We found out later that the elevator was only used to send pastries up to the shop above.) Downstairs, we entered a modern pastry kitchen with a bank of immaculate stainless-steel refrigerators and freezers along one wall. Many of the refrigerators had a digital panel showing the temperature and humidity. Today we see this advanced technology in most professional pastry kitchens, but fifteen years ago it was a futuristic scene. Our first thought was that those refrigerators and freezers held the secrets that would enable us to fulfill all of our cake- and pastry-making dreams. Little did we know at the time that the secret was not in the individual contents of the refrigerators, but in how the contents could be combined to create myriad variations of taste and texture.

Throughout our informal tour, the baker repeated *"Huit jours en avance,"* adding *"Pas de chemique"* (no chemicals) and *"Pas de congélation"* (no freezing). As it turned out, this no-chemicals credo was a novel idea, even in Paris, which at the time was experiencing a renaissance in Old World baking techniques. But, it was the litany "eight days in advance" that still puzzled us.

When we asked the pastry chef if we could watch him work, he agreed and began by laying clean towels on one of the work surfaces. We sat nearby—Joe with his camera and me with my notebook—as he worked. First he made *pâte sucré,* a sweet tart dough. When he finished mixing the dough, he placed it on the table and pounded it with his rolling pin, then divided it into eight separate *patons,* or large square pieces of dough. He carefully wrapped each one in plastic wrap. "This is for tomorrow," he said, gesturing toward one piece. Pointing to the others, he said, "These are for the rest of the week," and shuffled off to put them in one of the freezers. And with that exchange, we began to learn more about the vast difference between freezing during the production phase and freezing after a product is made (a taboo in almost any pâtisserie).

Next, the pastry chef made croissant dough, demonstrating its advance storage potential: the dough is made the first day, the butter is rolled in the second day, and the croissants are shaped and baked the third day. More important, on the second day, *patons* for the entire week's production can be frozen. He also made *pâte feuilleté,* or puff pastry, which can be made well in advance. It is the classic example of a dough that loves to be frozen. The old French bakers say that while the puff pastry dough "sleeps" in the freezer, some of its potent powers are softened. This gives the dough a more even consistency when it's "awakened" by the heat of the oven. *Pâte feuilleté* is just one example of how freezing and refrigeration are integral stages in the process and not just shortcuts.

The chef did the same thing with the brioche

as he had done with the other doughs, making some for the next day and the rest for future use. Joe and I were mesmerized. We couldn't tell if we were experiencing jet lag or were in some kind of trance. But one thing was clear: the significance of the "eight days in advance" mantra. If pastry chefs start just eight days in advance, their larders will be well enough stocked to enable them to quickly assemble many different pastries during high-production times. Proper use of refrigeration allows you to put out perfectly fresh product every day, every time.

Imagine a bank of refrigerators and freezers being filled to overflowing with every element of the pastry maker's art. All the elements are neatly stacked on trays or in containers and are labeled and dated. In some instances the products are covered to avoid crusting, but in other cases they are left uncovered because they might only sit for a few hours or they are too fragile to wrap. One refrigerator might contain doughs (*pâte sablé, pâte sucré, pâte feuilleté, pâte brisé,* and *pâte a pâté*). Another would hold the creams (*crème pâtissière* and *crème d'amandes*). Still another might contain fillings (such as prune, almond paste, raspberry, and apricot). Each product has its own shelf life and is made on a separate rotating schedule: seven to eight days for doughs, three to four days for the fillings, two or three days for the more vulnerable creams. The entire process is like that of an expert violin maker who makes a series of finely wrought elements—veneers, struts, pegs— and stores them until he is ready to assemble the instruments.

Almost every dessert in the pastry maker's repertoire is assembled from at least two of the two dozen or so basic building blocks. Common examples of this are napoleons, which are made with puff pastry, pastry cream, whipping cream, and raspberry jam; Princess Cake, made with genoise, pastry cream, raspberry jam, whipped cream, and marzipan; claufouti, made with tart dough, custard, and fresh fruit; and Chocolate Mousse Cake, made with devil's food cake, mousse, whipped cream, and chocolate ganache.

You can broaden your repertoire and create your own variations by learning to make only a handful of different elements—for example, puff pastry, tart dough, pastry cream, and chocolate ganache. With just these four building blocks to mix and match, you will be able to make dozens of different desserts. Here's a list of the most important building blocks you'll find in this book:

Doughs: tart dough, *pâte sucré,* puff pastry, croissant dough, Danish dough, pie dough, cream cheese dough, and *pâte à choux.*

Creams and fillings: almond paste, pastry cream, buttercream, Bavarian cream, whipping cream, and lemon curd.

Cakes: genoise, hazelnut, poppy seed, devil's food, and carrot.

Fruit: fresh, in jam form or puréed, or as a filling, flavoring, or decoration.

Chocolate: chocolate ganache, couverture chocolate, shaved chocolate.

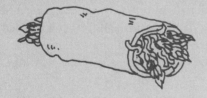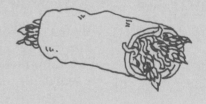

Croissant

Many people think that the croissant is related to the crescent roll because their shapes are similar. The word "croissant" is derived from the French word *accroissement,* which means "to increase." This technique of increasing by layering *(feuilletage)*—alternating layer upon layer of butter and dough—is symbolic of the practice of constructing pastries using many different elements or building blocks. (However, the building-block role of croissant dough itself is more evident in the technique than in its usage.) This technique is used in making Danish pastry, puff pastry, and, to some extent, in pie dough, in which the butter is left in chunks to create the flaky layers.

In France, the croissant is its own entity. Croissant dough is rarely used for other products, except *pain au chocolat* and *croissants aux amandes.* In American bakeries, croissant dough is used as the basis for many savory baked goods.

The croissant is the cornerstone of Gayle's Bakery. It was the first pastry I heard about and set out to make. In 1976, I read a description of the croissant in a *Gourmet* article about France. My fascination with France's seminal pastry began then and there and eventually evolved into the first chapter in the story of Gayle's Bakery. At the time, croissants were not yet available in California and, as a result, I had never tasted one. I found a croissant recipe in the *Joy of Cooking* and gave it a try. It was a disaster. I knew the croissants I made weren't the flaky, buttery pastries I had read about.

It was the summer of 1976, when I was working at Chez Panisse, that I heard about a croissant of unequaled taste and texture. A little restaurant called Fat Albert's was making them right in Chez Panisse's backyard. The minute I saw Fat Albert's croissants, I knew I'd found the flaky, glistening gems described in the *Gourmet* article. I immediately met the owner, Hildegard Marshall, and took one of her baking classes. It was from Hildy that I learned to mix croissant dough and roll in the butter properly. In fact, I learned many invaluable things from Hildy. Perhaps the most significant lesson was that the proportions of ingredients in a recipe are not nearly as important as how you put them together.

Like most other bakers and cooks, I always want to recreate the interesting foods I've seen and heard about. Hildy prepared me to do just that by demonstrating that a recipe is merely a road map—bakers can take so many different avenues and arrive at the same place. Now, after twenty years of baking professionally, I know firsthand that the end product is more than the sum of its parts—its essence transcends the basic ingredients and the way it was created.

Cornelus Van Peski was my pastry instructor and baking companion for the years preceding the bakery's opening and the next mentor in my quest to make the perfect croissant. Van was a European-trained chef, taskmaster, and perfectionist. He learned his craft alongside many a demanding Old World chef. He always followed instructions to the letter and never wasted anything in the kitchen; not even a little flour fell to the floor. I learned many things from him, but an allegiance to precision and consistency were, once again, the most enduring. (For more about Cornelus, see page 40.)

My croissant-making career began in the big, open kitchen of our modest Santa Cruz home. I rolled out my croissant dough on a wooden table that Joe "built" for me. The tabletop was a heavy 5-foot-long plank door, and the base was made of 4x4 posts shabbily nailed together with scrap wood. The top was unattached to the flimsy base, but so heavy that it rarely moved. One leg was shorter than the others and had to be shimmed with a folded newspaper.

I was waitressing at a local restaurant at the time. Every morning, as soon as I got up I'd remove the croissant dough from the refrigerator and roll and shape it. I would set the croissants on trays near the warm oven to rise while I showered and dressed for work. Then I baked and delivered them to a cookware shop downtown on my way to work the lunch shift. When I got home from work, I would mix the croissant dough and roll in the butter for the next day's batch. And the cycle continued. Five days a week.

The money I made from selling croissants went to buy more ingredients. Whatever small amount was left over was combined with my waitressing wages and went toward financing the bakery.

Joe and I remember those days with mixed emotions. There were hundred-pound sacks of flour stacked in the kitchen. Sixty-eight-pound blocks of butter often tumbled out of the refrigerator. Flour dust was everywhere, even on the television. Our dog Ria had a dust broom tail that automatically wagged when she walked, leaving designs in the flour dust on the coffee table. Eventually, we agreed: it was time to get the "baking thing" out of the house.

When we opened the bakery, two years after I had begun making croissants, the croissant was one of the featured items on the menu. Croissants weren't popular back then. People didn't know what to think of them, but we persisted. Even our landlady said, "I don't think you'll make it if you don't sell donuts." We never did.

It's difficult to learn the subtleties of a process until you know some basics. Fortunately, we had some practical experience before we visited the basement bakery in Paris. We knew what we wanted to learn (why certain techniques yield certain results and how to manipulate the process to achieve such results) and what our primary goal was (to make a croissant that was flaky and crispy outside and tender, layered, and flavorful inside). Since you may not have experimented with croissant dough before, here's a quick overview of the most important things we've learned—in Paris and at our bakery—about making perfect croissants:

- There are three ways to insert the butter into the dough. Some recipes call for working in the butter in two flat sheets between alternating layers of dough. Others call for rolling in the butter in a flat block, as is done for puff pastry, then giving the dough a three-fold turn. Still other recipes call for working in half of the butter, doing a three-fold turn, then adding the other half of butter and doing another three-fold turn.

- There are acceptable variations on the number of turns. Three turns is considered standard. In general, the more turns, the less flaky the pastry and the more homogeneous the interior of the croissant. Conversely, the fewer turns, the more the dough and butter separate, creating a flakier texture.

- For a flakier croissant you can eliminate two turns and add one four-fold turn (like the "book turn," used for puff pastry, which is described on page 84). Another variation for added flakiness is to give the dough two turns the first day, then let it rest in the refrigerator overnight, and give it one turn the next morning before making the croissants.

- Cold butter is essential. It helps keep the butter and dough separate. But, as we have learned through trial and error, if the butter is almost frozen, it creates lumps that break up under the dough and it often melts out during baking.

- By working with multiple blocks of dough (for us, it was twelve 10-pound blocks at a time) we found that the necessary relaxing and chilling of the dough in the refrigerator becomes the time a baker needs to work and sheet the other doughs. It's a continuous process.

- The French method calls for letting the dough rise overnight in the refrigerator, then rolling in the butter the next day. The French use milk powder and water instead of fresh whole milk. The dough-to-butter ratio—universal proportions in all French pâtisseries—was nearly the same as what we were using: 1,500 grams of dough to 500 grams of butter.

- In large-production bakeries, croissants can be cut by stacking three or four long strips of very cold dough on top of one another and cutting the triangles three or four at a time.

- Refrigeration and freezing are not only essential for staging and holding work in progress, they also age the dough, allowing the yeasty flavors to dissipate and deeper flavors to develop. Indeed, the flavor of a French croissant comes not only from the butter and milk powder but from the age of the dough. It is true that the whole process can be condensed into a single day and still achieve the same flakiness and look of the finished croissant, but the flavor will not be the same.

We hope you find the art of croissant making as satisfying and fun as we do, and offer just one warning: croissants will get the best of you if you are afraid of them. They are not easy, but if you stick with it, you'll master them and be glad you did (and so will your friends, family, and co-workers!).

Doing the Roll-In and Turns

Roll-in doughs have layers of butter meshed with layers of dough (about 250 layers in croissant dough and 2,400 in puff pastry!). They create flaky pastries and are fundamental to the art of pastry making. We include three types of roll-in doughs in this book: croissant dough, Danish pastry, and puff pastry.

The process begins with mixing the dough (called *le detrempe*) and chilling it. "Roll-in" refers to the process of incorporating butter into dough, called *le beurrage* in French. Because pastries made with roll-in doughs should be tender, it is not desirable to develop the gluten in the dough through prolonged kneading. It is only necessary that the dough be smooth and free of dry spots. Therefore, the dough is mixed just until the dry and wet ingredients are evenly combined. The dough rests in the refrigerator, covered to prevent a crust from forming, for several hours. Then, the butter is rolled in. Letting a roll-in dough rest in the refrigerator after mixing allows the gluten to relax while the dough chills.

In the simplest method, the dough is rolled out into a rectangle, and a sheet of butter is placed on one side of the dough. The other half of the dough is folded over to cover the butter, the edges of the two halves are pinched closed, and the whole piece of dough is rolled out and folded again. The dough is then covered in plastic wrap or a split-open plastic food storage bag (which is thicker and therefore easier to handle repeatedly) and refrigerated. It is extremely important that the dough remain cold throughout the roll-in process.

After the roll-in is completed, the dough is given "turns," which means it is rolled it out to a certain thickness, then folded, usually in thirds or quarters. After each turn, the dough is covered and placed in the refrigerator to rest and chill. This process is repeated as many as four times, depending on the dough.

BUTTER AND DOUGH CONSISTENCY

The butter has to be the right temperature and consistency before it can be rolled into the dough. Optimally, the dough and butter should be the same consistency and temperature. If the butter is too soft (warm), it will seep out of the dough as you roll it. If it is too hard (that is, appreciably harder and colder than the dough), it will break up or crack under the dough.

PREPARING THE BUTTER

We use two methods for preparing the butter for a roll-in dough. One calls for cold, hard butter, the other for softer butter. Follow the instructions given in the recipes, but use common sense. If it is a very cold or warm day, the methods and times may need to be adjusted. Remember, the consistency and temperature of both butter and dough must be the same. Practice is the best way to perfect this crucial step.

DOING THE TURNS

Most croissant methods call for three turns, each of which entails rolling the dough out to $1/4$ inch thick, brushing off the excess flour (so the dough will adhere to itself when folded), and folding the dough into thirds. To help yourself remember which turn you are on, make an indentation in the top of the dough with your finger after you complete a turn.

There is one rule about making turns that is very important to the consistency of the finished product. When beginning a turn, always have the open edge of one of the long sides of the dough on your right. The short edges should be at the top and bottom.

When rolling the dough out, always begin in the center and roll toward one end, then return to the center and roll the other way. Keep changing the direction, first rolling up and down and then rolling side to side (also rolling from the center outward). It is important that the dough be of even thickness when rolled out. It will be a little more difficult to roll after each turn because the gluten becomes more developed. Be forceful with the dough without being reckless. And remember, the faster you can finish each turn, the colder the dough will remain.

When the dough rests in the refrigerator between turns, it may rise quite a bit. If it has been refrigerated overnight, it will definitely rise. When this happens, gently flatten the dough with your hands to expel the

(continued)

THE RECIPES

air before rolling it out and doing another turn.

The length of time to chill the dough between turns varies depending on the refrigerator, but 20 to 30 minutes is usually enough. The length of chilling time after the first turn is crucial; if the dough is in the refrigerator too long, the butter under the layers of dough, which is still fairly thick at this stage, becomes too hard. With each turn, the layers of but-ter and dough get thinner and this is not such a problem. A good way to tell whether the butter is too hard is to feel the dough. Can you feel the butter underneath the dough layer? If you can, the butter is too hard and you should leave the dough out on the work surface for 5 to 10 minutes before proceeding.

Completing the Final Roll and Shaping, Rising, and Baking Pastries

After you've completed the turns, you'll roll the dough out one final time and form the pastries. Here are a few tips that will make these steps easier:

• Work as quickly as you can. If the dough begins to get soft, return it to the refrigerator for 20 minutes.

• Make sure that there is always enough flour on the work surface so that the dough doesn't stick. Lift the dough several times as you roll it to make sure it is not sticking. You will notice that when you pick it up, the dough will shrink back, which is natural. While rolling it out, pick up the edges between your thumb and fingers and check the thickness. Run your fingers all around the perimeter of the dough and make sure to feel the middle, too. This will tell you how much and where you need to roll. Achieving the right measurements and thickness can be tricky without this step.

• Remember, the dimensions given in the recipes are guidelines. For beginners, it may be difficult to achieve these measurements.

• When cutting the dough in a long line, keep your eye on the end of the line, not on where you are cutting. This will help you cut straighter.

RISING

Roll-in doughs rise for two reasons: First, because there's yeast in the dough (puff pastry is the exception). Second, because the heat of the oven causes the thin layers of butter to bubble and blister, creating the flaky layered effect.

The rising times given are estimates. The temperature outside and in your kitchen will vary. Pastries should rise slowly in a fairly cool place. If they rise in a spot that's too warm, they'll rise quickly on the outside but not on the inside, creating a bad interior texture. As the pastries rise, check them often by gently squeezing them between your fingers to see how they feel. When ready to bake, they should have a marshmallowlike feel—soft, but with a little resilience.

BAKING

It is important to bake the pastries long enough. If they don't have a rich medium brown color after baking the specified time, leave them in the oven and check them every 1 1/2 to 2 minutes. A pale pastry will not have a good caramelized flavor.

GAYLE'S CROISSANTS

This recipe is a slight variation of the one we use every day at the bakery. (We use milk powder at the bakery, but call for fresh milk here because it's easier to bake with when making smaller batches.) We use this recipe to make Downtowners (page 51), Ham and Cheese Croissants (page 53), and Asparagus-Cheese Croissants (page 54).

BAKER'S BASICS TO REVIEW

Measuring Dry Ingredients, page 21

Doing the Roll-In and Turns, page 34

Completing the Final Roll and Shaping, Rising,
   and Baking Pastries, page 35

CROISSANT DOUGH

1/4 cup warm water

1 package (1/4 ounce) active dry yeast

4 cups unbleached all-purpose flour

1/4 cup sugar

1 tablespoon salt

1/4 cup (2 ounces) butter, at room temperature

1 cup cold milk

———

1 1/2 cups (12 ounces) cold unsalted butter

EGG GLAZE

1 egg

2 tablespoons milk

To make the dough, place the water in a small bowl, sprinkle the yeast on top, and let sit undisturbed for approximately 5 minutes. Stir to fully dissolve.

In a medium mixing bowl, combine the flour, sugar, and salt. Pinch off small pieces of the 1/4 cup of butter, sprinkle them over the dry ingredients, then rub them into the flour by hand until they are almost fully dissolved. Stir the yeast mixture and add it to the flour mixture. Add the cold milk.

With a wooden spoon, mix the wet and dry ingredients just until evenly combined and all dry spots have disappeared. The dough will be of medium stiffness, like a moist bread dough. The dough may also be mixed in an electric mixer fitted with a dough hook; just be careful not to overmix it or it will become too elastic to roll out.

Turn the dough out onto a lightly floured surface and gently knead for about 1 minute. Place the dough on a floured baking sheet and cover with plastic wrap or a split-open plastic food storage bag. Refrigerate the dough for at least 5 hours; overnight is preferable.

To roll-in the butter, remove the butter from the refrigerator. Leaving the butter in its wrappers, with a wooden rolling pin pound each stick lightly but firmly on all four sides until softened. Unwrap the sticks and join them together. On a lightly floured surface, using the rolling pin, mold the butter into a flat block measuring 5 x 5 x ³/₄ inch. Work quickly, making sure the butter is soft but still cold. If it gets warm, return it to the refrigerator for several minutes.

Remove the dough from the refrigerator, place it on a lightly floured table, and roll it into a 12 x 6-inch rectangle.

Place the cold butter on the right half of the dough, then fold the other half of the dough over the butter. Pinch the edges to seal.

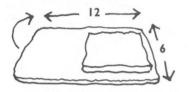

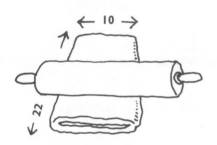

With the folded edge on your left, roll the dough out lengthwise so that it measures 22 x 10 inches.

Next, fold the bottom third up and the top third down. This is the *beurrage.*

Cover the dough, place it on a baking sheet, and refrigerate for 45 minutes.

For the turns, remove the dough from the refrigerator and place it on a lightly floured surface. Position the dough so that the folded edge running the length of the dough is on the left. Make sure the pinched edges are still sealed. Roll the dough out lengthwise so it measures approximately 22 x 10 x ¹/₂ inches. Fold the dough in thirds, beginning with the lower third, as before. (You have just completed one turn.)

Place the dough on the baking sheet. With your finger, make one small indentation on an edge of the dough to indicate one turn has been made. (Keeping track of how many turns have been made is critical.) Cover and refrigerate the dough for 45 minutes. Remove the dough from the refrigerator, transfer it to the lightly floured surface, and repeat the process to complete the second turn. After another 45 minutes, repeat the process to complete the third turn, always making sure that the dough remains cold but not too cold. Cover the dough and return it to the refrigerater to rest at least 5 hours (overnight is preferable).

Line two baking sheets with parchment paper.

To form the croissants, roll the dough out to exactly 25 x 14 x ¼ inches. Cut the dough in half lengthwise to make two 7-inch-wide strips. Using a pastry wheel or a long chef's knife, cut the strips into triangles, each with a base of 4 to 5 inches.

Starting with the base of one triangle, fold ¼ inch of the dough over onto itself and begin rolling the triangle up to the point. Gently stretch the dough by pulling on the tip as you roll it; this will result in more rolls and make a prettier croissant.

Repeat with the remaining triangles. If this process takes more than 10 minutes, return half of the triangles to the refrigerator and remove them a few at a time.

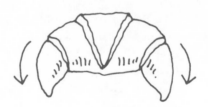

Place the croissants at least 2 inches apart on the prepared baking sheets. Turn each end in toward the center (the tip of the rolled-up triangle should be tucked under) and pinch them firmly together to form the croissant shape.

Whisk the egg and milk together to make the glaze. Lightly brush each croissant with the glaze and let rise, uncovered, in a cool place (65° to 75°) for 1 1/2 to 2 hours.

Preheat the oven to 400° and move the croissants to a warmer place (75° to 80°) near the oven to rise for 1 to 1 1/2 more hours. The croissants will be slightly puffy and have almost doubled in size when they are ready to be baked.

Brush the croissants with a second coat of glaze. Place the baking sheets on the center rack of the oven and bake for 15 to 17 minutes, or until golden brown.

NOTE: Croissants can be formed, proofed, and baked the same day, or they can be formed and stored in the refrigerator overnight and baked the next day. If you wish to bake the croissants the next day, place the formed but unrisen croissants on a baking sheet, cover with plastic wrap, and store overnight in the refrigerator. The next morning, remove them from the refrigerator, uncover, and let rise, then bake as directed. Croissants formed and baked the same day have a bold appearance and flaky crust. Next-day croissants are less yeasty tasting, more buttery, and have the nuances of a richly fermented dough.

Unbaked and unrisen croissants can be frozen for up to 2 weeks. Freeze on baking sheets until frozen and then transfer to airtight freezer bags. The day before you want to bake the croissants, remove them from the freezer, place on baking sheets, cover with plastic wrap, and refrigerate. The next day, let them rise at room temperature for 2 to 2 1/2 hours. Preheat the oven to 400° and bake for 15 to 17 minutes.

Cornelus Van Peski: The Croissant Master

One of the people who inspired me and was so important to me in the days before we opened Gayle's was my European pastry teacher, Cornelus Van Peski.

Recently, a woman came to the back window at Gayle's and asked if I had known Cornelus Van Peski. The woman told me that her husband had commissioned chef Van Peski to make a romantic meal for one of their first dates. She had only met the "loveable munchkin chef" very briefly, but his warmth and humor had stayed with her for many years.

Several years before the bakery opened, I met "Van," as I called him, through a mutual friend who said I had to meet this wonderful, Old World Danish baker in Carmel, California. My first visit to his adobe home reaffirmed my faith in what I was doing. Already retired at the time, Van, too, was making croissants out of his home and selling them to delighted friends and uptown shops. Since I had been doing the same thing in Santa Cruz, I found it reassuring that a professional was making a go of it at home.

Van was raised in The Hague, Holland, and had been trained in luxury hotels in the European way. That meant long hours of study first as an apprentice, later living in the hotel with only a few hours off on Sundays. It also meant that he learned to cook and bake with serious attention to detail and cleanliness.

After coming to the United States, he worked at Neil DeVaughn's, the first restaurant established on the abandoned Cannery Row in Monterey, California. For twenty-nine years, his tasks included baking breads in 2-pound coffee cans for eggs Benedict, making crab bisque from crab shells, and serving his ever-popular cheese fondue. Against the will of the restaurant's owner, he fed stray cats, dogs, and hungry seagulls at the restaurant's backdoor. He loved to feed anyone who was hungry.

After retiring from Neil DeVaughn's, Van gradually developed a reputation as a well-respected pastry chef on the Monterey peninsula. He was generous in his knowledge and shared all he knew (except, as I later found out, his prized croissant recipe). In his home kitchen, he baked an endless stream of goodies, which were often bartered or exchanged for small sums of money with truly appreciative locals and friends.

Van's kitchen was set up for professional use: it was large, well equipped and homey, with a small Santa Fe–style wood-burning fireplace in the corner. My first morning with him, we decided to focus on croissants and began sharing recipes and techniques. The first thing I noticed was that he loved to sing while he baked. He must have known the words to a thousand songs. Years later, his wife would tell me that you could determine how well an experimental recipe was turning out by whether Van was singing in a different language (he spoke five and probably sang in six). The music became happier and more intense as he got closer and closer to his goal.

Van generously shared all of his experience, which I needed, having been self-taught. We made his croissant; we made my croissant. We spent many hours comparing the two and extracting the best qualities of both. We finally came up with what we both agreed was the best.

Van usually made me lunch after our morning testing. His food was homestyle European—rich, but subtle. He made complex soups and perfect custards that were slowly baked. We spent many hours going over the cookbooks that he had acquired during the years.

Appropriately, Van's funeral was a celebration of his life. It was held where he had often walked with friends, among the poppies on a bluff overlooking the Pacific Ocean. Dozens of friends shared funny, heartwarming stories about the man who had touched their lives with his magic personality and sensational food.

The customer who had come to our window didn't know Van well enough to have attended that final celebration. But she knew his magic firsthand—she was still married to the fellow who had asked Van to make that memorable meal.

❧ ❧ ❧

PAIN D'AMANDES

DON'T TOSS OUT THOSE DAY-OLD CROISSANTS!

Here are a few of our favorite ways to use day-old croissants. These informal recipes don't call for exact amounts, so use your own judgment and have fun.

SAVORY BREAD PUDDING

Blanch 1 cup of asparagus pieces and sauté the same amount of mushrooms. Combine several beaten eggs, 1/4 to 1/2 cup heavy whipping cream, and about 1 cup of grated jack or sharp Cheddar cheese. Mix it all together and add a little salt and freshly ground pepper and a pinch of freshly ground nutmeg.

Tear a half dozen or so day-old croissants into 3 or 4 pieces each. Combine the croissant pieces and the rest of the ingredients in a heat-proof casserole, filling it halfway to the top.

Bake in a 400° oven until just cooked through and a little crispy on top. Serve warm.

CROISSANT AUX AMANDES

Make a mixture of about 1 cup of almond paste, 1/2 cup sugar, and 1 to 2 beaten eggs (add only enough egg to make a fluffy, not runny, mixture). Whip until fluffy in a heavy-duty tabletop mixer fitted with the whisk attachment. In a separate pan, combine 1/2 cup water, 1/2 cup rum,

(continued)

There has probably never been a pastry called *pain d'amande* in the history of France (gramatically it should be *pain aux amandes),* but when we started the bakery, I wanted an almond paste–filled croissant. I had never heard of one, so I created my own and named it Pain d'Amandes. It probably doesn't make sense to the French, but our customers sure know what it means: buttery croissant dough wrapped around not-too-sweet marzipan that has been enriched with eggs, butter, and raisins. You can make these any size you wish; you may want to make them smaller because they are rich. Pain d'Amandes can be frozen for up to 2 weeks. (Follow the freezing instructions for Gayles' Croissants, on page 36.)

BAKER'S BASICS TO REVIEW

Measuring Dry Ingredients, page 21

Folding, page 20

Completing the Final Roll and Shaping, Rising, and Baking Pastries, page 35

FILLING

7 ounces marzipan or almond paste (page 261)

1/4 cup sugar

2 tablespoons (2 ounces) butter, at room temperature

1 large egg, slightly beaten

2 teaspoons pure vanilla extract

1 cup all-purpose flour

1/2 cup raisins or currants (optional)

———

1 recipe Croissant Dough (page 36)

EGG GLAZE

1 large egg

2 tablespoons milk

———

1 cup thinly sliced almonds

Confectioners' sugar, for dusting

Cut the marzipan into 1/2-inch pieces. Place the marzipan and sugar in a food processor fitted with the metal blade and pulse until crumbly. Add the butter, egg, and vanilla and process until smooth. Add the flour and process until the mixture holds together and looks like a soft cookie dough. Transfer the mixture to a bowl and fold in the raisins with a wooden spoon. The marzipan filling makes about 1³/4 cups and can be stored in the refrigerator for up to 4 days or in the freezer for up to 2 weeks. If frozen, thaw the filling in the refrigerator the night before you plan to use it.

Line a baking sheet with parchment paper. In a small bowl, whisk together the egg and milk to make the glaze. Roll the croissant dough out to 28 x 12 x ¹/4 inches. Cut the dough in half widthwise to make three 4-inch-wide strips. Cut each strip into 7-inch-long pieces (still 4 inches wide). Turn each 7 x 4-inch piece of dough so the short edge is toward you and lightly brush glaze over half of each piece.

Place 2 heaping tablespoons of the marzipan mixture on the unglazed half of each piece. Fold the glazed half over the marzipan and gently press to seal all seams.

Place the pastries on the prepared baking sheet (they can be placed close to each other), cover, and let rest in the refrigerator overnight or for at least 5 hours.

The next day, separate the pastries a bit on the baking sheet. Preheat the oven to 375°. Brush the pastries with the glaze and let rise until they are puffy and feel like marshmallows.

Brush the risen pastries with the glaze a second time, then sprinkle with the sliced almonds. Place the baking sheet on the center rack in the oven and bake for approximately 20 minutes, or until golden brown. When completely cool, dust with confectioners' sugar.

and ¹/2 cup sugar. Heat until almost boiling, then let cool.

Slice day-old croissants lengthwise down the middle, not cutting them completely through so that the top and bottom halves are hinged. Drop each croissant into the liquid, soak very briefly (just until slightly wet), then remove.

Put the almond mixture in a pastry bag and pipe some inside each of the croissants. Fold the tops of the croissant over the almond filling, then pipe a little of the almond mixture on the top of each croissant and dip them in slivered almonds.

Place croissants on a baking sheet and bake in a preheated 400° oven until the almond paste puffs and the almonds are golden brown. Serve warm or at room temperature, with a light dusting of confectioners' sugar.

CROISSANT JAMBON

Slice day-old croissants down the middle lengthwise. Fill them with a few slices of your favorite ham, about ¹/4 cup of grated Gruyère or Swiss cheese, and 1 table-spoon or so of Béchamel Sauce (see page 000). Place on a baking sheet and heat in a preheated 400° oven for about 10 minutes. Serve warm.

CHOCOLATINES

MAKES 12 PASTRIES

These unbelievably satisfying delights were among the first eight items we sold when we opened the bakery. They come and go off our menu, but they have many devotees. Traditionally, French schoolchildren buy these treats on their way home from school.

EGG GLAZE
1 egg
2 tablespoons milk

---

1 recipe Croissant Dough (page 36)
1½ cups (12 ounces) semisweet chocolate chips

Whisk together the egg and milk to make the glaze. Line a baking sheet with parchment paper.

Roll the croissant dough out to 28 x 12 x ¼ inches. Cut the dough width-wise into three 4-inch-wide strips. Cut each strip into 7-inch-long pieces (still 4 inches wide). Turn each 7 x 4-inch piece of dough so the short edge is toward you and lightly brush glaze over the entire surface. Sprinkle approximately 3 tablespoons of chocolate chips onto the middle third of each piece.

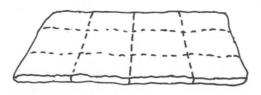

glaze

Fold the lower third over the chips and the upper third over that. Gently seal with your fingers.

Repeat the process with the rest of the dough rectangles. Place each Chocolatine seam side down on the prepared baking sheet.

Let the Chocolatines rest, covered, in the refrigerator for at least 5 hours or, preferably, overnight.

Line two baking sheets with parchment paper and divide the pastries between them, leaving approximately 2 inches between each one to allow space for rising. Brush them with the glaze and let rise until they are puffy and feel like marshmallows. Cover the remaining glaze with plastic wrap and store in the refrigerator. Preheat the oven to 375°.

Brush the risen pastries with the glaze a second time, then cut three diagonal slashes on the top of each Chocolatine. Place the baking sheets on the center rack in the oven and bake for approximately 20 minutes, or until golden brown.

CROISSANT AU LEVAIN

MAKES 36 TO 40 CROISSANTS

Traditionally, Croissant au Levain starts with a piece of *levain* or starter, from a rustic country bread called *pain de campagne,* which is made with whole-wheat flour. Croissant au Levain needs a long fermentation to develop its wide-open texture and deep flavor.

A professional baker might use a firm starter that is renewed with fresh flour and water several times a day. For the home baker, a liquid refrigerator starter works quite well. Notice the addition of a little yeast, which gives the sourdough an extra "push," especially in the oven.

Keep in mind two important points when baking sourdough goods: First, an excess of acidity in a starter reduces its ability to rise the dough, so keep your starter fresh by mixing some of your refrigerator sour with flour and water and letting it sit out several hours before you use it (see below for exact amounts). When a starter has been refreshed, it gets stronger and helps the dough rise. Second, anything made with sourdough will need a long fermentation process.

BAKER'S BASICS TO REVIEW
    Making a Firm Levain Sourdough Starter, page 48
    Making a Liquid Sourdough Starter (Refrigerator Sour) from
        a Firm Levain, page 49
    Measuring Dry Ingredients, page 21
    Doing the Roll-In and Turns, page 34
    Completing the Final Roll and Shaping, Rising, and
        Baking Pastries, page 35

SPONGE
    ¹/₂ cup Liquid Sourdough Starter (page 49)
    ¹/₄ cup water
    ¹/₂ cup whole-wheat flour

    1 package ($^1/_4$ ounce) active dry yeast

    2 cups warm water

    $^1/_2$ cup (4 ounces) butter, softened and cut into small chunks

    Scant $^1/_2$ cup powdered milk

    7 cups bread flour

    2 tablespoons salt

    $^1/_2$ cup sugar

———

    $2^1/_2$ cups (20 ounces) cold butter

EGG GLAZE

    1 egg

    2 tablespoons cold water

In a medium bowl, make the sponge, diluting the starter with the water. Add the whole-wheat flour and mix with a wooden spoon until smooth. The mixture will be the consistency of a thick batter. Let rise 5 to 6 hours, or until doubled.

For the dough, dilute the yeast in $^1/_4$ cup of the warm water. Set aside until creamy, about 10 minutes.

Place the sponge and the remaining $1^3/_4$ cups of water in a large bowl. Add the $^1/_2$ cup of butter and the milk powder and mix with a wooden spoon until moderately incorporated. Add the yeast mixture and stir to combine.

In a small bowl, combine the bread flour, salt, and sugar. Slowly add the dry mixture to the wet mixture, stirring with a wooden spoon or plastic dough scraper. Mix only until all the dry ingredients are incorporated. The dough will be damp and sticky but workable. Knead the dough no more than a few minutes on a lightly floured surface, working out any dry spots. Cover with a damp towel and let rise for 1 hour at room temperature.

Punch the dough down, then shape it into a flat 12 x 6 x 3-inch square. Cover the dough in plastic wrap or a split-open plastic food storage bag, and refrigerate for 12 to 15 hours.

For the roll-in, wrap all of the butter in parchment paper and pound it with a rolling pin until it is soft and malleable. Then, remove the parchment paper and, on the lightly floured work surface, with the rolling pin and a metal dough scraper alternately roll and shape the butter into a rectangle measuring 10 x 10 x $^1/_2$ inches thick.

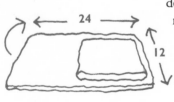

Remove the dough from the refrigerator and roll it out into a 24 x 12-inch rectangle. Place the slab of butter on the right half of the dough, fold the other half of the dough over the butter, and pinch the edges together to form a flat pillow.

Cover the dough pillow and transfer it to the refrigerator to rest for 10 minutes. To complete the first turn, remove the dough from the refrigerator and roll it out to approximately 30 x 12 inches. Fold the dough in thirds, then re-cover and let it rest in the refrigerator for at least 30 minutes.

Complete the second turn, rolling the dough out the opposite way and folding it in thirds again. Cover the dough and store overnight in the refrigerator. Repeat the process one more time the next day.

After the third turn is completed, cut the dough in half. Cover one half and return it to the refrigerator. Roll the other half into a 16-inch-wide rectangle $1/8$-inch-thick and cut it into two 8-inch-wide strips. Cut each strip into 9 or 10 triangles with 5-inch bases.

Starting with the base of the triangles, fold $1/4$ inch of the dough over onto itself and begin rolling the triangle up to the point. Gently stretch the dough by pulling on the tip as you roll it. Leave the pointed ends straight instead of curling into horns.

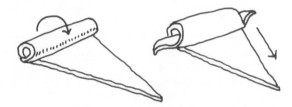

Repeat the process with the remaining half of the refrigerated dough or reserve it in the refrigerator for up to 2 days or in the freezer for up to 2 weeks.

Line two baking sheets with parchment paper. Place the croissants at least 2 inches apart on the prepared baking sheets. Whisk together the egg and water to make the glaze. Lightly brush each croissant with the glaze. Let rise, uncovered, for 4 to 5 hours at room temperature.

Preheat the oven to 400°. Brush the croissants once more with the glaze. Place the baking sheets on the center rack in the oven and bake for 18 minutes, or until golden brown.

SAMPLE TIMETABLE

FIRST DAY
3 P.M.: make sponge   9 P.M.: make dough and let rise   10 P.M.: refrigerate dough

SECOND DAY
9 A.M.: to 11 A.M.: do roll-in (2 turns)   11 A.M.: refrigerate dough

THIRD DAY
8 A.M.: do final turn, roll out dough, shape croissants, proof   2 to 3 P.M.: bake

---

Making a Firm Levain Sourdough Starter

An active sourdough starter can be made at home in 3 to 5 days. To start, you make a small ball of dough about the size of a walnut. French bakers call this the *chef* because it is the "chief" or first leavening agent in the process. After the *chef* has been refreshed with new flour and water one time, it becomes what French bakers call the *levain,* a natural leavener or "mother" as American bakers call it. After you are sure the levain is active, you can use it to make a liquid refrigerator sourdough starter that can be used for anything from bread to pancakes. Sourdough starter is used in Croissant au Levain (page 45), Sourdough Panettone (page 294), and Bob Hirsch's Sourdough Waffles (page 297). We recommend starting a *chef* at 8 P.M.

CHEF

> 1/2 cup whole-wheat flour
>
> Scant 1/4 cup warm water
>
> 1/8 teaspoon ground cumin
>
> 1/2 teaspoon milk

To make the chef, place the flour in a mound on a work surface and make a well in the middle. Pour about two-thirds of the warm water into the well and add the cumin and milk. With your index finger, start mixing the liquid with a little of the flour in the wall around the well. Pull in more and more of the flour to form a paste and, eventually, a firm dough. If the mixture is too dry, use some of the remaining water, adding it gradually until you have a pliable dough. The chef should be the same consistency as a bread dough, firm but somewhat sticky, and should spring back a little when touched.

Knead the dough for 5 to 8 minutes, then place the ball of dough in a ceramic or plastic container, cover it with a damp cloth, and let it rise at room temperature in a draft-free place for 24 to 36 hours. A crust will form on top of the chef, but inside it will be inflated and moist, with a spongy consistency. The aroma of cumin will still be evident and the dough will smell sour but fragrant and appealing.

Begin the next step, the first refreshment, at 8 P.M. the next evening.

FIRST REFRESHMENT

> 1/2 cup all-purpose flour
>
> 1 tablespoon chef
>
> Scant 1/4 cup warm water

Place the flour in a mound on a work surface and make a well in the middle. After removing and discarding any crust that has formed on the surface, break up the chef into small pieces. Place the pieces of the chef in the middle of the well. Pour in the warm water and stir and work the chef with your fingers until it is completely dissolved. Mix as directed for making the chef, adding a little more flour or water if necessary to make a dough that is firm but not too dry. It should be smooth and stand up in a small ball, but spring back when lightly pressed. This is the levain.

Transfer the levain to a bowl, cover with a damp towel, and let rise at room temperature for 12 to 18 hours. When ready, the levain will have risen noticeably and fallen slightly. It will still have a pleasing, slightly alcohol-like aroma. Inside, it will be inflated with tiny bubbles.

For the second refreshment, begin at 8 A.M. the next morning. (It can be done as late as 1 P.M., depending on its activity.)

SECOND REFRESHMENT

> 1/2 cup all-purpose flour
>
> 1/4 cup levain (from the previous step)
>
> Scant 1/4 cup warm water

Place the flour in a mound on a work surface and make a well in the middle. Place the levain in the well, add the water, and mix as directed for the first refreshment. Place a pan of water in the oven. Transfer the dough to a bowl, and cover with a damp towel. Set the bowl in the oven, warmed only by the pilot light (between 80° and 90°), and let the dough rise for 5 to 6 hours. The dough should increase in volume to three times its original size.

Making a Liquid Sourdough Starter (Refrigerator Sour) from a Firm Levain

Although some professional bakers use firm starters (they can be evaluated and controlled more easily), home bakers will get better results using a liquid starter because its acidity can be controlled by keeping it in the refrigertator.

Liquid starter can be used to make anything from bread to muffins, panettone to pancakes.

LIQUID SOURDOUGH STARTER (REFRIGERATOR SOUR)

1 cup active (5 to 6 hours old) Firm
    Levain Sourdough Starter
    (page 48)
2 cups warm water
1 1/2 cups all-purpose or bread flour

Chop the firm levain into pieces and place it in a large wide-mouthed jar. Add 1 cup of the warm water and stir the mixture to partially dilute the dough. Add 3/4 cup of the all-purpose flour and stir vigorously for 2 to 3 minutes so that the mixture is well combined. Leave the soupy mixture in a draft-free place at room temperature for at least 8 hours or, preferably, overnight.

When the starter has risen to twice its size, it is refreshed one last time before it is ready for regular use. Add the remaining 1 cup of water and 3/4 cup all-purpose flour. Mix again to fully incorporate. Leave the mixture at room temperature for 4 to 8 hours, then place it, covered, in the refrigerator. Use as directed.

CARE AND USAGE

Liquid sourdough starter can be stored in the refrigerator indefinitely, provided it is refreshed periodically. The liquid starter is best when used on a weekly basis, but it can be refreshed and stored up to 14 days. Each time you use 1 cup of the starter, it must be replenished with 1/2 cup of water and 3/4 cup all-purpose flour. Add the water first and stir until the mixture has a liquid consistency. Then slowly add the flour and stir until it is fully incorporated. Leave the starter in a warm, draft-free place for 3 to 4 hours, then return it to the refrigerator for storage. Any excess liquid that separates from the top of the starter should always be poured off before it is refreshed with the 1/2 cup of water and 3/4 cup of flour.

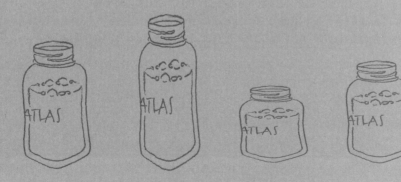

WHOLE-WHEAT CROISSANTS

MAKES 24 CROISSANTS

This is a variation of Gayle's Croissants (page 36). It's helpful to try the croissant recipe several times before attempting this one.

BAKER'S BASICS TO REVIEW
Measuring Dry Ingredients, page 21

DOUGH
$^1/_2$ cup water (warmed to 125°)
1 cup milk
2 packages ($^1/_2$ ounce) active dry yeast
3 cups whole-wheat flour
1 cup all-purpose flour
1 tablespoon salt
$^1/_4$ cup honey
2 tablespoons vegetable oil
1 egg

———

$^1/_2$ cup (4 ounces) unsalted butter

Follow the instructions for Gayle's Croissants (page 36), but make the following adjustments:

1. Make sure the dough is moist but not too sticky. If it sticks to the floured surface when mixed, add up to $^1/_4$ cup all-purpose flour to achieve a dough that is soft, smooth, and satiny.

2. After mixing and before the roll-in process, the dough can be left in the refrigerator for as little as 12 hours and as long as 36 hours.

3. If the dough becomes more elastic during the roll-in process, let it sit up to 1 hour longer in the refrigerator between turns. If the butter gets too hard to roll out when it has been refrigerated for 1 hour, let the dough rest, unrefrigerated, for 10 to 15 minutes before rolling out.

4. Use an egg glaze made of 1 egg and 2 to 3 tablespoons of milk. (The extra tablespoon of milk prevents the croissants from overbrowning.) They may be glazed several times during rising to prevent them from crusting over.

5. Rise 30 to 60 minutes longer for the final rising.

6. Bake at 375° (a lower temperature than for the basic croissants) for 17 to 20 minutes. Whole-wheat croissants tend to overbrown in the oven.

DOWNTOWNERS

MAKES 12 BUNS

These are often called Morning Buns. We named our version after the bakery that originally made them, the Downtown Bakery and Creamery in Healdsburg, California.

EGG GLAZE

1 egg
2 tablespoons milk

CINNAMON SUGAR

2 teaspoons ground cinnamon
1/4 cup granulated sugar
1/4 cup plus 2 tablespoons firmly packed brown sugar

———

1/2 recipe (22 ounces) Croissant Dough (page 36),
    or 1/4 recipe (19 ounces) Croissant au Levain (page 45)

———

1/4 cup granulated sugar, for finishing (optional)

In a small bowl, whisk together the egg and milk to make the glaze. In another small bowl, combine the cinnamon and sugars. Roll out the dough to 18 x 12 x 1/4 inches. Brush the entire piece of dough with a light coat of the glaze. Sprinkle the cinnamon-sugar mixture evenly over the entire surface of the dough. With the 18-inch side of dough nearest you, tightly roll the dough jelly-roll style so that you have a log about 1 1/2 to 2 inches in diameter and 18 inches long. Pinch the seam and edges to seal and brush away any excess cinnamon and sugar.

With a metal dough cutter (or the back edge of a knife), make slight indentations on the dough log at 1 1/2-inch intervals (there should be 12 sections), then cut into pieces. Place each piece in a separate cup of a nonstick or lightly buttered muffin pan. Let rise, uncovered, at room temperature for 2 1/2 to 3 hours, or until fully risen and slightly higher than the rim of the muffin cups.

Preheat the oven to 350°. Place the pan on the center rack in the oven and bake for 25 to 30 minutes, or until golden brown and puffy.

Place the 1/4 cup granulated sugar on a large tray or platter about the same size as the muffin pan. Turn the hot buns out onto the platter and immediately roll each one in the sugar until well coated. Let cool before serving.

GARLIC-CHEESE PRETZELS

MAKES 8 PRETZELS

Years ago, I destroyed a piece of croissant dough because it stuck when I passed it through the dough sheeter (a machine with two stainless-steel rollers and two canvas conveyor belts). It looked like a torn sweatshirt when it came out the other side. I pondered my next move and then decided to try working grated Cheddar cheese into the gnarled dough. The result became one of our most popular savory treats.

1/2 recipe (22 ounces) Croissant Dough (page 36),
   or 1/4 recipe (19 ounces) Croissant au Levain (page 45)
1 1/2 cups loosely packed grated sharp Cheddar cheese

EGG GLAZE
1 egg
2 tablespoons cold milk
_____

Garlic salt

Roll the dough out to measure 15 x 8 inches. In the center of the dough, place 3/4 cup of the grated cheese. Fold the left third of the dough over the cheese. Place the remaining 3/4 cup cheese on the folded dough, then fold the right third of dough over the cheese. (You should have three layers of dough with cheese between two of the layers.)

Seal the edges of the dough by pressing them with the rolling pin. Roll the dough out to measure 14 x 8 x 3/8 inches. Slicing lengthwise, cut eight 1-inch strips 14 inches long. Stretch piece until it is about 20 inches long, then twist it into a 24-inch-long corkscrew shape. Holding both ends of one strip, twist the tips together about 3 inches from the ends of the rope. Fold the rounded side down over the twisted ends, pinching them together firmly to secure.

Repeat until all the strips have been formed into pretzels. Line two baking sheets with parchment paper. Place

the pretzels on the prepared baking sheets. In a small bowl, whisk together the egg and milk to make the glaze. Brush the pretzels with the glaze, then sprinkle with garlic salt. Let rise, uncovered, at room temperature for $1^{1}/_{2}$ to 2 hours, or until doubled in size. Preheat the oven to 375°.

Place the baking sheets on the center rack in the oven and bake for 20 to 25 minutes, or until a rich brown color.

HAM AND CHEESE CROISSANTS

MAKES 6 CROISSANTS

A savory treat made with croissant dough that is a meal in itself. These filled croissants are one of our more popular items.

$^{1}/_{2}$ recipe (22 ounces) Croissant Dough (page 36),
or $^{1}/_{4}$ recipe (19 ounces) Croissant au Levain (page 45)
1 tablespoon Dijon mustard
$^{1}/_{2}$ pound ham, thinly sliced
2 cups grated Swiss cheese

EGG GLAZE
1 egg
2 tablespoons cold milk

Roll the dough out to measure 17 x 11 x $^{1}/_{4}$ inches. Cut the dough in half lengthwise, then into six $5^{1}/_{2}$-inch squares.

Coat the top side of each square of dough with $^{1}/_{2}$ teaspoon of the mustard, leaving a $^{1}/_{2}$-inch border uncoated. Divide the ham and cheese evenly among the 6 squares, again leaving a $^{1}/_{2}$-inch border uncovered.

Fold each square of dough into a triangle and press the edges together to firmly seal. In a small bowl, whisk together the egg and milk to make the glaze. Line a baking sheet with parchment paper. Place the triangles on the prepared baking sheet and brush them with the glaze. Let rise at room temperature for 2 hours, or until doubled in size. When the triangles have 30 minutes left to rise, preheat the oven to 400°.

Place the baking sheet on the center rack in the oven and bake for 15 to 17 minutes, or until golden brown.

Let cool completely on baking sheets before serving. To store longer than a few hours, place croissants in a plastic bag and refrigerate.

ASPARAGUS-CHEESE CROISSANTS

MAKES 6 CROISSANTS

This is a vegetarian version of the previous recipe.

> 30 thin asparagus spears ($1/4$ inch in diameter)
> $1/2$ recipe (22 ounces) Croissant Dough (page 36),
>   or $1/4$ recipe (19 ounces) Croissant au Levain (page 45)
> 1 tablespoon Dijon mustard
> 2 cups grated Swiss cheese

EGG GLAZE
> 1 egg
> 2 tablespoons cold milk

Trim the asparagus to about $6^{1}/2$ inches in length. Bring a pot of salted water to a boil. Add the asparagus and blanch for 5 to 6 minutes, or just until spears are tender. Test asparagus every minute after they've been blanching for 4 minutes; overcooked asparagus will make the pastry soggy. Drain well. Alternatively, steam the asparagus for 5 to 8 minutes, or until tender.

Line a baking sheet with parchment paper. Roll the dough out to measure 15 x 10 x $1/4$ inch. Cut the dough in half lengthwise. Cut each half into three 5-inch squares.

Coat the top side of each square with $1/2$ teaspoon of the mustard, leaving a $1/2$-inch border uncoated. Place 5 asparagus spears in the middle of each square of dough. Divide the cheese equally among the 6 squares, sprinkling it evenly over the asparagus and making sure that it covers all but the $1/2$-inch border around the edges of the dough.

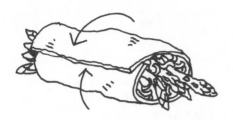

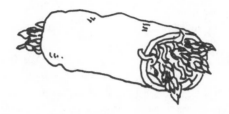

Fold one edge of the square toward the center so that it is parallel to the asparagus and covers the spears. Fold the other side toward the center so that it completely covers the other folded half, meeting the outside edge and leaving the two short ends open. Turn each pastry over and place seam side down on the prepared baking sheet.

Repeat until all squares are folded.

In a small bowl, whisk together the egg and milk to make the glaze. Brush the pastries with the glaze. Let the pastries rise, uncovered, at room temperature for $1\frac{1}{2}$ hours, or until doubled in size. Preheat the oven to 400°.

Place the baking sheet on the center rack in the oven and bake for 16 to 18 minutes, or until golden brown.

Let cool completely on the baking sheet before serving. To store longer than a few hours, place croissants in a plastic bag and refrigerate.

Jean-Claude Poilpre and Le Feyeux

Joe recalls one of our favorite bakers in Paris:

❦   ❦   ❦

Two years after the bakery opened, Gayle said we had to go to Paris. I went grudgingly because I was tired and sleep-deprived. I'll never forget that first day in Paris. We were both suffering from jet lag as we wandered through the Montmartre District—the center of the food trade, where fishmongers, butchers, foie gras and wild mushroom suppliers, and professional kitchenware shops mingle with the district's open-air markets, cafes, and the bustle of everyday Parisian life.

Half-asleep, we inadvertently found ourselves at the door of the Fédération de Boulanger et Pâtissier (the Parisian bakers' federation). Gayle stopped abruptly on the street and said, "Let's go up and ask if there's someone we can study with." "Gayle, I'm tired," I protested. The next thing I knew, we were upstairs sitting in front of a young lady who spoke only French. Somehow we managed to convey what we wanted. *"Cette homme* (this man)," she said as she pointed at a door labeled "Le President."

Inside we met Monsieur Lasse, who was friendly and cooperative. Never one to mince words, Gayle got right to the point: "We're bakers from California and we're looking for a baker in Paris who will let us watch his production." I sunk deeper into my chair, half from fatigue, half from embarrassment.

We were so overwhelmed by having the chance to speak directly with the president that we never noticed what was on the wall behind us: a huge board blanketed with pink, yellow, and blue cards, each containing the name and address of a baker in Paris—all 1,200 of them. M. Lasse

surveyed the cards and picked one. The name he gave us was Jean-Claude Poilpre, who owned a bakery called Le Feyeux. It was our first formal introduction to a Parisian baker.

When we met Jean-Claude Poilpre, we realized why M. Lasse matched us up with him. Jean-Claude is a genuine humanist with a great sense of humor. Jean-Claude is proud of his bakery and wanted to show us everything. On that first visit, and on every visit since, he has always made the time to show us some aspect of his production no matter how busy he is. On our second visit, we spent nine days at his bakery and came away with 110 recipes. More important, what we saw inspired us to expand our own little bakery into a food emporium with a labyrinthine work area where we could make anything we could imagine. (And we eventually did just that. Today, the only type of desserts we don't make at Gayle's that the pastry chefs make at Le Feyeux are chocolate candies and ice cream.)

At Le Feyeux, we learned that separate rooms for separate processes help focus production. Each type of product turns out best when prepared in a certain environment. For example, it's not good to make whipped cream near the ovens; chocolate loathes humidity; and rolling the butter into croissant dough must be done in a cool area. What's good for the baguette isn't always good for the petit four.

We also learned that French bakers regard each recipe as a formula that can be etched in one's memory. At Le Feyeux they had a large laminated card on which the small batch sizes for each and every recipe were written (in metric, of course). Most recipes were based on a kilo of flour. So the croissant recipe, for example, called for 25 grams of salt and 80 grams of sugar per kilo of flour. One of the apprentices' first lessons is to memorize the proportions. Simply by multiplying the proportions by the desired batch size, the bakers adjust the amounts in their heads, a trick that is virtually impossible with our measuring system.

Jean-Claude and his wife Pierrette, who runs the retail shop, appear ready to retire soon. Their son Frederique, who was just a tyke when we met him on our first visit is now twenty years old and going away to school. The Poilpres have spent close to twenty years working ten to twelve hours a day, six days a week to pay off the bakery that they bought from its original owner, Monsieur Feyeux. It has not been an easy life. Like all French bakers, the Poilpres have to serve three masters at all times: the consumer, who always wants the perfect baguette, baked three times a day, for the perfect (low) price; the bakers' federation, which regulates wages and apprenticeship programs; and the government, which levies high taxes, mandates the ingredients that can be used, and has controlled the price of bread for centuries. Because of all this and perhaps because many bakeries and cafes in Paris are closing each year due to competition from fast food outlets, the Poilpres are probably relieved that Frederique is not planning to follow in their footsteps.

The first time we meet most bakers, it's usually in the middle of the day, which is the end of their workday and means they have the

time and inclination to talk. If we strike up a good relationship and they invite us back, which happened that day in 1980 with Jean-Claude, we return for a pre-dawn visit to watch their production in full swing.

When Gayle and I made our first early morning visit to Le Feyeux, it was to watch the bread being made. It was dark outside and Paris was still asleep—except for the bakers, of course. The day before, Jean-Claude had told me to knock on the door and someone would let us in. We knocked and knocked, but no one heard us. After 15 minutes or so, an apprentice came around the corner on his way into work. Gayle and I told him why we were there. He simply turned the knob and opened the door. Like the Poilpres' hearts, the door had been open to us all the time.

❀ ❀ ❀

Danish Pastry

BEFORE YOU BEGIN

Before beginning the recipes in this chapter, turn to page 34 and read "Doing the Roll-In and Turns." The technique for rolling in the butter and giving the dough turns is the same for Danish as for croissant and puff pastry dough, but the process for Danish pastry is a bit simpler because the dough is softer and easier to roll out. If you have ever wanted to try a roll-in dough, and love sweet things for breakfast, these are the perfect recipes to start with.

Many of the pastries in this chapter can be filled with different fillings in addition to the ones specifically called for. So before you start a recipe, check out our basic filling recipes, which are at the end of the chapter. Then, mix and match them as you wish.

True American baking is a compilation of our combined heritage, but Americans have taken to Danish pastries like the French have taken to croissants and the Italians to biscotti. Bakeries all over the country have been making Danish pastries since the early 1930s, but a decade or so after the sweet rolls were introduced here, they suffered the indignities of mass production. With the advent of the supermarket, Danish pastries were delivered to the masses in cardboard boxes covered with cellophane. They were made with shortening, loaded with artificial flavorings, and laced with preservatives for long shelf life. Old-fashioned Danish pastries are a sweet pastry dough made with butter and rolled the same way as croissants. The differences are that Danish pastry dough is a little sweeter, is richer (because it has eggs and additional milk), and is often flavored with vanilla extract or lemon zest. The butter and dough create a very delicate pastry that can easily be made at home. Danish pastries are filled with ricotta cheese, pastry cream, fresh fruit compotes, and homemade jams. At Gayle's, we make more than twenty different ones, most of which are included in this chapter.

DANISH PASTRY DOUGH

MAKES 4¹/₂ POUNDS OF DOUGH

The principles of making Danish pastry are the same as for croissant dough. The only real difference is that Danish dough is sweeter and richer. It is a wonderfully versatile dough. We recommend making this quantity of dough because the process is time-consuming, the dough turns out better, and any extra can be frozen for future use.

BAKER'S BASICS TO REVIEW

Measuring Dry Ingredients, page 21
Doing the Roll-In and Turns, page 34

---

2 cups milk
2 packages (¹/₂ ounce) active dry yeast
2 large eggs
¹/₂ teaspoon pure vanilla extract
7 cups all-purpose flour
¹/₃ cup plus I tablespoon sugar
I¹/₂ teaspoons salt
2 cups (I pound) unsalted butter, at room temperature

Warm the milk to 110°. Sprinkle the yeast over the milk and let it dissolve for 5 minutes, then whisk to fully dissolve. Add the eggs and vanilla and whisk just until mixed.

Mix the flour, sugar, and salt together in a large bowl. Using your fingertips and palms, rub 3 tablespoons of the butter into the flour mixture, rubbing just until the butter is no longer visible in the flour.

Add the wet ingredients to the flour mixture, stirring with a wooden spoon until incorporated. Knead the dough on a floured work surface just until smooth; there should be no dry spots left. Be careful not to overknead. The dough should be slightly wet.

Lightly flour a baking sheet. Place the dough on the prepared baking sheet and shape it into a rough rectangle. Dust the top with flour and cover with plastic wrap. Refrigerate for 1 hour.

Transfer the dough from the baking sheet to the lightly floured work surface, and roll out into a 26 x 13 x ³/₈-inch rectangle. Brush off any excess flour. Position the rectangle so that one of the short sides is closest to you.

The butter should be soft enough to spread, but not so soft that

Danish Pastry

59

it has started to melt. By hand, smear the butter evenly over the lower two-thirds of the dough, leaving a ^{1}/2-inch unbuttered border around side and bottom edges.

Fold the upper third of the dough toward the center of the rectangle, then fold the lowest third over that.

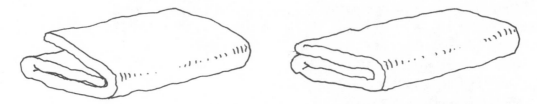

With your fingers, crimp the short edges and the seam on top to seal in the butter. Turn the dough so that the long, crimped edge is on your right.

With one of the short sides closest to you, gently roll the dough out into a 21 x 13 x ^{3}/8-inch rectangle, using only enough flour to keep the dough from sticking to the work surface and rolling pin. Brush off the excess flour. Fold the top third of the dough toward the middle, then the lower third up over that. Place on the baking sheet. Cover with plastic wrap and refrigerate for 45 minutes. Repeat this process three more times, refrigerating the dough for 30 minutes between each turn.

After all of the turns are complete, let the dough rest in the refrigerator for at least 5 hours (overnight is best) before using as directed. At this point, the dough can be refrigerated for up to 2 days or frozen for up to 2 weeks. Freeze on a baking sheet, well sealed with plastic wrap.

RASPBERRY AND
PASTRY CREAM FIGURE EIGHTS

MAKES 12 PASTRIES

We make several types of Danish using the traditional figure-eight shape. They are fun to eat because there are two completely different flavors—one at each end. Some people like to eat them by taking alternating bites from each end; others just eat the Danish from one end to the other. At Gayle's, we make all our fillings, with the exception of the jam fillings, from scratch.

BAKER'S BASICS TO REVIEW
Storing Desserts and Pastries, page 23

$1/2$ recipe ($2^1/4$ pounds) Danish Pastry Dough (page 59)

EGG GLAZE
1 large egg
2 tablespoons milk

---

1 cup homemade raspberry jam
1 cup Pastry Cream (page 127)
Clear Glaze (page 81)
Sugar Glaze (page 81)

Line two large baking sheets with parchment paper.

Lightly flour the work surface. Roll the dough out to measure 12 x 12 x $1/2$ inches. Dust off any excess flour. With a sharp knife, cut the dough into 1-inch strips.

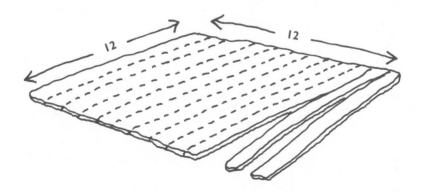

(continued)

Place one 12 x 1-inch strip horizontally on the work surface. Place one palm on each end of the dough and begin to apply light pressure, simultaneously rolling the dough under your right hand away from you and the dough under your left hand toward you. This will begin to twist the dough. Continue the gentle rolling motion, until the entire strip, which should remain 12 to 14 inches long, is twisted.

Shape the strip of twisted dough into a reverse "S" shape. Bend the top end of the dough down so that it extends past the middle of the "S."

On the other side, bring the bottom end of the dough up so that it also extends past the middle of the "S."

Pinch the middle of the pastry to secure the ends, then invert the figure eight onto the prepared baking sheet.

To make a pocket for the fillings, form a depression in the center of the circles by gently pressing with your fingers to flatten the middle. This also seals the bottom of the dough so that the filling doesn't leak out during baking.

Form the rest of the figure eights the same way and place 6 on each of the baking sheets, leaving enough room between each one for them to double in size.

In a small bowl, whisk together the egg and milk to make the glaze. Brush each pastry with the glaze. Place about 1 tablespoon of jam in one end of each figure eight and 1 tablespoon of pastry cream in the other end.

Let the pastries rise at room temperature in a draft-free place for 1 1/2 hours, or until they have doubled in size and feel like a marshmallow when pressed gently with a finger. Preheat the oven to 350° about 30 minutes before baking.

Place the baking sheets on the center rack in the oven and bake for 15 to 20 minutes, or until the pastries are golden brown on the top and bottom. Let cool on the baking sheets for 5 minutes. With a pastry brush, coat the pastries with the Clear Glaze. When the figure eights have cooled completely, dip a fork in the Sugar Glaze and wave it diagonally over the pastries to decorate them with thin lines of glaze. Let the glaze set before serving or storing.

FIGURE-EIGHT VARIATIONS

Apricot, strawberry, or your favorite jam can be substituted for the raspberry jam. For other variations, use any of the fillings on pages 79 and 80.

APPLE AND CHEESE
FIGURE EIGHTS

MAKES 12 PASTRIES

PETITE FIGURE
EIGHTS

*These smaller versions of
the standard-sized figure
eights may disappear twice
as fast, so you might make a
double batch. They are
perfect for a Sunday brunch.
To make Petite Figure Eights,
follow the instructions for the
Raspberry and Pastry Cream
Figure Eights (page 61), using
any of the recommended
fillings (see the Apple and
Cheese Figure Eights recipe,
right), with the following
adjustments:*

*• Cut the 12 x 12 x 1/2-inch
sheet of dough in half,
then cut each half into
twelve 6 x 1-inch strips
(you will have 24 strips).*

*• After forming the pastries,
place 3/4 (for cheese-based
fillings) to 1 1/2 teaspoons
of filling in each end of the
figure eights. Rise, bake,
and glaze as instructed on
page 63, but decrease the
baking time to 10 to 15
minutes.*

Makes 24 pastries.

1/2 recipe (2 1/4 pounds) Danish Pastry Dough (page 59)

EGG GLAZE
1 large egg
2 tablespoons milk

———

1/2 cup Cheese Filling (page 80)
1 cup Apple Filling (page 80)
1 cup Streusel Topping (page 81)
Clear Glaze (page 81)
Sugar Glaze (page 81)

Follow the instructions for the Raspberry and Pastry Cream Figure Eights (page 61) to make 12 shaped, egg-glazed, unfilled pastries.

Place about 1 1/2 teaspoons of the Cheese Filling in one end of each figure eight and 1 tablespoon of Apple Filling in the other end. Sprinkle 1 teaspoon of the Streusel Topping over the Apple Filling in each pastry. Rise, bake, and glaze as directed for Raspberry and Pastry Cream Figure Eights.

STRAWBERRY AND
CHEESE SNAILS

MAKES 12 PASTRIES

Snails are an old-fashioned American breakfast treat that may seem like a lot of work, but we guarantee you'll become a legend if you make them.

BAKER'S BASICS TO REVIEW
Filling and Using a Nylon Pastry Bag, page 20
Storing Desserts and Pastries, page 23

———

1/2 recipe (2 1/4 pounds) Danish Pastry Dough (page 59)

EGG GLAZE
1 large egg
2 tablespoons milk

———

1 1/2 cups Cheese Filling (page 80)
1 1/2 cups homemade strawberry jam
1 cup Streusel Topping (page 81)

———

Clear Glaze (page 81)
Sugar Glaze (page 81)

LEMON SNAIL VARIATION

Make as directed for the Strawberry and Cheese Snails (left), but fill each snail with 2 tablespoons English Lemon Curd (page 173) instead of the cheese and strawberry jam.

Line two large baking sheets with parchment paper.

Lightly flour the work surface. Roll the dough out to measure 12 x 12 x 1/2 inches. Dust off any excess flour. With a sharp knife, cut the dough into 1-inch strips.

Place one of the strips horizontally on the work surface. Place one palm on each end of the dough and begin to apply light pressure, simultaneously rolling the dough under your right hand away from you and the dough under your left hand toward you. This will begin to twist the dough. Continue the gentle rolling motion, until the entire strip, which should remain 12 to 14 inches long, is twisted.

Take the left end of the dough and gently press the very tip onto the work surface, flattening it slightly. Lift the right end of the dough and circle it around the pinched end in a spiral motion, keeping the dough flat on the work surface.

When the dough is completely wrapped into a spiral, tuck 1 inch

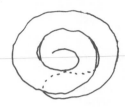

of the right end under the pastry and pinch together to seal. Gently place the snail on one of the prepared baking sheets. Repeat to form the rest of the snails. Place 6 snails on each of the baking sheets, leaving enough room between each one for them to double in size.

To make a pocket for the filling, form a depression in the center of the snails by gently pressing with your fingers to flatten the middle. This also seals the bottom of the dough so that the filling doesn't leak out during baking.

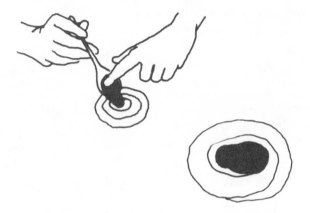

In a small bowl, whisk together the egg and milk to make the glaze. Brush each pastry with the glaze.

Fill a pastry bag fitted with a 1/2-inch tip with the Cheese Filling. Pipe about 1 tablespoon of the filling around the outer edge of the pocket of each snail. Alternately, use a spoon to place the Cheese Filling in the pocket. (Be careful to leave space in the middle for the jam.) Fill the centers with about 1 tablespoon of jam.

Sprinkle 1 tablespoon of the Streusel Topping over the fillings. Let the pastries rise at room temperature in a draft-free place for 1 1/2 hours, or until they have doubled in size and feel like a marshmallow when pressed gently with a finger. Preheat the oven to 350° about 30 minutes before baking.

Place the baking sheets on the center rack in the oven and bake for 15 minutes, or until the pastries are brown on the top and bottom. Let cool on the baking sheets for 5 minutes. With a pastry brush, coat the tops with the Clear Glaze. When the snails have cooled completely, dip a fork in the Sugar Glaze and wave it diagonally over the pastries to decorate them with thin lines of glaze. Let the glaze set before serving or storing.

BLUEBERRY AND PASTRY CREAM SNAILS

MAKES 12 PASTRIES

These are a wonderful alternative to the Strawberry and Cheese Snails. The smooth custard and tangy blueberries are a killer combo.

BAKER'S BASICS TO REVIEW
Filling and Using a Nylon Pastry Bag, page 20.

———

1/2 recipe (2 1/4 pounds) Danish Pastry Dough (page 59)

EGG GLAZE
1 large egg
2 tablespoons milk

———

1 1/2 cups Pastry Cream (page 127)
Blueberry Filling (page 79)
1 cup Streusel Topping (page 81)
Clear Glaze (page 81)
Sugar Glaze (page 81)

Follow the directions for the Strawberry and Cheese Snails (page 65) to make 12 shaped, egg-glazed, unfilled pastries.

Fill a pastry bag fitted with a 1/2-inch tip with the Pastry Cream. Pipe about 2 tablespoons of the filling around the outer edge of the pocket of each snail. Alternately, use a spoon to place the Pastry Cream in the pocket. (Be careful to leave space in the center for the filling.) Fill the centers with about 1 tablespoon of Blueberry Filling. Sprinkle 1 tablespoon of the Streusel Topping over the fillings. Rise, bake, and glaze as directed for the Strawberry and Cheese Snails.

PETITE SNAILS

These miniature versions of the standard-sized pastries are perfect for a breakfast buffet. To make Petite Snails, follow the instructions for the Strawberry and Cheese Snails (page 65), using any of the fillings on pages 79 and 80, with the following adjustments:

• Cut the 12 x 12 x 1/2-inch sheet of dough in half, then cut twelve 6 x 1-inch strips from each half (you will have 24 strips).

• After forming the pastries, place 1 1/2 teaspoons to 1 tablespoon of filling in each snail. Rise, bake, and glaze according to the instructions on page 66, but decrease the baking time to 10 to 15 minutes.

Makes 24 pastries.

PECAN SCHNECKEN

MAKES 24 PASTRIES

This is the most decadent of all Danish pastries. They're also fun to make. People won't believe you actually made them, and they're easy, too. The butter, brown sugar, and honey make them deliciously sticky as well as sweet.

1 recipe Danish Pastry Dough (page 59)

BROWN SUGAR–HONEY GOO
1 cup (8 ounces) butter, at room temperature
2 cups firmly packed brown sugar
1/3 cup honey
2 tablespoons plus 1/2 teaspoon cornstarch
1/8 teaspoon salt

———

3 cups coarsely chopped pecans

EGG GLAZE
1 large egg
2 tablespoons milk

FILLING
1 cup granulated sugar
1 cup firmly packed brown sugar
2 tablespoons ground cinnamon

Butter the cups and tops of two 12-cup muffin pans. Line two baking sheets with parchment paper.

To make the "goo," with a handheld mixer beat the butter until smooth. Add the brown sugar and mix until well incorporated. Mix in the honey. Add the cornstarch and salt and mix well to combine.

Divide the goo evenly among the muffin cups, filling them about 1/2 inch high. Divide the pecans among the muffin cups, sprinkling them over the goo.

Lightly flour a work surface. Roll the dough out to measure 24 x 12 x 1/8 inches, positioning one of the long sides nearest you. In a small bowl, whisk together the egg and milk to make the glaze. In a separate bowl, combine the filling ingredients. Generously brush the dough with the glaze. Spread the filling evenly over the glazed surface, leaving a 1/2-inch border along the bottom edge.

Beginning with the top edge of the dough, fold 3/4 inch of dough over onto itself and flatten it gently. Repeat this step. With the folded strip of dough, begin rolling the sheet into a log shape, creating a little tension while rolling so that the log is tight. (The log should not be so tight that the dough tears nor should it be so loose that the filling falls out.)

Pinch the ends of the log to seal in the filling. Trim away $3/4$ inch from each end. Cut the dough into $1\frac{1}{2}$-inch-wide slices.

Place them in the muffin cups with one of the cut sides up.

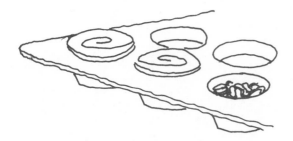

Let the pastries rise at room temperature in a draft-free place for $1\frac{1}{2}$ hours, or until they have increased in size to one and a half times their original volume. Preheat the oven to 350° about 30 minutes before baking.

Set the muffin tins on two unlined baking sheets. Place the baking sheets on the upper rack in the oven and bake for 20 to 25 minutes, or until the tops of the pastries are golden and you can lift them up and see whether the dough is baked all the way through.

Turn the pastries out nut side up onto two clean baking sheets. Spoon any brown sugar mixture remaining in the muffin tins over the pastries. Wait about 5 minutes, then scrape up any of the brown sugar mixture and nuts that may have fallen off the pastries and put it back on top of them. Let the pastries cool, periodically lifting them with a spatula to prevent them from sticking to the baking sheets.

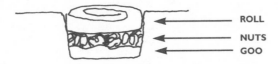

ROLL
NUTS
GOO

CHEESE DANISH

There are many recipes for Cheese Danish. Ours uses ricotta cheese for the filling. It has quite a following.

BAKER'S BASICS TO REVIEW
Storing Desserts and Pastries, page 23

1/2 recipe (2 1/4 pounds) Danish Pastry Dough (page 59)
1 1/2 cups Cheese Filling (page 80)

EGG GLAZE
1 large egg
2 tablespoons milk

Clear Glaze (page 81)
Sugar Glaze (page 81)

Line two baking sheets with parchment paper.

Lightly flour a work surface. Roll the dough out to measure 26 1/4 x 11 x 1/4 inches. Brush off excess flour. Cut the dough in half lengthwise. Cut each half into 5 pieces that are 5 1/4 inches long. Place about 2 tablespoons of the filling in the center of each square. Lift the top right corner and bottom left corner of dough and pinch them together over the cheese. Lift the two remaining corners of dough up to meet the pinched pieces and pinch all 4 together to seal well. (They have a tendency to come apart during rising and baking.) Repeat this process with the remaining squares.

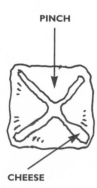

PINCH

CHEESE

Transfer the pastries to the prepared baking sheets, leaving enough room between each one for them to double in size. In a small bowl, whisk together the egg and milk to make the glaze. Brush each pastry well with the glaze.

Let the pastries rise at room temperature in a draft-free place for 1 hour 15 minutes, or until they have doubled in size and feel like a marshmallow when pressed gently with a finger. Preheat the oven to 350° about 30 minutes before baking.

Just before baking, gently pinch the four corners together again to firmly seal, being careful not to deflate the pastry. Place the baking sheets on the center rack in the oven and bake for 15 to 20 minutes, or until the pastries are golden brown on the top and bottom. Cool on the baking sheets for 5 minutes. With a pastry brush, coat the tops with the Clear Glaze. When the pastries have cooled completely, dip a fork in the Sugar Glaze and wave it diagonally over the pastries to decorate them with thin lines of glaze. Let the glaze set before serving or storing.

CHRISTOPHER'S BUNS

MAKES 9 BUNS

One of the things we like to do at Gayle's is encourage our staff members to bring in and try out recipes they want the bakery to sell. If we all like the results, we put it on the menu. Such was the case in 1994 when Christopher Love, then the head of our dough department, brought in this recipe. There was never a question about selling it—one bite was all it took to convince us. These rich, spiral-shaped rolls have cinnamon swirled inside and a butter and cream cheese glaze that melts slightly as they cool.

BAKER'S BASICS TO REVIEW
Storing Desserts and Pastries, page 23

---

^{1}/2 recipe (2^1/4 pounds) Danish Pastry Dough (page 59)

EGG GLAZE
1 large egg
2 tablespoons milk

CINNAMON SUGAR
1 cup sugar
1 tablespoon plus 1 teaspoon ground cinnamon

---

^{1}/3 cup raisins (optional)

CREAM CHEESE GLAZE
3 ounces cream cheese, at room temperature
^{3}/4 cup butter, at room temperature
1^3/4 cups confectioners' sugar
2 teaspoons pure vanilla extract

Butter a 13 x 9-inch pan with sides that are at least 2 inches high.
Lightly flour a work surface. Roll the dough out to measure 18 x 16 x ^{1}/4 inches, with one of the long sides nearest you. Brush off any excess flour.
In a small bowl, whisk together the egg and milk to make the Egg Glaze.

Danish Pastry

With a pastry brush, apply a thin coat of Egg Glaze over the entire surface of the dough. Spread the cinnamon sugar mixture evenly over the surface, leaving a $1/2$-inch border along the bottom edge. Sprinkle the raisins evenly over the cinnamon sugar.

Beginning at the top of the dough, fold $1/2$ inch of dough over onto itself and press it down firmly. With the doubled-up strip of dough, begin rolling the sheet into a log shape, creating a little tension while rolling so that the log is tight. (The log should not be so tight that the dough tears nor should it be so loose that the filling falls out.) Pinch the ends of the log to seal in the filling.

Cut the log into 2-inch-wide slices and place them in the pan with one of the cut sides up.

Let the buns rise at room temperature in a draft-free place for 2 hours, or until they have doubled in size and feel like a marshmallow when pressed gently with a finger. Preheat the oven to 350° about 30 minutes before baking.

Place the baking sheet on the center rack in the oven and decrease the heat to 325°. Bake for 25 to 30 minutes, or until golden brown (including the buns in the center of the pan). Set the pan on a rack, and let the buns cool in the pan until slightly warm and almost room temperature.

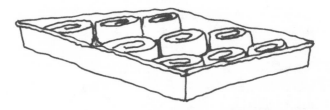

To make the Cream Cheese Glaze, with a handheld mixer or by hand, blend all of the ingredients until smooth. With a rubber spatula, spread the glaze evenly over the top of the buns.

RASPBERRY-ALMOND-CHOCOLATE DANISH

MAKES 12 PASTRIES

This breakfast roll combines three of our favorite baking ingredients. The pastries are rich, but they are good. They are another invention of Gayle's former dough department manager, Christopher Love.

BAKER'S BASICS TO REVIEW

Melting Chocolate, page 21

Storing Desserts and Pastries, page 23

———

$^1/_2$ recipe ($2^1/_4$ pounds) Danish Pastry Dough (page 59)

$1^1/_4$ cups Pain d'Amande filling (page 42)

$^1/_3$ cup homemade raspberry jam

EGG GLAZE

1 large egg

2 tablespoons milk

———

Clear Glaze (page 81)

1 cup semisweet chocolate chips

Line two large baking sheets with parchment paper.

Lightly flour a work surface. Roll the dough out to measure 18 x 13$^1/_2$ x $^1/_4$ inches. Dust off any excess flour. Cut the dough in thirds horizontally and quarters vertically to make twelve 4$^1/_2$ x 4$^1/_2$-inch squares.

Pinch off about 2 tablespoons of almond filling and form it into a log shape about 2$^1/_2$ inches long. Place the log of filling diagonally across the center of a square of dough. With a spoon, place 1 tablespoon of raspberry jam in a line alongside the log of filling. Repeat for the remaining 11 squares.

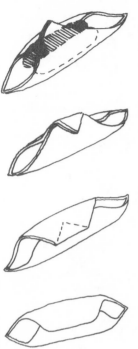

Bring the two points of the dough in the middle of the filling toward the center and pinch hard to seal. Then, fold them over twice and press gently to flatten. The pastry will now be shaped like a cigar. Repeat for the remaining squares.

Transfer the pastries to the prepared baking sheets, leaving enough room between each one for them to double in size. In a small bowl, whisk together the egg and milk to make the Egg Glaze. With a pastry brush, coat the top of each pastry with the Egg Glaze.

Let the pastries rise at room temperature in a draft-free place for 1½ hours, or until they have doubled in size and feel like a marshmallow when pressed gently with a finger. Preheat the oven to 350° about 30 minutes before baking.

Place the baking sheets on the center rack in the oven and bake for 15 minutes, or until the pastries are brown on the top and bottom. Let them cool on the baking sheets for 5 minutes, then brush with the Clear Glaze.

While the pastries are cooling, melt the chocolate chips in the top of a double boiler over low heat. When the pastries are completely cool, drizzle the tops with the melted chocolate by dipping a fork in the chocolate and waving it diagonally over them. Let the chocolate set before serving or storing.

BEAR CLAWS

MAKES 10 PASTRIES

In the professional baker's world, these pastries are lifesavers. We always have a lot of cake crumbs left over from trimming cakes, and bear claws are the perfect use for them. This filling calls for using only very fresh scraps, as stale ones will not produce the desired flavor. When you are trimming your cakes, be sure to wrap the scraps tightly and freeze them immediately.

½ recipe (2¼ pounds) Danish Pastry Dough (page 59)
Bear Claw Filling, at room temperature (page 79)

EGG GLAZE
1 large egg
2 tablespoons milk

———

1¼ cups sliced almonds
Clear Glaze (page 81)
Sugar Glaze (page 81)

Line two large baking sheets with parchment paper.

Lightly flour a work surface. Roll the dough out to measure 26 x 11 x ¼ inches. Brush off any excess flour. With a pastry cutter or sharp knife, cut the dough in half lengthwise.

Pinch off small pieces of the filling and shape them into 1-inch-wide strips. Place the strips lengthwise along the top third of each piece of dough, making a continuous strip of filling that runs the length of the pieces of dough.

Working with one length of dough, fold the top third over the filling. Then, fold the filled section over the last third so that the seam is in the center underneath the folded dough. Repeat with the other piece of dough. You will have two 26-inch-long logs of filled dough.

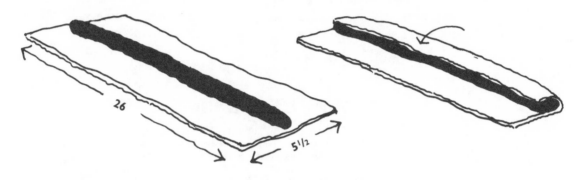

With the heal of your hand, flatten one long side of each log. Cut each log into five 5¼-inch pieces. Then, make cuts along the flattened edge of each piece about ¾ inch into the log and ½ inch apart.

In a small bowl, whisk together the egg and milk to make the Egg Glaze. With a pastry brush, coat each pastry with the Egg Glaze. Place the almonds on a plate. Invert each pastry onto the almonds and press gently to adhere the nuts to the pastry. Transfer the pastries, almond side up, to the prepared

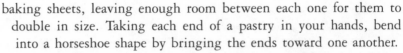

baking sheets, leaving enough room between each one for them to double in size. Taking each end of a pastry in your hands, bend into a horseshoe shape by bringing the ends toward one another.

Pinch each end to seal in the filling, and repeat for the remaining pastries.

Let the pastries rise at room temperature in a draft-free place for 1¹/₂ hours, or until they have doubled in size and feel like a marshmallow when pressed gently with a finger. Preheat the oven to 350° about 30 minutes before baking.

Place the baking sheets on the center rack in the oven and bake for 20 minutes, or until they are golden brown on the top and bottom. Let cool on the baking sheets for 5 minutes, then brush them with Clear Glaze. When the pastries are completely cool, drizzle them with the Sugar Glaze by dipping a fork in the glaze and waving it diagonally over them.

APPLE BEAR CLAW DANISH BRAID

MAKES TWO 4 X 10-INCH PASTRIES

This is a beautiful braided pastry that's a perfect treat to make for a special friend or for your family. The addition of baked apples to the filling is irresistible.

BAKER'S BASICS TO REVIEW
Storing Desserts and Pastries, page 23

---

¹/₂ recipe (2¹/₄ pounds) Danish Pastry Dough (page 59)
Bear Claw Filling, at room temperature (page 79)
Apple Filling (page 80)

EGG GLAZE
1 large egg
2 tablespoons milk

---

1 cup Streusel Topping (page 81)
Clear Glaze (page 81)
Sugar Glaze (page 81)

Line two large baking sheets with parchment paper.

Lightly flour a work surface. Roll the dough out to measure 20 x 10 x ¹/₃ inches. Brush off any excess flour. Cut the dough in half widthwise to make two 10-inch squares. Along the sides of each square, cut 3-inch-long, 1-inch-wide diagonal strips. Transfer the squares to the prepared baking sheets. Divide the Bear Claw Filling in half, form each half into a log, and place one log in the middle of each square of dough. Spoon half of the Apple Filling over the strips of Bear Claw Filling on each square of dough.

Fold about 2 inches of dough at the top and bottom of the squares toward the center over the end of the strips of filling. Starting at the bottom of each square, fold the right strip of dough

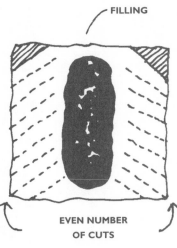

FILLING

EVEN NUMBER OF CUTS

toward the middle and lay it over the filling, then lay the left strip over the right. Alternating right and left, move up the pastry, laying each strip over the previous one. Trim away any excess dough that may hang over the top or bottom.

In a small bowl, whisk together the egg and milk to make the Egg Glaze. With a pastry brush, generously coat the top of the pastries with the Egg Glaze. Sprinkle the Streusel Topping over the pastries.

Let the pastries rise at room temperature in a draft-free place for 2 hours, or until they have doubled in size and feel like a marshmallow when pressed gently with a finger. Preheat the oven to 350° about 30 minutes before baking.

Place the baking sheets on the center rack in the oven and bake for 20 to 25 minutes, or until they are golden brown on the top and bottom. After the pastries have cooled for 5 minutes, brush the tops with Clear Glaze. When the braids have cooled completely, drizzle the pastries with Sugar Glaze by dipping a fork in the glaze and waving it diagonally over the top of them.

MULTIFRUIT DANISH RING

MAKES ONE 9-INCH RING

This pastry features a combination of all of the fillings we use for Danish pastry. It is a nice alternative to making individual pastries for a party. The ring serves 8 and can be made with any fillings you like. The different colors of the fillings make this a visual treat.

BAKER'S BASICS TO REVIEW
   Storing Desserts and Pastries, page 23

1/2 recipe (2 1/4 pounds) Danish Pastry Dough (page 59)
1 cup Pastry Cream (page 127), at room temperature
1 cup Cheese Filling (page 80), at room temperature
16 tablespoons assorted fruit fillings (such as raspberry jam,
   Blueberry Filling [page 79], strawberry jam, and apricot jam)
1/2 cup Streusel Topping (page 81)
Clear Glaze (page 81)
Sugar Glaze (page 81)

Butter a 9-inch springform or removable-bottom cake pan.

Lightly flour a work surface. Roll out the dough to measure 21 x 10 1/2 x 1/3 inches. Brush off any excess flour. Cut the dough in half lengthwise, then cut it into eight 5 1/4 x 5 1/4-inch squares.

Fold each square in half. Pinch the ends together to seal, making eight pockets 5 1/4 inches long and 2 5/8 inches high. Place 6 pockets of dough, with the openings facing up, around the inside edge of the cake pan and 2 in the center. Push the pockets down slightly as you place them in the pan so they stand up straight.

Carefully spoon 2 tablespoons of Pastry Cream into 4 of the pockets. Spoon 2 tablespoons of Cheese Filling into 4 other pockets. Spoon 2 tablespoons of one of the fruit fillings on top the Pastry Cream and Cheese Filling in each pocket, using whatever combination you like.

Let the ring rise at room temperature in a draft-free place for 2 hours, or until it feels like a marshmallow when pressed gently with a finger. Sprinkle the top with the Streusel Topping. Preheat the oven to 350° about 30 minutes before baking.

Place the pan on the center rack in the oven and decrease the heat to 325°. Bake for 35 to 45 minutes, or until the edges are brown and the center is golden brown. If the top begins to brown too quickly, lay a piece of aluminum foil loosely over the ring. To check for doneness, open the springform pan or push up the bottom of the false-bottom cake pan, using a spatula to check the bottom of the ring. The entire bottom of the ring should be brown. If it is not, return it to the oven for another 10 minutes, then recheck it. (It's easy to underbake this ring because it's so packed full of fillings.) Transfer the ring to a cooling rack and let it rest for 5 minutes. With a pastry brush, coat the tops with the Clear Glaze. When the ring has cooled completely, dip a fork in the Sugar Glaze and wave it diagonally over the pastries to decorate them with thin lines of glaze. Let the glaze set before serving or storing.

BLUEBERRY FILLING

MAKES 1 1/3 CUPS

2 1/2 cups (12 ounces) fresh or frozen blueberries (thawed, if frozen)
1/4 cup sugar
2 tablespoons freshly squeezed lemon juice
1 tablespoon water
1 tablespoon cornstarch

Place the blueberries and sugar in a heavy saucepan over medium heat. Bring the mixture to a simmer. Meanwhile, combine the lemon juice, water, and cornstarch, mixing until the cornstarch is dissolved. When the berries start to simmer, whisk the cornstarch liquid to mix it again and add it to the berries, stirring continuously. Stir until the mixture thickens, about 1 to 2 minutes. Cool and store in the refrigerator until ready to use. This filling will keep for up to 5 days in the refrigerator. It does not freeze well.

BEAR CLAW FILLING

MAKES 2 1/2 CUPS

8 cups (1 1/2 pounds) lightly packed cake scraps (see Note)
1 1/2 teaspoons almond extract
2 tablespoons Myers's rum (optional)
1/4 to 3/4 cup water
1/2 large egg, lightly beaten
2 tablespoons (1 ounce) butter, melted and cooled

Combine all of the ingredients in the bowl of a heavy-duty mixer fitted with the flat beater. Mix on low speed until smooth. The consistency should be soft but firm enough to hold its shape. Store in the refrigerator for up to 3 days and in the freezer for up to 2 weeks.

NOTE: We recommend primarily using chocolate cake (such as our Devil's Food Cake, page 199). We also use Vanilla Genoise (page 195), Spice Cake (page 203), and Hazelnut Sponge Cake (page 201). Any type of cake except angel food will work. If you don't have cake scraps on hand, you may be able to buy an unfrosted cake from a local bakery. Or, buy a frozen unfrosted cake at the supermarket or bake one from scratch. Cut the entire cake into small scraps, wrapping and freezing any extra for future use.

APPLE FILLING

MAKES 2½ CUPS

2 to 3 large (1 pound 2½ ounces) Pippin apples
2 tablespoons sugar
¼ teaspoon ground cinnamon
1 tablespoon all-purpose flour
4 tablespoons water

Peel, core, and cut the apples into ½-inch pieces. Combine with the remaining filling ingredients in a heavy saucepan and cook over very low heat, stirring frequently. Simmer the mixture just until the apples are soft, about 10 to 15 minutes. Cool and store in the refrigerator until ready to use. Stores for up to 3 days in the refrigerator and up to 2 weeks in the freezer.

CHEESE FILLING

MAKES 2 CUPS

1 cup (8 ounces) ricotta cheese
6 tablespoons sugar
⅛ teaspoon salt
1 tablespoon orange zest
1 large egg, lightly beaten
3 tablespoons butter, melted and cooled

Place all filling ingredients in a bowl and stir just until blended. Store in the refrigerator for up to 3 days. (Do not freeze; it ruins the ricotta's texture.)

CLEAR GLAZE

MAKES ABOUT 1/2 CUP

1/2 cup sugar
1/4 cup water
1 tablespoon light corn syrup

In a heavy saucepan, bring all of the ingredients to a rapid boil. Remove from the heat and let cool. Store in the refrigerator for up to 1 month.

SUGAR GLAZE

MAKES 1 1/4 CUPS

2 cups confectioners' sugar
4 tablespoons water

Whisk ingredients together until completely smooth. If the glaze is too thick, add 1 teaspoon of water at a time until it is still white, but liquid enough to drizzle off of a fork onto the pastries.

Store in an airtight container at room temperature for up to 1 week. (The glaze does not have to be refrigerated.)

STREUSEL TOPPING

MAKES 2 CUPS

3/4 cup all-purpose flour
1/3 cup granulated sugar
1/3 cup firmly packed brown sugar
1/4 teaspoon ground cinnamon
1/2 cup (4 ounces) very cold butter, cut into 1/2-inch pieces

Combine all of the dry ingredients in the bowl of a food processor fitted with the metal blade. Add the butter and pulse several times until the mixture is a crumbly consistency. Alternately, use a pastry blender or two knives to cut in the butter. Be careful not to overmix or the topping will become doughlike. Refrigerate for up to 1 week or freeze for up to 1 month.

Puff Pastry

Puff pastry should have several qualities, but flakiness and tenderness are the most important ones. It should shrink very little when it is rolled out and baked; it should be able to expand to great heights for certain uses, and, at the same time, it should be able to create thin, crisp sheets when "docked" (pricked all over) before it is baked.

Classic puff pastry dough is made from nothing more than flour, salt, and water. After it has been refrigerated, the block of dough (which weighs about 8 pounds) is rolled at the corners to form a crude star shape, with the points tapered and the center thick. A block of cold unsalted butter is placed in the middle, the flaps of the four points of the star are folded over to encase the butter like an envelope. (In our basic recipe [see page 85], the butter is chopped into chunks, frozen, and mixed right into the dough instead of being added in a large block. It's much easier and yields a consistently good product.) The dough is then fed through a sheeter, and a series of four-fold turns, called "book turns," are done. This series of sheetings and turns produces the layered butter and dough effect, which, when baked, creates the thousands of crispy layers that the French call *millefeuille.*

Making puff pastry or *pâte feuilleté* was one of the most difficult skills for us to learn. We studied it at two Paris bakeries, Le Feyeux and Le Moule a Gateaux. The roll-in and turns weren't hard to perfect because the techniques are similar to those used for croissants. But to get a classic puff pastry that could achieve the rise and flakiness we wanted was for quite some time too difficult for our bakers to do on a daily basis. Finally, when Lindsey Shere's book *Chez Panisse Desserts* was published, we discovered a simpler recipe called Clay's Quick Puff Pastry. We tried it.

The baker at Gayle's who adjusted the recipe to fit our large-scale needs either got the proportions wrong or decided that the dough needed a little more butter to make a puff pastry with the qualities we wanted. Or, the baker may have been influenced by our belief that butter is good and more butter is better. However the recipe came about, it has worked well for us ever since. At the bakery, we make the dough two or three times a week, eight to ten squares at a time. The dough can also be frozen, then thawed in the refrigerator for a day or two before you plan to use it. Just as with croissants and Danish pastry, refrigeration and freezing are important in the process. Refrigeration gives the baker more control over the flavor of the dough and, if done right, freezing produces more consistent rising capabilities.

Puff pastry can be used for many products. At Gayle's, we use it for Apple-Nut Turnovers (page 89), Palm Leaves (page 94), Crocodiles (page 86), numerous appetizers, Napoleons (page 87), Ham in Puff Pastry (page 92), and Parmesan Cheese Sticks (page 90). Puff pastry is also used in several pastries we don't make at Gayle's, including *Chaussons aux Pommes* (page 89), *Sfogliatta* (page 87), and *Tarte Tatin* (page 277). Even though we've been making puff pastry for decades, it's still one of the most time-consuming things we do at the bakery. Fortunately, it's also one of the tastiest. Just ask our customers!

Lindsey Shere: Portrait of an Uncompromising Baker

Back in 1976, I spent two weeks with Lindsey Shere, one of the original owners of Chez Panisse in Berkeley, while she was training me to fill in for her for the summer. In those two weeks I learned a new respect for baking, pastries, and ingredients. Ordering fruit was even enlightening. Lindsey only uses organic, locally grown seasonal fruits, and she treats every detail with care and attention. The quality of the butter, the organic flour, and the jams and jellies that are made by her staff all play an important role in her magical desserts. Lindsey has been making her legendary Almond Tarte for twenty-five years. It's the picture of perfection every time—and it's not easy to make. The creamy nougat that surrounds the almonds in the filling must be watched every step of the way, or as Lindsey says, "It looks like corn flakes."

At Chez Panisse, pastries are not just made at the beginning of the day, as they are at many restaurants. Instead, each pastry is either made to order or is made every hour, as the desserts run out. That kind of freshness can't help but showcase the excellence of the ingredients and technique.

Many people may not know that Lindsey is as active in fostering and furthering the Chez Panisse vision of supporting local growers as is the restaurant's primary founder, Alice Waters. Lindsey has perhaps an even closer relationship today with farmers from whom she buys produce than she may have had back in 1976, when I first noticed the connection. To Lindsey, an orange isn't just an orange. Instead—as stated on the dessert menu—it might be Jim Churchill's orange. This is an important distinction for an idea

(continued)

that was once dismissed as a counterculture concept and has always been the core of the Chez Panisse philosophy. Lindsey and the other Chez Panisse professionals hold that buying direct from the grower puts a restaurant in a position of power. By knowing the source of an orange, a restaurant or bakery can become more than a place for hedonistic indulgences. It becomes an institution that can dictate social and economic change. By directly supporting the very farmer who grows our food, we complete our connection to the land, making us responsible for the food we eat and its effect on the environment that sustains us.

This is a serious and lofty pursuit that requires constant dedication. Thus, to some, Lindsey might appear a little too serious. Even her husband, Charles, admits she is too committed at times. He tells how Lindsey won't eat fresh bread if there's a day-old loaf in the house. This reflects one of Lindsey's basic values—she's an idealist who puts ecology before her own pleasure. In a world where many of us compromise too easily, Lindsey lives by her standards on a daily basis.

In the end, Lindsey's commitment to quality filters down to how something tastes and feels on the palate. She tastes food unlike anyone else I've met. I once saw her try a tart and I'll never forget the way she delicately broke off a piece, slowly and gently sliding it into her mouth without touching the fork with her lips. I could see her evaluating the flavors and textures while staring off into the distance and, after what seemed like an eternity, finally swallowing the bite. She had just tasted more in that one minute than most of us taste in a week.   ❧ ❧ ❧

Doing Book Turns

Like croissant and Danish dough, puff pastry is also given turns to create the buttery, flaky texture characteristic of fine pastries. However, unlike croissant and Danish doughs, puff pastry is often given four-fold book turns, which are different than the three-fold turns used for the other two doughs.

To complete one book turn after the butter has been rolled in, roll out the dough into a long rectangle. Fold the top and bottom quarters of the rectangular sheet of puff pastry dough to meet in the center. Then, holding a doubled-up section of dough in each hand, fold the halves toward each other to end up with one 4-layer piece of dough hinged like a book cover. Proceed as the recipe directs.

❧ ❧ ❧

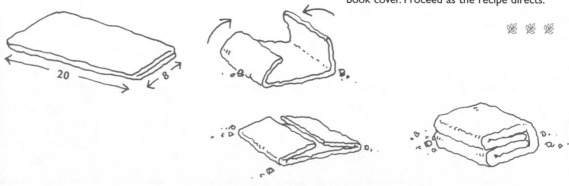

THE RECIPES

BASIC PUFF PASTRY DOUGH

MAKES 2 POUNDS

The pastry flour for this recipe can be purchased in bulk at health food stores or through baking supply catalogs (see page 317). At the bakery we use two-thirds all-purpose and one-third pastry flour, but if you can't find pastry flour, all-purpose flour will work fine (the dough just might not be quite as tender).

BAKER'S BASICS TO REVIEW

Measuring Dry Ingredients, page 21
Doing the Roll-In and Turns, page 34
Doing Book Turns, page 84

———

1 pound (16 ounces) unsalted butter, cut into $^1/_2$-inch cubes
$2^1/_4$ cups all-purpose flour
1 cup plus 2 tablespoons pastry flour
1 teaspoon salt
$^1/_2$ cup plus 3 tablespoons ice water
1 tablespoon freshly squeezed lemon juice

THAWING FROZEN PUFF PASTRY DOUGH

Frozen dough should be thawed at room temperature for 45 minutes to 1 hour, then transferred to the refrigerator, where it should rest for at least 1 hour before it is used. Or, transfer the dough from the freezer to the refrigerator to thaw the night before you plan to use it.

Freeze the butter cubes for at least 2 hours.

In a large bowl, combine the flours and salt. When the butter is frozen, combine the ice water and lemon juice, which should total $^3/_4$ cup. Mix the frozen butter into the flour mixture, then slowly add the liquid, stirring with a wooden spoon. The dough will come together in a pebbly, irregular mass that will barely stick together when squeezed. If the mixture is too crumbly to bind together, add 1 extra tablespoon of water at a time (up to 4 tablespoons), being careful not to make it too wet.

Turn the dough onto a lightly floured surface and press into a square. It will be very crumbly and difficult to handle. With a rolling pin, roll the dough into a 15 x 8-inch rectangle. It will crumble apart at the edges (it smooths out eventually). Fold the dough in thirds (a three-fold turn), patching as necessary.

Rotate the dough one-quarter turn, so that the seams are at the top and bottom. Roll the dough out again, this time to measure 20 x 8 inches. Give the dough a four-fold book turn. Rotate the dough one-quarter turn, so that the seams are on the top and bottom. Then, roll out again to 20 x 8 and give the dough a three-fold turn. Cover the dough with plastic wrap and let it rest in the refrigerator for 1 hour. Remove the dough from the refrigerator, again roll it into a 20 x 8-inch rectangle, and give it another three-fold turn. Immediately roll the dough out to 20 x 8 inches and give it one last three-fold turn. If the dough starts to soften, refrigerate for 15 minutes before starting the final turn.

Wrap the dough and refrigerate overnight for use the next day, or freeze for up to 10 days.

CROCODILE

MAKES ONE 16 X 7-INCH PASTRY

PIZZA PARISIENNE

Here's a conceptual recipe for a savory treat we used to see in Parisian pastry shops back in the early eighties. Follow the recipe for Napoleons (page 87) to make one 16 x 8-inch sheet of baked puff pastry. Trim 1 inch off the length of the sheet, so it measures 15 x 8 inches. Cut the sheet into twenty 3 x 2-inch rectangles. Coat each rectangle with tomato sauce, then top with 2 slices of fresh tomato, 2 crisscrossed anchovy fillets, and 2 pitted kalamata olives. Garnish with minced parsley and serve at room temperature. Makes 20 pastries.

One day, our friend Dr. Kenny Bloom brought us an Alligator from a Los Angeles bakery. Months later, we were in Southern California and dropped by the bakery. We asked them for the recipe, and they declined. So we put our heads together and came up with our own variation. It's been a bestseller ever since we started making it back in 1989.

1/2 cup (4 ounces) butter
2/3 cup firmly packed brown sugar

EGG GLAZE
1 egg
2 tablespoons milk

———

1/2 recipe (1 pound) Basic Puff Pastry Dough (page 85)
2/3 cup chopped pecans
40 pecan halves
1/4 cup Clear Glaze (page 81)

MAPLE GLAZE
6 tablespoons confectioners' sugar
2 teaspoons maple syrup
1 teaspoon water

Line a baking sheet with parchment. Have ready another baking sheet that fits just inside the first one (for flattening the pastry while it bakes). Melt the butter in a small saucepan and stir in the brown sugar. Set aside to cool. In a small bowl, whisk together the egg and milk to make the glaze.

On a lightly floured surface, roll the puff pastry into a rectangle roughly measuring 19 x 16 x 1/8 inches. Trim the dough to 17 x 14 x 1/8 inches, reserving the scraps for another use (see page 93).

Brush the entire surface of the dough with a light to medium coating of Egg Glaze. Reserve the remaining glaze. Spread the brown sugar–butter mixture down the center of the dough in a 15 x 5-inch rectangle, leaving a 1-inch border along the 14-inch-long edges and a 4 1/2-inch border along each 17-inch side. Sprinkle the chopped pecans over the filling.

Fold the 17-inch-long sides of the dough over the filling, overlapping them slightly, and press lightly to seal. (The dough will now be about 7 inches wide.) Fold the ends over 3/4 inch and pinch to seal. The finished piece will measure 16 x 7 inches.

Gently flip the crocodile over onto the prepared baking sheet. Brush it again with the glaze and place it in the freezer for at least 20 minutes or, preferably, for overnight. At this point, the crocodile can be frozen for up to 1 week. If freezing the crocodile overnight or longer, cover the Egg Glaze with plastic wrap and refrigerate, or make more later.

Preheat the oven to 350°. Take the crocodile directly from the freezer and place it on the center rack in the oven. Bake for 10 minutes, then remove from the oven. Again brush the top of the pastry with a light coat of the remaining glaze, then arrange the pecan halves in rows 8 pecans long and 5 pecans across, gently pressing them in place.

Place another piece of parchment paper on top of the crocodile, then set the second baking sheet on top and press down lightly. Return the pastry to the center rack in the oven, leaving the baking sheet on top, and bake for 35 to 40 minutes more, or until golden brown. (Due to the thinness of the dough, some of the butter will leak out during baking.)

Remove from the oven and, while still hot, brush with the Simple Syrup. To make the Maple Glaze, combine the confectioners' sugar, maple syrup, and water with a fork until the glaze has a smooth consistency and runs off the fork. When the Crocodile has cooled for 5 to 10 minutes, dip a fork into the Maple Glaze and drizzle it over the top of the pastry in a squiggly pattern.

When the glaze has hardened and the pastry is completely cool, trim $1/4$ inch off the ends, then cut into 2-inch slices, making sure one row of pecans is in the center of each slice.

SFOGLIATTA

We had this simple dessert at one of our favorite restaurants in Rome. All you need to make it are three 8-inch discs of puff pastry. Make three 9 x 9-inch sheets of puff pastry, following the recipe for Napoleons (see below). Using a cake cardboard (see page 187) or the bottom of a tart pan as a guide, carefully cut the puff pastry into 3 discs. Bake as for Napoleons. Combine 2 cups stiff whipped cream (page 258) and 2 cups Pastry Cream (page 127). Top 2 of the discs with one-half of the whipped cream. Stack the discs, placing the uncoated disc on top.

Place the stack in the refrigerator for several hours to give the filling time to set up, then dust the top with confectioners' sugar. To serve, using a serrated knife gently cut the stack into pie-shaped wedges. Makes one 3-layer, 8-inch pastry.

NAPOLEONS (MILLEFEUILLE)

MAKES 4 PASTRIES

Although *millefeuille* literally means "a thousand sheets," the French use it (as they do the word *feuilleté*) to mean puff pastry. *Millefeuille* is also the name given to the wonderful pastries known to the rest of the world as napoleons.

BAKER'S BASICS TO REVIEW
Whipping Cream, page 258
Folding, page 20

$1/2$ recipe (1 pound) Basic Puff Pastry Dough (page 85)
$1/4$ to $1/3$ cup raspberry jam
1 cup Pastry Cream (page 127)
1 cup whipped cream (page 258)
$1/4$ cup confectioners' sugar, for dusting

Preheat the oven to 325°. Line an 18 x 11-inch or larger baking sheet with parchment paper. Have ready another baking sheet that fits just inside the first one (for flattening the pastry while it bakes).

Lightly flour a work surface and the top of the dough. Roll out the puff pastry to 18 x 10 x $1/8$ inch. Starting from one end, roll the dough onto the rolling pin so it can be transferred to the prepared baking sheet.

With the tines of a fork, prick the dough 30 to 40 times all over its surface to prevent it from overinflating as it bakes. Place the baking sheet on the center rack in the oven and bake for 10 minutes. The dough will puff a little but color only slightly.

Remove the baking sheet from the oven. Place a clean sheet of parchment paper over the dough, then place the second baking sheet on top of the dough and push it down to flatten the puff pastry. Return the baking sheets to the center rack in the oven and bake for 15 minutes, then check to make sure the pastry isn't rising too much. If it expands over $1/2$ inch high, again press down the top baking sheet and return the pastry to the oven. Bake 15 minutes more, or until the pastry is golden brown.

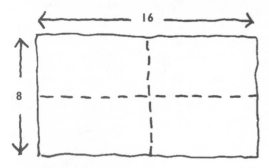

Remove the pastry from the oven. Remove the top baking sheet and let the pastry cool on the bottom sheet. With a sharp knife and a ruler, trim the pastry into a perfect 16 x 8-inch rectangle. Cut this rectangle into 4 smaller rectangles, each measuring 8 x 4 inches. Cut a 4 x 2-inch strip from each rectangle and set aside.

In a small bowl, fold the pastry cream into the whipped cream; set aside. Gently coat the remaining four 6 x 4-inch strips with a thin layer of raspberry jam.

Carefully spread each of the raspberry-coated pieces with a $1/4$-inch-thick layer of the pastry cream mixture, leaving a $1/8$-inch border around all edges. With the knife and ruler in hand, cut each of the four coated 6 x 4-inch rectangles into three 4 x 2-inch strips so you have 4 sets of 3 coated strips. (Clean the knife after cutting the pasty each time.)

With the knife, stack 3 coated strips for each of the 4 pastries (using up 12 coated strips in all), then top each stack with 1 uncoated strip.

Using a fine sieve, dust the top of the stacks with confectioners' sugar. With the back of a butter knife, create a cross-hatched pattern on top of each pastry.

Napoleons may be served immediately or refrigerated for up to 6 hours. If refrigerated, let them sit at room temperature for 45 minutes before serving.

APPLE-NUT TURNOVERS

MAKES 4 TURNOVERS

These turnovers are a little smaller than the ones we make at the bakery. At this size, they are easier to make and eat.

BAKER'S BASICS TO REVIEW
Toasting Nuts, page 23

FILLING
2 apples (such as Pippin, Golden Delicious, or Gravenstein), peeled, cored, and chopped into 1/2-inch pieces
2 tablespoons firmly packed brown sugar
2 tablespoons water
1 tablespoon plus 1 teaspoon all-purpose flour
1/4 teaspoon ground cinnamon
1/4 teaspoon pure vanilla extract
———
1/3 recipe (about 11 ounces) Basic Puff Pastry Dough (page 85)
4 tablespoons chopped toasted almonds (page 23)

EGG GLAZE
1 egg
2 tablespoons milk

SIMPLE SYRUP
3 tablespoons water
3 tablespoons granulated sugar
———
Confectioners' sugar, for dusting

Preheat the oven to 325°. Line a baking sheet with parchment paper.

Place all the filling ingredients in a small nonreactive saucepan. Heat over medium-low heat, stirring continuously for 10 to 15 minutes, or until the apples are tender. If the apples do not release enough moisture and the mixture is dry after 5 minutes, add 1 to 5 tablespoons of water, 1 tablespoon at a time, until the mixture renders a small amount of light syrup. Set aside and let cool.

Roll out the dough to a thickness of 1/8 inch. It should measure at least 10 x 10 inches. (Be aware that the dough tends to shrink.) Cut the dough into 4 pieces measuring 4 x 4 inches. Reserve the scraps for another use (see page 93). Place the squares on the work surface. Divide the cooled filling among the 4 squares. Sprinkle the almonds over the filling. Fold each square into a triangle and squeeze the edges firmly enough to seal but not to crush them.

CHAUSSONS AUX POMMES

Gayle's Apple-Nut Turnovers (left) are the Capitola, California, version of the oval-shaped French chaussons aux pommes. We created the triangular version because the traditional shape produced too many dough scraps. The oval varieties are also beautiful; look for them if you visit France or follow these steps to make your own:

Follow the instructions for Apple-Nut Turnovers, but double the filling recipe and roll the dough out to measure 14 x 7 inches. Make a 6 x 4-inch oval template out of cardboard. Using the template and a sharp knife, cut 3 ovals from the sheet of dough.

Place one-third of the filling on one half of each oval, leaving a 3/4-inch border around the edge.

Fold the unfilled half over the filling and press the edges together.

(continued)

Place the turnovers on the prepared baking sheet. In a small bowl, whisk together the egg and milk to make the glaze. Lightly brush the turnovers with the glaze. Place the baking sheet on the center rack in the oven and bake for 1 hour and 20 minutes, or until golden brown.

When the turnovers have 5 minutes left to bake, make the Simple Syrup. Combine the water and sugar in a small saucepan over medium-high heat, stirring frequently. Bring to a boil, then remove from heat and let cool.

Remove the turnovers from the oven and brush with a light coating of Simple Syrup. Let cool. Serve as is or dust lightly with confectioners' sugar.

NOTE: If you want to make larger, fluffier turnovers like the ones we make at Gayle's, use 20 ounces of dough and double the filling recipe (but not the Egg Glaze and Simple Syrup recipes). Roll the dough out to $1/4$ inch thick, cut it into 5-inch squares, and try to get as much filling into each turnover as possible while still being able to fold and seal them. Bake as directed for the smaller turnovers.

PARMESAN CHEESE STICKS

MAKES 8 LARGE OR 16 SMALL STICKS

A simple savory pastry that is a perfect appetizer.

$1/2$ recipe (1 pound) Basic Puff Pastry Dough (page 85)

EGG GLAZE
1 large egg
2 tablespoons milk

———

1 cup grated Parmesan cheese

Preheat the oven to 350°. Line a baking sheet with parchment paper.

On a lightly floured work surface, roll the dough out to $1/8$ inch thick. With a sharp knife, cut the dough into a 28 x 7-inch rectangle.

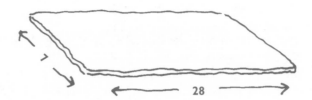

Fold the dough in thirds to create crease marks, then unfold and cut it into three equal pieces along the fold lines.

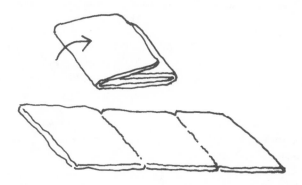

In a small bowl, whisk together the egg and milk to make the glaze. Lightly coat the top of one piece of dough with the glaze. Sprinkle 1/4 cup of the Parmesan over the glaze. Coat the top of the second piece with glaze, then place it glaze side down on top of the first. Glaze the other side of the second piece and sprinkle with another 1/4 cup of Parmesan. Coat the top of the third piece with glaze, then place it glaze side down on the other two stacked pieces. Glaze the other side of the piece of dough on top and sprinkle it with 1/4 cup of the Parmesan. Invert the stack of dough pieces and coat the final unglazed side with the glaze and then sprinkle with the remaining 1/4 cup of Parmesan.

Cut the stack of dough into eight 1-inch-wide, 7-inch-long, 3/4-inch-high strips using a ruler and chef's knife. At this point, the strip may be left whole or cut in half to create sixteen 3 1/2-inch-long cheese sticks. Twist each strip into a tight corkscrew shape (they will untwist some during baking, so they should be tightly twisted to begin with) and place on the prepared baking sheet.

Place the baking sheet on the center rack in the oven and bake for 30 to 40 minutes, or until golden brown. Let the sticks cool on the baking sheet, then serve at room temperature.

HAM IN PUFF PASTRY (JAMBON FEUILLETÉ)

MAKES 6 TO 10 APPETIZERS

We first saw this at a charcuterie in the south of France and wondered what it was. Years later, we learned how to make it at Le Feyeux bakery in Paris. It is a savory appetizer filled with ham, béchamel sauce, and cheese.

BÉCHAMEL SAUCE
  2 tablespoons butter
  1 1/2 tablespoons all-purpose flour
  1 cup milk

FEUILLETÉ
  1/3 recipe (about 11 ounces) Basic Puff Pastry (page 85)
  3 ounces ham, thinly sliced
  1 1/2 ounces Gruyère cheese, grated

EGG GLAZE
  1 large egg
  2 tablespoons milk

To make the sauce, begin several hours before you plan to assemble the pastries because the sauce needs to be refrigerated before it is used. In a small saucepan over medium-low heat, melt the butter. Sprinkle in the flour while stirring continuously for 5 to 6 minutes, or until the mixture thickens. It will be bubbly, but should not brown. Remove from the heat and let cool a few minutes, then return to the heat and whisk in the milk. Stir over medium heat for 15 to 20 minutes more, or until the mixture thickens. The sauce is done when it is the consistency of mayonnaise and drips, not runs, off the spoon. Set aside to cool, then refrigerate.

Preheat the oven to 400°. Line a baking sheet with parchment paper.

Roll the dough out into a 16 x 12 x 1/8-inch rectangle. Trim into a perfect 15 x 10-inch rectangle, then cut it in half so you have two pieces measuring 10 x 7 1/2 inches. Reserve the scraps for another use (see page 93). Place one sheet of the puff pastry on the prepared baking sheet.

Thinly coat the puff pastry on the baking sheet with one-third of the sauce, leaving a 3/4-inch border. Top with one-half of the ham, slightly overlapping the slices and still leaving the border. Cover the ham with another coating of sauce, then top with one-half of the cheese. Repeat the process, adding another layer of ham, sauce, and cheese.

Carefully place the remaining sheet of puff pastry on top of the ham-, sauce-, and cheese-topped dough, lining up the edges, and press together firmly. Using the tines of a fork, crimp the edges of the dough to seal it.

In a small bowl, whisk together the egg and milk. Brush the top of the pastry with the glaze. Place the pastry in the refrigerator, uncovered, for 10 minutes. Remove the pastry from the refrigerator and, with the back of a small paring knife, lightly score 2 or 3 diagonal lines at 2-inch intervals into the top of the pastry. Switching the direction of the knife, score another 2 or 3 diagonal lines in the opposite direction into the top of the pastry, or copy this pattern:

With an ice pick or a toothpick, poke 3 or 4 holes in top of the pastry to allow air to escape during baking. Place the baking sheet on the center rack in the oven and immediately decrease the oven temperature to 325°. After 30 minutes, move the tray to the lower oven rack and bake for another 30 minutes, or until the pastry is golden brown and the bottom is well browned (lift it gently with a wide spatula to check).

Let the pastry cool completely on the baking tray, then slice and serve at room temperature.

SAVE THOSE PUFF PASTRY SCRAPS!

Puff pastry scraps, which in the language of the French pâtissier are called rognures, can be saved and reused. Just store them, tightly covered in plastic wrap or sealed in airtight plastic bags, in the refrigerator or freezer. Then, incorporate them into any remaining piece of unrolled puff pastry by lifting one of the folds of the square of dough and placing the scraps, as flat as possible, inside. Cover the scraps with the flap and roll out as usual.

Scraps can also be used, without reincorporating them into unrolled dough, by laying them on top of one another, rolling them out flat with a rolling pin, and lining small appetizer tins with them. The pastry cups can then be filled with any kind of cheese filling or with a tomato sauce, anchovy, and Parmesan cheese mixture (similar to the topping on page 86—see sidebar). Bake the appetizers for 15 to 20 minutes, or until the filling is cooked and the crust is puffy and golden.

PALM LEAVES (PALMIERS)

MAKES TWENTY-FOUR 2½-INCH PASTRIES

These flaky, irresistible little cookies are great with ice cream, fruit compotes, and all by themselves. The cookies need at least 1 hour to rest before baking, so be sure to allow enough time for this step.

¼ recipe (½ pound) Basic Puff Pastry Dough (page 85)
½ cup sugar

Begin making the cookies 1 to 6 hours before you plan to bake them. Spread 1 tablespoon of the sugar on the work surface. Place the dough on top of the sugar, then spread 1 tablespoon of sugar on top of the dough. Press the rolling pin into the dough at ½-inch intervals to flatten it and adhere the sugar to the dough.

Roll the dough out into a 6 x 6-inch square. Spread 2 tablespoons of sugar on the work surface and place the dough on top of the sugar. Top the dough with 2 more tablespoons of sugar. Roll the dough out into a 10½ x 10½ x ⅛-inch square. Trim the dough into a perfect 10-inch square.

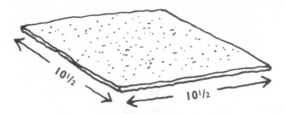

Fold two of the outer edges of dough 2½ inches in toward the middle, leaving a 5-inch sugar-coated single layer in the middle.

Roll the rolling pin over the folded flaps to flatten them.

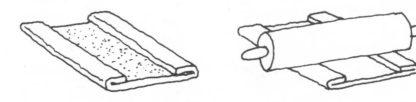

Fold the folded edges toward the middle once more, so you have two double folds in the center. Lightly roll the rolling pin over the dough to just compress the pieces.

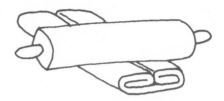

Lay the rolling pin lengthwise over the middle of the fold between the crease in the dough and press.

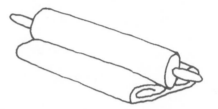

Fold the two flaps together to resemble a man's wallet, then roll over the dough lengthwise one last time to flatten it. Cut off the two ragged ends of the dough.

Cover the flattened dough log in plastic wrap and let it rest in the refrigerator for at least 1 hour and no longer than 6 hours. (The longer the dough sits in the refrigerator, the more likely the sugar will dissolve into a runny syrup.)

Preheat the oven to 350° 20 minutes before removing the dough from the refrigerator. Line a baking sheet with parchment paper. Unwrap the pastry and cut the log into 3/8-inch pieces. Dip both sides of each piece in the remaining 2 tablespoons of sugar just to lightly coat them. Lay the cookies 2 inches apart on the prepared baking sheet.

Place the baking sheet on the center rack in the oven and bake for 10 minutes. Remove from the oven and, using a metal spatula, flip any of the cookies that are rising unevenly. (If necessary, they may also be lightly flattened with the spatula.) Return the cookies to the oven for another 10 minutes, and bake until golden and crispy (any cookies that are still pale may be left in the oven a few extra minutes).

Pies and Tarts

When you use that familiar saying "as American as apple pie," do you ever wonder where pie actually originated? Most likely, early European immigrants brought their favorite pie recipes to America, and those recipes evolved into the beloved desserts Americans have been serving forth ever since. Each country has its own special pie or pielike dessert, but none are quite like our all-American classics. Through the years, American bakers have reinvented these Old World pies by baking them in deeper dishes and using a wider variety of fillings. In celebration of these simple yet satistfying desserts, you'll find pies of every kind—including your favorite custard-, nut-, and fruit-based ones—in this chapter.

You'll discover that pies are quite simple to make. Here's a brief pie-making primer to get you started:

- **Ingredients:** All ingredients should be at room temperature, unless otherwise stated.

- **Measuring:** Always have everything measured out before beginning to make the recipe. Flour and other dry ingredients are measured by the fluff and scoop method described on page 21.

- **Mixing:** For complete instructions for mixing pie dough, see page 99. Follow the instructions carefully the first few times. After that, you'll know the method by heart and will make flawless pie shells every time. Most pie fillings can be mixed by hand, with a handheld mixer, or with a tabletop mixer.

- **Baking:** Re-read the information about pie plates and pizza pans on page 15. We prefer to begin baking many pies on the lower rack, then to move them up to the center rack midway through baking. This creates a nicely baked lower crust and prevents the top from browning too much. If the top crust browns too quickly, place aluminum foil loosely over the pie while it finishes baking.

- **Cooling:** Always remove the pie from the baking sheet and place it on a cooling rack to cool. Pies are best when they have cooled just enough to hold their shape when sliced.

- **Storage:** Always let pies cool to room temperature before storing. Custard-based pies can be stored in the refrigerator for up to 3 days. All other pies can be stored at room temperature for 1 day, then refrigerated for up to 4 days. Reheat pies in a 325° oven for 10 to 25 minutes (exact warming times are given in each recipe) before serving.

  We do not recommend freezing pies, but if you must do so, carefully wrap them in aluminum foil, place in an airtight plastic bag, and freeze for up to 2 weeks. Thaw in the refrigerator overnight and warm in a 325° oven for 15 to 25 minutes before serving.

Although pies have been common in this country since colonial times, tarts are relatively new to Americans. When we began seeing the French tart in American restaurants back in the 1970s, we were excited about this wonderful addition to the nation's dessert menus. Tarts are a more delicate version of our American pie. The use of fresh fruit makes them perfect for spring and summer entertaining. Making fresh fruit tarts is an easy and rewarding artistic exercise for home bakers; serving a tart with the fruit arranged in a beautiful design is so satisfying. The tarts in this chapter are based on the recipes I was taught in Paris and the techniques I learned at Chez Panisse.

   As is true for all dessert making, the trick to making great pies and tarts is practicing the skills regularly, which enables you to master the nuances of the process. If you read the hints, tips, and techniques on pages 98, 105, 109, and 123, and keep practicing, we guarantee you'll make pies and tarts you're proud to serve for any occasion.

Rolling Out Pie Crusts

The pie dough used in this book is best rolled at room temperature, but it can also be rolled out after it has been refrigerated. Just let it rest at room temperature for 10 minutes before rolling.

To roll out a bottom crust, lightly flour your work surface. A wood or marble surface is best. If possible, use a rolling pin that has no handles because it is easier to feel the texture and thickness of dough under the pin as you roll. Begin rolling the disc of pie dough from the center out, turning the disc one-quarter turn clockwise after every two or three rolls. This will help achieve a round crust and ensure even flour distribution during rolling. Add a little flour if necessary during rolling so that the crust does not stick. Turn the dough over once or twice early in the rolling process to achieve a smoother surface on both sides.

For bottom crusts, roll out the dough until it measures 1 inch larger than the rim of the pie plate, rolling the edges of the dough a little thinner than the rest of the crust (because they will be doubled up when turned under and fluted). Place the pie plate next to the rolled-out crust, fold the dough in half and transfer it to the pie plate. Gently unfold the dough and fit it snugly into the pie plate. Trim the edges of the dough, leaving ³/₄ inch hanging over the rim of the pie plate.

For top crusts, roll out the dough to measure 1¹/₂ inches larger than the rim of the pie plate or large enough to cover the filling and extend ³/₄ inch beyond the rim of the pie plate. As for the bottom crust, roll the edges of the dough a little thinner than the rest of the crust. Place the filled pie next to the rolled-out crust. Fold the rolled crust in half and then in quarters. Transfer the folded crust to the top of the filled pie. Unfold the crust over the filling and trim it to the same size as the bottom crust. It is important to have at least ³/₄ inch of dough on each crust hanging over the pie plate rim.

🌿 🌿 🌿

Fluting Pie Crusts

There are many ways to flute the edge of a pie crust. Anyway it is fluted, the rim of the dough should be high enough to hold in all of the filling as the pie bakes. Here's one basic technique. Once you have it down, experiment with other methods for variety.

To flute the bottom crust of one-crust and lattice crust–topped pies, fold the edge of the crust under so that it is doubled up and even with the outside rim of the pan. Hold the thumb and index finger of your left hand about 1 inch apart and place them outside a section of the edge. Placing a knuckle of your right hand between your left thumb and index finger, gently press in opposite directions to make a ¹/₂-inch-long "V" shaped curve in the dough. Repeat, working your way around the pie until the entire edge is fluted.

For two-crust pies (other than lattice crust or topless pies) do not fold or flute the edge of the bottom crust until the top crust is placed on the pie. Fold the top and bottom crusts under together so that they just meet the rim of the pie pan. This seals in any juices that may bubble up during baking.

Flute both crusts together, as described for the bottom crust.

🌿 🌿 🌿

PIE DOUGH

MAKES TWO 10-INCH BOTTOM CRUSTS
OR ONE 10-INCH DOUBLE CRUST

For years, pie dough was the bane of my pastry-making existence. I had studied French pastries and knew how to make a terrific croissant but still couldn't make a good pie dough. While visiting my friend Markita Lerch in Aspen, Colorado, I confessed to my pie dough–making shortcomings. To console me, she made the most ethereal fresh cherry pie, using this dough.

Since then, I've never even tried another pie dough. I have included directions for making this dough by hand or in the food processor. It turns out better when mixed by hand, but if the directions are followed precisely, the food processor dough produces a good crust.

BAKER'S BASICS TO REVIEW
Measuring Dry Ingredients, page 21

---

4 Ice cubes
water
2¹/₂ cups all-purpose flour
I cup (8 ounces) cold butter, cut into ¹/₂-inch cubes

To make the dough by hand, place the ice cubes in a 1-cup measure and fill it with water. Set aside. Measure the flour into a large bowl. Add the cubed butter and toss with your hands to coat the cubes with flour.

Working quickly, rub the flour and butter cubes between your thumbs and index fingers to break up the butter and blend. Continue until all of the butter is broken up into about ¹/₈-inch pieces, being careful not to overwork it. There should be plenty of dry spots intermixed with the flour-coated butter pieces. It's always safe to stop before you think you should.

Next, rub the flour and butter between your palms, sliding your right hand away from you and your left hand toward you. I call this "sheeting." It is important to sheet in only one direction and to sheet only once before letting the dough fall back into the bowl. Continue until all of the butter cubes resemble flattened leaves. Again, don't overwork the dough; stop before you think you should.

Remove the ice cubes from the water and pour all but ¹/₂ cup of

IT'S BETTER WITH BUTTER

There are as many opinions about the merits of using butter versus shortening in pie dough as there are pie makers. No one is right or wrong. Pie crust preferences are probably most heavily influenced by the kind of crust we grew up eating or the one we found most pleasing when we first started baking pies.

Proponents of shortening say it produces a flaky crust. The problem with shortening is that it also leaves a greasy film on the upper palate. Personally, I don't think the trade-off is worth it or necessary. I think you'll find that our recipe produces a very tender, flaky crust with a rich buttery flavor. The method may be a little more labor intensive than you're used to, but I bet you'll join us butter believers after you try it!

*Our pie dough recipe,
like most others, calls for an
inexact amount of water.
Why? Because sometimes
you need more water, sometimes you need less. When
the weather is damp and
rainy, pie dough needs much
less water than it does on
sunny, dry days. Try using less
water at first: you can always
add more, 1 tablespoon at a
time, if you need it.*

the water out of the measuring cup. Pour the remaining $1/2$ cup of water into the dough. Toss the dough with a fork just until it is mixed. The dough should look flaky and coarse and should not hold together. Again, stop before you think you should; at this stage, it is very easy to overmix the dough, which results in a tough crust.

Pour the dough out onto a lightly floured surface and gently push it together with your hands. The dough will begin to come together as you roll it out. If the dough looks at all smooth, it has been overworked.

Divide the dough into 2 pieces and gently shape the pieces into flat round discs. The dough can now be worked, covered with plastic wrap, and refrigerated for up to to 3 days, or covered in plastic wrap and frozen for up to 2 weeks. If the dough has been frozen, let it thaw overnight in the refrigerator before rolling it out. The dough is best rolled out either at room temperature or after it has rested unrefrigerated for 10 minutes.

To make the dough in a food processor, place 4 ice cubes in a 1-cup measure and fill it with water. Set aside. Fit the food processor with the metal blade and measure the flour into the bowl of the processor. Add the butter and toss with your hands to coat the cubes with flour. Pulse until the butter pieces are the size of peas.

Remove the ice cubes from the water and pour out all but $1/2$ cup of the water. Pour the remaining $1/2$ cup of water through the feed tube of the food processor while pulsing. Stop when the mixture just begins to come together. It should still look dry and crumbly.

Turn the dough out onto a lightly floured surface and gently push it together with your hands. Divide the dough into 2 pieces and gently shape the pieces into flat round discs. The dough can now be worked and rolled out, covered and refrigerated for up to 3 days, or covered in plastic wrap and frozen for up to 2 weeks. If the dough has been frozen, let it thaw overnight in the refrigerator before rolling it out. It is best rolled out either at room tempera-ture or after it has rested unrefrigerated for 10 minutes.

APPLE PIE

MAKES ONE 10-INCH PIE

This pie has a streusel topping and is sometimes called a French or Dutch Apple Pie. It is buttery and almost has a caramel taste because of the butter and sugar in the topping. No one guesses that the reason this pie is so deliciously rich is there's a little heavy cream in the filling.

BAKER'S BASICS TO REVIEW

Measuring Dry Ingredients, page 21
Rolling Out Pie Crusts, page 98
Fluting Pie Crusts, page 98

STREUSEL

1 cup all-purpose flour
1/2 cup firmly packed brown sugar
1/2 cup granulated sugar
1/2 teaspoon ground cinnamon
3/4 cup (6 ounces) cold unsalted butter, cut into 1/2-inch pieces

FILLING

4 pounds Granny Smith or other baking apples
    (about 10 cups sliced)
1 tablespoon flour
1/2 cup granulated sugar
1/2 teaspoon ground cinnamon

1/2 recipe Pie Dough (page 99)
1/2 cup heavy whipping cream

To make the streusel, place the dry ingredients in a food processor fitted with the metal blade and pulse several times to mix. Add the butter and pulse until the mixture is crumbly. Set aside.

Preheat the oven to 325°.

To make the filling, peel, core, and cut the apples into 1/4-inch slices. Combine the flour, granulated sugar, and cinnamon in a separate bowl.

Roll out the pie dough and fit it into a 10-inch pie plate. Flute the edge of the crust.

Toss the apples with the sugar mixture and place them in the pie shell. They will be mounded very high. Press them down slightly. Pour the whipping cream over the apples.

Gently apply the streusel to the apples, pressing it into the slices. The streusel should cover the apples completely but not touch the edge of the pie shell.

Place the pie on the lower rack in the oven. Bake for 25 minutes, then transfer the pie to the center rack and continue baking for approximately 1 hour, or until the apples are softened but slightly firm when tested with a skewer. Set the pie on a wire rack to cool.

This apple pie is best about 1 hour after it comes out of the oven. Left-over pie can be warmed in a 325° oven for 15 minutes before serving.

NOTE: Four pounds, or 10 cups, of apples may seem like a lot of apples. It is! When baked, this pie is very tall. We use Granny Smith apples at the bakery because they are readily available all year, but you may substitute your favorite baking apple. Just keep in mind that the results may vary because apples vary in water content. (We find that even Granny Smith apples have different water contents from month to month.) If you know that the apples you're using are on the watery side, you may want to add an additional tablespoon of flour to the cinnamon-sugar mixture they're tossed with.

Gayle's, Capitola, California

PUMPKIN PIE

There's nothing newfangled about this pie. It is a straightforward, old-fashioned pumpkin pie—perfect comfort food for the holidays. This version is creamy and a little spicy.

BAKER'S BASICS TO REVIEW

Rolling Out Pie Crusts, page 98
Prebaking Pie Shells, page 109
Fluting Pie Crusts, page 98

1/2 recipe Pie Dough (page 99)
1 16-ounce can pumpkin purée
2 large eggs, at room temperature
1/2 cup granulated sugar
1/4 cup firmly packed dark brown sugar
1/2 teaspoon salt
1 teaspoon ground cinnamon
1 teaspoon ground ginger
1/4 teaspoon ground cloves
1/2 cup milk
1/2 cup evaporated milk

Preheat the oven to 375°.

Roll out the pie dough and fit it into a 10-inch pie plate. Flute the edge of the crust. Line the pie shell with parchment paper and fill it with 2 1/2 cups of dried beans or rice. Bake the shell on the lower rack in the oven for 15 minutes. Remove the paper and beans or rice and place the partially baked shell on a wire rack to cool.

Place the pumpkin purée in a large bowl, and, using a handheld whisk, add the eggs one at a time, waiting until the first one is incorporated before adding the second. Add the sugars, salt, and spices and beat to incorporate. Whisk in the milk and evaporated milk.

Pour the mixture into the cool prebaked pie shell. Place the pie on the lower rack in the oven. Bake for 30 minutes, then transfer the pie to the center rack and continue baking until the filling is set, about 15 minutes. For a creamy custardlike filling, take the pie out of the oven when a 2- or 3-inch-diameter area in the center has not quite set up. The pie will continue to cook while it cools, creating a wonderful, creamy texture. If you prefer a firmer filling, leave the pie in the oven until it is completely set up.

Set the pie on a wire rack to cool. This pie is best at room temperature the day it is baked, but it keeps, well covered, in the refrigerator for up to 3 days.

THANKSGIVING AT GAYLE'S

Thanksgiving pie production is choreographed with amazing precision at the bakery. It has to be, or there's no way we could make the 2,000-plus pumpkin pies we turn out during the 5 days before Thanksgiving each year. Would you believe that 800 of those pies are made in our 40 x 30-foot bake-off room the afternoon before Thanksgiving?

Preparation for the big event starts long in advance. Our bakers perform the physically demanding job of making 120 pounds of all-butter pie dough for five straight days before the holiday. To ensure consistency and quality, the same baker forms all of the shells. Each morning the baker begins by rolling out the dough on the sheeter, a tabletop machine that flattens the dough to 1/8 inch thick. Next, the baker cuts each shell and fits it into the pie tin by hand. One year, we tried using an expensive commercial pie press to speed up the process, but the heat of the machine played havoc with our all-butter pie dough and we had to go back to the hand method.

Five bakers work the pie bake-off shift. They work around the clock for 2 days. And this all happens while our normal production schedule continues. The bakers have to juggle space, trays, and equipment. Because oven time becomes so valuable, specific time slots

(continued)

PECAN PIE

MAKES ONE 10-INCH PIE

We make this pie every Thanksgiving and Christmas. It is a nice alternative (or addition!) to our Pumpkin Pie (page 103).

BAKER'S BASICS TO REVIEW
Measuring Dry Ingredients, page 21
Rolling Out Pie Crusts, page 98
Fluting Pie Crusts, page 98
Prebaking Pie Shells, page 109
Creaming, page 20

$1/2$ recipe Pie Dough (page 99)
2 tablespoons butter, at room temperature
$1/2$ cup firmly packed dark brown sugar
3 large eggs
2 tablespoons all-purpose flour
$1/4$ teaspoon salt
$1 1/2$ cups (12 ounces) light corn syrup
1 teaspoon pure vanilla extract
$2 1/4$ cups (8 ounces) pecan halves

Preheat the oven to 350°.

Roll out the pie dough and fit it into a 10-inch pie plate. Flute the edge of the crust. Line the pie shell with parchment paper and fill it with $2 1/2$ cups of dried beans or rice. Bake the shell on the lower rack in the oven for 15 minutes. Remove the paper and beans and place the partially baked shell on a wire rack to cool.

To make the filling, cream the butter and sugar with a wooden spoon. Add the eggs one at a time, beating well to incorporate each one before adding the next. In a small bowl, combine the flour and salt, then beat them into the butter mixture. Add the corn syrup and vanilla and again beat to incorporate.

Place the pecan halves in the prebaked shell and pour the filling over them. Place the pie on the center rack in the oven. Bake for approximately 45 to 50 minutes. The filling should be set in the center but still jiggle a little when you shake the pie plate.

Set the pie on a wire rack to cool. This pie is best the day it is made, but you can make it a day ahead and keep it in the refrigerator if you wish. Warm leftover pie in a 300° oven for 10 to 15 minutes before serving.

Making a Lattice Crust

Re-read "Rolling Out Pie Crusts" and "Fluting Pie Crusts," page 98, then roll out one disc of pie dough (1/2 recipe) for a 10-inch pie on a lightly floured surface to measure about 12 x 10 x 1/8 inch. If you prefer thicker lattice crusts, roll the dough out to 1/4 inch thick. Cut the dough into 1/2-inch-wide strips with a fluted pie-cutting wheel or a sharp knife. You will have about 12 strips.

Lay 6 strips parallel to each other and equidistant across the filled pie shell. The edges of the strips should extend slightly beyond the rim of the pie. Pinch together one end of each strip and the edge of the bottom crust to secure well.

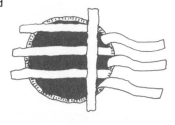

Working from top to bottom, lift the unsecured end of the second strip and gently bend it back to rest on the work surface. Repeat with the fourth and sixth strips, leaving the first, third, and fifth strips laying over the filling. Lay a strip of dough across the first, third, and fifth strips.

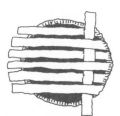

Lay the second, fourth, and sixth strips back over the pie.

Now lift the unsecured ends of the first, third, and fifth strips and bend them

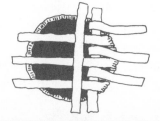

back to rest on the work surface. Lay another strip across the second, fourth, and sixth strips.

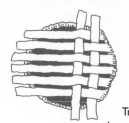

Lay the first, third, and fifth strips back over the pie.

Continue alternating the strips until you have 6 strips going one way and 6 going the opposite way. Trim the excess dough from the unsecured ends of the strips so they meet the inside edge of the bottom crust.

To make a tighter (or looser) lattice crust, simply cut and weave more or fewer strips.

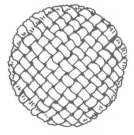

Seal the ends of the strips to the bottom crust by gently pinching them together. Glaze and bake lattice crust as directed in each recipe.

❧ ❧ ❧

STRAWBERRY-RHUBARB PIE

Sometimes we aren't able to make this pie for a year or two because there's such a small window of time when rhubarb is available in Capitola. We try to keep our eyes open every spring and fall to make sure we don't miss it, then hope that strawberries are available. This pie has achieved cult status with some of our customers.

BAKER'S BASICS TO REVIEW
Baking Fruit Pies, page 109
Rolling Out Pie Crusts, page 98
Fluting Pie Crusts, page 98
Prebaking Pie Shells, page 109
Zesting Citrus, page 24
Making a Lattice Crust, page 105

1 recipe Pie Dough (page 99)
1 to 1 1/4 cups sugar
1/4 cup cornstarch
1/2 teaspoon ground nutmeg
1 tablespoon grated orange zest
3 cups halved fresh strawberries
11 ounces fresh rhubarb, cut into 1/2-inch pieces (about 3 cups)

EGG GLAZE
1 large egg
2 tablespoons milk

Preheat the oven to 400°.

Roll out one disc of the pie dough and fit it into a 10-inch pie plate. Flute the edge of the crust. Line the pie shell with parchment paper and fill it with 2 1/2 cups of dried beans or rice. Bake the shell on the lower rack in the oven for 15 minutes. Remove the paper and beans or rice and place the partially baked shell on a wire rack to cool.

In a large bowl, combine the sugar, cornstarch, nutmeg, and orange zest. Add the fruit and toss to coat well. Let stand for 10 to 15 minutes.

To make the lattice crust, roll out the second disc of pie dough and cut it into 12 strips.

Pour the fruit mixture into the cooled prebaked pie shell. Assemble the lattice crust over the filling. Trim the ends of the lattice strips and press to seal with the bottom crust.

In a small bowl, whisk together the egg and milk to make the glaze. Using a pastry brush, coat the lattice strips with the glaze.

Place the pie on the lower rack in the oven. Bake for 40 minutes, then decrease the temperature to 375°. Move the pie to the center rack, and continue baking for 30 minutes, or until the crust is golden brown and the center of the filling is bubbling.

Set the pie on a wire rack to cool. This pie is best at room temperature 2 to 3 hours after it is baked. It keeps well covered in the refrigerator for up to 3 days. Warm leftover pie in a 300° oven for 10 to 15 minutes before serving.

OLALLIEBERRY PIE

MAKES ONE 9-INCH PIE

Here on the central coast of California, we live in the heart of blackberry country. We are especially blessed to be near the Gizdich Ranch, one of the best berry farms in the country. Nita Gizdich and her family not only grow the best apples, they also grow the best olallieberries anywhere. Olallieberries are a cross between black loganberries and Young berries. The name olallie comes from the Chinook Indians of the Columbia River Valley who called all blackberries *olallie.* If olallieberries are not available in your area, substitute any other type of blackberries.

BAKER'S BASICS TO REVIEW
Baking Fruit Pies, page 109
Rolling Out Pie Crusts, page 98
Fluting Pie Crusts, page 98
Making a Lattice Crust, page 105

1 recipe Pie Dough (page 99)
3/4 cup sugar
4 tablespoons cornstarch
8 cups olallieberries or any other blackberries (see Note)

EGG GLAZE
1 large egg
2 tablespoons milk

Preheat the oven to 400°.

Roll out one disc of the pie dough and fit it into a 9-inch pie plate. Flute the edge of the crust.

In a medium bowl, combine the sugar and cornstarch. Add the berries and toss to coat well. Let stand for 5 to 10 minutes.

To make the lattice crust, roll out the second disc of pie dough and cut it into 12 strips.

Pour the berries into the pie shell. If some of the sugar and cornstarch have settled on the bottom of the mixing bowl, pour them over the top of the berries. Working quickly so the pie shell doesn't get soggy, assemble the lattice crust over the filling. Trim the ends of the lattice strips and press to seal with the bottom crust.

In a small bowl, whisk together the egg and milk to make the glaze. With a pastry brush, coat the lattice strips with the glaze.

Place the pie on the lower rack in the oven. Bake for 25 minutes, then decrease the heat to 375°, move the pie to the center rack, and continue baking for 30 to 45 minutes, or until the crust is golden brown and the center of the filling is bubbling.

Set the pie on a wire rack to cool. This pie is best at room temperature 2 to 3 hours after it is baked. It keeps well covered in the refrigerator for up to 3 days. Warm leftover pie in a 300° oven for 10 to 15 minutes before serving.

NOTE: Blackberries can be hard to find and, even when in season, they can be very tart and may require additional sugar to taste (add it a couple of tablespoons at a time). Of course sweet fresh berries are best, but frozen ones can be used. Just thaw them in a single layer at room temperature on a baking sheet for about 1 hour. Drain off any liquid before using.

Baking Fruit Pies

The sugar and water content vary so much from one fruit to another, and even among the same kind of fruit when it is grown and harvested under different conditions, that it is impossible to standardize baking instructions for fruit pies. As a result, customized baking directions are given for each fruit pie in this book (Strawberry-Rhubarb Pie, page 106; Olallieberry Pie, page 107; Cherry Pie, page 112; Green Tomato Pie, page 267; and Apricot Pie, page 268).

For fruit pie fillings to set properly, it is imperative that you observe the baking temperatures and times given in the recipes and that you monitor the pie as it bakes. (As always, it is also important to know your oven's idiosyncrasies and make adjustments as necessary. For more about this, see "Adjusting Oven Temperatures and Baking Times," page 18.) Check the pie 5 minutes before the first baking stage is complete. If the bottom is browning nicely, move the pie to the center rack and decrease the oven temperature as directed. While the pie continues to bake, check it every 15 minutes to make sure the filling is setting up and the crust is not browning too quickly. If the top crust is browning too quickly, mold a piece of aluminum foil into a pie shape and lay it over the pie as it finishes baking. The pie is perfectly baked when the juices are bubbling at least 2 inches in from the edge and the center has thickened and does not jiggle when the pie is moved. Optimally, the center should also be bubbling. The top and bottom crusts should be a deep golden brown color. The more fruit pies you bake, the better you will be able to judge the sweetness and juiciness of the fruit you are working with and make whatever slight adjustments to the oven temperature and baking times that may be necessary.

🌺 🌺 🌺

Prebaking Pie Shells

There are two kinds of prebaked pie shells: fully baked and partially baked shells. Partially baked shells are prebaked for about 15 minutes before they are filled to give them the extra strength they need to hold together, stay crisp, and support wetter pie fillings. Once filled, partially baked shells finish baking along with the filling and, sometimes, a top crust. Fully baked shells are used for pies with puddinglike fillings, such as our Lemon Meringue Pie (page 114). For these pies, the fillings and shells are cooked independently, then combined and baked briefly or not at all.

To make a fully baked 10-inch pie shell, make the pie dough (see page 99), roll it out, fit into the pie plate, and flute the edge (see page 98). Immediately chill the shell in the refrigerator for 30 minutes. If the shell has been preformed and frozen, thaw it at room temperature for 20 minutes.

Meanwhile, preheat the oven to 450°.

Line the pie shell with a 12-inch circle of parchment paper or waxed paper and fill it with 2½ cups of dried beans or rice. The beans or rice weigh down the bottom and hold up the sides of the crust as it bakes, so spread them out to the edges and place more near the sides than in the center.

Set the pie shell on a baking sheet and place on the center rack in the oven. Bake for 10 minutes, then decrease the heat to 375° and bake for 5 minutes more. Remove the pie shell from the oven. Grasp the edges of the parchment paper or waxed paper and slowly lift it and the beans or rice out of the shell. Prick the bottom of the pie shell in 3 or 4 places with the point of a sharp knife to prevent the shell from forming bubbles as it finishes baking.

Return the shell to the oven and bake for 15 to 18 minutes, or until it is golden brown. Transfer the shell from the baking sheet to a wire rack and let cool completely before filling.

🌺 🌺 🌺

VEGETARIAN
MINCEMEAT PIE

MAKES ONE 9-INCH PIE

Finding or developing the perfect mincemeat pie has been a challenge we've struggled with for years. For a long time, we used a high-quality canned mincemeat (a real departure from our fresh-, homemade-only philosophy) because none of us could find a good recipe. Finally, Louisa got fed up with the canned variety and solicited the help of our friend and baking guru, Marion Cunningham. With the suggestions and ideas of Marion and our head pastry baker, Linda Younger, Louisa produced this meatless recipe. Filled with sweet chunks of fresh fruit, a healthy splash of brandy, and plenty of butter, it's a decadent treat for vegetarians and nonvegetarians alike. Note that the filling should be started 2 days before baking the pie.

BAKER'S BASICS TO REVIEW
Zesting Citrus, page 24
Rolling Out Pie Crusts, page 98
Fluting Pie Crusts, page 98
Making a Lattice Crust, page 105

FILLING
1 1/2 cups peeled, cored, 1/2-inch dice baking apples
    (about 10 ounces unprepared)
1 cup peeled, cored, 1/2-inch dice slightly firm ripe pears
    (about 8 ounces unprepared)
3/4 cup raisins
3/4 cup currants
1/3 cup candied orange peel, cut into 1/4-inch pieces (see Note)
1 tablespoon grated lemon zest
3 tablespoons freshly squeezed lemon juice
1/4 cup apple juice
1/2 cup (4 ounces) unsalted butter, cut into 1/2-inch pieces
1/4 cup brandy
1/4 cup firmly packed dark brown sugar
1/2 teaspoon ground cinnamon
1/4 teaspoon ground nutmeg
1/4 teaspoon mace
1/2 teaspoon allspice

1 recipe Pie Dough (page 99)
4 tablespoons all-purpose flour

EGG GLAZE
1 large egg
1 tablespoon milk

Two days before baking the pie, combine the apples and pears, raisins, currants, zest, candied orange peel, fruit juices, butter, and brandy in a large mixing bowl. In a separate bowl, combine the brown sugar and spices. Add the sugar-spice mixture to the bowl of fruit, toss to combine, cover, and refrigerate. Stir the mixture at least twice a day for 2 days. (The fruit can be prepared just prior to baking if necessary, but the filling is much better when the flavors of the ingredients have had a few days to marry.)

Preheat the oven to 350°.

Roll out one disc of the pie dough and fit it into a 9-inch pie plate. Flute the edge of the crust.

To make the lattice crust, roll out the second disc of pie dough and cut it into 12 strips.

Remove the mincemeat filling from the refrigerator. Add the flour and toss to coat well. Spoon the filling into the pie shell. Working quickly so the pie shell doesn't become soggy, assemble the lattice crust over the filling. Trim the ends of the lattice strips and press to seal with the bottom crust.

In a small bowl, whisk together the egg and milk to make the glaze. Using a pastry brush, coat the lattice strips with the glaze.

Place the pie on the center rack in the oven. Bake for 45 minutes, or until the crust is a dark golden brown and the filling is bubbling.

Set the pie on a wire rack to cool. This pie keeps very well at room temperature for up to 3 days; in fact, it gets better after the first day.

NOTE: If you can't find pre-made candied orange peel, or the type you find is not satisfactory, make your own (see the recipe at right). It's very simple and much better than any store-bought variety.

CANDIED ORANGE PEEL

This recipe is an adaptation of Lindsey Shere's recipe in Chez Panisse Desserts, a book I use all the time.

Cut 2 oranges in quarters, then remove the peel. Place the peel in a nonreactive saucepan and cover with cold water. Bring the water to a boil and simmer until the white pith is translucent, about 10 minutes. Remove the pan from the heat and let the peel stand in the hot water for 15 minutes. Drain and remove from the pan. Let cool slightly.

In the same saucepan, combine 1 cup sugar, 1/2 cup water, and 2 tablespoons light corn syrup. Scrape off as much of the white pith on the peel as possible. Cut the peel into 1/4-inch strips and add to the syrup in the saucepan. Cook over medium heat until the peel is translucent and tender, about 10 minutes. Increase the heat and boil the mixture for 4 minutes. Meanwhile, cover a baking sheet with 1 cup of sugar.

Drain the cooked peel well, then place on the baking sheet and toss with the sugar until all pieces are fully coated. Separate the pieces and lay them on a clean baking sheet to dry. When completely dry, store the peel in an airtight container for up to 3 months. Makes about 1 cup.

CHERRY PIE

In California, we can't seem to get the sour baking cherries that make this pie so wonderful. In Colorado, my friend Markita Lerch gets them every spring. We were lucky enough to be visiting during the cherry harvest one year, and she baked a cherry pie I'll never forget. The filling was made of firm but tender, sweet and tangy baking cherries, with just enough natural juices to surround them in the glistening filling.

Since then, I've tried to duplicate that pie both at the bakery and at home. We have come close at the bakery using a very good frozen sour cherry. But for home use, grocery stores usually carry only the frozen sweet cherries (which make a very bad pie) or canned sour cherries, which are soft and discolored. Instead of settling for either in our home kitchens, we use jarred Czechoslovakian cherries imported by international food purveyors (look for them at Middle Eastern markets and other specialty markets that import international foods). They make very good cherry pies, cobblers, and crisps.

BAKER'S BASICS TO REVIEW

Baking Fruit Pies, page 109

Measuring Dry Ingredients, page 21

Rolling Out Pie Crusts, page 98

Fluting Pie Crusts, page 98

Making a Lattice Crust, page 105

---

1 recipe Pie Dough (page 99)

FILLING

1 cup sugar

4 tablespoons cornstarch

1 tablespoon all-purpose flour

6 cups (about three 24-ounce jars) sour baking cherries, well drained

EGG GLAZE

1 large egg

2 tablespoons milk

Preheat the oven to 400°.

Roll out one disc of the pie dough and fit it into a 10-inch pie plate. Flute the edge of the crust.

To make the lattice crust, roll out the second disc of pie dough and cut it into 12 strips.

In a large bowl, combine the sugar, cornstarch, and flour. Add the cherries and toss gently to combine well.

Pour the filling into the pie shell. Working quickly so the bottom crust does not get soggy, assemble the lattice crust over the filling. Trim the ends of the strips and press to seal with the bottom crust.

In a small bowl, whisk together the egg and milk to make a glaze. Using a pastry brush, coat the lattice strips with the glaze.

Place the pie on the lower rack in the oven. Bake for 20 minutes, then decrease the oven to 350°, move the pie to the center rack and continue baking for 40 minutes to 1 hour, or until the crust is golden brown and the center of the filling is bubbling.

Set the pie on a wire rack to cool. This pie is best at room temperature 2 to 3 hours after it is baked. It keeps well covered in the refrigerator for up to 3 days. Warm leftover pie in a 300° oven for 10 to 15 minutes before serving.

LEMON MERINGUE PIE

Although the ingredients and proportions are fairly standard for this pie, our technique is a little unusual. We feel the additional steps are well worth the effort. We have discovered that it is very important for the filling to be warm when the meringue is applied. This helps seal the meringue to the filling so the two don't separate when cut. Instead of pouring the filling directly into the crust right after it is made and letting it cool, the filling is kept warm in the double boiler until the meringue is ready.

Some meringues develop beads of moisture, are chunky and unappetizing, or fall apart when cut. Heating the egg whites and sugar together before whipping solves these problems and makes a silky smooth meringue that slices beautifully. (Not even one drop of moisture beaded up on the meringue when we tested the recipe during a major rainstorm.)

BAKER'S BASICS TO REVIEW
> Prebaking Pie Shells, page 109
> Separating Eggs, page 22
> Zesting Citrus, page 24
> Whipping Egg Whites and Making Meringues, page 198

FILLING
> 1½ cups sugar
> ½ cup plus 2 tablespoons cornstarch
> 2½ cups cold water
> 5 large egg yolks
> 2 tablespoons (1 ounce) butter
> 2 tablespoons lemon zest
> ½ cup freshly squeezed, strained lemon juice
>
> ———
>
> 1 10-inch fully baked pie crust, cooled (page 109)

MERINGUE
> 5 large egg whites
> ¾ cup sugar
> ¼ teaspoon cream of tartar

Preheat the oven to 400°.

Start the filling only when you are ready to prepare the whole pie; this pie cannot be made in stages. In the top of a double boiler, off the heat, combine the sugar and cornstarch. Add the water and, using a whisk, stir until the mixture is well dissolved, making sure no cornstarch lumps remain. Whisk in the egg yolks and stir until the mixture is smooth.

Place the egg mixture over boiling water, and cook, whisking continuously. After about 7 minutes, the mixture will thicken rapidly. After it has thickened, cook for 1 minute. Whisk in the butter, then remove from the heat. Quickly whisk in the lemon zest and juice and stir until blended. Immediately cover the mixture to keep it warm. Set aside.

To make the meringue, make sure all your mixing equipment is grease free. Then, with a whisk combine the egg whites, sugar, and cream of tartar in the bowl of a tabletop mixer. Place the bowl over a pan of barely simmering water. Stir continuously with the whisk until the mixture is just warm to the touch.

Return the bowl to the mixer, fit the mixer with the whip attachment, and whip at high speed until the meringue forms soft peaks, about 2 minutes. The meringue should be glossy and smooth, not chunky.

Pour the lemon filling into the cooled fully baked 10-inch pie shell and spread it out evenly.

So that the meringue is easy to spread evenly, place it 3 or 4 places on the filling, rather than piling it all in the center. (If you have a cake turntable, placing the pie on it while applying the meringue makes the process easier.) Using an icing spatula, spread the meringue completely over the surface of the pie. Make sure the meringue meets the outside rim of the crust all the way around the pie (so that it will create a seal with the crust when baked). Place the remaining meringue in the center of the pie. Use the spatula to shape the meringue into the classic dome, complete with swirls that will brown nicely.

Place the pie on the center rack in the oven and bake for 6 minutes. Most of the meringue will be a very light brown, with some areas still white and the higher peaks a darker brown.

Set the pie on a wire rack in a draft-free location and let cool for 4 hours before serving.

This pie is best the day it is made. It may be stored uncovered at room temperature overnight, but some liquid will form under the crust the next day.

NOTE: This recipe must be made in a 10-inch pie plate. It makes too much filling to work in a 9-inch pie plate.

KEY LIME PIE

This pie is as easy as it is decadent. The secret is using a really good Key lime juice. If you are lucky enough to live in Florida, you're home free. We use Nellie and Joe's Famous Key West Lime Juice (see page 317 for ordering information). The pie filling can also be used as a custard to layer with fresh seasonal fruit.

BAKER'S BASICS TO REVIEW

Whipping Cream, page 258

Filling and Using a Nylon Pastry Bag, page 20

Piping Borders and Other Decorations, page 215

GRAHAM CRACKER CRUST

1/2 cup (4 ounces) unsalted butter

1 1/2 cups graham cracker crumbs

FILLING

8 ounces cream cheese, at room temperature

1 (14-ounce) can sweetened condensed milk

1/2 cup Key lime juice (see above and page 317)

1/2 teaspoon pure vanilla extract

TOPPING

1 cup heavy whipping cream

1 tablespoon sugar

1 teaspoon pure vanilla extract

To make the crust, preheat the oven to 350°.

Melt the butter and cool slightly. In a medium bowl, combine the melted butter and graham cracker crumbs. The mixture will be a little crumbly. With your fingers, press the crust into a 9-inch pie plate. Bake on the center rack in the oven for 5 minutes. Set on a wire rack to cool.

To make the filling, beat the cream cheese in the bowl of a tabletop mixer until smooth. Slowly add the condensed milk in a steady stream, beating until well incorporated and scraping the sides of the bowl several times. Add the lime juice and vanilla, again mixing well and scraping the sides of the bowl.

Pour the filling into the prebaked pie shell, cover with plastic wrap and refrigerate for at least 5 hours.

Just before serving, whip the cream with the sugar and vanilla until stiff peaks form. Decorate the pie using a pastry bag to pipe swirls or rosettes on top or by spreading the whipping cream over the filling with a spatula.

Let the pie sit at room temperature 30 minutes before serving so the crust will be easier to cut. This pie can be stored in the refrigerator for up to 3 days.

BANANA CREAM PIE

MAKES ONE 9-INCH PIE

We have many requests for this pie. The trick to achieving an intense banana flavor is combining the bananas with the custard while it is still hot.

BAKER'S BASICS TO REVIEW
Separating Eggs, page 22
Whipping Cream, page 258
Filling and Using a Nylon Pastry Bag, page 20
Piping Borders and Other Decorations, page 215

FILLING
3/4 cup sugar
1/2 cup cornstarch
1/4 teaspoon salt
4 cups milk
5 large egg yolks, lightly beaten
2 teaspoons pure vanilla extract
2 bananas
2 tablespoons freshly squeezed orange juice

—

1 (9-inch) prebaked Graham Cracker Crust, cooled (page 116)

TOPPING
1 cup heavy whipping cream
1 tablespoon sugar
1 tablespoon Myers's rum or pure vanilla extract

Combine the sugar, cornstarch, and salt in a heavy saucepan, stirring to mix. Add the milk and egg yolks, whisk to combine and bring the mixture to a boil over medium heat, stirring continuously. After the mixture has come to a boil, continue to cook, while stirring, for 1 minute. Remove the custard from the heat and whisk in the vanilla.

Peel the bananas and cut into 1/2-inch-thick slices. Place in a medium bowl, add the orange juice and toss to coat well. Drain off any excess juice.

Place one-third of the hot custard in the cool prebaked pie shell. Place one-half of the banana slices on top the custard. Pour another third of the custard over the bananas, making sure to cover them completely. Place remaining bananas on the second layer of custard and top with the remaining custard, covering all of the bananas, but keeping the filling from touching the rim of the shell. Place the pie, uncovered, in the refrigerator for 1 hour. Cover with plastic wrap and refrigerate for 2 to 5 hours.

Just before serving, whip the cream to soft peaks. Add the sugar and rum and continue whipping until stiff peaks form. Decorate the pie using a pastry bag to pipe swirls or rosettes on top or by spreading the whipping cream over the filling with a spatula.

Let the pie sit at room temperature for 30 minutes before serving. This pie keeps in the refrigerator for up to 3 days.

CHOCOLATE-APRICOT TORTE

MAKES ONE 9-INCH TORTE

Many years ago, we had a customer whom everyone called Pesto Bruce (because he made and sold pesto out of his home). He gave us this wonderful recipe and I will always be grateful. (Thanks, Bruce, wherever you are!)

We make this torte in the winter when locally grown fresh fruit is not available. It is really easy and stores beautifully. The flavors of bitter chocolate, walnuts, and dried apricots are magical together—it's one of my favorites.

BAKER'S BASICS TO REVIEW
Measuring Dry Ingredients, page 21

FILLING
8 ounces dried apricots
$^1/_2$ cup sugar
2 tablespoons all-purpose flour
2 tablespoons freshly squeezed lemon juice
Water to cover fruit

CRUST
1$^1/_2$ ounces unsweetened chocolate, cut into $^1/_2$-inch pieces
1$^1/_2$ cups all-purpose flour
$^1/_2$ cup firmly packed brown sugar
1 cup walnut pieces
6 tablespoons (3 ounces) cold butter, cut into $^1/_2$-inch cubes
1 tablespoon water
1 teaspoon pure vanilla extract

Preheat the oven to 350°.

Place all of the filling ingredients in a heavy saucepan. Bring to a boil, stirring to mix well. Decrease the heat and simmer until the fruit is soft and the liquid has thickened, about 5 minutes, depending on how hard the apricots are. Let the mixture cool and coarsely purée it in a food processor or blender. Set aside.

To make the crust, coarsely chop the chocolate in a food processor. Turn off the processor and add the flour and brown sugar. Process just until mixed. Add the walnuts and process again just until mixed. Add the butter and process until it is in very small pieces. Add the water and vanilla and pulse until the crust mixture is crumbly.

Spoon one-half of the crust mixture into a 9-inch springform pan or a pan with a removable bottom and sides at least 2 inches high. It will be crumbly, don't worry. With your hands, press the crust down over the bottom of the pan until it is as flat and smooth as possible. Spoon the filling into the crust, distributing it evenly and leaving 1/2 inch of the crust exposed all the way around the edge of the torte.

Sprinkle some of the remaining crust mixture around the edge to seal in the filling, then sprinkle the rest over the filling and gently pat down so that no filling shows.

Place the torte on the center rack in the oven. Bake for 25 to 35 minutes, or until golden brown. Set the torte on a wire rack to cool. When completely cool, remove the torte from the pan and serve at room temperature.

The finished torte will keep, tightly covered with aluminum foil, at room temperature for 4 days. Or, it can be refrigerated for up to 1 week or frozen for up to 2 weeks.

NOTE: If you wish, you can make the crust and the filling in advance and store them, well covered, in the refrigerator for up to 4 days or in the freezer for up to 2 weeks. When you want to bake the torte, let the ingredients come to room temperature and then assemble as the recipe directs.

CLAFOUTI

There are many versions of this baked fresh fruit dessert. Some have no crust, others do. Ours is a simple combination of pie dough, custard filling, and seasonal fresh fruit. This is a great dessert for spring and fall when figs, pears, and plums are in season. This dessert is comfort food at its best.

BAKER'S BASICS TO REVIEW
Measuring Dry Ingredients, page 21
Rolling Out Pie Crusts, page 98

$^1/_2$ recipe Pie Dough (page 99)
6 fresh plums, cut into 6 wedges, or 15 figs,
    cut in half (see Note)
$^1/_3$ cup sugar
2 tablespoons all-purpose flour
1 large egg
1 cup milk
1 teaspoon pure vanilla extract, Grand Marnier,
    or other liqueur

Roll out the pie dough to $^1/_8$ inch thick. Transfer the dough to the tart pan by rolling it around the rolling pin, then unrolling it over a 9-inch fluted tart pan with a removable bottom.

With one hand, lift the edge of the dough slightly while you gently guide it with your other hand into the curve where the sides and bottom of the pan meet, carefully tucking the dough into the flutes along the side of the pan. Work all the way around the pan, until the dough is fitted snugly into it. You can use a bit of pressure to make sure that it pressed into the sides of the pan. This will prevent the dough from pulling away from the pan while it bakes. If the dough tears, patch it with another small piece of dough that has no flour on it.

Trim away all but ¹/₂ inch of the excess dough extending beyond the sides of the pan.

Fold the excess dough toward the center of the pan, and press against the sides to create a double thickness of dough that extends ¹/₄ inch above the rim of the pan.

Arrange the fruit pieces cut side up in the tart shell. (The fruit can be arranged randomly, in a spiral, or in concentric circles.)

In a medium bowl, combine the sugar and flour. Add the egg and beat with a whisk until fully incorporated and shiny. Add the milk and vanilla and whisk until smooth.

Pour the milk mixture between the fruit, being careful not to pour it over the fruit. Place the tart on the lower rack in the oven. Bake for 40 minutes, then move the pan to the center rack and continue baking until the clafouti is light golden brown, approximately 5 to 15 minutes. Set the tart on a wire rack and let cool. When cool, depan and serve. This tart is best within 2 hours after it is baked.

NOTE: Fresh fruit at its peak is essential to this recipe. It is also important to determine the liquid content of the fruit; try to use ripe but firm fruit. Fruit that is too juicy will weep in the baking process and result in a runny clafouti. Other fruits you might substitute for the plums or figs include apricots, pie or baking sour cherries, peaches, nectarines, blueberries, and raspberries.

TART DOUGH

**MAKES TWO 9-INCH CRUSTS
OR ABOUT TWELVE 3-INCH TARTLET SHELLS**

This dough is the backbone of all the fresh fruit tarts we make at Gayle's. It is very hardy and can stand up to the moisture of pastry cream and fresh fruit for hours. We bet the crisp cookielike crust will quickly become one of your favorites, too, because it's so easy to make and use. It's one of the recipes we learned at the Le Feyeux bakery in Paris. They have been making it for twenty years.

BAKER'S BASICS TO REVIEW
Measuring Dry Ingredients, page 21

---

^{1}/$_2$ cup (4 ounces) butter, at room temperature
(use chilled butter for food processor method)
^{1}/$_2$ cup sugar
2 large eggs
1^3/$_4$ cups all-purpose flour

To make the dough in a tabletop mixer, fit the mixer with the flat beater. In the bowl of the mixer, beat the butter on medium speed until smooth. Add the sugar and beat until incorporated. Add the eggs, one at a time, waiting until the first one is incorporated before adding the second. Add the flour all at once and mix slowly just until incorporated.

To make the dough in a food processor, combine the flour and sugar in the bowl fitted with the metal blade. Pulse several times to blend the ingredients. Cut the butter into ^{1}/$_2$-inch cubes and toss in the flour mixture to coat well. Pulse several times, or until the mixture resembles cornmeal. Add the eggs and pulse just until they are incorporated and the mixture has begun to hold together.

Transfer the dough to a lightly floured surface and divide it in half. Shape each half into a round, flat disc, handling them as little as possible. Cover the discs in plastic wrap and refrigerate for at least 2 hours. The dough keeps in the refrigerator for up to 4 days or in the freezer for up to 2 weeks.

Roll out and bake tart dough as directed in each recipe.

Checking Tart Dough Consistency

When rolling out tart dough, the temperature and consistency of the dough is very important. Remove the dough from the refrigerator approximately 5 minutes before you plan to use it. When the dough is ready to be rolled out, it should be cold but slightly malleable. If it is too cold and stiff, it will crack when you try to roll it. If it is too soft, it will stick to the work surface and rolling pin and will be difficult to fit in the tart pan.

Using Fruit Glazes

Homemade jams and jellies make the best fruit glazes, but a good store-bought variety will work just fine. Do not use the packaged powdered glaze that is sold for coating strawberries; it is artificial tasting, poorly colored, and too thick.

We prefer to use currant jelly to glaze darker fruits, such as berries, and apricot jam for lighter fruits, such as peaches. To make a fruit glaze from a jam, purée the jam in a food processor or blender, then strain it through a fine sieve. Warm and use as directed.

FRESH FRUIT TART

In California, the selection of fresh fruit is abundant. For the best berries, we go to the farmers' market, where each vendor is known for his or her specialty. For this tart, take the extra time to find the best locally grown fruit in season. It's worth the trouble because the fruit is really the star. Assemble the tart 5 hours or less before you plan to serve it—the somewhat delicate pastry doesn't hold up much longer.

BAKER'S BASICS TO REVIEW
Checking Tart Dough Consistency, page 123
Folding, page 20
Using Fruit Glazes, page 123

$^{1}/_{2}$ recipe Tart Dough (page 122)
2$^{1}/_{2}$ to 3 cups mixed fresh fruit (such as strawberries, raspberries, blackberries, blueberries, kiwifruit, peaches, nectarines, bananas, and seedless grapes)
1 cup fruit glaze (see Note and page 123)
1 cup Pastry Cream (page 127)
1 tablespoon Myers's rum, Grand Marnier, or your favorite liqueur

Place the chilled dough on a lightly floured work surface and let it rest for 5 minutes. Lightly flour the top of the dough, then roll it into a $^{1}/_{8}$-inch-thick circle that is at least 12 inches in diameter. Keep both sides lightly floured to prevent the dough from sticking to the surface or the rolling pin.

Transfer the dough to the tart pan by rolling it around the rolling pin, then unrolling it over a 9-inch fluted tart pan with a removable bottom.

With one hand, lift the edge of the dough slightly while you gently guide it with your other hand into the curve where the sides and bottom of the pan meet, carefully tucking the dough into the flutes along the side of the pan. Work all the way around the pan, until the dough is fitted snugly into it. You can use a bit of pressure to make sure that the dough is pressed into the sides of the pan. This will prevent the dough from pulling away from the pan while it bakes. If the dough tears, patch it with another small piece of dough that has no flour on it. With a sharp paring knife, scrape off the excess dough.

Gently pinch together the rim of the dough and the sides of the pan to make sure they are sealed. Cover the shell with plastic wrap and refrigerate for at least 30 minutes or as long as overnight before baking. (At this point, the shell may be covered with plastic wrap and frozen for up to 2 weeks. If frozen, thaw it in the refrigerator for at least 5 hours before baking.)

Preheat the oven to 350°.

To bake the tart shell, unwrap the chilled shell. Place the shell on the center rack in the oven. Bake for 7 minutes, then remove from the oven and check to be sure the sides are not collapsing. If they are, gently push them back into place with a dinner knife. If air pockets are forming on the bottom of the shell, prick with a toothpick to deflate them. Return the shell to the oven and continue baking until it is golden brown, about 13 minutes. The top of the sides will be a little darker. Let the shell cool in the pan on a wire rack.

To remove the tart shell from the pan, simply place your hand under the pan, touching only the removable bottom. Gently loosen the sides of the shell from the sides of the pan by prying the ring away from the bottom disc. The tart ring will fall away from the shell onto your arm.

Set the shell on the work surface and, using a serrated knife, gently loosen it from the bottom of the pan by carefully sliding the blade between the pan and the shell. (This becomes easier with practice.) The tart shell may be left on the bottom of the pan and served off of it if you prefer.

Except for raspberries and blackberries, prepare the fruit by washing and drying it very well, then removing any stems. Peel and slice the peaches, nectarines, kiwifruit, and bananas. Do not wash berries; use a pastry brush to clean away any dirt instead.

Heat the glaze, stirring frequently, in a heavy saucepan over medium heat just until it bubbles. With a pastry brush, coat the bottom and inside edges of the shell with glaze. Do not brush or drip glaze over the edge or it will show after the tart is filled. Let the glaze dry for 30 minutes.

Fold the rum into the Pastry Cream. Spread the cream evenly over the bottom of the tart shell, being careful to keep any cream from touching the sides above the level that the fruit will reach when arranged on the tart.

Arranging the fruit is an individual exercise. You may want to put the strawberries on whole or slice them. You may want to use only one type of fruit or as many as six kinds to create an elaborate mosaic. Try laying the sliced fruit in concentric overlapping circles. Use your imagination, and have fun.

When the fruit is arranged on the Pastry Cream, rewarm the glaze and gently brush it on the fruit. Be careful not to apply too much glaze or it will look gloppy. Do not get any glaze on the tart shell. The goal is to make the fruit look like it glistens naturally.

This pastry is best at room temperature, which intensifies the natural sweetness of the fruit, but it should not sit out of the refrigerator longer than 30 minutes because the Pastry Cream is perishable. If stored in the refrigerator, remove it 30 minutes before serving.

NOTE: For darker fruits, such as berries, use a currant jelly glaze. For lighter fruits, such as peaches, use an apricot jam glaze.

FRESH FRUIT TARTLETS

MAKES 12 TARTLETS

We make close to 400 of these tartlets every week during the height of the summer season. Because they are easy-to-handle, individual pastries, they are perfect for picnics and tailgate parties.

BAKER'S BASICS TO REVIEW
Checking Tart Dough Consistency, page 123
Using Fruit Glazes, page 123

---

1 recipe Tart Dough (page 122)
1/2 cup fruit glaze (see Note, page 125, and page 123)
1 cup Pastry Cream (page 127)
1 tablespoon Myers's rum, Grand Marnier, or your favorite liqueur
3 to 4 cups mixed fresh fruit (such as strawberries, raspberries, blackberries, blueberries, kiwifruit, peaches, nectarines, bananas, and seedless grapes)

Follow the instructions for the Fresh Fruit Tart (page 124), with the following adjustments:

Cut twelve 4-inch rounds out of the tart dough. Fit the rounds into 3-inch tartlet tins. Set the tartlet shells on a baking sheet and place on the center rack in the oven. Bake for 5 minutes, then check sides and bottom of each shell as directed. Bake for 10 to 12 minutes more, or until golden brown. Transfer the shells from the baking sheet to a wire rack to cool. They will easily slip out of the tins.

Brush the tartlet shells with the glaze, fill with Pastry Cream and fruit, and glaze as directed for the Fruit Tart.

PASTRY CREAM

MAKES 3 CUPS

This is such a versatile component in the pastry maker's world. It is used for all kinds of pastries, including tarts, cakes, éclairs, and breakfast Danish. A few spoonfuls of leftover pastry cream and fresh fruit can also transform a simple dessert, such as a brownie, cookie, or slice of our Lemon Bread (page 169), into a special treat. Other uses for pastry cream include just spooning it out of the bowl right into your mouth (or a young helper's mouth).

1 1/2 cups half-and-half
6 tablespoons cornstarch
1/2 cup sugar
1/2 cup water
4 large egg yolks, at room temperature
1 teaspoon pure vanilla extract

In a heavy saucepan, warm the half-and-half over medium heat until it begins to simmer. Meanwhile, in a medium bowl, mix the cornstarch with the sugar. Using a whisk, whip in the water until smooth. Add the egg yolks and beat to incorporate.

When the half-and-half is simmering, slowly add about one-half of it to the cornstarch mixture, whisking continuously to incorporate. Whisk this mixture into the simmering half-and-half and continue to whisk vigorously until the pastry cream thickens, about 2 to 5 minutes. It is very important to whisk continuously or the pastry cream may form lumps.

When the pastry cream has thickened, remove it from the heat, add the vanilla, and transfer it to a glass or metal bowl with a plastic lid. (A bowl covered by a plate works well, too.) Stir the mixture frequently while it is cooling to prevent a skin from forming on top.

Refrigerate the pastry cream after it has cooled. It keeps in the refrigerator for up to 3 days, but should not be frozen because it will become watery and lose its smooth texture.

NOTE: If you have cooked the pastry cream too quickly or too long and it develops lumps, don't worry. It happens to the best of us. First, remove it from the heat and try to whisk it until it smooths out. If that doesn't work, wait until it cools, then run it through a fine sieve or quickly blend it in a food processor until smooth. As you practice making pastry cream, you will become familiar with what it should look like when it is done.

Cookies

When most of us began baking as children, it was alongside Mom and a tray full of cookies. Cookies are such forgiving things—they turn out well, even in the reckless hands of children.

Cookies are not unique to the United States, although Americans have adopted them as their national pastry. Because of this, we're especially religious about sampling the local cookie specialties when we travel. One of our favorite places to sample is a little bakery called Wittamers in Brussels, Belgium, that specializes in tiny buttery wonders sold by the pound. Fauchon, the huge food emporium in Paris, also makes cookies we can't pass up. We cart home at least two tins of them on every visit. In fact, almost every bakery in Europe has a cookie that would make you travel hundreds of miles just to rekindle the memory of it. In the United States we never pass up Greenberg's in New York City or Tom's Cookies in Macy's Cellar in San Francisco.

In this chapter, we have included the recipes for all of the cookies we bake at Gayle's. We don't bake them all every day. Instead, we rotate them every two months or so, giving our customers just enough time to get really hooked. Whenever the cookie varieties change, shouts of protest ring out until our customers find another favorite.

There are several types of cookies—bar cookies, drop cookies, hand-shaped cookies, refrigerator (icebox) cookies—and a lot of ways to make them. Using different forming and baking techniques, depending on whether you like your cookies soft, crispy, or chewy, can help you customize the results.

Here are some guidelines to help you achieve the ideal cookie for you:

- **Ingredients:** All ingredients should be at room temperature, unless otherwise stated.

- **Measuring:** Always measure out all ingredients before beginning to make the cookies. Flour and other dry ingredients are measured by the fluff and scoop method (see page 21).

- **Mixing:** Cookies may be mixed in a number of ways. To mix with a tabletop mixer, use the flat beater and begin on a lower speed, progressing to medium-high at the end of each mixing phase. Be very careful not to over-mix, and do not leave the mixer unattended. Mix the cookie dough only until each addition is incorporated. Using a sturdy handheld mixer makes it easier to avoid overmixing, but some cookie doughs in this chapter are too firm to mix with a handheld mixer.

Mixing by hand is a good way to get a feel for the dough, but it can be tiring, as some doughs are stiff and hard to mix for any length of time. If you prefer this mode of mixing, by all means, use it. It's a tried-and-true method.

- **Shaping cookies:** At Gayle's, we use an ice cream scoop instead of a regular tablespoon to drop unbaked cookies on baking sheets. It saves lots of time and makes uniform cookies. After dropping the dough on the sheet you may leave it rounded the way it comes from the scoop or flatten it. Ice cream scoops come in all sizes; look for one that makes the perfect size cookie for your family. Cookies may also be shaped using the log method (for more about this, see "Forming Cookies Using the Log Method," page 140).

- **Pans:** Baking sheets measuring 17 x 11 inches are a good size for cookies because they are large enough to hold plenty of cookies but small enough for two to fit on the center rack of most ovens. If your oven is too hot on the bottom, use two baking sheets, one stacked inside the other for added thickness.

There is nothing wrong with well-worn, seasoned baking sheets. In fact, they are better, so don't waste your time scrubbing every little stain off of a baking sheet. A well-seasoned pan does not need to be buttered for most cookies. The cookies may not spread quite as much as on a buttered or parchment paper–lined sheet, but if you form them using the log method they will spread very little anyway.

- **Preparing baking sheets:** Parchment paper is a wonderful tool for baking cookies. It keeps your pans clean and makes it easy to remove baked cookies. If you butter a baking sheet, do so only the first time you use it for each batch of cookies. After that, simply wipe the sheet with a paper towel; enough butter will remain on the sheet to keep the cookies from sticking to it. If you are baking on seasoned sheets (see "Pans," above), it's not necessary to line them with parchment paper or butter them.

- **Baking:** Ovens vary so be careful. (For more about this, see "Ovens," page 15, and "Adjusting Oven Temperatures and Baking Times," page 18.) Check the cookies at least 5 minutes before the baking time is over. If you want chewy cookies, bake them 3 to 5 minutes less and remove them from the oven when they are just turning golden. If you like crispy cookies, bake them until they are dark golden brown. If time allows, always bake a few cookies before you bake a whole sheetful to see how the dough bakes in your oven.

- **Cooling:** Cookies that have been transferred to a cooling rack right after baking will be crisper; cookies that cool on the baking sheet will be chewier. Many bakers believe cookies must cool on a rack. At Gayle's, we let cookies cool on their baking sheets and they turn out fine. It's really up to you and your particular taste.

- **Storing:** Let the cookies cool completely before storing them in an airtight container. If you store them in a tin, use one small enough to just hold the cookies so there is very little headroom between them and the top of the container. The more headroom they have, the faster they get stale.

If you want to freeze cookies, double-bag them in resealable bags. If you like crispy cookies, bring them to room temperature, then crisp them in a 325° oven for 3 to 5 minutes.

ROCKY-ROAD BROWNIES

From ice cream to cookies, Rocky Road is an American favorite. These are rich, gloriously sticky, and make our customers very happy.

BAKER'S BASICS TO REVIEW
Measuring Dry Ingredients, page 21
Melting Chocolate, page 21

----

4 ounces unsweetened chocolate
1 cup (8 ounces) butter
4 large eggs
2 cups granulated sugar
1/4 teaspoon salt
1 teaspoon pure vanilla extract
1 cup all-purpose flour
1 1/2 cups diced almonds

FROSTING
2 ounces unsweetened chocolate
1/2 cup (4 ounces) butter
2 1/2 cups confectioners' sugar
6 tablespoons milk
1 teaspoon pure vanilla extract
1 1/2 cups miniature marshmallows

Preheat the oven to 325°. Butter a 15 x 10-inch glass baking pan.

In the top of a double boiler, melt the chocolate and butter over low heat, stirring frequently. Remove from the heat and transfer the mixture to a bowl. With a handheld electric mixer, beat in the eggs, sugar, salt, and vanilla. Stir in the flour until well blended. Stir in the almonds.

Spread the mixture in the prepared pan. Place the pan on the center rack in the oven and bake for 20 to 25 minutes, or until a toothpick inserted in the center comes out clean. Don't overbake or the brownies will be dry. Cool in the pan on a wire rack to room temperature.

To make the frosting, melt the chocolate in the top of a double boiler over low heat, stirring frequently. Remove from the heat and let cool.

With a handheld mixer, beat the butter and confectioners' sugar until smooth. Beat in the milk, pure vanilla extract, and melted chocolate and stir in the marshmallows. Spread the frosting on the brownies. Let the frosting set before cutting the brownies.

RASPBERRY-WALNUT
BROWNIES

MAKES TWENTY-FIVE 2 X 3-INCH BROWNIES

These brownies are among the cookies that rotate in and out of our case. Every time they are "discontinued," dozens of frantic customers remind us just how gooey and unbelievably satisfying they are. The key to these brownies is to slightly underbake them.

BAKER'S BASICS TO REVIEW

Measuring Dry Ingredients, page 21

Toasting Nuts, page 23

Melting Chocolate, page 21

Folding, page 20

BROWNIES

9 ounces unsweetened chocolate, cut into $1/2$-inch pieces

1 cup plus 1 tablespoon (9 ounces) unsalted butter

2 teaspoons pure vanilla extract

$1/4$ cup raspberry jam

6 large eggs

3 cups sugar

$1^1/2$ cups all-purpose flour

$1/4$ teaspoon salt

$1^1/2$ cups toasted walnuts, finely chopped (optional)

ICING

4 ounces bittersweet chocolate

$1/2$ cup (4 ounces) butter, at room temperature

2 ounces cream cheese, at room temperature

$2^1/3$ cups confectioners' sugar

Preheat the oven to 325°. Butter a 15 x 10-inch glass baking pan.

Melt the chocolate in the top of a double boiler over barely simmering water. In a separate saucepan, melt the butter. Add the melted butter to the melted chocolate, stirring continuously. Stir in the pure vanilla extract and raspberry jam.

Whip the eggs in the bowl of a tabletop mixer fitted with the whip attachment for 1 minute. With the mixer on high speed, slowly add the sugar and whip for 10 minutes.

Combine the flour and salt and place them in a sifter. Transfer the whipped eggs to a wide-mouthed bowl for easier folding. Sift the flour and salt into the egg batter, folding it in with a rubber spatula in four additions. Fold in the chocolate mixture, then the walnuts.

Pour the brownie batter into the prepared pan. Bake on the center rack in the oven for approximately 25 to 30 minutes. It's important to check the brownies during baking. They are done when a toothpick inserted in the center comes out almost clean. Overbaking makes them dry. Let the brownies cool in the pan on a wire rack.

When the brownies are completely cool, make the icing. Melt the chocolate in the top of a double boiler over barely simmering water. Let the chocolate cool.

With an electric mixer, beat the butter and cream cheese on medium speed until smooth. Beat in the sugar and melted chocolate. Spread the icing evenly over the brownies.

RASPBERRY-WALNUT BROWNIE VARIATION

Omit the raspberry jam and nuts and press 1 basket of fresh raspberries into the batter after pouring it into the pan. Make sure that the raspberries are fully immersed in the batter.

LEMON LUST

MAKES TWENTY-FIVE 2 X 3-INCH BARS

We had been making lemon bars for several years and they always sold well. About four years ago, Joe and I took a trip to England and saw a pastry called Lemon Lust in a bakery window. We loved the name. When we returned, we renamed our lemon bars Lemon Lust. Sales tripled! It just shows what a little marketing can do.

BAKER'S BASICS TO REVIEW
> Measuring Dry Ingredients, page 21
> Zesting Citrus, page 24

CRUST
> 1 cup (8 ounces) cold butter
> 1/2 cup confectioners' sugar
> 1/4 teaspoon salt
> 2 cups all-purpose flour

FILLING
> 1/2 teaspoon baking powder
> 1/4 cup all-purpose flour
> 4 large eggs
> 2 cups granulated sugar
> 1/4 cup freshly squeezed lemon juice
> 2 tablespoons grated lemon zest

> Confectioners' sugar, for dusting

Preheat the oven to 350°.

To make the crust in a food processor, cut the butter into 1/2-inch pieces and return it to the refrigerator. In the bowl of the food processor fitted with the metal blade, place the confectioners' sugar, salt, and flour. Pulse until well blended. Add the chilled butter and toss with your hands to coat the pieces with flour. Process the mixture until it looks like a fine meal, about 15 seconds.

To make the crust by hand, cut the butter into 1/2-inch pieces and return it to the refrigerator. In a bowl, combine the confectioners' sugar, salt, and flour. Add the chilled butter and toss to coat it with flour. With a fork or a pastry blender, cut in the butter until the mixture looks like a fine meal.

Transfer the crust dough to a 15 x 10-inch glass baking pan and press firmly onto the bottom. Place the pan on the center rack in the oven and bake for 15 minutes.

While the crust bakes, make the filling. Combine the baking powder and flour. In a separate bowl, beat the eggs with a handheld whisk until they are well mixed. Add the sugar and beat until it is fully incorporated. Add the baking powder and flour in small amounts, beating after each addition. Whisk in the lemon juice and zest.

Pour the filling over the hot crust and bake for 15 to 20 minutes, or until the filling has set and is golden brown. Let the bars cool in the pan on a wire rack. When completely cool, dust with confectioners' sugar and serve.

CHEWY CHOCOLATE-OATMEAL BARS

MAKES TWENTY-FIVE 2 X 3-INCH BARS

The combination of chocolate and oatmeal are irresistible. Somehow, the oatmeal makes us feel like we're eating something healthy!

BAKER'S BASICS TO REVIEW
Measuring Dry Ingredients, page 21
Toasting Nuts, page 23
Creaming, page 20
Melting Chocolate, page 21

CRUST
1/2 cup (4 ounces) butter, at room temperature
1 cup firmly packed dark brown sugar
1 teaspoon pure vanilla extract
1 large egg
1 1/2 cups rolled oats (quick-cooking or regular)
1 1/4 cups all-purpose flour
1/2 teaspoon baking soda
1/4 teaspoon salt
1/2 cup toasted pecans, coarsely chopped

FILLING
7 ounces (one-half 14-ounce can) sweetened condensed milk
1 cup semisweet chocolate chips
1/2 cup shredded sweetened coconut
1/2 cup pecans, coarsely chopped
1 tablespoon butter
1/4 teaspoon salt
1 teaspoon pure vanilla extract

Preheat the oven to 350°. Butter a 15 x 10-inch glass baking pan.

To make the crust, in the bowl of a tabletop mixer fitted with the flat beater, cream the butter and the sugar until smooth. Add the vanilla and egg and mix thoroughly. In another bowl, combine the oatmeal, flour, baking soda, salt, and pecans. Add the dry ingredients to the creamed mixture and mix just until incorporated.

Pack two-thirds of the crust mixture into the bottom of the prepared pan. Reserve the remaining crust mixture.

To make the filling, combine the milk and chocolate in the top of a double boiler over low heat, stirring as it melts. When melted, remove from the heat. Add the coconut, pecans, butter, salt, and vanilla and mix until smooth.

Spread the filling evenly over the bottom crust. Top with the remaining crust mixture, sprinkling pieces of it over the filling.

Place the pan on the center rack in the oven and bake for about 20 minutes, or until the crust is slightly brown. Be careful not to overbake or the bars will be dry.

HEALTHY LOWFAT BRAN BARS

MAKES TWELVE 3¹/₄ X 3-INCH BARS

This recipe is Joe's answer to a request for a healthful dessert. The bars have a wonderful flavor.

BAKER'S BASICS TO REVIEW
Measuring Dry Ingredients, page 21

———

1 cup whole-wheat flour
1¹/₄ cups rolled oats
1³/₄ cups diced almonds
1¹/₄ cups bran flakes
1¹/₂ cups raisins or chopped dried apricots
1 cup honey

Preheat the oven to 325°. Line a 13 x 9-inch baking sheet with parchment paper.

In a tabletop mixer fitted with the flat beater, combine the flour, oats, almonds, bran flakes, and raisins. With the mixer on the lowest speed, pour in the honey. Mix just until there are no dry spots. The mixture will be a dry, sticky paste that will mold together when pinched between your fingers.

Press the mixture onto the prepared baking sheet, making it as even and as flat as possible. Place another sheet of parchment paper on top. Using the side of a jar or wine bottle, roll over the mixture until it is perfectly flat and completely fills the pan. Remove the top piece of parchment paper. With the end of a small dowel or a chopstick, make three rows of $^{1}/_{4}$-inch-deep indentations across the pan. The rows should be $3^{1}/_{4}$ inches apart. Then, make two rows of indentations 3 inches apart.

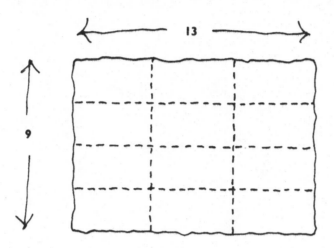

Bake on the center rack in the oven for 25 to 30 minutes, or until the bars puff slightly, are golden in the center and darker around the edges, and spring back when gently pressed with a fingertip.

Let cool on the baking sheet for 15 minutes. When still slightly warm, cut into bars, using the rows of indentations as guides. Run the knife around the edge of the pan to loosen the edges. Remove each bar with a metal spatula and transfer to a wire rack to finish cooling.

SUGARLESS RASPBERRY-OATMEAL BARS

MAKES TEN 2 X 3-INCH BARS

One of our bakers, Christopher Love, developed this recipe for us because so many of our customers requested a sugar-free cookie.

BAKER'S BASICS TO REVIEW
Measuring Dry Ingredients, page 21
Creaming, page 20

1/2 cup (4 ounces) butter, at room temperature
1 cup Fruitsource (see Note)
1 large egg
1 1/2 cups rolled oats (quick-cooking or regular)
1 1/4 cups all-purpose flour
1 teaspoon pure vanilla extract
1/2 teaspoon baking soda
1/2 teaspoon salt
1/2 cup pecans
1/2 cup dates, chopped
1 cup sugar-free raspberry jam

Preheat the oven to 350°. Butter a 10 x 6 x 1-inch baking pan.

In the bowl of a tabletop mixer fitted with the flat beater, cream the butter and Fruitsource. Add the egg and mix until incorporated. Add the oats, flour, vanilla, baking soda, and salt and mix for about 1 minute, or just until well combined. Add the pecans and dates and mix until incorporated.

Pat two-thirds of the dough into the bottom and about 1 inch up the sides of the pan, making sure it is evenly distributed and being careful not to compact it.

Spread the jam over the dough, leaving a 1/2-inch border around the edges. Crumble the remaining dough over the jam.

Place the pan on the center rack in the oven and bake for 30 to 35 minutes, or until the jam is bubbling and the top of the oatmeal dough just begins to brown. Cool completely in the pan on a wire rack, then cut into squares.

NOTE: Fruitsource is a sweetener made from fruit. You can find it in powdered form at most health food stores.

CHOCOLATE MACAROONS

MAKES 8 TO 25 COOKIES

This recipe is straight out of *Maida Heatter's Book of Great Chocolate Desserts*. We have been making this rich, chewy cookie for years, but we've adapted the recipe to fit our bakery style. It's one of the items in the showcase that none of us at the bakery can pass up. We make 165 at a time and they're gone in 2 days.

BAKER'S BASICS TO REVIEW
Separating Eggs, page 22
Melting Chocolate, page 21
Whipping Egg Whites and Making Meringues, page 198
Folding, page 20

————

4 ounces semisweet chocolate
2 ounces unsweetened chocolate
2 large egg whites, at room temperature
Pinch of salt
$^1/_2$ cup sugar
I teaspoon pure vanilla extract
$2^3/_4$ cups shredded sweetened coconut

Preheat the oven to 325°. Lightly butter or line two large baking sheets with parchment paper.

Melt both chocolates in the top of a double boiler over barely simmering water. Remove the chocolate from the heat and let cool for about 15 minutes.

In the bowl of a tabletop mixer or with a handheld electric mixer, beat the egg whites and salt on high speed until soft peaks form. Slowly add the sugar, then the vanilla. Whip into a very stiff meringue, about 5 minutes. With the mixer on slow speed, add the chocolate and mix just until incorporated. Transfer the mixture to a large bowl and fold in the coconut with a spatula.

Using an ice cream scoop or a spoon ranging from teaspoon to standard ice cream scoop size, shape and drop the cookies 2 inches apart on the prepared baking sheets. Bake on the center rack in the oven for 15 to 20 minutes (depending on the size of the cookies), checking frequently. When done, the cookies should be crisp on the outside and chewy and moist on the inside; be careful not to overbake. The macaroons should lift off the sheets without sticking. Transfer the cookies from the baking sheets to a wire rack to cool.

Forming Cookies Using the Log Method

This is a professional baker's method for shaping cookies. It's fast and allows you to make the dough ahead of time, then to bake the cookies right before you serve them so they are as fresh as possible. The log method is also used when bakers want to save part of the dough for another time, or when they want the cookies to be flatter and more symmetrical and consistent in size.

The following cookies, which are normally formed with a spoon and dropped onto a baking sheet, may also be formed using the log method:

- Ginger-Molasses Cookies (page 150)
- Peanut Butter–Chocolate Chunk Cookies (page 143)
- Spritz Cookies (page 151)
- Fudge Crackle Cookies (page 142)
- White Chocolate–Macadamia Nut Cookies (page 144)
- Lemon–Poppy Seed Cookies (page 152)
- Oatmeal Cookies (page 146)
- Chocolate Chip Cookies (page 147)
- Anahola Chocolate Chip Cookies (page 148)
- Cocos (page 149)
- Pecan Clouds (page 153)

After mixing the dough, lay a piece of plastic wrap, measuring at least 15 inches long, on the work surface. Spoon the dough onto the center of the plastic wrap in a long straight line. The dough should be about 2 to 3 inches in diameter, but does not need to be shaped into a perfect log at this point. Fold the plastic wrap lengthwise over the dough once and begin to roll it into a log shape, smoothing out any lumps and holes as you go. Make the log $2^{1}/_{2}$ to 3 inches in diameter and as long as you wish. Or, you may want to make 2 or 3 shorter logs. When the log is shaped, wrap it in plastic wrap and refrigerate for up to 3 days or freeze for up to 2 weeks. If the dough has been frozen, let it thaw in the refrigerator overnight before cutting.

When you are ready to bake the cookies, preheat the oven for at least 20 minutes. Remove the cookies from the refrigerator, unwrap the log, and slice it into $^{1}/_{4}$- to $^{1}/_{2}$-inch discs. The thickness of the disc determines the crispness and delicacy of the cookie. Experiment with one tray at a time to see how a particular thickness works for each dough.

It is very important to watch the baking times carefully. A cookie that is $^{1}/_{4}$ inch thick will bake faster than one that is $^{1}/_{2}$ inch thick. For thinner cookies, check for doneness 5 minutes before the baking time is up.

HAZELNUT
MERINGUE COOKIES

MAKES 24 COOKIES

These cookies have very little fat. The only fat is in the nuts. They are great with ice cream, whether whole or crumbled over a scoop or two.

BAKER'S BASICS TO REVIEW
Separating Eggs, page 22
Whipping Egg Whites and Making Meringues, page 198
Folding, page 20

———

^{1}/$_2$ cup egg whites (about 3 large eggs), at room temperature
Pinch of salt
3 ^{1}/$_2$ cups confectioners' sugar
^{1}/$_4$ teaspoon cream of tartar
^{1}/$_2$ teaspoon ground cinnamon
1 teaspoon pure vanilla extract
2 ^{3}/$_4$ cups ground hazelnuts (see Note)

Preheat the oven to 225°. Line a large baking sheet with parchment paper.

In the bowl of a tabletop mixer fitted with the whip attachment, beat the eggs whites and salt until foamy, first checking to be sure the bowl and whip are grease-free.

In a separate bowl, combine the sugar, cream of tartar, and cinnamon. When the eggs are foamy, add the sugar mixture very slowly with the machine on medium speed. When the sugar is fully incorporated, increase the speed to high and whip the egg whites for 15 minutes. Using a rubber spatula, quickly fold in the vanilla and hazelnuts by hand, being careful not to deflate the egg whites.

With a spoon, drop 2 tablespoons of the dough at least 2 inches apart onto the prepared baking sheet. Place the sheet on the center rack in the oven and bake for 30 minutes. Test for doneness by lifting a cookie and pressing gently on the bottom. It should feel firm, but still be soft on the inside. Let the cookies cool completely on the sheet.

NOTE: Grind the hazelnuts in a food processor by pulsing several times, or just long enough to grind them but not so long that they become pastelike.

FUDGE CRACKLE COOKIES

MAKES 40 COOKIES

These cookies taste a little like brownies and have a wonderfully chewy texture.

BAKER'S BASICS TO REVIEW
Measuring Dry Ingredients, page 21
Melting Chocolate, page 21

$^{1}/_{2}$ cup (4 ounces) butter

6 ounces unsweetened chocolate

2 cups sugar

4 large eggs

2 teaspoons pure vanilla extract

1 cup pecans, finely chopped

2 cups all-purpose flour

2 teaspoons baking powder

$^{1}/_{2}$ teaspoon salt

Sugar, for coating

FUDGE CRACKLE COOKIE VARIATION

Refrigerate the dough for 5 hours. Shape into logs, refrigerate or freeze, then slice into discs and bake, as directed for the log method of forming cookies (page 140).

Melt the butter and chocolate in the top of a double boiler over barely simmering water. Set aside to cool.

In the bowl of a tabletop mixer fitted with the flat beater, beat the sugar, eggs, and vanilla until smooth, blend in the chocolate-butter mixture, then add the pecans and mix well.

In a separate bowl, combine the flour, baking powder, and salt, then add them to the batter. Mix just until incorporated. The dough should be very soft at this point. Cover the bowl with plastic wrap and refrigerate for at least 5 hours.

To bake the cookies, preheat the oven to 325°. Line two baking sheets with parchment paper.

Remove the dough from the refrigerator, then pinch off one-third of it. To keep the rest of the dough firm while you work, return it to the refrigerator. Place the sugar on a large shallow plate.

Take about 2 tablespoons of dough. Form it into a ball and roll it in the sugar. Place the ball on one of the baking sheets and repeat, placing the cookies at least 2 inches apart, until all of the dough (including the remaining two-thirds in the refrigerator) has been rolled. Bake on the center rack in the oven for about 12 minutes. The cookies will have a slight crust on the top but feel soft to the touch. Immediately transfer the cookies to wire racks to cool.

PEANUT BUTTER–
CHOCOLATE CHUNK COOKIES

MAKES ABOUT 45 COOKIES

If you like Reese's Peanut Butter Cups, you will love these cookies.

BAKER'S BASICS TO REVIEW
Measuring Dry Ingredients, page 21
Creaming, page 20
Folding, page 20

----

1 cup (8 ounces) butter, at room temperature
1 cup chunky or smooth peanut butter, at room temperature
1 cup granulated sugar
1 cup firmly packed brown sugar
2 large eggs
1 teaspoon pure vanilla extract
2 cups all-purpose flour
1 teaspoon baking soda
5 ounces semisweet chocolate, cut into 1/2-inch pieces
1/4 cup unroasted or roasted, unsalted peanuts

Preheat the oven to 350°. Line two baking sheets with parchment paper.

In the bowl of a tabletop mixer fitted with the flat beater, cream the butter and peanut butter. Add the sugars and mix until fully incorporated and smooth. Beat in the eggs, one at a time, waiting until the first is incorporated before adding the second. Mix in the vanilla.

In a separate bowl, combine the flour and baking soda. Pour the dry ingredients into the creamed mixture and beat until fully incorporated. With a rubber spatula, fold in the chocolate and nuts by hand.

Using a spoon, drop 2-inch balls of dough about 2 inches apart onto the baking sheets. Bake on the center rack in the oven for approximately 13 minutes. Let the cookies cool on the baking sheet for 1 minute, then transfer to a wire rack to finish cooling.

**PEANUT BUTTER–
CHOCOLATE CHUNK
COOKIE VARIATION**

Shape dough into logs, refrigerate or freeze, then slice into discs and bake, as directed for the log method of forming cookies (page 140).

WHITE CHOCOLATE–
MACADAMIA NUT COOKIES

MAKES 50 COOKIES

These cookies are similar to blondies. The addition of macadamia nuts makes them even more rich.

BAKER'S BASICS TO REVIEW
Measuring Dry Ingredients, page 21
Creaming, page 20

---

1 1/2 cups (12 ounces) butter, at room temperature
1 1/4 cups granulated sugar
1 1/2 cups firmly packed brown sugar
2 large eggs
1 teaspoon pure vanilla extract
5 cups all-purpose flour
2 tablespoons baking powder
1 tablespoon baking soda
1/4 teaspoon salt
12 ounces white chocolate, cut into 1/2-inch chunks,
       or 1 to 1 1/2 cups white chocolate chips
1 1/4 cups unsalted macadamia nuts (see Note)

**WHITE CHOCOLATE–
MACADAMIA NUT
COOKIE VARIATION**

*Shape dough into logs,
refrigerate or freeze, then
slice into discs and bake, as
directed for the log method of
forming cookies (page 140).*

Preheat the oven to 325°. Line two baking sheets with parchment paper.

In the bowl of a tabletop mixer fitted with the flat beater, cream the butter and both sugars until smooth. Add the eggs, one at a time, waiting before the first is incorporated before adding the second. Mix in the vanilla.

In a separate bowl, combine the flour, baking powder, baking soda, and salt. Add the dry ingredients to the creamed mixture and mix just until incorporated. Transfer the batter to a large bowl and, with a rubber spatula, fold in the chocolate and macadamia nuts by hand.

Scoop out 2-tablespoon-sized balls of dough and drop them at least 2 inches apart on a baking sheet. Bake on the center rack in the oven for 13 minutes, or just until the cookies begin to turn golden. Don't overbake; these cookies should be soft and chewy.

NOTE: If you can only find salted macadamia nuts, place the nuts in a sieve and wash them. Spread them out on a paper towel to dry before using.

TRIPLE CHOCOLATE
CHUNK COOKIES

MAKES ABOUT 40 TO 50 COOKIES

A chocolate lover's dream come true—three kinds of chocolate in one cookie!

BAKER'S BASICS TO REVIEW

Measuring Dry Ingredients, page 21
Toasting Nuts, page 23
Melting Chocolate, page 21
Creaming, page 20

———

7 ounces semisweet chocolate
1 cup (8 ounces) butter, at room temperature
1 cup granulated sugar
1 cup firmly packed dark brown sugar
2 large eggs
1 teaspoon pure vanilla extract
3 1/4 cups all-purpose flour
1 tablespoon plus 1 teaspoon baking powder
2 teaspoons baking soda
2 pinches salt
8 ounces semisweet chocolate, cut into 3/4-inch chunks
8 ounces white chocolate, cut into 3/4-inch chunks,
    or 1 to 1 1/2 cups white chocolate chips
1 1/2 cups toasted pecan pieces

Preheat the oven to 325°.

Melt the 7 ounces of chocolate in the top of a double boiler over barely simmering water. Set aside to cool.

In a tabletop mixer fitted with the flat beater, cream the butter and sugars until smooth. Add the eggs, one at a time, waiting until the first is incorporated before adding the second. Add the vanilla and melted chocolate and mix until well blended.

In a separate bowl, mix the flour, baking powder, baking soda, and salt together. Add the dry ingredients to the batter and mix until smooth. Be careful not to overmix. Add the chocolate pieces and pecans and mix just until incorporated.

With a spoon, drop 2 tablespoons of the dough at least 2 inches apart onto the baking sheets. Bake on the center rack in the oven for 14 minutes.

TRIPLE CHOCOLATE COOKIE VARIATIONS

Substitute 1 pound semisweet chocolate for the chunks, omitting the white chocolate, and use walnuts instead of pecans. Shape dough into logs, refrigerate or freeze, then slice into discs and bake, as directed for the log method of forming cookies (page 140).

OATMEAL COOKIES

MAKES 40 TO 48 COOKIES

We have been making this tried-and-true recipe since the day we opened the bakery. It's one of my favorites because it reminds me of childhood afternoons when my mother and I would stand around the kitchen talking while spreading butter on one oatmeal cookie after another.

BAKER'S BASICS TO REVIEW
Separating Eggs, page 22
Measuring Dry Ingredients, page 21
Creaming, page 20

---

1 cup (8 ounces) butter, at room temperature
3/4 cup granulated sugar
1 1/4 cups firmly packed brown sugar
2 large eggs
1 large egg yolk
1 teaspoon pure vanilla extract
3/4 teaspoon ground cinnamon
2 cups all-purpose flour
3/4 teaspoon salt
3/4 teaspoon baking soda
3 1/2 cups rolled oats (quick-cooking or regular)
1 1/4 cups raisins, soaked and drained

OATMEAL COOKIE VARIATION

Shape dough into logs, refrigerate or freeze, then slice into discs and bake, as directed for the log method of forming cookies (page 140).

Preheat the oven to 350°. Line two baking sheets with parchment paper.

In the bowl of a tabletop mixer fitted with the flat beater, cream the butter and sugars. Add the eggs, one at a time, waiting until the first is incorporated before adding the second. Mix in the vanilla.

In a separate bowl, combine the cinnamon, flour, salt, and baking soda. Add the dry ingredients to the creamed mixture and mix just until incorporated. Add the oats and raisins and mix until incorporated, but do not overmix. The cookie dough will be somewhat moist.

Using two tablespoons, drop about 2 tablespoons of cookie dough 2 inches apart on the prepared baking sheets. Bake on the center rack in the oven for 12 to 14 minutes, or until golden brown and still soft when gently pressed.

CHOCOLATE CHIP COOKIES

MAKES 48 COOKIES

There must be hundreds of chocolate chip cookie recipes. We love this one because it's particularly buttery and chewy.

BAKER'S BASICS TO REVIEW
Measuring Dry Ingredients, page 21
Creaming, page 20

---

1 cup (8 ounces) butter, at room temperature
3/4 cup granulated sugar
1 1/4 cups firmly packed brown sugar
2 large eggs
3/4 teaspoon pure vanilla extract
3 3/4 cups all-purpose flour
2 teaspoons baking soda
1 1/4 teaspoons baking powder
1/2 teaspoon salt
2 cups semisweet chocolate chips
3/4 cup walnut pieces

Preheat the oven to 350°. Line two large baking sheets with parchment paper.

In the bowl of a tabletop mixer fitted with the flat beater, cream the butter. Add the sugars and beat until well combined. Beat in 1 egg and the vanilla. Add the remaining egg and beat just until incorporated.

In a separate bowl, combine the flour, baking soda, baking powder, and salt. Add the dry ingredients to the creamed mixture and and mix gently until just barely incorporated. Add the chocolate chips and walnuts and combine just until incorporated; do not overmix. The cookie dough will be moist and should hold together.

Using two tablespoons, drop about 2 tablespoons of dough on the prepared baking sheets. Do not flatten the cookies. Bake on the center rack in the oven for 12 to 14 minutes, or until golden brown and still soft when gently pressed.

CHOCOLATE CHIP COOKIE VARIATION

Shape dough into logs, refrigerate or freeze, then slice into discs and bake, as directed for the log method of forming cookies (page 140).

ANAHOLA
CHOCOLATE CHIP COOKIES

MAKES 24 COOKIES

Joe learned this recipe from Michelle Ahearn at Michelle's Cafe in Kapaa, Kauai, when we went to teach her how to make *francese* (Joe's Italian-style French bread). One of the rewards was a new angle on the chocolate chip cookie. When baked, these cookies resemble the mountains on the west coast of Kauai—they're mounded in the center and flat around the edges.

BAKER'S BASICS TO REVIEW
Separating Eggs, page 22
Measuring Dry Ingredients, page 21
Creaming, page 20

3/4 cup (6 ounces) unsalted butter, at room temperature
1/4 cup (2 ounces) margarine, at room temperature
1 cup firmly packed light brown sugar
2/3 cup granulated sugar
1 large egg, plus 1 egg yolk
1 teaspoon pure vanilla extract
2 cups all-purpose flour
2/3 cup rolled oats, finely ground (in a food processor or blender)
1 teaspoon baking soda
Scant 1/2 teaspoon salt
1 1/3 cups semisweet chocolate chips
1 1/3 cups walnut pieces

ANAHOLA CHOCOLATE CHIP COOKIE VARIATION

Shape dough into logs, refrigerate or freeze, then cut dough into 1-inch square chunks. Place 2 chunks together for each cookie and bake, as directed for the log method of forming cookies (page 140).

Preheat the oven to 350°. Line two large baking sheets with parchment paper.

In the bowl of a tabletop mixer fitted with the flat beater, cream the butter and margarine until fluffy. Add the sugars and mix until incorporated.

In a small bowl, beat the egg and egg yolk. Add the vanilla. Slowly add the egg-vanilla mixture to the creamed mixture and combine well.

In a separate bowl, combine the flour, oats, baking soda, and salt. Add the dry ingredients to the creamed mixture and mix to blend well.

Remove the beater from the mixer and, using a wooden spoon, gently incorporate the chocolate chips and walnut pieces into the dough, being careful not to break up the walnuts.

Using two tablespoons, drop 2 generous tablespoons of dough 2 1/2 inches apart on the prepared baking sheets. Do not flatten the cookies. Bake on the center rack in the oven for 15 minutes, or until golden brown.

COCOS

I learned to make these cookies while staying on the island of Fin in Denmark. This is an adaptation of an adaptation that Flo Braker did after she tasted them.

BAKER'S BASICS TO REVIEW
Separating Eggs, page 22
Measuring Dry Ingredients, page 21
Creaming, page 20

———

1¹/₂ cups all-purpose flour
2¹/₂ cups unsweetened shredded coconut
1¹/₄ cups plus 2 tablespoons unsalted butter, at room temperature
1 cup sugar
1 large egg yolk

In a medium bowl, mix the flour and coconut together to combine. Set aside.

In the bowl of a tabletop mixer fitted with the flat beater, cream the butter until smooth. Add the sugar and cream again. Add the egg yolk, beating until well combined and slightly fluffy. Scrape down the sides of the bowl with a plastic dough scraper. Gradually add the coconut and flour mixture, mixing just until completely incorporated.

Divide the dough into 4 equal portions. On a lightly floured surface, roll each portion into a log about 9 inches long and 1¹/₂ inches in diameter. Wrap each log in plastic wrap and refrigerate until firm, at least 4 hours. The dough can be refrigerated for up to 3 days or double-wrapped and frozen for up to 2 weeks.

To bake the cookies, preheat the oven to 325°. Line two baking sheets with parchment paper.

Remove dough logs from the refrigerator, unwrap them, and slice into ¹/₂-inch thick rounds. Place them 1 inch apart on the baking sheet. Bake on the center rack in the oven for 15 minutes, or until light golden around the edges. Let the cookies cool on the baking sheets for 5 minutes, then transfer them to a wire rack to finish cooling.

HOW COCOS CAME TO GAYLE'S

I was in Denmark when I tasted an ethereal coconut cookie called a Coco at the bakery across the street from the country inn where I was staying. While I waited for a ride to the airport on my last day there, I decided to stop into the local bakery, a quaint Old World–style building with a thatched roof, to chat with the cookie baker. He didn't speak a word of English, but since the method of creaming butter and gently mixing cookie dough is a universal technique, I was able to jot down the recipe just by deciphering his simple hand gestures...and I still made it to the airport just in time to catch my plane.

GINGER-MOLASSES COOKIES

MAKES ABOUT 50 COOKIES

Dentists' standard advice to stay away from sugar doesn't hold true in Capitola. Dentist Bob Schellentrager, whose office is across the street from Gayle's, gave us his favorite cookie recipe to make at the bakery so that his wife Judy wouldn't have to bake them so often. They are absolutely toothsome.

BAKER'S BASICS TO REVIEW
Measuring Dry Ingredients, page 21

———

3/4 cup (6 ounces) butter
1 1/4 cups sugar
1/4 cup light molasses
1 large egg
2 teaspoons baking soda
2 cups all-purpose flour
1/2 teaspoon ground cloves
1/2 teaspoon ground ginger
1 teaspoon ground cinnamon
1/2 teaspoon salt

GINGER-MOLASSES COOKIE VARIATION

Shape dough into logs, refrigerate or freeze, then slice into discs and bake, as directed for the log method of forming cookies (page 140).

Preheat the oven to 375°. Lightly butter three baking sheets or line with parchment paper.

Melt the butter and pour it into a large mixing bowl. Let it cool. Add 1 cup of the sugar, the molasses, and the egg and beat well.

Sift together the baking soda, flour, cloves, ginger, cinnamon, and salt. Add the sifted ingredients to the butter mixture and mix well. Cover the bowl and place in the refrigerator to chill for 15 minutes.

Place the remaining 1/4 cup sugar on a flat plate. Scoop out the cookie dough by the tablespoonful, roll each scoop into a 1-inch ball, then coat with the sugar. Arrange the balls 2 inches apart on the baking sheets. Bake on the center rack in the oven for 8 minutes for chewy cookies or 10 minutes for crispy cookies.

SPRITZ COOKIES

There is something very nurturing about these simple little jam-filled cookies—we've been making them since our opening day. They are easy to make and the dough keeps well in the refrigerator or freezer.

BAKER'S BASICS TO REVIEW
Measuring Dry Ingredients, page 21
Creaming, page 20

———

3/4 cup (6 ounces) butter, at room temperature
3/4 cup sugar
1 large egg
1 teaspoon pure vanilla extract
2 cups cake flour
2 to 3 tablespoons apricot jam
2 to 3 tablespoons raspberry jam

Preheat the oven to 325°. Line two baking sheets with parchment paper.

In the bowl of a tabletop mixer fitted with the flat beater, cream the butter and sugar. Add the egg and vanilla and mix until smooth. Add the flour and mix just until incorporated.

Pinch off walnut-sized pieces of dough, roll them into balls and place on baking sheets. With your index finger, make an impression in the center of each ball at least halfway to the bottom of the cookie. Fill the indentations with 1/2 teaspoon of apricot jam or raspberry jam.

Bake on the center rack in the oven for 12 minutes, or until the dough is set but not browned and the jam is bubbling. Transfer the cookies from the baking sheets to a wire rack to cool.

SPRITZ COOKIE VARIATION

Shape dough into logs, refrigerate or freeze, then slice into discs and bake, as directed for the log method of forming cookies (page 140).

LEMON–POPPY SEED COOKIES

At Gayle's, we make these in batches twelve times the size of the one given here. That's enough to last us for only 3 or 4 days! We use a small, 1-inch scoop to portion the cookies.

BAKER'S BASICS TO REVIEW
    Measuring Dry Ingredients, page 21
    Zesting Citrus, page 24
    Creaming, page 20

2 tablespoons poppy seeds
1/2 cup (4 ounces) butter, at room temperature
1 cup sugar
1 large egg
1/4 teaspoon pure vanilla extract
2 tablespoons grated lemon zest
1 3/4 cups all-purpose flour
1/4 teaspoon salt

LEMON–POPPY SEED VARIATION

Shape dough into logs, refrigerate or freeze, then slice into discs and bake, as directed for the log method of forming cookies (page 140).

Preheat the oven to 325°.

Place the poppy seeds on a baking sheet and toast for 4 to 5 minutes, or just until they start to brown. Set aside.

In the bowl of a tabletop mixer fitted with the flat beater, cream the butter and sugar. Add the eggs and vanilla and mix to incorporate. Add the lemon zest and poppy seeds and mix. Add the flour and salt and mix once more to incorporate completely.

Divide the dough into two flat, circular pieces and cover each with plastic wrap. Place the dough in the refrigerator for at least 1 hour or overnight. The dough may also be frozen for up to 2 weeks at this point.

To bake the cookies, preheat the oven to 325°. Line two baking sheets with parchment paper. Remove the dough from the refrigerator and let it come to almost room temperature. Remove the plastic wrap, pinch off walnut-sized pieces, and roll them into balls. Place the balls 2 inches apart on baking sheets. Bake on the center rack in the oven for 15 minutes, or just until the cookies become golden brown. Transfer the cookies from the baking sheets to a wire rack to cool.

PECAN CLOUDS

MAKES ABOUT 72 COOKIES

When made with walnuts, these cookies are known as Mexican Wedding Cookies. We use pecans instead of walnuts. They are covered with lots of confectioners' sugar and nestled together in our showcase, where they look like little clouds.

BAKER'S BASICS TO REVIEW
    Measuring Dry Ingredients, page 21
    Creaming, page 20

1¼ cups plus 2 tablespoons (11 ounces) butter,
    at room temperature
¾ cup confectioners' sugar, sifted
1½ teaspoons pure vanilla extract
3⅓ cups cake flour
Scant ½ teaspoon salt
1 cup plus 2 tablespoons finely ground pecans (see Note)
1 cup confectioners' sugar, for coating

Preheat the oven to 325°.

In the bowl of a tabletop mixer fitted with the flat beater, cream the butter, sugar, and vanilla. Mix in the flour and salt. Add the ground pecans and mix gently, just until incorporated.

To form the cookies, pinch off walnut-sized pieces of dough and roll them into balls. Place the balls 2 inches apart on baking sheets. Bake on the center rack in the oven for about 12 minutes. The cookies should be hard but not brown. Let the cookies cool completely on the baking sheets.

Place the 1 cup of confectioners' sugar in a shallow bowl. Roll each cooled cookie in the sugar until generously coated. Store in an airtight container.

NOTE: Grind the pecans in a food processor by pulsing several times, or just long enough to grind them but not so long that they become pastelike.

PECAN CLOUD VARIATION

Shape dough into logs, refrigerate or freeze, bring to room temperature, slice into discs, roll into balls, and bake, as directed for the log method of forming cookies (page 140).

BACI DI DAMA

We first tasted these cookies in Florence, Italy. The chocolate ganache and hazelnut butter cookies are a heavenly combination. We came home with the idea but not the recipe, so we experimented with our butter cookie and it worked.

BAKER'S BASICS TO REVIEW
Measuring Dry Ingredients, page 21
Toasting Nuts, pages 23
Creaming, page 20

1¼ cups (10 ounces) unsalted butter, at room temperature
1 cup sifted confectioners' sugar
2 teaspoons pure vanilla extract
1 large egg
2⅔ cups all-purpose flour
¼ teaspoon salt
¾ cup ground toasted, skinned hazelnuts (page 23; see also Note)
Chocolate Ganache (page 262; see also Note)

In the bowl of a tabletop mixer fitted with the flat beater, cream the butter, confectioners' sugar, and vanilla until smooth. Add the egg and mix until incorporated.

In a separate bowl, combine the flour, salt, and ground hazelnuts. Add the dry ingredients to the creamed mixture and mix until completely incorporated.

Form the dough into a flat disc, cover it in plastic wrap, and refrigerate for at least 2 hours or overnight.

Preheat the oven to 325°. Butter two baking sheets or line with parchment paper.

Remove the dough from the refrigerator and place it on a lightly floured work surface. Lightly flour the top of the dough. Roll the dough out to ⅛ inch thick. Cut out circles using a 2-inch round cutter. When all of the dough has been used, press the remaining dough together and refrigerate for 30 minutes. Re-roll and cut out the dough as before. Dough trimmings can be shaped into miniature crescent shapes and baked.

Place the cookies on the prepared baking sheets (they can be close to each other because they will not spread). Bake on the center rack in the oven for 7 minutes, then check for doneness. They should be light brown. Bake for 3 more minutes, checking frequently because they brown quickly at the end of the baking time.

Let the cookies cool on the baking sheets. When they have completely cooled, spread about 1 teaspoon Chocolate Ganache on half of them. Top with the remaining cookies to make little sandwiches. Let the cookies rest on the sheets until the chocolate sets. If you want to eat the cookies sooner, place them in the refrigerator for about 10 minutes to set the chocolate more quickly.

NOTE: Make the Chocolate Ganache filling at least 5 hours (or even 1 day ahead) before making the cookies. It must be a spreadable consistency when used.

Grind the toasted, skinned hazelnuts in a food processor by pulsing several times, or just long enough to grind them but not so long that they become pastelike.

BACI DI DAMA VARIATION

Shape dough into logs, refrigerate or freeze, then slice into discs and bake, as directed for the log method of forming cookies (page 140).

LAVENDER SHORTBREAD

MAKES ABOUT 48 COOKIES

When we asked local cookbook author Fran Raboff if we could make this shortbread at the bakery, she said, "Talk to Renee." So we did. Inspired by Santa Cruz gardening expert Renee Shepherd's shortbread, which appeared in her book, *Recipes from a Kitchen Garden,* our recipe makes 500 cookies. After some figuring and head scratching, we came up with this version for home bakers.

BAKER'S BASICS TO REVIEW
Measuring Dry Ingredients, page 21
Creaming, page 20

———

1 1/2 cups (12 ounces) butter, at room temperature
2/3 cup granulated sugar
2 tablespoons finely chopped fresh or dried organic lavender blossoms
2 teaspoons chopped fresh mint
2 1/3 cups all-purpose flour
1/2 cup cornstarch
1/4 teaspoon salt
1/2 cup confectioners' sugar, for dusting

In the bowl of a tabletop mixer fitted with the flat beater, cream the butter, sugar, lavender, and mint until light and fluffy. Add the flour, cornstarch, and salt and mix until incorporated.

Divide the dough into 2 equal blocks. Flatten the blocks, seal each in plastic wrap, and refrigerate until firm, about 1 to 2 hours or overnight.

Preheat the oven to 325°.

On a very lightly floured work surface, roll out each block of dough to measure 9 x 8 x ¼ inches. Using a metal spatula or dough scraper, square up the sides of the dough and lift it off the table from time to time to prevent it from sticking as you roll it out.

With a fluted pastry wheel cutter or a knife, cut the sheets of dough into 2 x 1½-inch rectangles.

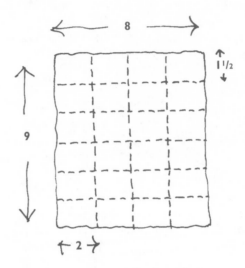

Place the rectangles evenly spaced on a sheet. Bake on the center rack in the oven for 12 to 14 minutes, or until pale gold, not browned. Let the cookies cool on the baking sheets for 5 minutes, then transfer them to a wire rack to finish cooling. When the cookies are completely cool, dust lightly with confectioners' sugar.

THE RECIPES

HAZELNUT TWIST COOKIES

MAKES ABOUT 30 COOKIES

The large-grained crystallized sugar called for in this recipe can be found in specialty food shops.

1/4 recipe (8 ounces) Basic Puff Pastry Dough (page 85)

CINNAMON SUGAR
2 tablespoons granulated sugar
3 tablespoons firmly packed brown sugar
1 teaspoon ground cinnamon

EGG GLAZE
1 large egg
1 tablespoon of milk

1/3 to 1/2 cup crystallized sugar or granulated sugar
3/4 cup finely chopped hazelnuts

Preheat the oven to 350°. Line a baking sheet with parchment paper.

Roll out the dough to measure 15 x 5 inches. It will be about 1/4 inch thick. Shape the sides of the dough with a ruler or the back edge of a chef's knife blade to make them even.

In a small bowl, combine the Cinnamon Sugar ingredients. In a separate small bowl, whisk together the egg and milk to make the glaze.

Brush the dough lightly with glaze, then sprinkle with one-half of the Cinnamon Sugar. Coat with one-half of the crystallized sugar and one-half of the chopped hazelnuts. (A lot will fall off.) Flip the dough over and repeat the three-step process.

Using a ruler and chef's knife, cut the dough into 5-inch-long, 3/8-inch-wide strips. Discard the irregular end scraps. Twist each strip into a tight corkscrew shape (they will untwist some during baking, so they should be tightly twisted to begin with) and place on the prepared baking sheet. (The cookies will be about 4 inches long when twisted.) Bake on the center rack in the oven for 20 to 25 minutes, or until they are very crunchy and a rich, golden color.

FLORENTINES

These aren't really cookies, although we sell them as such—they're more of a chocolate nougat candy. They have always been one of my favorites. Many years ago, before we opened the bakery, I found the perfect Florentine in a shop in Aspen, Colorado. The baker wouldn't share his recipe, so I created this one. We think it's even better than his.

BAKER'S BASICS TO REVIEW
Measuring Dry Ingredients, page 21
Melting Chocolate, page 21

---

1 cup sliced almonds
Scant 1/4 cup finely minced Candied Orange Peel (page 111)
1/4 cup all-purpose flour
6 tablespoons (3 ounces) butter
2/3 cup plus 1 tablespoon sugar
2 1/2 tablespoons honey
4 tablespoons heavy whipping cream
1 1/2 cups semisweet chocolate chips

Preheat the oven to 375°. Line four large baking sheets with parchment paper.

In a small bowl, combine the almonds, orange peel, and flour. Set aside.

In a heavy, nonreactive saucepan, place the butter, sugar, honey, and cream. Cook over medium-high heat, stirring continuously, for about 8 to 10 minutes. Using a candy thermometer, test the temperature of the mixture. When it reaches 248°, add the almonds, orange peel, and flour. Cook and continue to stir until the mixture pulls away from the sides of the pan, about 6 minutes. Let the dough cool until you can handle it.

Working quickly, take a heaping teaspoon of the dough, roll into a ball, and place on the baking sheet. Continue with the rest of the dough, placing the balls 3 inches apart in rows 4 cookies long and 2 cookies wide. Bake on the center rack in the oven for 5 minutes, or until each cookie has spread to 3 1/2 inches in diameter and set up slightly but is still soft; do not overbake. Let the cookies cool on the baking sheets.

In the top of a double boiler, melt the chocolate chips over barely simmering water. Using a serrated knife or a plastic pastry comb with 1/4-inch teeth, spread the melted chocolate on the bottom of the cooled cookies. Let the cookies dry, chocolate side up, on the baking sheets. Store cookies in an airtight container.

Muffins, Cream Puffs, and Other Bakery Goodies

This chapter includes the items in our repertoire that have a huge following but don't have a place in the other chapters. It's an eclectic selection, ranging from muffins, quick breads, and scones to bread pudding and cream puffs, yet the recipes have one feature in common: they're some of the simplest, quickest items to make. Even the cream puffs and éclairs are easier than you might think.

The techniques used in this chapter vary as much as the recipes, so guidelines and specific directions appear within each recipe. However, because we've included multiple muffin and quick bread recipes, we've compiled the following useful tips for your reference.

Muffins are characterized by a bumpy top and a dense, moist interior. They are great for breakfast or a snack, but are also wonderful with dinner. Quick breads are usually sweet, like cake, but they are denser and are baked in loaf pans.

- **Measuring:** Always have everything measured out before beginning the recipe. Flour should be measured by the fluff and scoop method. For more about this, see "Measuring Dry Ingredients," page 21.

- **Mixing:** It is easy to overmix muffins and quick breads. To avoid overmixing, mix only until most of the dry spots are gone when combining dry and wet ingredients. A perfectly mixed batter should still have a few dry spots, which will absorb moisture and disappear during baking.

- **Making batter in advance:** Many people believe muffins must be baked right after they are mixed. This is not so. You can make muffin batter in advance if you follow certain rules. At the bakery, we make enough batter for 2 days and refrigerate half. We store it in airtight containers overnight and don't stir it in the morning before scooping it into the muffin pans. If some of the liquid from the batter has pooled on top, it is all right to stir it very gently once or twice.

- **Pan preparation:** Be sure to butter muffin pans and loaf pans, even the nonstick kind.

- **Filling muffin pans:** We like to use an ice cream scoop to deposit the batter in the pans; it measures a specific amount and keeps the top of the muffin pan clean.

- **Baking:** Overbaking is just about the worst mistake you can make with muffins and quick breads, so always check them 10 minutes before the baking time is up. Most of these muffin recipes require two 12-cup muffin pans or one 18- or 24-cup pan. If your oven is not big enough to accommodate two 12-cup muffin pans on the center rack, bake one panful at a time. Placing one pan on the lower oven rack and one on the center rack inhibits correct baking. Remember, ovens vary. Knowing your oven is crucial to good baking. For more about this, see "Ovens," page 15, and "Adjusting Oven Temperatures and Baking Times," page 18.

- **Testing for doneness:** When you have baked a particular muffin or quick bread several times, you will know when it is properly baked just by the color and look of it. We also recommend using one or all of the following methods of testing for doneness:

  1. Insert a toothpick in the center of a muffin in the center of the pan or in the middle of a quick bread loaf. It should come out clean or with just a few crumbs on it, not with raw dough on it. This indicates that the batter has set, but has not overbaked.

  2. With your fingers, gently press or squeeze the top of muffins or quick breads while they are baking. When ready, they should feel firm, have no soft area in the center, and lift out of the pan easily.

  3. Take a muffin out of the pan and break it apart. It should look moist and crumbly, not gummy or underdone.

- **Storing:** Muffins and quick breads keep very well. Let them cool completely, at least 1 hour, before storing. For overnight storage, place the muffins (in a single layer) or quick bread in a plastic bag and store at room temperature. To keep for 2 to 4 days, store in the refrigerator and warm slightly before serving. To store for 4 days to 1 month, seal in double airtight plastic bags and keep in the freezer. Place in the refrigerator the night before serving. Warm slightly in a 325° oven for about 10 minutes before serving.

PUMPKIN-NUT MUFFINS

These muffins are like pieces of pumpkin pie. They are perfect for fall; we start making them around Halloween and don't stop until Thanksgiving.

BAKER'S BASICS TO REVIEW
Measuring Dry Ingredients, page 21

———

3 large eggs
2¼ cups sugar
³⁄₄ cup (6 ounces) butter, melted and cooled
1²⁄₃ cups canned pumpkin purée
3¹⁄₃ cups all-purpose flour
1 tablespoon baking soda
¹⁄₂ teaspoon salt
¹⁄₂ teaspoon ground cinnamon
¹⁄₂ teaspoon ground nutmeg
¹⁄₂ teaspoon ground cloves
¹⁄₄ teaspoon ground allspice
³⁄₄ cup coarsely chopped walnuts
¹⁄₃ cup raisins
Streusel Muffin Topping (page 162)

Preheat oven to 400°. Butter one large or two small muffin pans.

In a large bowl, mix the eggs, sugar, butter, and pumpkin purée with a wooden spoon until smooth.

In a small bowl, combine the flour, baking soda, salt, and spices, tossing to mix well. Add the dry ingredients, along with the walnuts and raisins, to the wet ingredients, mixing just until incorporated and a few dry spots remain; do not overmix.

Scoop or spoon the batter into the prepared muffin pan(s), filling 18 of the cups three-quarters full. Sprinkle 1 tablespoon of the streusel mixture over each muffin. Place the muffin pan(s) on the center rack in the oven and bake for approximately 15 to 20 minutes. The topping should be golden brown and the muffins should spring back when gently pressed. Let the muffins cool in the pan(s) on a wire rack.

ORANGE-
OLALLIEBERRY MUFFINS

MAKES 18 MUFFINS

With their orangy aroma and pockets of soft berries, these are very popular.

BAKER'S BASICS TO REVIEW

Measuring Dry Ingredients, page 21

Zesting Citrus, page 24

STREUSEL MUFFIN TOPPING

1/4 cup all-purpose flour

2 tablespoons sugar

2 tablespoons firmly packed brown sugar

1/8 teaspoon ground cinnamon

3 tablespoons (1 1/2 ounces) very cold butter, cut into 1/2-inch pieces

MUFFINS

3 cups all-purpose flour

1 cup granulated sugar

1 tablespoon baking powder

1 1/2 teaspoons baking soda

1/2 teaspoon salt

1/3 cup finely grated orange zest

2/3 cup coarsely chopped walnuts

2 large eggs

1 1/2 cups sour cream, at room temperature

3/4 cup freshly squeezed orange juice

2 tablespoons (1 ounce) butter, melted and cooled

3 cups frozen or fresh olallieberries or other blackberries,
    coarsely chopped (see Note)

Preheat the oven to 400°. Butter one large or two small muffin pans.

To make the streusel, combine all of the dry ingredients in the bowl of a food processor fitted with the metal blade. Pulse to mix. Add the butter and pulse several times, or until the mixture is crumbly. Be careful not to over-mix or you will end up with a dough instead of a batter. Set aside.

To make the muffins, combine the flour, granulated sugar, baking pow-der, baking soda, and salt in a medium bowl. Add the orange zest and wal-nuts and mix to combine. In a separate bowl, combine the eggs, sour cream, orange juice, and melted butter. Add to the dry ingredients, mixing just until incorporated and a few dry spots remain; do not overmix. Fold the berries into the batter. Immediately scoop or spoon the batter into 18 of the prepared muf-fin pan(s), filling the cups two-thirds full.

Sprinkle 1 tablespoon of the streusel mixture over each muffin. Place the muffin pan(s) on the center rack in the oven and bake for 14 minutes. The streusel should be golden brown and the muffins should spring back when gently pressed. Remove the muffins from the pan(s) and let cool on a wire rack.

NOTE: Fresh berries discolor the batter more than frozen berries.

REDUCED-FAT APPLE-CARROT MUFFINS

MAKES 12 MUFFINS

These tasty, healthful muffins have a fresh apple flavor and aren't too sweet.

BAKER'S BASICS TO REVIEW
Measuring Dry Ingredients, page 21
Zesting Citrus, page 24

MUFFINS
$^1/_3$ cup raisins
2 tablespoons water
1 cup all-purpose flour
1 cup whole-wheat flour
1 $^1/_2$ teaspoons ground cinnamon
1 teaspoon baking soda
1 teaspoon baking powder
$^1/_4$ teaspoon salt
$^1/_3$ cup granulated sugar
$^1/_2$ teaspoon grated lemon zest
1 cup coarsely grated green apples
2 cups coarsely grated carrots
1 large egg
2 tablespoons (1 ounce) butter, melted and cooled
1 teaspoon pure vanilla extract
2 tablespoons canola oil
$^1/_3$ cup firmly packed brown sugar
$^1/_4$ cup light molasses
$^1/_4$ cup apple juice

GLAZE
1 cup confectioners' sugar
2 tablespoons apple juice

Preheat the oven to 400°. Butter one 12-cup muffin pan.

Place the raisins in a small bowl, add the water, and set aside to soak.

Combine the dry ingredients in a medium bowl. Add the lemon zest, apple, and carrot, then toss gently with a rubber spatula just until mixed.

In a separate bowl, whisk together the egg, butter, vanilla, oil, brown sugar, molasses, and juice. Add this mixture, along with the raisins and water, to the dry ingredients, mixing just until incorporated and a few dry spots remain; be careful not to overmix. Immediately scoop or spoon the batter into the prepared muffin pan.

Place the muffin pan on the center rack in the oven and bake for 13 minutes, or until the muffins are golden brown and spring back when gently pressed. Remove the muffins from the pan and let cool on a wire rack.

To make the glaze, whisk together the confectioners' sugar and apple juice in a small bowl. When the muffins have cooled for 10 minutes, brush them with the glaze.

MOSTLY ORGANIC
BRAN MUFFINS

MAKES 24 MUFFINS

When a new organic produce barn opened forty miles away in Carmel Valley, the owners came to us and asked if we would supply them with organic bread and muffins. We were so flattered that we created this muffin for them. The reason we call it "mostly organic" is that sometimes it's difficult to get all of the organic ingredients. Fortunately, the muffins are just as moist and delicious even if you can't find organic vanilla.

BAKER'S BASICS TO REVIEW
Measuring Dry Ingredients, page 21
Folding, page 20

———

1 1/2 cups organic wheat bran

1 cup organic rolled oats

2/3 cup organic raisins

3/4 cup organic applesauce

1 1/2 cups coarsely chopped organic walnuts

3 cups buttermilk

3 large hormone-free eggs

1/2 cup organic canola oil

1/4 cup unsulphured molasses

¹/4 cup organic maple syrup

1 tablespoon organic pure vanilla extract

³/4 cup puréed organic bananas

2¹/4 cups organic whole-wheat flour

2 tablespoons baking soda

Preheat the oven to 400°. Butter two muffin pans.

Combine the wheat bran, oats, raisins, applesauce, walnuts, and butter-milk in a very large bowl.

In another bowl, whisk together the eggs, oil, molasses, maple syrup, vanilla, and bananas.

In a small bowl, combine the flour and baking soda.

Fold the banana mixture into the bran mixture until just mixed. Fold the flour and baking soda into the batter, mixing just until incorporated and a few dry spots remain; do not overmix.

Scoop or spoon the batter into the prepared muffin pans. Place the muffin pans on the center rack in the oven and bake for 14 minutes, or until they are golden brown and spring back when gently pressed. (These muffins are moist and slightly dense, so make sure they are baked through before removing them from the oven.) Remove the muffins from the pans and let cool on a wire rack.

NOTE: This recipe makes a rather large batch, but the muffins keep well. For storage instructions, see "Storing," page 160.

CRANBERRY-ORANGE MUFFINS

MAKES 18 MUFFINS

We make these muffins every year from November 1 through the holidays. They have an intense orange flavor and are not too sweet.

BAKER'S BASICS TO REVIEW
   Measuring Dry Ingredients, page 21
   Zesting Citrus, page 24

ORANGE GLAZE
   1 tablespoon (1/2 ounce) butter, at room temperature
   1 tablespoon grated orange zest
   1 cup confectioners' sugar
   2 tablespoons milk
   1 teaspoon pure vanilla extract

MUFFINS
   3 cups all-purpose flour
   1 cup granulated sugar
   1 tablespoon baking powder
   1 1/2 teaspoons baking soda
   1/2 teaspoon salt
   1/3 cup finely grated orange zest
   2/3 cup coarsely chopped walnuts
   2 large eggs
   1 1/2 cups sour cream, at room temperature
   3/4 cup freshly squeezed orange juice
   2 tablespoons (1 ounce) butter, melted and cooled
   3 cups chopped fresh cranberries

To make the glaze, mix all the ingredients until smooth. Set aside.

To make the muffins, follow the recipe for Orange-Olallieberry Muffins (page 162), but substitute the cranberries for the olallieberries. Brush the Orange Glaze on the muffins after they have cooled for 10 minutes.

JALAPEÑO-CORN MUFFINS

MAKES 18 MUFFINS

We serve these in our Rosticceria with some of the daily specials, such as chili. None of us can resist them. The amount of jalapeño may seem like a lot, but it's not too much because the chiles mellow when baked.

BAKER'S BASICS TO REVIEW
Measuring Dry Ingredients, page 21
Folding, page 20

———

1/2 cup (4 ounces) unsalted butter, melted and cooled
2 cups cornmeal
2 cups all-purpose flour
1/4 cup sugar
2 teaspoons salt
1 tablespoon baking powder
3 large eggs
2 cups heavy whipping cream
1 cup fresh or canned corn
1 cup stemmed, seeded, and finely chopped red bell pepper
1/4 cup plus 2 tablespoons stemmed, seeded, and finely chopped
  fresh jalapeño chiles
3/4 cup grated sharp Cheddar cheese

Preheat the oven to 400°. Butter one large or two small muffin pans. Melt the butter and set aside to cool.

In a large bowl, combine the dry ingredients. In a separate bowl, whisk together the eggs, cream, and cooled butter. Add to the dry ingredients, mixing just until incorporated and a few dry spots remain; do not overmix. Fold in the corn, bell pepper, and jalapeños until just incorporated.

Scoop or spoon the batter into 18 of the prepared muffin pan cups. Sprinkle each muffin with a few teaspoons of the cheese. Place the muffin pan(s) on the center rack in the oven and bake for 16 minutes, or until slightly golden. Let the muffins cool in the pan(s) on a wire rack.

PRUNE-ARMAGNAC GINGERBREAD

MAKES ONE 9¹/₂ X 3¹/₂-INCH LOAF

We make this every fall. The moist, rich "cake" is made in a loaf pan and smells divine while baking. It keeps well and is delicious alone or with whipped cream.

BAKER'S BASICS TO REVIEW
Measuring Dry Ingredients, page 21
Creaming, page 20

I cup prunes, pitted and coarsely chopped
¹/₄ cup Armagnac or brandy
2 teaspoons peeled, grated fresh ginger
¹/₂ cup (4 ounces) butter, at room temperature
³/₄ cup firmly packed dark brown sugar
¹/₂ cup light molasses
2 large eggs
I¹/₂ cups all-purpose flour
I teaspoon baking soda
I teaspoon ground cinnamon
¹/₂ teaspoon ground ginger
¹/₂ teaspoon ground cloves
Pinch of ground cayenne pepper
¹/₄ teaspoon salt
¹/₄ cup strong black coffee
¹/₂ teaspoon pure vanilla extract
¹/₄ cup crystallized ginger, finely chopped

Preheat the oven to 300°. Butter a 9¹/₂ x 3¹/₂-inch loaf pan.

In a saucepan, combine the prunes, Armagnac, and ginger over medium heat, stirring frequently, until almost all of the liquid is evaporated. Remove from the heat and let cool.

In the bowl of a tabletop mixer fitted with the flat beater, cream the butter and sugar until light and fluffy. Add the molasses in a stream, beating slowly until it is well incorporated. Add the eggs, one at a time, waiting until the first is incorporated before adding the second. Blend just until the batter is smooth.

In another bowl, combine the flour, baking soda, spices, and salt. In a separate bowl, combine the coffee and vanilla. Alternately add the dry ingredients and coffee mixture to the creamed batter in several small additions, scraping the bowl after each addition. Add the prune mixture and crystallized ginger and mix just until incorporated.

Pour the batter into the prepared loaf pan. Place the pan on the center rack in the oven and bake for about 35 minutes, or until a toothpick comes out with a few crumbs on it when inserted in the center. Let cool in the pan on a wire rack.

When the gingerbread has almost cooled, remove it from the pan and place on the rack to finish cooling. Covered in plastic wrap, this bread will keep for up to 2 weeks.

LEMON BREAD

MAKES TWO 9 X 5-INCH LOAVES

We've been making this tea cake since we opened, and it's still one of our best sellers. Undoubtedly, it's so popular because it's simple and fresh tasting. The lemon zest in the batter adds a fresh-off-the-tree flavor. You can eat it plain or serve with fresh berries in the summer or stewed rhubarb in the winter. The ways to serve this cake are endless.

BAKER'S BASICS TO REVIEW
Measuring Dry Ingredients, page 21
Zesting Citrus, page 24
Creaming, page 20

BREAD
1/2 cup (4 ounces) butter, at room temperature
2 1/4 cups sugar
4 large eggs
2 2/3 cups all-purpose flour
1 1/4 teaspoons salt
2 1/2 teaspoons baking powder
1 1/3 cups milk, at room temperature
2 tablespoons grated lemon zest

LEMON SOAKING SOLUTION
1/4 cup freshly squeezed lemon juice
1/2 cup sugar

Preheat the oven to 350°. Butter two 9 x 5-inch loaf pans.

In the bowl of a tabletop mixer fitted with the flat beater, cream the butter and sugar until fluffy. Add the eggs, one at a time, waiting until each is incorporated before adding the next.

In a separate bowl, combine the flour, salt, and baking powder.

BLUEBERRY-LEMON MUFFINS

The tartness of blueberries and the sharpness of lemon zest make them perfect partners in these muffins, which are great for brunches, picnics, hikes, or any other excuse you can think of.

To make Blueberry-Lemon Muffins, prepare the batter as directed for the Lemon Bread (see left). Fold in 2 cups of fresh or thawed frozen blueberries, then pour the batter into two large well-buttered muffin pans. Bake at 350° for about 18 minutes, or until the muffins are golden brown and spring back when gently pressed. Makes about 36 muffins.

Beginning and ending with the milk, alternately add the milk and dry ingredients to the batter in 3 or 4 additions, mixing thoroughly after each addition. Add the lemon zest and mix just until blended.

Pour the batter into the prepared loaf pans, filling them a little more than half full. (There should be some space above the baked loaves so that the soaking solution can be poured over them.) Place the pans on the center rack in the oven and bake for approximately 30 to 35 minutes, or until the loaves are golden brown and spring back when gently pressed.

To make the soaking solution, combine the juice and sugar in a small bowl, stirring frequently to dissolve the sugar. When the loaves come out of the oven, pour the soaking solution over them. It will take a little while for the solution to soak in. Let the breads cool in the pans on a wire rack. When completely cool, remove the loaves from the pans.

HONEY CAKE

MAKES ONE 10-INCH CAKE

This recipe was given to us by Kenny Bloom, a longtime friend whom we met while remodeling the first bakery site. Kenny poked his head in the door as I was scraping the floor and Joe was scraping the ceiling. We've been friends ever since. This is his mother Judy's recipe for a wonderfully spicy quick bread.

BAKER'S BASICS TO REVIEW
Measuring Dry Ingredients, page 21
Separating Eggs, page 22
Preparing Cake Pans, page 189

---

2 1/4 cups all-purpose flour
1 1/2 teaspoons baking powder
3/4 teaspoon baking soda
1/4 teaspoon ground ginger
1/4 teaspoon ground nutmeg
1/4 teaspoon ground allspice
1/2 teaspoon ground cinnamon
2 tablespoons vegetable oil
1 cup sugar
2 large egg yolks
1/2 cup honey
1 teaspoon pure vanilla extract
1 cup brewed coffee, cooled
1/2 cup walnuts, chopped
1/4 cup currants

Preheat the oven to 350°. Butter and flour a 10-inch Bundt pan.

In a bowl, combine the flour, baking powder, baking soda, and spices. In another bowl, combine the vegetable oil and sugar. Stir in the egg yolks, one at a time, waiting until the first is incorporated before adding the second. In a third bowl, combine the honey, vanilla, and coffee.

Beginning and ending with the coffee mixture, alternately add the coffee and the flour mixtures to the egg mixture, incorporating well after each addition. Add the walnuts and currants and stir to blend well.

Pour the batter in the prepared pan. Place the pan on the center rack in the oven and bake for 35 minutes, or until the cake slightly pulls away from the sides of the pan. Let cool in the pan on a wire rack.

BREAD PUDDING

MAKES ONE 13 X 9-INCH BREAD PUDDING

We have so many kinds of breads left over every day that it was hard to decide which kind to use for our bread pudding. This recipe calls for the types we think are ideal, but you may substitute whatever you have on hand.

> 5 (^{1}/2-inch-thick) slices day-old cinnamon bread (see Note)
> ^{1}/4 cup (2 ounces) butter, at room temperature
> 2 day-old croissants, cut into bite-sized pieces
> 5 large eggs
> ^{3}/4 cup sugar
> 1 tablespoon pure vanilla extract
> 2^1/2 cups heavy whipping cream
> 1 teaspoon ground cinnamon
> ^{1}/4 teaspoon ground nutmeg
> Whole nutmeg, for grating

Preheat the oven to 325°.

Butter one side of each slice of bread. Layer the slices, butter side down, alternating with the croissant pieces, in a 13 x 9-inch pan with sides at least 2 inches high.

In the bowl of a tabletop mixer fitted with the whip attachment, beat the eggs until thick, fluffy, pale yellow, and more than double in volume, about 5 minutes. Add the sugar and vanilla and beat until well incorporated. Add the cream, cinnamon, and nutmeg and mix on low speed until well incorporated. Pour the egg mixture slowly over the bread. You may need to wait a few minutes for the bread to absorb a portion of the liquid before pouring on more. Grate the whole nutmeg over the pudding.

Place the baking pan in a roasting pan or any other large pan. Pour water into the roasting pan until it reaches halfway up the outside of the bread pudding pan (this is called a water bath). Place the pans on the center rack in the oven and bake for about 20 to 25 minutes, or until the pudding is set but still jiggles in the center. (The pudding will continue to set as it cools.) Do not overbake or the pudding will be dry and rubbery. Remove from the oven and immediately take the pan of bread pudding out of the water bath.

This dessert is best warm from the oven. If served later, serve at room temperature. Because of the perishable ingredients used, don't let it sit at room temperature for more than 8 hours.

NOTE: We used 5 slices from a standard-sized loaf for this recipe. If you are using a small loaf, add 1 more slice. The bread should be no more than 2 days old or it may absorb too much liquid.

LEMON CREAM SCONES

MAKES 8 SCONES

These scones are wonderfully moist when baked correctly. They taste even better when served with the English Lemon Curd (page 173).

BAKER'S BASICS TO REVIEW
Measuring Dry Ingredients, page 21
Zesting Citrus, page 24

2 cups all-purpose flour
$1/4$ cup sugar
2 teaspoons baking powder
$1/8$ teaspoon salt
$1/2$ cup heavy whipping cream
1 large egg
$1 1/2$ teaspoons pure vanilla extract
$1 1/2$ teaspoons grated lemon zest
$1/3$ cup ($2 2/3$ ounces) unsalted butter, chilled
$1/2$ cup currants (optional)

EGG GLAZE (OPTIONAL)
1 large egg
1 teaspoon water

Preheat the oven to 350°.

In the bowl of a food processor fitted with the metal blade, place the flour, sugar, baking powder, and salt. Pulse several times to combine the ingredients.

In another bowl, mix the cream, egg, vanilla, and zest. Set aside.

Cut the butter into 1/2-inch pieces and sprinkle them over the flour. Pulse several times, or until the mixture resembles coarse crumbs.

Transfer the dough to a bowl and add the cream mixture. Stir to combine. Stir in the currants, being careful not to overmix.

Turn the dough out onto a lightly floured surface. With floured hands, gently pat the dough into an 8-inch circle and transfer to an ungreased baking sheet. With a serrated knife, cut into 8 wedges. In a small bowl, whisk together the egg and water to make the glaze. Using a pastry brush, coat the scones with the glaze.

Place the baking sheet on the center rack in the oven and bake for 19 to 22 minutes, or until the top is lightly browned and a toothpick comes out clean when inserted in the center. Let the scones cool on the baking sheet on a wire rack for 5 minutes.

ENGLISH LEMON CURD

MAKES 1 1/4 CUPS

When Joe and I visited England in 1992, we ate more than our share of scones with lemon curd. Scones and lemon curd just go together naturally. Lemon curd is also a great filling for cakes or a topping, along with whipped cream, for the Lemon Bread (page 169).

BAKER'S BASICS TO REVIEW
Zesting Citrus, page 24

3 large eggs
1/2 to 3/4 cup sugar (use less for a more tart flavor)
1/4 cup freshly squeezed lemon juice
2 tablespoons (1 ounce) unsalted butter
2 tablespoons grated lemon zest

In the top of a double boiler, whisk the eggs and sugar until smooth. Add the rest of the ingredients and cook over medium heat, whisking continuously, until the mixture resembles slightly whipped cream.

Remove it from the heat, cover, and stir frequently as it cools. When cool, strain and store in the refrigerator for up to 4 days.

CREAM CHEESE PASTRY DOUGH

MAKES ABOUT 2³/₄ POUNDS

This dough is one of the most versatile items in a pastry maker's recipe book. We use it for sweet and savory goods, such as the Pecan Tassies (page 175), Rugelach (page 176), and Mushroom Turnovers (page 177). Other good uses include miniature pizzas, pot pie crusts, and cheese straws. Consider using it whenever you would use a pie dough; it's richer than pie dough and adds depth of flavor.

BAKER'S BASICS TO REVIEW
Measuring Dry Ingredients, page 21
Creaming, page 20

––––––

2 cups (1 pound) butter, at room temperature
12 ounces cream cheese, at room temperature
4 cups all-purpose flour

In the bowl of a tabletop mixer fitted with the flat beater, cream the butter and cream cheese until fully blended. Add the flour and mix just until incorporated.

Form the dough into a 1-inch-thick rectangle. Cover with plastic wrap and refrigerate for at least 2 hours. Let the dough rest at room temperature for at least 20 minutes before rolling it out. This dough may be refrigerated for up to 3 days and frozen for up to 2 weeks.

PECAN TASSIES

MAKES 36 TASSIES

These little southern morsels are much sought after at the bakery. They taste like miniature pecan pies and have earned every bit of their zealous following.

BAKER'S BASICS TO REVIEW
Creaming, page 20

---

2 tablespoons butter, at room temperature
1 1/2 cups firmly packed brown sugar
2 large eggs
1 1/2 teaspoons pure vanilla extract
1/3 recipe (about 1 pound) Cream Cheese Pastry Dough (page 174)
1 1/4 cups pecans, coarsely chopped

Preheat the oven to 350°.

Cream the butter and brown sugar until smooth. Add the eggs and vanilla and mix until fully incorporated.

Roll the dough out to 1/8 inch thick. Using a 3-inch round cutter, make 36 rounds. Gently fit the rounds into miniature muffin or gem pans. The edges of the shells should extend 1/8 inch over the top of each cup; trim any excess dough. Let the shells rest, uncovered, in the refrigerator for about 10 minutes.

Fill each shell halfway with pecan pieces. Spoon the brown sugar mixture over the pecans, filling the shells to within 1/8 inch from the top.

Place the pans on the center rack in the oven and bake for approximately 15 minutes, or until the shells are golden brown and the filling is just set. Do not overbake; the filling should be slightly gooey in the center when the tassies are cool. Let cool in the pans for 5 minutes, then remove from the pans and finish cooling on wire racks.

RUGELACH

MAKES ABOUT 30 RUGELACH

These little pastries are light and rich at the same time. They are very easy to make and are a fun project for kids.

- 1/4 cup firmly packed brown sugar
- 1/2 cup granulated sugar
- 1 tablespoon ground cinnamon
- 1/2 recipe (22 ounces) Cream Cheese Pastry Dough (page 174)
- 1/2 cup walnuts, finely chopped
- 1 cup currants

Preheat the oven to 350°. Line one large baking sheet with parchment paper.

In a small bowl, combine the sugars and cinnamon.

On a lightly floured work surface, roll out the dough into a 1/8-inch-thick rectangle. Sprinkle the cinnamon mixture generously over the dough. Cut long 4-inch-wide strips of dough from the rectangle. Using a pastry wheel or a long chef's

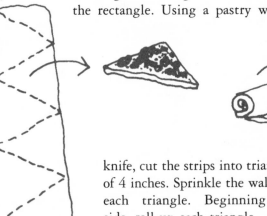

knife, cut the strips into triangles, each with a base of 4 inches. Sprinkle the walnuts and currants over each triangle. Beginning with the shortest side, roll up each triangle.

Place the triangles on the prepared baking sheet. Set the baking sheet on the center rack in the oven and bake for approximately 15 minutes, or until golden. These are best the same day they are baked or the day after. Store in an airtight container.

MUSHROOM TURNOVERS

MAKES 24 TURNOVERS

These turnovers are great hors d'oeuvres or a savory accompaniment to soups and salads.

FILLING

3 tablespoons (1½ ounces) butter
1 cup finely chopped yellow onions
10½ ounces mushrooms, cleaned and finely chopped
   (about 4 cups)
6 ounces cream cheese
¾ teaspoon thyme, dried or freshly chopped
¾ teaspoon salt
¼ teaspoon freshly ground black pepper

———

1 recipe Cream Cheese Pastry Dough (page 174)

EGG GLAZE

1 large egg
2 tablespoons milk

Preheat the oven to 350°.

To make the filling, melt the butter in a skillet over medium-high heat. Add the onions and mushrooms and sauté, stirring occasionally, until all of the moisture has cooked out of the vegetables. Add the cream cheese in 3 parts, stirring until each addition is well incorporated before adding the next. Stir in the thyme, salt, and pepper. Remove from the heat and let cool. At this point, the filling may be refrigerated for up to 3 days.

On a lightly floured surface, roll out the dough to 24 x 16 x ⅛ inches. Cut the dough into 4-inch squares. In a small bowl, whisk together the egg and milk to make the glaze. Using a pastry brush, lightly coat each square with the glaze. Spoon 1 tablespoon of filling in the center of each square. Taking one corner, fold it to meet the opposite corner, making a triangle and enclosing the filling. Press the edges gently to seal. Repeat to fill the rest of the squares.

Place the triangles on a baking sheet and brush the top of them with the glaze. Place the baking sheet on the center rack in the oven and bake for 20 to 25 minutes, or until golden brown.

These turnovers can be stored in an airtight plastic bag and frozen for up to 2 weeks. Defrost by bringing to room temperature while covered. Reheat in a 325° oven for 5 minutes.

CHEESE WAFERS

MAKES ABOUT 50 WAFERS

These luscious little hors d'oeuvres are so easy to make you'll want to have the dough in your freezer all the time. The recipe is from our friend Barbara Hart, who lived in Mexico and threw the biggest and best parties you ever saw.

BAKER'S BASICS TO REVIEW
Measuring Dry Ingredients, page 21

- 1 pound extra-sharp Cheddar cheese, grated, at room temperature
- 1 cup (8 ounces) butter, at room temperature
- 1 cup finely chopped pecans
- 2 cups all-purpose flour
- 1 teaspoon ground cayenne pepper
- 1 tablespoon sage, dried or freshly chopped

Place all of the ingredients in the bowl of a food processor fitted with the metal blade. Process just until the mixture forms a ball.

Divide the dough into 4 equal pieces and place each piece on a sheet of plastic wrap. Roll the dough into a log and seal well in the plastic wrap. Refrigerate overnight. If you are in a hurry, you can freeze the logs for 1 hour before baking.

Preheat the oven to 350°. Line two baking sheets with parchment paper.

Cut the logs into 1/2-inch slices. Arrange the slices on the prepared baking sheets. Bake on the center rack of the oven for 10 to 12 minutes, or until slightly golden. Be careful not to overbake. Transfer the wafers to wire racks to cool.

NOTE: The wafers are only good for 2 days, even when stored in an airtight container, so it's better to keep the dough in the refrigerator or freezer and bake the wafers the day you plan to serve them.

PÂTE À CHOUX

Pâte à choux is a light, eggy pastry shell used for Cream Puffs (page 180), Chocolate Éclairs (page 182), and Paris-Brest (page 184).

BAKER'S BASICS TO REVIEW
Measuring Dry Ingredients, page 21

1/2 cup water

4 tablespoons unsalted butter

1 tablespoon sugar

2 pinches salt

3/4 cup all-purpose flour

3 large eggs, at room temperature

Ten minutes before beginning the choux pastry, preheat the oven to 375°. Place the water, butter, sugar, and salt in a heavy saucepan with a handle and bring to a boil. While the paste is on the heat, add the flour all at once. Stir vigorously with a wooden spoon until the mixture comes away from the sides of the pan and forms a ball.

Remove the paste from the heat and add the eggs, one at a time, beating well to incorporate each one before adding the next. After the third egg is added, beat until the mixture is smooth. Use immediately.

CREAM PUFFS

MAKES 20 TO 25 CREAM PUFFS

CHOCOLATE-FILLED CREAM PUFFS

Substitute 1/2 cup cooled Chocolate Ganache (page 262) for the vanilla, folding it into the whipped cream once the stiff peaks have formed.

CHOCOLATE-TOPPED CREAM PUFFS

To top the cream puffs with Chocolate Ganache (page 262), follow the instructions for topping éclairs on page 183.

MINIATURE CREAM PUFFS

Cream Puffs may be made in any size. At Gayle's, we sometimes make tiny 1-inch puffs for special orders. They make wonderful bite-sized pastries for parties. To make the mini-puffs, use a 1/4-inch pastry tip to pipe the shells. Bake as directed for the full-sized puffs, but check them 5 minutes before the baking time is up. Makes 40 to 50 miniature puffs.

I still can't resist sneaking a cream puff out of the case every so often. All that whipped cream nestled into a crispy shell is just irresistible.

BAKER'S BASICS TO REVIEW

Filling and Using a Nylon Pastry Bag, page 20

Whipping Cream, page 258

Piping Borders and Other Decorations, page 215

———

1 recipe hot Pâte à Choux (page 179)

FILLING

1 1/2 cups heavy whipping cream

2 to 3 tablespoons granulated sugar

1 1/2 teaspoons pure vanilla extract, or 2 tablespoons Grand Marnier, Chambord, Myers's rum, or crème de menthe

———

Confectioners' sugar

Preheat the oven to 375°. Lightly butter two baking sheets or line with parchment paper. Fit a pastry bag with a 3/4- to 1-inch plain tip.

To make the puff shells, place the hot paste in the pastry bag. Holding the bag at a 45-degree angle, with the tip 1/4 inch away from one of the prepared baking sheets, pipe a ball that is 1 1/4 to 1 1/2 inches in diameter and 1 inch high. After completing the shape, stop applying pressure, then pull up on the tip so that you do not create a "tail." Repeat to form the rest of the cream puffs, placing them 2 inches apart. To smooth the tops, dip your index finger in a glass of water and run it over the top of each puff. Repeat until all balls are smoothed, wetting your finger every other time.

Place the baking sheets on the center rack in the oven. Bake for 15 minutes at 375°, then decrease the heat to 325° and bake for 15 more minutes. While the puff shells are baking, fit a second pastry bag with a 1/2- to 1-inch plain or star tip. Let the puffs cool on the baking sheets completely. (At this point, the puff shells can be frozen in airtight plastic bags. To fill frozen puffs, slice off the top one-third and crisp both halves in a 300° oven for 10 minutes. Let cool before filling.)

Fill the cream puffs as close to serving time as possible. As soon as the cream puffs are completely cool, gently whip the cream. Add the sugar and vanilla (or liqueurs) and whip until stiff peaks form. Slice off the top one-third of the puff shells. Place the whipped cream in the second prepared pastry bag. Pipe a spiral of about 3 tablespoons of filling in the bottom of each cream puff. Alternatively, use a small spoon to scoop the whipped cream into the puffs.

Place the tops on the cream puffs and sift confectioners' sugar over them. Refrigerate, uncovered, until ready to serve. The puffs should be served the same day they are made.

CHOCOLATE ÉCLAIRS

MAKES 12 ÉCLAIRS

CHOCOLATE-FILLED ÉCLAIRS

Substitute ¹/₂ cup cooled Chocolate Ganache (page 262) for the vanilla, folding it into the filling after the Pastry Cream has been folded in.

MINIATURE ÉCLAIRS

Sometimes it's nice to enjoy these very rich pastries in smaller sizes. Try piping 1-inch-long éclairs with a ¹/₄-inch tip. Bake as directed for the full-size éclairs, but check them 5 minutes before the the baking time is up. Makes 24 to 30 miniature puffs.

Over the years, I've watched many people eat éclairs and noticed that there's always a look of total joy and contentment on their faces. Keep a few napkins handy. These are definitely gooey.

BAKER'S BASICS TO REVIEW
Filling and Using a Nylon Pastry Bag, page 20
Whipping Cream, page 258
Folding, page 20
Piping Borders and Other Decorations, page 215

———

¹/₃ recipe (1¹/₂ cups) Chocolate Ganache (page 262)
1 recipe hot Pâte à Choux (page 179)

FILLING
³/₄ cup heavy whipping cream
1¹/₂ tablespoons sugar
1 teaspoon pure vanilla extract, or 1¹/₂ tablespoons liqueur, such as
    Grand Marnier, Chambord, Myers's rum, or crème de menthe
1 cup Pastry Cream (page 127)

Make the ganache following the directions on page 262, letting it cool until it is soft but still at room temperature, about 1 hour.

Preheat the oven to 375°. Lightly butter two baking sheets or line with parchment paper. Fit a pastry bag with a ³/₄- to 1-inch plain tip.

To make the puff shells, place the hot paste in the pastry bag. Holding the bag at a 45-degree angle, with the tip ¹/₄ inch away from one of the prepared baking sheets, pipe a 3-inch-long, 1-inch-high log. After completing the shape, stop applying pressure, then pull up on the tip so that you do not create a "tail." Repeat to form the rest of the shells, placing them 2 inches apart. To smooth the tops, dip your index finger in a glass of water and run it over the top of each shell. Repeat, wetting your finger every other time, until all logs are smoothed.

Place the baking sheets on the center rack in the oven. Bake for 20 minutes at 375°, then decrease the heat to 325° and bake for 15 more minutes. While the puff shells are baking, fit a second pastry bag with a ¹/₂- to 1-inch plain or star tip. Let the puffs cool on the baking sheets completely. (At this point, the puff shells can be frozen in airtight plastic bags. To fill frozen shells, slice off the top one-third of the shells and crisp both halves in a 300° oven for 10 minutes. Let cool before filling.)

As soon as the éclair shells are completely cool, gently whip the cream. Add the sugar and vanilla (or liqueurs) and whip until stiff peaks form. Fold in the Pastry Cream. Slice off the top one-third of the shells. Place the filling in the second prepared pastry bag. Pipe a spiral of 5 to 6 tablespoons in the bottom of each shell. Alternatively, use a small spoon to scoop the filling into the shells.

To top the éclairs, make sure that the ganache is soft and at room temperature. Dip the top of each shell in the ganache and set it on a filled bottom. Refrigerate, uncovered, until ready to serve. The éclairs should be served the day they are made.

PARIS-BREST

MAKES TWO 8-INCH PASTRIES

This was one of the first pastries we ever made at Gayle's, and I'm still very sentimental about it. It is named for the first train to travel between Paris and Brest, France. If you like the taste of caramelized nuts, you'll love this pastry. We've recommended reviewing the directions for leveling and cutting cakes into layers because the techniques are helpful when cutting the rings in half.

BAKER'S BASICS TO REVIEW

Filling and Using a Nylon Pastry Bag, page 20
Whipping Cream, page 258
Folding, page 20
Leveling and Cutting Cakes into Layers, page 20
Piping Borders and Other Decorations, page 191

—

1 recipe hot Pâte à Choux (page 179)
1/4 cup thinly sliced almonds

FILLING

1 cup heavy whipping cream
2 tablespoons butter, at room temperature
1 cup Hazelnut Nougat (page 185)
1 cup Pastry Cream (page 127)

—

Confectioners' sugar

Preheat the oven to 375°. Line two baking sheets with parchment paper or lightly butter them. Using the bottom of an 8-inch cake pan and a pencil, trace an 8-inch circle on the parchment on each of the baking sheets. If you are buttering the sheets, use the tip of a cotton swab to trace the circles. Fit a pastry bag with a 3/4- to 1-inch plain tip.

Place the hot paste in the pastry bag. Holding the bag at a 45-degree angle, with the tip 1/4 inch away from one of the prepared baking sheets, pipe around the circle to make a 1 1/2-inch-wide, 1-inch-high ring. After completing the ring, stop applying pressure, then pull up on the tip so that you do not create a "tail." Repeat to form the other ring. Dip your index finger in water and run it over the seams to smooth. Sprinkle the top of the rings with the almonds, hand-placing any that fall off and gently pressing to adhere them.

Place the baking sheet on the center rack in the oven. Bake for 20 minutes, then decrease the heat to 325° and bake for 15 more minutes. While the rings are baking, fit a second pastry bag with a 1/2-inch plain or star tip. Let the rings cool on the baking sheets completely. (At this point, the rings can be frozen in airtight plastic bags. To fill frozen rings, slice as directed below and crisp both halves in a 300° oven for 10 minutes. Let cool before filling.)

As soon as the rings are completely cool, whip the cream just until it forms stiff peaks. (If it is any stiffer, it will be difficult to incorporate into the other filling ingredients.) Set aside.

In the bowl of a tabletop mixer fitted with the flat beater, beat the butter and nougat until smooth. Add the Pastry Cream and mix thoroughly. Fold the Pastry Cream mixture into the whipped cream. Chill until ready to use.

With the tip of a sharp knife, make a hole in the side of each ring. Insert the tip of a serrated knife in the hole. Gently cut the ring in half horizontally, being careful not to twist the knife. (If you break the ring while cutting it in half, don't despair. Any accidents will be concealed by the confectioners' sugar.)

Place the filling in the second prepared pastry bag. Pipe half of the filling into each of the bottom halves of the rings so that it shows slightly on either side. Alternatively, use a small spoon to scoop the filling into the shells.

Place the tops on the rings and dust them with confectioners' sugar. Refrigerate, uncovered, until 30 minutes before serving. These pastries should be served the same day they are made.

HAZELNUT NOUGAT

MAKES 1 1/2 CUPS

1 cup sugar
1/2 cup water
1 1/2 cups whole toasted, skinned hazelnuts (page 23)

Place the sugar and water in a heavy saucepan. Using a candy thermometer, boil the mixture, without stirring, to the hard crack stage, 350°. The mixture will be a dark amber color.

Add the hazelnuts and pour the mixture out onto a buttered baking sheet; set aside to harden. After the candy has hardened completely, turn it out onto the work surface and break it into large pieces. Pulverize the pieces in a food processor until the candy resembles brown sugar. Store in an airtight container.

Cakes, Icings, and Decorations

Of all desserts and baked goods, cakes are extra special because they bring to mind joyous occasions—birthdays, holidays, weddings, celebrations of all kinds. As bakers, we love cakes because they take so many forms—from simple to grand—and can feature an unlimited combination of flavors and textures. Creating cakes out of just the right combination of elements gives us the chance to evoke a feeling or mood. We most enjoy making cakes whose names, shapes, and decorations elicit those emotional and sensory responses. We remember the thrill of seeing uncluttered cakes lining the case at Cocolat in Berkeley and the fantastical creations at Fauchon in Paris, of learning to make huge sheets of the incredible Opera Cake (page 231) from a visiting French baker, and of successfully replicating a Princess Cake (page 217) using nothing more than a single slice as a guide. The next time you have something special to celebrate, we hope you'll share our enthusiasm for these wonderful desserts by turning to this chapter, which includes our favorite and most popular cakes, best tips for cake-making success, and easy-to-follow icing and decorating instructions.

Most of the cakes we make at Gayle's are fairly simple classic American- and European-style favorites, but they taste much more complex. That's because we use only the freshest, highest-quality ingredients and we ice each of the 50 to 125 cakes the very same day they go in the showcases. We know our customers taste the difference and so will your guests. You wouldn't believe how many times customers have told us that their weddings were the only ones where they've seen people not only eat the wedding cake but also line up for seconds.

We've found that many people think they don't have time to make cakes (and we're happy to help them out!), but that's not really true. Generally speaking, cakes are a combination of components or building blocks that can be made in advance and then assembled when time allows. And, it doesn't take that much practice to make great-tasting, great-looking cakes. If you're still not convinced, try some of the simpler recipes in this chapter. (We've included recipes for bakers of all skill levels.) The trick is to start with the easier cakes, mastering a technique or two, and then apply what you've learned to a more complex recipe. Once you learn how cake batters are supposed to look, feel, and bake, and after you've tried the basic assembly and decorating skills, you'll be a more confident cake baker. In the meantime, your cakes may not be technically perfect, but they'll taste great, and your friends and family will appreciate the love that went into them.

It is possible to successfully bake and decorate cakes without using a lot of tools. In addition to the basic equipment listed on pages 13–17, you'll need the following essentials. If you have a difficult time finding cake-decorating equipment at specialty kitchenware stores, see page 317 for mail-order sources.

- Cake-decorating turntable: Icing cakes with the help of a turntable is a pleasure. Turntables are affordable and well worth the investment, especially if you've priced quality bakery cakes lately; we recommend owning one even if you only make three or four cakes a year. An alternative is to set a plastic turntable or lazy Susan on an inverted saucepan just slightly smaller than the diameter of the turntable. To eliminate the lip on the plastic turntable, cut or buy a couple of cardboard circles to fit just inside the lip. When using a homemade turntable, be very careful when turning it so you don't knock it off the saucepan.

- Long serrated knife: A sharp, sturdy serrated knife with a 14-inch-long blade is best for leveling and cutting cakes into layers. (We affectionately refer to ours as cake saws.) As an alternative, you may use a serrated knife with a blade at least 3 inches longer than the diameter of the cake.

- Metal icing spatula: One flexible metal icing spatula with a 8-inch-long, 1¼-inch-wide blade is really all you need. Choose one that is fairly stiff. Don't let the spatula get nicked or bent, and replace it if it does. It is also nice to have a smaller (4-inch-long, ¾-inch-wide) spatula for delicate jobs and to reach tight spots. An offset metal spatula works well for spreading mixtures in pans, and some people swear by them for decorating.

- Cake cardboards: Whatever did bakers do before these were invented? Their smooth, level surface makes icing and transferring cakes, as well as clean-up, much easier. Store-bought cardboards are sturdy corrugated cardboard circles with a white top. If you prefer, you may make your own cake cardboards by cutting circles out of cardboard boxes and covering them with aluminum foil. When a cake cardboard larger than the size of the cake is called for (such as a 10-inch cardboard for a 9-inch cake) and you don't have one, you may substitute a platter with a completely flat area that is at least as large as the specified size of the cardboard.

- Decorating tips: The cakes in this book use an assortment of the following pastry bag tips: #1 and #2 open-star tips, #5 and #6 plain-tube tips, and a #104 rose tip. Tips are inexpensive and fun to experiment with. Keep plenty on hand (and take care to keep them out of the garbage disposal and out from underfoot).

We have given storage guidelines within each recipe, but recommend that you also observe these general rules:

- To store un-iced cakes, place the completely cooled cake on a cardboard circle the same size as the cake. Wrap it thoroughly in plastic wrap, making sure no cake is exposed to air. Place the wrapped cake in a plastic bag and tie a knot in the end. Label and date the bag, if desired. We recommend freezing rather than refrigerating un-iced cakes, even if they will be used the next day.

- If an iced cake must be refrigerated overnight, place it in an airtight plastic cake container. If you don't have one, use a cardboard cake box taped tightly shut.

- Serve cakes iced with whipped cream the day they are made because they absorb refrigerator odors very easily.

- Buttercream-iced cakes are best the day they are made because they also absorb refrigerator odors, but they are still good the next day.

- For best flavor and texture, always remove cakes filled and/or iced with buttercream or ganache from the refrigerator at least 2 hours before serving. Remove cakes filled and/or iced with whipped cream 30 minutes before serving.

- Remember that cakes iced and/or filled with buttercream, whipped cream, and especially ganache will melt in direct sunlight.

Preparing Cake Pans

Take the time to prepare your pans thoroughly and carefully. It is worth the effort because your cakes will depan without tearing and have a smooth surface that is easier to ice.

To line a cake pan, set the pan on parchment paper or waxed paper and trace around the base with a knife point or pencil. Cut out the circle of parchment or waxed paper and set aside. Lightly but evenly coat the sides of the pan with soft, not melted, butter. Don't butter the bottom of the pan. Place about 1 tablespoon of flour in the pan. Tilt and roll the pan in a circular motion, letting the flour adhere to the butter. Holding the pan over the sink or another cake pan, turn the pan over and tap the bottom to release any excess flour. Place the circle of parchment or waxed paper in the bottom of the pan.

If you are preparing more than one pan, cut all of the paper liners first and set aside. Next, butter all the pans, then flour one pan, tapping the excess flour from pan to pan until all are buttered and floured. Last, place the liners in the pans.

❧ ❧ ❧

Mixing Cake Batters and Filling Pans

Because timing is so important when mixing cakes, always start by bringing all ingredients to room temperature (unless otherwise specified), measuring them, and assembling the equipment you'll need. Then, read the recipe instructions carefully. Once you begin to make the batter, proceed from start to finish without stopping.

BUTTER-BASED BATTERS

Butter-based cakes, such as devil's food and spice cakes, are the most popular cakes in the United States and the kind most of us probably think of when we plan to bake a cake. The secret to producing their fine, moist crumb is correctly combining the ingredients to form a velvety smooth batter. Follow these steps to make perfect butter-based cake batters:

1. Make sure the butter is at room temperature, but not overly soft or starting to melt.

2. Thoroughly cream the butter with the sugar, which produces the tiny air bubbles that are responsible for the basic structure of these cakes.

3. Make sure the eggs are at room temperature and add them gradually, so they can be incorporated easily without deflating the air bubbles that developed during creaming. The eggs in butter-based cakes add flavor, richness, and volume.

4. When adding the dry and wet ingredients to the batter, blend just enough so that they are well incorporated, without overmixing and toughening the batter. When adding dry and wet ingredients alternately, always start with the dry ingredients and end with wet ones.

5. Be sure to scrape down the sides and bottom of the mixing bowl after each step and to tap off any flour that collects on the beater or spatula.

EGG-BASED BATTERS

Sponge or foam cakes, like vanilla genoise, orange chiffon, and angel food, are egg-based cakes known for their volume and light springy texture. These cakes get their loft from eggs that are aerated through whipping and then solidifed by baking, leaving the air bubbles that create a soft, spongy cake.

Two techniques are especially important in making a batter that is as light and has as much loft as possible. First, whip the eggs or egg whites until they reach

(continued)

the specified consistency. Follow the whipping times given in the recipes; don't under- or overwhip the eggs. Then, when folding in the flour, work quickly but gently so you don't deflate the batter and lose volume.

Handle the finished batter delicately as you transfer it to the pan and immediately place it in the oven. Be forewarned: more than any other type of cake, egg-based cakes are the most likely to fall when the oven door is opened, and are most often underbaked rather than overbaked.

FILLING PANS

Divide the batter evenly between the pans. Spread it out to the edges then smooth and level the top using a rubber spatula, a plastic bowl scraper, or your hand. The easiest way to tell if you have the same amount in each pan is to stick the tip of your finger into the batter. The batter should come up to the same place on your finger in each of the pans.

Baking Cakes

Always bake cakes in a preheated oven. Many bakers believe that placing filled cake pans on a baking sheet makes the cake easier to handle, turn, and take in and out of the oven without sticking a finger or oven mitts in it. If your oven bakes hotter on the bottom, you should definitely use a baking sheet.

Cakes should be checked partway through baking. Usually, by the time you can smell a cake, it is time to at least peek at it through the oven window (if your oven has one). The trick is knowing when to open the oven door and test for doneness or to turn the pans for even baking without causing the cake to fall. A good rule of thumb is to wait to open the oven door until three-quarters of the baking time has lapsed. Again, if your oven has a window, peek through it first. If the cake still looks liquidy, don't open the door. (If your oven doesn't have a window, slowly open the door just enough to see inside.) If you think the cake might be ready, test it without moving it if possible. If you must pull the pan closer to you, do it slowly.

Most cakes are done when they just begin to pull away from the sides of the pan, when they spring back when pressed gently, and when a toothpick inserted in the center comes out clean (without any raw batter clinging to it).

Cooling and Depanning Cakes

When you remove cakes from the oven, set them on a cooling rack, away from drafts. If it looks like any part of the cake is sticking to the sides of the pan, immediately loosen it by running a small knife or metal icing spatula around the edge of the cake to prevent it from tearing as it contracts and cools.

Unless otherwise specified, let the cake cool in the pan for 15 minutes. Then, place a second cooling rack on top of the cake and invert it onto the rack. Carefully lift away the pan. Place the first rack on top of the cake and again invert it so that the top is facing up. Let the cake cool completely on the rack before using or wrapping.

Leveling and Cutting Cakes into Layers

There are two reasons to properly level and cut cakes into layers. First, the cake is much easier to fill and ice, and second, the cake will look more beautiful when it is sliced and served.

Cakes should be completely cool when they are leveled and cut into layers. If the cake has been frozen, let it thaw for about 1 hour. The three exceptions in this book are the Hazelnut Sponge Cake (page 201) and Carrot Cake (page 209), which should be cut frozen, and the Vanilla Genoise (page 195), which should be thawed for only 30 minutes.

Cakes must be leveled before they are cut into layers. Always level cakes (and cut into layers) when they are sitting top side up on the work surface, not on a cake-decorating turntable. If you have made two or three layers in separate pans, all should be leveled to the same height. The parchment or waxed paper pan liner should be left on the bottom of the cake, but cake cardboards should be removed.

A serrated knife with a 14-inch blade is ideal for leveling cakes and cutting them into layers. If you don't have one, use a serrated knife with a blade at least 3 inches longer than the diameter of the cake. To begin, cut off any crisp dark edges, crust, or mounded areas on the top that may have developed during baking. Next, to ensure a more level cut, score the cake by placing one palm on the top of the cake and turning the cake as you make a 1/4-inch-deep track all the way around the sides with the serrated knife. Then, using the track as a guide for the knife, cut through the cake with a gentle sawing motion.

After the top is leveled, look at the cake and review the recipe to determine the number of layers you need to cut. Using the same scoring technique described for leveling, cut the cake into layers.

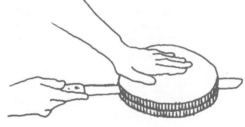

To separate and transfer thin layers more easily and prevent them from cracking when handled, slide cardboard rounds under the layers before lifting them off the cake. Fill and assemble as recipe directs.

Once you've cut the cake into layers, assembling it is a breeze. Filling and icing cakes may seem a bit difficult, but you'll get the hang of it quickly. Many people don't think twice about spreading peanut butter or mayonnaise on bread, but are intimidated by filling and icing a cake. Just like anything else, all it takes is practice and a little confidence.

ASSEMBLING CAKES

To assemble a cake, carefully look over the cut layers. If one layer is a little taller than the others, use it for the bottom of the cake. The weight of the other layers will compress it. If the layers are slightly uneven, don't worry; you can compensate for any unevenness by placing the tallest part of one layer over the shortest part of the another layer. Use the layer with the parchment or waxed paper pan liner on the bottom for the top of the cake, placing it cut side down on the previous layer. Its smooth surface and sharp edges will make icing the cake much easier. Don't peel off the pan liner until the top layer is placed on the cake (but be sure to remember to remove it!). If you've cut the cake into layers but can't ice it right away, leave the paper liner on the top layer and cover the cake with plastic wrap to prevent it from drying out.

SOAKING CAKES

Most of the cakes in this book call for brushing the layers with soaking solution (page 257) as the cake is assembled. This is essential for any cake made with Vanilla Genoise (page 195), and ideal for all of the others, except for the Hazelnut Sponge Cake (page 201) and Carrot Cake (page 209), which should not be soaked. The amount of "soak" to use depends on the type and age of the cake, whether it was slightly overbaked, and your personal preference. Europeans tend to like their layers noticeably soaked; Americans seem to prefer just enough soaking to make a decidedly moist cake.

Start with the bottom layer once it is resting on the cardboard round. Apply the soaking solution by dipping a 1- or 2-inch pastry brush into the solution and brushing it onto the top of the cake. (Never brush soaking solution on the sides of the cake layers.) A few crumbs will be raised as the solution is brushed on. Use just enough solution for the surface of the cake to slightly change color, but not so much that it pools on the surface. Be especially careful not to oversoak the bottom layer. The cake will quickly absorb the soak. Soak the remaining layers as they are placed on the cake.

FILLING CAKES

Use a cake-decorating turntable and a metal icing spatula when filling (and icing) cakes. If you are right-handed, control the turntable with your left hand, rotating it away from you as you work. Remember that you control the turntable, not vice versa.

To fill and assemble the layers, begin by placing some of the filling on top of the bottom (soaked) layer. Holding the spatula so the long edge touches the cake and is parallel to the turntable, spread the filling with a push-and-pull motion; push the filling out to the edge of the cake, angling the spatula away from you, then pull it back with the blade angled toward you.

If using a lot of a very soft filling, such as a pastry cream, try the trick we use at the bakery: Fill a pastry bag fitted with a #1 or #2 star tip and pipe a border of the icing that will be used on the exterior of the cake around the outside edge on top of the layer. Then, spread the filling evenly within the piped border, which will hold in the filling and stabilize the cake. Place the next layer over the first, brush with soaking solution, and spread with filling. Repeat for additional layers.

Once the cake is assembled spread any icing over-hanging between the layers onto the sides of the cake. To prepare for the next step, skim coating, wipe crumbs and any excess soaking solution and icing off the turntable and exposed cardboard.

SKIM COATING A CAKE

Skim coating cakes—that is, covering them with a thin preliminary coat of icing—and briefly chilling them until the icing firms up, is one of the most important steps in making a beautifully iced cake with a uniform shape. Skim coating works with any type of icing. Also called crumb coating, skim coating seals in the crumbs, helps establish the shape of a cake, and makes the final coat of icing adhere much better. Although skim coating requires some downtime, it probably saves time in the long run.

If you have icing mixed with cake crumbs left over from filling the cake, use it for the skim coat. Always start by mounding plenty of icing on the area to be covered. We have given generous amounts of icing for

all of the recipes in this book, so don't worry about having enough to complete the job. Using plenty of icing makes it possible to avoid raising a lot of crumbs as the icing is spread.

With the spatula, spread the icing out to the edges, using the push-and-pull technique (as described for filling, see opposite). Scrape off the crumbs and excess icing on one spot on the rim of the icing bowl every three or four strokes. Keep a moist towel near the turntable to use as needed. Spread the coat of icing as thin as possible on the cake, filling in any tears or depressions to create a level top that meets the sides at a perfect right angle. Don't worry if the icing is a little thicker in some places than in others.

To allow the skim coat to set up, refrigerate cakes, uncovered, for about 15 minutes. Cakes that are skim coated with a ganache or whipped cream icing should chill for at least 15 minutes; chill buttercream-iced cakes for at least 30 minutes or, ideally, 1 hour. The final icing is put on skim-coated cakes immediately after they are removed from the refrigerator.

APPLYING THE FINAL COAT OF ICING

To put the final coat of icing on a cake, place a generous mound of icing (about 2 cups for a 9-inch cake) on the center of the top of the cake. Spread it out to the edges with the icing spatula, using the push-and-pull technique (as described for filling, see opposite). The icing should be fairly smooth and level, but doesn't have to be absolutely perfect; it will be smoothed yet again once the sides are covered. Leave the lip of icing that occurs naturally around the top

(continued)

edge and hangs down toward the sides; you will use it when icing the sides of the cake.

Start icing the sides with about ¼ cup of icing on the end of your spatula. Holding the spatula almost perpendicular to the turntable, meet the overhanging lip of icing on the top and, working from top to bottom, spread the icing onto the sides of the cake. Repeat this process until the sides of the cake are completely covered.

If the cake is seated on a cardboard round the same size as the cake, use the outside edge of the cardboard as a guide as you smooth the sides. Holding the edge of the spatula blade at a 45-degree angle to the cake, rest the tip of the spatula on the turntable with the blade up against the edge of the cardboard, not the cake, then pull the spatula toward you as you turn the turntable away from you (work in one direction only). If the cake is on a larger cardboard, rest the tip of the spatula on the cardboard with the blade up against the cake.

Once the final coat of icing is on the sides, do a final smoothing, leaving the little lip that occurs around the top of the cake.

SMOOTHING THE TOP

Before giving the top its final smoothing, the last step in icing a cake, always wipe off your spatula with a clean towel. Hold the flat part of the spatula blade parallel to the cake and angle the blade toward you. Using light pressure, pull the lip around the top edge of the cake into the middle. Repeat until the lip disap-

pears and the top is smooth. If using whipped cream, wetting the spatula will make it easier to smooth out any remaining flaws. If using buttercream or ganache, heat the spatula slightly over a stovetop burner or under hot water.

Another professional trick is knowing when to quit. A few imperfections won't affect anyone's enjoyment of the cake—you're probably the only one who will notice!

VANILLA GENOISE
LAYER CAKE

MAKES ONE 9-INCH 2-, 3-, OR 4-LAYER CAKE

Vanilla genoise is the only vanilla cake we sell at Gayle's. We do not make a traditional American white cake, even for wedding cakes. When asked to describe it, we say it is a French butter sponge cake, light and eggy, with a wonderful texture.

Genoise is the main building block in our cake repertoire. It is the perfect base for many classics, including princess cakes, petits fours, and rolled cakes like bûche de noël. It is so versatile it can even be used in an English trifle.

BAKER'S BASICS TO REVIEW

> Preparing Cake Pans, page 189
> Measuring Dry Ingredients, page 21
> Folding, page 20
> Mixing Cake Batters and Filling Pans, page 189
> Baking Cakes, page 190
> Cooling and Depanning Cakes, page 190

> 5 large eggs
> 3/4 cup sugar
> 2 tablespoons (1 ounce) unsalted butter
> 1 teaspoon pure vanilla extract
> 1 cup cake flour, sifted

Preheat the oven to 350°. Butter, flour, and line one 9-inch-diameter x 2-inch-deep cake pan or two 9-inch-diameter x 1½-inch-deep pans (see Note) with parchment paper. Bring a saucepan of water to a boil.

Using a whisk, stir the eggs in the bowl of a mixer fitted with the whip attachment. Whisk in the sugar. Place the mixer bowl over the saucepan of boiling water. (The water should be at least 2 inches below the bottom of the bowl.) To prevent the eggs from cooking, use your hand like a whisk to stir the mixture continuously until it feels quite warm. The eggs should remain liquid and not become opaque or cooked. (Failing to mix continuously will result in very sweet scrambled eggs!) When warm, immediately remove the bowl from the heat, place on the mixer, and start whipping on high speed. Whip the eggs without stopping for 3½ to 4 minutes.

While the eggs are whipping, melt the butter and pour it into a small bowl. Add the vanilla. Place the flour in the sifter and set aside.

The egg mixture is ready when the eggs have just cooled and at least

VANILLA GENOISE TIPS

• *Always pre-measure ingredients and assemble equipment before starting.*

• *Once you start making the cake, complete all steps without stopping. If you stop at any point, the batter won't work.*

• *Never double the recipe. If you do, the egg batter will overflow the bowl during whipping.*

• *Genoise may be cut into layers as soon as it is cool. If it has been refrigerated, cut it as soon as you remove it from the refrigerator. If it has been frozen, let it thaw about 30 minutes, then cut. If you wait much longer, the cake will be too soft to cut. When properly made in one 9-inch-diameter x 2-inch-deep pan, this cake can be cut into three 5/8-inch layers.*

• *Don't panic if your cake has some sticky spots in the center of the top after it has been frozen. To remove them, evenly level the whole top by slicing just under the soft spot.*

(continued)

tripled in volume. When you lift the whip out of the bowl, the batter should fall off the whip in ribbons.

Take the bowl off the mixer and sift a little less than one-fourth (a scant 1/4 cup) of the flour over the surface of the batter. Gently fold in the flour using the rubber spatula or your hand. You will hear the batter crunch if you are too rough. Repeat until all the flour is completely incorporated.

Pour a generous cup of the batter over the melted butter mixture in the small bowl. Thoroughly fold the batter into the butter. Slowly pour the butter mixture over the remaining batter in the mixer bowl in a circular motion. (If you add the butter mixture too quickly the butter will sink, reducing the volume and toughening the cake.) Gently fold together until none of the darker butter mixture is visible.

Carefully pour the batter into the prepared 9-inch-diameter x 2-inch-deep pan; it should be about two-thirds full. If using two 9-inch-diameter x 1 1/2-inch-deep pans and making a 3-layer cake, pour one-third of the batter into one pan and the remaining two-thirds into the other pan. If making a 2- or 4-layer cake using two 9-inch-diameter x 1 1/2-inch-deep pans, divide the batter equally between the pans.

Set the cake pan(s) on a baking sheet and immediately place on the center rack in the oven. If using a 9-inch-diameter x 2-inch-deep cake pan, bake for about 30 minutes and wait to open the oven until the cake has baked at least 25 minutes or it may fall. If using two pans, bake for about 20 minutes and wait to open the oven until the cake has baked at least 15 minutes. The cake is done when it just starts to pull away from the sides of the pan. (The cake will not spring back when gently pressed and a toothpick will not come out clean when it is ready.)

After removing the cake from the oven, immediately run a metal icing spatula or knife around the inside of the pan(s) to loosen the cake. Let cool 5 minutes, then depan. The cake may be stored, well wrapped, in the refrigerator for 1 day, or frozen for up to 1 week. Assemble as recipe directs.

NOTE: For optimum moistness, this cake is best baked in a 9-inch-diameter x 2-inch-deep cake pan, then cut into layers. If you don't have one, use two 9-inch-diameter x 1 1/2-inch-deep pans.

• Always cut off the top layer first and place it cut side down on the cardboard. Do not place it cut side up or it will stick to the cardboard.

• If you precut the cake layers before icing the cake, keep them covered with plastic wrap. Vanilla genoise dries out very quickly when left unwrapped.

• Vanilla genoise should always be moistened with a soaking solution (for more about this, see "Assembling, Soaking, Filling, and Icing Cakes" page 192).

VANILLA GENOISE SHEET CAKE

MAKES ONE 15 X 10-X ⁵/₈-INCH CAKE

We use this cake for our Bûche de Noël (page 306) and Petits Fours (page 245), but you can also use it as a base for your favorite jelly roll cake.

> 4 large eggs
> ¹/₂ cup plus 2 tablespoons sugar
> 1¹/₂ tablespoons (³/₄ ounce) unsalted butter
> ³/₄ teaspoon pure vanilla extract
> ³/₄ cup plus 1 tablespoon sifted cake flour

Preheat the oven to 350°. Follow the directions for Vanilla Genoise Layer Cake (page 195) with the following adjustments:

• Line the bottom of a 15 x 10-inch jelly roll pan with parchment paper or waxed paper, securing the paper in place with a tiny dab of butter under each corner.

• Whip the batter for only about 3 minutes before removing it from the mixer.

• Using a plastic bowl scraper, spread the batter into the prepared pan. Work quickly and make it as level as possible.

• Place the cake on the center rack in the oven and bake for 10 to 13 minutes. When the genoise just starts to color and pull away from the sides of the pan, remove the cake from the oven and place it on a rack.

• Let the cake cool completely in the pan on the rack. The cake may be stored, well wrapped in the pan, in the refrigerator overnight, or frozen for up to 1 week.

• Assemble as recipe directs.

Whipping Egg Whites and Making Meringues

Many recipes are based on a combination of egg whites and sugar, and although the amounts, methods, and techniques vary to create different results, most involve whipping. Proper whipping of egg whites is not as mystifying or difficult as many people think. Following two basic rules will usually result in successfully whipped egg whites. First, always use equipment that is totally grease-free. Second, if you're unsure how long to whip the whites, it's usually better to underwhip than overwhip them. This is especially true when whipping egg whites with a tabletop or handheld mixer; once you've checked their consistency, you can whip them just a bit longer with a whisk if necessary.

Here's an overview of the most common ways to whip egg whites:

Egg whites at soft peak are usually whipped without sugar at medium to high speed. They will just barely hold a peak, still look foamy, and slide around freely in the bowl.

Egg whites at stiff peak are usually whipped without sugar at high speed until they will hold their shape and bend only slightly when the whip is lifted away. They should be smooth and slightly wet, not chunky or dry.

A **cold meringue** is made by whipping egg whites until soft peaks form, then adding sugar and whipping until stiff and glossy.

A **warm meringue** is made by combining egg whites and sugar then heating the mixture slightly in the top of a double boiler over warm water before whipping. This stable meringue performs well when folded into another mixture.

Italian meringue is made by pouring a hot sugar syrup into a cold meringue as it is whipping. This stiff meringue is most often used in unbaked recipes.

DEVIL'S FOOD CAKE

**MAKES ONE 9-INCH 2-LAYER CAKE WITH 1-INCH-THICK LAYERS
OR ONE 9-INCH 3-LAYER CAKE WITH ⅝-INCH-THICK LAYERS**

We occasionally test our old standards, such as this recipe, against other recipes to make sure we're still making the best. This one has stood up to the test very well. We have even tested it against Louisa's father's devil's food cake recipe, which she once thought was the best she'd ever tasted. As well as being moist, ours has a rich, rounded flavor most devil's food cakes can't match.

BAKER'S BASICS TO REVIEW

Separating Eggs, page 22
Preparing Cake Pans, page 189
Measuring Dry Ingredients, page 21
Creaming, page 20
Whipping Egg Whites and Making Meringues, page 198
Folding, page 20
Mixing Cake Batters and Filling Pans, page 189
Baking Cakes, page 190
Cooling and Depanning Cakes, page 190

CUSTARD

½ cup milk
1 cup firmly packed light brown sugar
1 large egg yolk
3 ounces unsweetened chocolate, coarsely chopped

CAKE

½ cup (4 ounces) unsalted butter
1 cup granulated sugar
2 large eggs, separated
2 cups cake flour
1 teaspoon baking soda
½ teaspoon salt
½ cup milk
¼ cup water
1 teaspoon pure vanilla extract

Begin to prepare the custard at least 1 hour before mixing the cake. In the top of a double boiler, whisk together the milk, brown sugar, and egg yolk. Cook over boiling water, whisking occasionally, until hot, about 5 minutes. Add the chocolate and continue to cook and whisk until the mixture has slightly thickened, about 6 to 8 minutes. Remove from the heat and pour the mixture into another bowl to speed cooling. Let the mixture cool, whisking occasionally, until it is at room temperature, about 30 minutes.

Preheat oven to 350°. Butter, flour, and line two or three 9-inch cake pans with parchment paper.

Cream the butter in the bowl of a tabletop mixer fitted with the flat beater. With the mixer running on medium speed, gradually add the sugar. Increase the speed to high and beat until light and fluffy, about 1 minute. With the mixer on medium speed, add the egg yolks one at a time, waiting until the first is incorporated before adding the second. Beat until well blended, about 30 seconds.

Sift together into a medium bowl the flour, baking soda, and salt. In a separate bowl, combine the milk, water, and vanilla. With the mixer on medium-low speed, alternately beat in the dry ingredients and the milk mixture in thirds, waiting until each addition is incorporated before adding the next. Stop the mixer and add all the chocolate custard. With the mixer on medium speed, blend until smooth. Set aside.

In a separate bowl, whip the egg whites until stiff but not dry. Gently fold the egg whites into the batter. Pour the batter into the prepared pans. If making a 3-layer cake, pour one-third of the batter into one pan and the remaining two-thirds into the other pan. If making a 2- or 4-layer cake, divide the batter equally between the pans.

Set the pans on a baking sheet and place on the center rack in the oven. Bake for about 30 minutes, or until the cake springs back when gently pressed and a toothpick comes out clean when inserted in the center. This cake tends to dome and develop a crust if the oven is too hot, so adjust the temperature accordingly.

Let cool completely in the pans on wire racks, then depan. This cake may be stored, well wrapped, in the refrigerator for 2 days or in the freezer for 2 weeks. Assemble as recipe directs.

HAZELNUT SPONGE CAKE

MAKES ONE 9-INCH 2-LAYER CAKE

This light, moist, perfectly nutty cake is very versatile. It pairs well with many flavors of icings. We particularly like it with raspberry, mocha, chocolate, buttercream, or whipped cream, or any combination thereof. This recipe makes enough for the Opera Cake (page 231) or any two-layer European-style torte. If you prefer a taller cake, double the recipe and make four layers.

BAKER'S BASICS TO REVIEW

Toasting Nuts, page 23
Preparing Cake Pans, page 189
Measuring Dry Ingredients, page 21
Separating Eggs, page 22
Whipping Egg Whites and Making Meringues, page 198
Folding, page 20
Mixing Cake Batters and Filling Pans, page 189
Baking Cakes, page 190
Cooling and Depanning Cakes, page 190

———

1 cup lightly packed, finely ground toasted, skinned hazelnuts
    (page 23; see also Note)
1/3 cup unseasoned bread crumbs
1 tablespoon cake flour
5 large eggs
1/2 cup plus 1/3 cup sugar

Preheat the oven to 325°. Butter, flour, and line two 9-inch cake pans with parchment paper.

Combine the ground hazelnuts, bread crumbs, and flour in the bowl of a food processor fitted with the metal blade. Process for about 10 seconds. (These ingredients may also be combined by hand, but the cake's texture will not be as fine.) Set aside.

Separate 4 of the eggs. Add the remaining whole egg to the egg yolks. In the bowl of a tabletop mixer fitted with the whip attachment, whip the egg yolks at high speed until fluffy. With the mixer running, gradually add 1/2 cup of the sugar and whip until thick and lemon-colored, about 1 minute. Remove the bowl from the mixer and, using a rubber spatula, gently fold in the nut mixture.

In another bowl, whip the egg whites on high speed until foamy. With the mixer still running, gradually add the remaining 1/3 cup sugar and whip until the meringue holds stiff peaks, about 1 minute. Fold one-third of the meringue

HAZELNUT SPONGE CAKE TIPS

• The top of this cake is fairly sticky. Don't worry if some of the cake sticks to the knife or your hand during leveling, or if it sticks to the plastic wrap if it has been wrapped and frozen.

• If the cake has been frozen, level and cut it into layers immediately after removing from the freezer.

• Because it is so moist, Hazelnut Sponge Cake should not be brushed with soaking solution.

into the nut mixture to lighten it, then gently but thoroughly fold in the remaining meringue. Make sure no white pockets or streaks of meringue remain.

Pour the batter into the prepared pans. Set the pans on a baking sheet and place the sheet on the center rack in the oven. Bake for 22 to 24 minutes, or until the top is light golden, the sides are pulling away from the pan, and a toothpick comes out clean when inserted in the center. The center of the cake will also have fallen slightly.

Remove the pans from the oven and place on cooling racks. Immediately run a metal icing spatula or knife around the inside of the pans to loosen the cake, so that it won't cling to the sides of the pan and tear as it cools. Let cool completely in the pans on wire racks, then depan.

The cake may be stored, well wrapped, in the freezer for up to 1 week. Do not store it in the refrigerator. Assemble as recipe directs.

NOTE: Grind the toasted, skinned hazelnuts in a food processor by pulsing several times, stopping when they are finely ground but not pastelike.

POPPY SEED CAKE

MAKES ONE 9-INCH 3-LAYER CAKE

The poppy seeds' crunch and earthy flavor give this moist, rich cake, which is almost like pound cake, a satisfying taste and texture.

BAKER'S BASICS TO REVIEW

Separating Eggs, page 22
Preparing Cake Pans, page 189
Measuring Dry Ingredients, page 21
Creaming, page 20
Whipping Egg Whites and Making Meringues, page 198
Folding, page 20
Mixing Cake Batters and Filling Pans, page 189
Baking Cakes, page 190
Cooling and Depanning Cakes, page 190

---

1 cup poppy seeds
1 cup milk
1 cup (8 ounces) unsalted butter
2¼ cups sugar
5 large eggs, separated
2 teaspoons pure vanilla extract
3½ cups cake flour

1 teaspoon baking powder

¹/₂ teaspoon salt

In a small bowl, combine the poppy seeds and milk. Set aside at room temperature for 1 hour to soften slightly.

Preheat oven to 350°. Butter, flour, and line three 9-inch cake pans with parchment paper.

Cream the butter in the bowl of a tabletop mixer fitted with the flat beater. With the mixer running on medium speed, gradually add the sugar. Increase the speed to high and beat until light and fluffy, about 1 minute. With the mixer on medium speed, add the egg yolks one at a time, waiting until each is incorporated before adding the next. Blend in the vanilla.

Sift together into a medium bowl the flour, baking powder, and salt. With the mixer on medium-low speed, alternately beat in the dry ingredients and poppy seed mixture in thirds, waiting until each addition is incorporated before adding the next.

In another bowl, whip the egg whites until stiff but not dry. Gently fold the egg whites into the batter. Pour the batter into the prepared pans.

Set the pans on a baking sheet and place on the center rack in the oven. Bake for about 30 to 35 minutes, or until the cake springs back when gently pressed and a toothpick comes out clean when inserted in the center.

Let cool completely in the pans on wire racks, then depan. The cake may be stored, well wrapped, in the refrigerator for 2 days or in the freezer for 2 weeks. Assemble as recipe directs.

SPICE CAKE

MAKES ONE 9-INCH 2-LAYER CAKE

This classic cake will fill your home with a comforting aroma as it bakes.

BAKER'S BASICS TO REVIEW
Separating Eggs, page 22
Measuring Dry Ingredients, page 21
Preparing Cake Pans, page 189
Creaming, page 20
Whipping Egg Whites and Making Meringues, page 198
Folding, page 20
Mixing Cake Batters and Filling Pans, page 189
Baking Cakes, page 190
Cooling and Depanning Cakes, page 190

3/4 cup (6 ounces) unsalted butter

1 1/2 cups sugar

3 large eggs, separated

1 1/2 teaspoons pure vanilla extract

2 1/3 cups cake flour

1/2 teaspoon baking soda

1 1/2 teaspoons baking powder

1 teaspoon ground cinnamon

1/2 teaspoon ground nutmeg

1/2 teaspoon ground cloves

1/2 teaspoon ground ginger

3/4 teaspoon salt

3/4 cup plus 2 tablespoons buttermilk

Preheat oven to 350°. Butter, flour, and line two 9-inch cake pans with parchment paper.

Cream the butter in the bowl of a tabletop mixer fitted with the flat beater. With the mixer running on medium speed, gradually add the sugar. Increase the speed to high and beat until light and fluffy, about 1 minute.

With the mixer running on medium speed, add the egg yolks one at a time, waiting until each is incorporated before adding the next. Blend in the vanilla.

Sift together twice, the flour, the baking soda, the baking powder, the spices, and the salt. With the mixer running on medium-low speed, alternately add the dry ingredients and buttermilk in thirds, waiting until each addition is incorporated before adding the next.

In a separate bowl, whip the egg whites until stiff but not dry. Gently fold the egg whites into the batter. Pour the batter into the prepared pans.

Set the pans on a baking sheet and place on the center rack in the oven. Bake for about 30 minutes, or until the cake springs back when gently pressed and a toothpick comes out clean when inserted in the center.

Let cool completely in the pans on wire racks. This cake may be stored, well wrapped, in the refrigerator for 2 days or in the freezer for 2 weeks. Assemble as recipe directs.

NOTE: Spice cake is delicious iced with caramel- or praline-flavored buttercream (for directions, see "Flavoring Buttercream and Whipped Cream," page 260, or Cream Cheese Icing, page 264).

BANANA CAKE

For this cake, use bananas so ripe they could almost be poured out of their skins.

BAKER'S BASICS TO REVIEW
Preparing Cake Pans, page 189
Measuring Dry Ingredients, page 21
Creaming, page 20
Mixing Cake Batters and Filling Pans, page 189
Baking Cakes, page 190
Cooling and Depanning Cakes, page 190

———

3/4 cup (6 ounces) unsalted butter
2 cups sugar
3 large eggs
2 1/2 cups cake flour
3/4 teaspoon baking powder
1 teaspoon baking soda
3/4 teaspoon salt
1 1/2 cups mashed bananas (about 3 large bananas)
1 1/2 teaspoons pure vanilla extract
3/4 cup buttermilk

Preheat oven to 350°. Butter, flour, and line two 9-inch cake pans with parchment paper.

Cream the butter in the bowl of a tabletop mixer fitted with the flat beater. With the mixer running on medium speed, gradually add the sugar. Increase the speed to high and beat until light and fluffy, about 1 minute. With the mixer running on medium speed, add the eggs one at a time, waiting until each is incorporated before adding the next.

Sift together into a medium bowl the flour, baking powder, baking soda, and salt. In a small bowl, combine the bananas, vanilla, and buttermilk.

With the mixer running on medium-low speed, alternately add the dry ingredients and banana mixture in thirds, waiting until each addition is incorporated before adding the next.

Pour the batter into the prepared pans. Set the pans on a baking sheet and place on the center rack in the oven. Bake for 30 to 35 minutes, or until the cake springs back when gently pressed and a toothpick comes out clean when inserted in the center.

Let cool completely in the pans on wire racks, then depan. This cake may be stored, well wrapped, in the refrigerator for 2 days or in the freezer for 2 weeks. Assemble as recipe directs.

VARIATIONS

We use Banana Cake to make our Banana-Coconut Cake, but you might experiment with other combinations. We especially like to fill and ice Banana Cake with Cream Cheese Icing or Chocolate Cream Cheese Icing (page 264).

ANGEL FOOD CAKE

This is the original fat-free cake, but we bet you won't feel like you've given up a thing when you taste it!

BAKER'S BASICS TO REVIEW
Measuring Dry Ingredients, page 21
Separating Eggs, page 22
Whipping Egg Whites and Making Meringues, page 198
Folding, page 20
Baking Cakes, page 190

———

1 cup sifted cake flour
1 1/2 cups sugar
1 1/2 cups egg whites, at room temperature (about 11 large whites)
2 tablespoons plus 1 teaspoon cold water
1 1/2 teaspoons cream of tartar
1 teaspoon pure vanilla extract or almond extract
1/2 teaspoon salt

Adjust the oven racks so that a 10-inch-diameter x 4-inch-deep tube pan will fit in the oven when placed on the center rack. Preheat the oven to 350°. Set the ungreased tube pan on a baking sheet.

Combine the flour and 1/2 cup of the sugar. Sift together three times. Set aside.

Bring a saucepan of water to a gentle simmer. Fit a tabletop mixer with the whip attachment. Combine the egg whites, water, cream of tartar, vanilla, and salt in the bowl of the mixer. Place the mixer bowl over the pan of barely simmering water. (The water should be at least 2 inches below the bottom of the bowl.) Using a whisk, stir the egg mixture continuously until it is just slightly warm to the touch. When warm, immediately remove the bowl from the heat, place on the mixer, and whip on medium speed just until soft peaks cling to the whip. The mixture will still be foamy but will have at least quadrupled in volume.

With the mixer running on medium speed, very gradually add the remaining 1 cup sugar. Stop whipping as soon as all of the sugar is incorporated.

Transfer the mixture to a large wide-mouthed mixing bowl. With a large spoon or your fingers, sprinkle a scant 1/4 cup of the flour mixture over the egg white mixture. Using a rubber spatula, gently but thoroughly fold the flour mixture into the egg whites until incorporated. Repeat this procedure until all of the flour mixture has been folded in. (Be sure to incorporate any flour that has collected on the edge of the bowl or the handle of the spatula.) Gently spread the batter in the pan and level the top. It will be about 2 inches below the edge of the pan.

Immediately place the cake in the oven. Do not open the oven until the cake has baked for 40 minutes or it may fall. Bake for 45 minutes, or until the top of the cake is a light golden brown, the cake springs back when gently pressed, and a toothpick comes out clean when inserted in the center. The cake will be $1/2$ to 1 inch below the edge of the pan.

Remove the cake from the oven and immediately invert the pan onto the neck of a wine bottle or a large funnel. Let the cake cool completely, suspended on the bottle, about 2 hours.

Remove the pan from the bottle and set it, cake side up, on the work surface. To depan, loosen the cake from the sides by inserting a metal icing spatula between the cake and the pan and gently working around the entire cake. Try to keep the spatula up against the side of the pan so you don't rough up the sides of the cake. Repeat this procedure around the cone in the center. With your hand, push up on the bottom of the pan, letting the sides of the pan fall onto your arm. With the bottom of the pan still attached to the cake, invert the cake onto a 9-inch cake cardboard or a serving platter. Separate the bottom of the pan from the cake by inserting the spatula between the two and working it all the way around. Lift off the bottom of the pan.

This cake may be stored at room temperature in an airtight cake container or covered in plastic wrap for 1 to 2 days. The cake may also be well wrapped and frozen for up to 1 week, but it will lose some of its volume and tenderness.

Making and Filling a Paper Pastry Bag

Paper pastry bags are great for small decorating jobs and are often more practical for home bakers than the large nylon bags because they don't have to be washed and rewashed every time you want to change colors or types of icing or filling.

To make a pastry bag out of parchment paper, cut a triangle that is 12 inches tall from its base to its top point with a 24-inch-long base. Lay the triangle on the work surface with the top point closest to you and the base away from you. Label the top right corner "A," the point closest to you "B," and the top left corner "C."

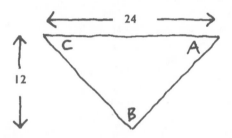

With your right thumb and index finger, take corner A and lift and roll it under and toward the center of the triangle until it meets corner B. The side of the paper at corner A that was facing the work surface should now be lying over corner B and still facing the work surface. The points should match up and the paper should form an open cone.

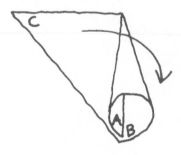

Switch hands and hold corners A and B in place with your left index finger and thumb. Reach across the paper with your right hand, grab corner C and wrap it over and around the open cone, sliding it under corner B.

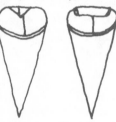

Hold the bag up in front of you, and adjust the corners so that they meet neatly together and a tight seam runs from the tip of the bag to the corners in your hand. If you wish, secure the seam with a piece of tape.

Keeping the corners firmly together, fold them down 1/2 inch toward the inside of the bag, then continue to roll them tightly until the top of the back of the bag (where the seam runs) is almost even with the front of the bag.

To fill the bag, with or without a decorating tip, hold the bag upright in your left hand. If using a decorator tip, place it in the bag and evenly snip off just enough of the end of the bag to allow the decorator tip to stick out. Then, using a spoon or spatula, drop the icing or filling into the bag without getting any on the outside.

Fill the bag two-thirds full, then fold over the top to seal in the icing or filling. If not using a decorator tip, evenly snip off the end of the bag, cutting only high enough to make the size of opening you desire. Procede to decorate as directed.

❀ ❀ ❀

CARROT CAKE WITH CREAM CHEESE ICING

MAKES ONE 9-INCH 2-LAYER CAKE

This traditional favorite is still very popular at the bakery. It is even ordered for wedding cakes. We decorate it with handpainted carrots.

BAKER'S BASICS TO REVIEW

Preparing Cake Pans, page 189

Measuring Dry Ingredients, page 21

Mixing Cake Batters and Filling Pans, page 189

Baking Cakes, page 190

Cooling and Depanning Cakes, page 190

Leveling and Cutting Cakes into Layers, page 191

Assembling, Soaking, Filling, and Icing Cakes, page 192

CAKE

1 1/2 cups vegetable oil

2 cups sugar

4 large eggs, lightly beaten

2 cups all purpose flour

2 teaspoons baking soda

2 teaspoons baking powder

2 teaspoons ground cinnamon

1 teaspoon salt

3 cups grated carrots (4 to 6)

1 cup chopped walnuts (optional)

1/2 cup raisins

———

1 recipe Cream Cheese Icing (page 264)

Preheat oven to 325°. Butter, flour, and line two 9-inch cake pans with parchment paper.

Combine the oil and sugar in the bowl of a tabletop mixer fitted with the flat beater. Add the eggs and mix on medium speed until well blended, about 1 minute.

Combine the dry ingredients, then sift. Add the dry ingredients to the oil-sugar mixture, mixing on medium speed until incorporated, about 1 minute.

Add the carrots, walnuts, and raisins. Mix on medium speed just until incorporated. Pour the batter into the prepared pans.

Set the pans on a baking sheet and place on the center rack in the oven. Bake for about 30 minutes, or until the cake starts to pull away from the sides of the pan and springs back when gently pressed.

CARROT CUPCAKES

This cake can easily be made in cupcake form. Preheat the oven to 325° and make the cake batter as directed. Line muffin tin(s) with 30 paper muffin cups and fill cups two-thirds full, using a ladle or large spoon. (Be careful you don't overfill the cups.) Bake on the center rack in the oven for 30 minutes. (The muffins will be still be soft when done.) Cool in the muffin pan(s)on a wire rack. When completely cool, the cupcakes may be wrapped well and frozen for up to 1 week. To prevent cupcakes from sticking to each other, do not stack them until they are frozen. Using a metal icing spatula, ice cupcakes with 1 recipe of Cream Cheese Icing (page 264). Alternatively, using a nylon pastry bag and a #1 or #2 star tip (see page 188), pipe large rosettes on top of the cupcakes.

Let cool completely in pans on racks, then depan. At this point, the cake may be stored, well wrapped, in the refrigerator for 1 day or in the freezer for 2 weeks.

To assemble the cake, level the tops of the cake layers, if necessary, while they are still frozen. The cake is also easier to ice when still slightly frozen. Place one layer leveled side up on a 9-inch cake cardboard. Using a metal icing spatula, spread the top of the layer with about 1 cup of the icing (it will be a thin coat). Place the other layer cut side down on top of the icing.

Skim coat the entire cake with a thin layer of the cream cheese icing. Place the cake in the refrigerator for about 30 minutes to let the skim coat harden.

Remove the cake from the refrigerator and set it on a serving platter. Ice the cake, swirling the icing with the rounded end of the spatula. Serve at room temperature. The iced cake will keep in an airtight cake container in the refrigerator for 3 days. If refrigerated, let it come to room temperature before serving.

ORANGE CHIFFON CAKE

MAKES ONE 10-INCH CAKE

This cake is an old-time favorite. Orange chiffon has several charms. It is light yet flavorful and relatively low in fat. The orange glaze hardens slightly as it cools and contrasts wonderfully with the soft, moist inside. This cake is fairly foolproof and smells heavenly when baking.

BAKER'S BASICS TO REVIEW
Measuring Dry Ingredients, page 21
Separating Eggs, page 22
Zesting Citrus, page 24
Preparing Cake Pans, page 189
Whipping Egg Whites and Making Meringues, page 198
Folding, page 20
Baking Cakes, page 190
Creaming, page 20

CAKE
2 1/4 cups cake flour
1 1/2 cups sugar
1 tablespoon baking powder
1 teaspoon salt
1/2 cup vegetable oil
6 large egg yolks
3/4 cup freshly squeezed orange juice

2 tablespoons minced orange zest

8 large egg whites

GLAZE

6 tablespoons (3 ounces) salted butter

2 tablespoons minced orange zest

3 cups confectioners' sugar, sifted

2 tablespoons milk

1 teaspoon pure vanilla extract

Adjust the oven racks so that a 10-inch-diameter x 4-inch-deep tube pan with a removable bottom will fit in the oven when placed on the center rack. Preheat the oven to 325°. Lightly butter and flour the tube pan (including the cone in the center). Set the tube pan on a baking sheet.

Sift together the flour, 3/4 cup of the sugar, the baking powder, and salt into a large mixing bowl.

In a small mixing bowl, whisk together the vegetable oil, egg yolks, orange juice and zest.

Whisk the oil mixture into the dry ingredients. Using a wooden spoon or whisk, beat until smooth, about 1 minute. Set aside.

In the bowl of a tabletop mixer fitted with the whip attachment, whip the egg whites on high speed until foamy. With the mixer running, gradually add the remaining 3/4 cup of sugar and whip until the meringue is glossy and forms stiff peaks, about 2 minutes.

With a rubber spatula, fold one-third of the meringue into the batter, then gently but thoroughly fold in the remaining meringue. The batter should hold its shape and should not be thin or runny. Pour the batter into the pan and smooth the top.

Immediately place the pan in the oven and bake for about 50 to 60 minutes, or until the cake springs back when gently pressed and a toothpick comes out clean when inserted in the center. Do not open the oven until the cake has baked for 45 minutes or it may fall.

Remove the cake from the oven and immediately invert the pan onto the neck of a wine bottle or large funnel. Let the cake cool, suspended on the bottle, for 1 hour. While the cake is cooling, prepare the glaze.

To make the glaze, fit the mixer with the flat beater. Cream the butter and zest in the bowl of the mixer. Add the confectioners' sugar and mix on medium-low speed, scraping the bowl twice. The mixture will be crumbly.

Add the milk and vanilla and beat on medium speed until fluffy, about 1 minute. The mixture may look slightly separated. Set aside until ready to use.

After the cake has cooled for 1 hour, it will still be slightly warm and is ready to be assembled. Remove the pan from the bottle and set it cake side up on the work surface. To depan, loosen the cake from the sides by inserting a metal icing spatula between the cake and the pan and gently working around the entire cake. Try to keep the spatula up against the side of the pan so you don't rough up the sides of the cake. Repeat this procedure around the cone in the center. With your hand, push up on the bottom of the pan, letting the sides of the pan fall onto your arm. With the bottom of the pan still attached to the cake, invert the cake onto a 9-inch cake cardboard. Separate the bottom of pan from the cake by inserting the spatula between the two and working it all the way around. Lift off the bottom of the pan. Place the cake on a cooling rack and set the rack on a baking sheet.

Using a metal icing spatula, immediately spread the entire cake, including the hole in the center, with the glaze. The cake will be soft, but the warmth of it will soften the glaze and allow you to spread it easily. If some of the glaze drips onto the baking sheet, just scrape it up and reuse it. When completely iced, transfer the cake to a serving platter.

This cake may be stored at room temperature in an airtight cake container for 3 days. If covering with plastic wrap, let the icing harden for 8 hours before wrapping.

BANANA-COCONUT CAKE

MAKES ONE 9-INCH 2-LAYER CAKE

Even better than Banana Cream Pie, this moist cake has a tropical quality. Make it when summer fruits are out of season.

BAKER'S BASICS TO REVIEW
Filling and Using a Nylon Pastry Bag, page 20
Leveling and Cutting Cakes into Layers, page 191
Assembling, Soaking, Filling, and Icing Cakes, page 192
Garnishing Cakes, page 214

1 Banana Cake (page 205)
1 recipe Soaking Solution (page 257)
4 cups prepared whipped cream (page 258)
1/3 recipe (1 cup) Pastry Cream (page 127)
2 bananas, sliced
2 cups coconut, toasted

Using a long serrated knife, level the cake layers. Place one cake layer leveled side up on a 9-inch cake cardboard. Brush the cake with Soaking Solution. Fill a pastry bag fitted with a #1 or #2 star tip and pipe a border of whipped cream around the outside edge of the cake to hold in the Pastry Cream. Using a metal icing spatula, spread the Pastry Cream on top of the cake, being careful to spread it to the edges. Lay the banana slices in tight concentric circles over the Pastry Cream. Place the other cake layer leveled side down over the Pastry Cream and bananas. Brush it with Soaking Solution. Using a metal icing spatula, skim coat the entire cake with a thin layer of the whipped cream, then refrigerate for 15 minutes. Ice the cake with the remaining whipped cream. The top should be perfectly level and form a right angle with the sides of the cake.

Slide the icing spatula under the cake cardboard and tilt the cake up enough to get the palm of your other hand underneath to lift it without touching the sides. Using the icing spatula, scrape off any whipping cream hanging over the edge of the cardboard.

To cover the sides of the cake with the coconut, continue to hold up the cake with one hand under the cake cardboard. Pick up a handful of the coconut in your other hand and, with your palm slightly cupped, gently press the coconut into the whipped cream, working from the bottom to the top. If desired, sprinkle the top with any remaining coconut. When the sides of the cake are completely covered, tap the cake cardboard to remove any excess coconut.

Transfer the cake to a serving platter and refrigerate until 30 minutes before serving. The cake should be served the day it is made because the bananas will turn brown after 1 day. The cake may be stored overnight in the refrigerator in an airtight container.

Garnishing with grated chocolate or toasted nuts or coconut is not only an easy way to decorate the sides of a cake, it adds flavor and texture. (It's also a great way to hide a less-than-perfect icing job.) Choose a flavor of garnish that complements the cake. To garnish the sides of the cake with chocolate, nuts, or coconut, slide the icing spatula under the cake cardboard and tilt the cake up enough to get the palm of your hand underneath it without touching the sides. Pick up a handful of the chocolate, nuts, or coconut in your other hand and, with your palm slightly cupped, gently press them into the icing on the side of the cake, working from the bottom to the top. When the sides are completely covered, tap the cake cardboard to remove any excess chocolate, nuts, or coconut. The amounts given here will cover the sides of a 9-inch, 3-layer cake.

Grated chocolate: Place 6 ounces of coarsely chopped semisweet chocolate in the bowl of a food processor fitted with the metal blade and pulse until finely grated. Semisweet chocolate in bar form may be finely grated using a metal cheese grater.

Toasted coconut: Spread one 7-ounce package of sweetened shredded coconut on a dry baking sheet. Bake in a preheated 350° oven for about 10 minutes, or until light golden. Let cool completely before using.

Toasted nuts: For garnishing cakes, we prefer to use almonds, pecans, and hazelnuts. For specific toasting instructions, read "Toasting Nuts," page 23.

FLOWER DECORATIONS

Almost twenty years ago, the nosegays of fresh flowers we put on cakes were considered unusual. Now flower garnishes are much more common, and just as beautiful. Whenever possible, use organically grown edible flowers such as violets, pansies, roses, and nasturtiums. Take every precaution to be sure the flowers you use are not poisonous. (Your local poison control center can provide you with a list.) To garnish a cake with flowers, insert their stems directly into the cake. The moisture in the cake and icing will keep them fresh for several hours.

Piping Borders and Other Decorations

The following decorating techniques are simple ways to dress up cakes. First, review the instructions for filling and using a nylon pastry bag (page 20) and for making and filling a paper pastry bag (page 208). So that you can control the bag easily, don't fill it more than two-thirds full. Using even pressure and release are the keys to uniform piping. The end results are also affected by a combination of elements, including the consistency, type, and temperature of the icing; the angle of the bag; and the size of the tip or opening in the end of the bag. Always "bleed" or squeeze the air out of the bag right before piping, even if you've just set the bag down for a minute or two.

To pipe icing, hold your arms fairly close to your body. If you are right-handed, make an open fist (with fingers curled down) with your right hand and grip the top of the bag. Use your left hand to steady the tip between your index and middle fingers, or just let the end of the bag rest on top of your left index finger. Your right arm and hand will do most of the work, squeezing and guiding the bag, which should be held at a 45-degree angle.

Before starting to pipe, gently squeeze it with your right hand to collapse any air bubbles in the icing or filling. As you use up the icing, twist the top of the bag and let the excess hang over your right wrist. If right-handed, you will work from left to right when piping borders, rotating the turntable away from you three or four times for a 9-inch cake. It is not necessary to keep the turntable moving the entire time.

Although there are many cake borders or "trims," as we call them, the shell, "S," and closed and open rosettes are beautiful and appropriate on just about any cake. All three can be made with a #1 or #2 star tip. You can vary the effect of each one by elongating or condensing the individual sections. To pipe a shell border, hold the bag at a 45-degree angle to the cake. Gently squeeze then release while moving the bag slightly to the right. Squeeze, release, and move the same amount for each shell to make a uniform border.

der. To vary the effect, make the shells farther apart by releasing more slowly and moving the bag farther to the right, creating larger "tails" for each shell.

To pipe and "S" scroll, start at the middle on the side of the cake. The scrolls are easier to space evenly if you start by piping 4 equidistant around the cake, then fill in the area between them with 4 more scrolls.

To pipe a rosette, hold the bag at a 45-degree angle to the cake. Start at 2 o'clock and pipe one continuous circle until the desired height is reached, beginning and ending at 2 o'clock. For open rosettes, make the circle more open.

Large individual rosettes may be used as a decoration as well as a border. Closed rosettes look great topped with a sprinkling of grated chocolate or chopped nuts. Open rosettes make nice holders for whole berries.

WRITING ON CAKES

Set aside a little buttercream icing or ganache or keep a small supply in the freezer to use for writing on cakes. Our Buttercream (page 259) is the perfect consistency for writing and can be colored as desired. Chocolate Ganache (page 262) looks sophisticated and is also great to write with; it should be very soft, but not liquid. To write on a cake, snip off the tip of a paper pastry bag, making an opening about the size of a pin head. Fill the bag with the icing or ganache and write away! This is another skill that really improves with practice: keep at it, developing your own style in the process.

LAYERED STRAWBERRY ANGEL FOOD CAKE

MAKES ONE 10-INCH 3-LAYER CAKE

This dramatic-looking cake is easy to assemble and an unusual way to use angel food cake.

BAKER'S BASICS TO REVIEW
Leveling and Cutting Cakes into Layers, page 191
Assembling, Soaking, Filling, and Icing Cakes, page 192
Filling and Using a Nylon Pastry Bag, page 20
Piping Borders and Other Decorations, page 215

1 Angel Food Cake (page 206)
4 cups prepared whipped cream (page 258)
1/2 recipe (1 1/2 cups) Pastry Cream (page 127)
2 to 3 cups strawberries, sliced 1/4 inch thick
8 to 10 whole glazed strawberries (page 123)
Confectioners' sugar

Using a serrated knife, cut the cake into 3 equal layers. Place the bottom (widest) layer cut side up on a 10-inch cake cardboard or a serving platter.

Using a pastry bag fitted with a large #1 or #2 star tip, pipe one 1-inch-thick "S" border of whipped cream around the outside and inside edges of the bottom layer. Using a metal icing spatula or pastry bag, spread or pipe one-half of the Pastry Cream between the borders.

Lay half of the strawberry slices overlapping on the Pastry Cream. Place the middle layer widest part down over the Pastry Cream and strawberries and repeat the filling process. Place the top layer cut side down on the second layer and sift confectioners' sugar over the top.

Place the whipped cream in a pastry bag fitted with a #1 or #2 star tip and pipe 8 to 10 large, evenly spaced rosettes around the top of the cake. Top each rosette with a whole glazed strawberry.

Serve this cake the day it is made, refrigerating it until 30 minutes before serving.

PRINCESS CAKE

MAKES ONE 9-INCH 3-LAYER CAKE

The Princess Cake elicits more oohs and aahs than any other cake in our cases. Its simple and elegant appearance so intrigues people, they have to taste it. The delicate genoise, rich pastry cream, fluffy whipped cream, and sweet marzipan in it all combine in a perfect balance of taste and texture. It is a classic that is wonderfully suited for special occasions, such as bridal and baby showers, sixteenth birthdays, and small weddings.

BAKER'S BASICS TO REVIEW

Leveling and Cutting Cakes into Layers, page 191
Assembling, Soaking, Filling, and Icing Cakes, page 192

———

1 recipe Marzipan, made at least 1 day in advance (page 261)
1 Vanilla Genoise Layer Cake (page 195)
1 recipe Soaking Solution (page 257)
1/3 cup raspberry jam
6 cups prepared whipped cream (page 258)
1/3 recipe (1 cup) Pastry Cream (page 127)
Confectioners' sugar
1 fresh organic pink or white rose

FIRST TIME MAKING A PRINCESS CAKE?

Before attempting to cover a cake with marzipan for the first time, practice covering an inverted 8- or 9-inch bowl. Once you are comfortable with this technique, gather up the marzipan, knead it into a ball, and re-roll to cover the cake.

Bring the marzipan to room temperature at least 1 hour before assembling the cake.

Using a long, serrated knife, level the vanilla genoise, then cut it into 3 even layers. Place the top of the cake cut side down on a 9-inch cake cardboard. Brush it lightly with Soaking Solution, being careful not to oversoak it. Spread the cake with a thin layer of the raspberry jam. (You should almost be able to see through it.) Spread a 1/4-inch-thick layer of the whipped cream over the raspberry jam. Set the middle layer of the cake on the whipped cream. Brush it with Soaking Solution and then spread it with a 3/8-inch layer of the Pastry Cream. Place the remaining cake layer cut side down on top of the Pastry Cream. Brush it with Soaking Solution.

Using a metal icing spatula, skim coat the sides of the cake, icing them with a 1/8-inch-thick coat of whipped cream. There should be just enough whipped cream to seal in all the crumbs and to prevent the marzipan from resting directly on the cake.

Mound all the remaining whipped cream on the top of the cake and, using a metal icing spatula, spread into a dome so that the cake almost looks like an upside-down bowl. Soften the edge where the top of the genoise ends and the dome begins by beveling it with the flat part of the spatula.

Lightly dust a work surface with confectioners' sugar. Place the marzipan on the surface and, using an 18-inch-wide rolling pin, roll out the marzipan as you would roll out pie dough into a 16-inch circle, 1/8 inch thick. Frequently dust the marzipan with plenty of confectioners' sugar and turn the circle to make sure the marzipan is not sticking to the work surface. Using your hand, brush off the excess confectioners' sugar. Don't worry if a lot of confectioners' sugar clings to the marzipan; it will be absorbed.

Set the cake near the rolled out marzipan about 6 inches away from the edge of the work surface so that you can see and reach around the entire cake. Loosely roll the marzipan onto the rolling pin, starting at the back and rolling toward you.

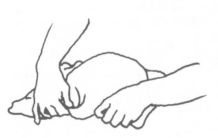Lift the rolling pin with the marzipan wrapped around it. Unroll the marzipan over the cake, starting at the front and unrolling toward the back while making sure to cover the entire cake and cardboard. When finished, some marzipan should drape onto the work surface all around the cake.

At this point, the dome of the cake will be smoothly covered but there will be folds or creases on the sides. To remove the folds and creases, lift the outside edge of the marzipan with one hand on either side of a fold and, without tearing or stretching, gently pull the marzipan out and down until the fold disappears.

Work your way around the cake. Once all the folds are eliminated, rub the palm of your hand around the side of the cake to further smooth it and eliminate air pockets.

With a rolling pizza cutter or small, sharp knife, carefully cut off the excess marzipan along the bottom edge of the cake cardboard. (The cardboard should not show.)

Slide the icing spatula under the cake cardboard and tilt the cake up enough to get the palm of your other hand underneath to lift it without touching the sides. Turn the cake, checking to make sure the cake and cardboard are completely covered with marzipan. If not, gently push the marzipan down using the palm of your other hand.

Set the cake down and sift a fine dusting of confectioners' sugar over it. Transfer to a serving platter.

Cut 3 elongated ovals about 3 inches long by 1 inch wide out of the remaining marzipan to make 3 rose leaf shapes. Lightly score the tops of the leaves with a knife to create veins. Gently bend each leaf into a leaflike curve. Place the leaves, spaced evenly apart, on the center of the domed cake top with the stem ends touching. Gently press the stem ends into the dome to secure the leaves to the top of the cake.

Cut the rose stem 2 inches below the flower. Lift the sepals so they will set over the marzipan leaves and insert the rose into the center of the dome.

The cake may be stored in the refrigerator for up to 2 days, but it is best the day it is made. Remove the cake from the refrigerator 30 minutes before serving.

Cakes, Icings, and Decorations

ITALIAN RUM CAKE

MAKES ONE 9-INCH 4-LAYER CAKE

Rich and satisfying yet light, Italian Rum Cake is a great way to end a special meal or celebration. In this cake, the moist vanilla genoise, smooth pastry cream, and fresh whipped cream are perfumed with Myers's rum. The crunchy candied almonds that cover this cake are the perfect contrast to the soft texture inside. This is a good cake to make if you are not confident of your cake-icing technique. The candied almond garnish covers a multitude of sins while still providing an impressive appearance.

BAKER'S BASICS TO REVIEW

    Separating Eggs, page 22
    Whipping Cream, page 258
    Leveling and Cutting Cakes into Layers, page 191
    Assembling, Soaking, Filling, and Icing Cakes, page 192
    Garnishing Cakes, page 214

CANDIED ALMOND GARNISH

    2 large egg whites
    2 tablespoons sugar
    2 cups sliced almonds

CAKE

    3 cups heavy whipping cream
    3 tablespoons sugar
    3 tablespoons Myers's rum
    1 Vanilla Genoise Layer Cake (page 195)
    1 recipe Soaking Solution (page 257)
    1/3 recipe (1 cup) Pastry Cream, flavored with 1 teaspoon
        Myers's rum (page 127)

Preheat the oven to 350°. Line a large baking sheet with parchment paper or aluminum foil.

To make the candied almonds, whip the egg whites and sugar with a fork or whisk in a medium mixing bowl until frothy. Add the almonds and stir until evenly coated. Spread them in as thin of a layer as possible over the entire baking sheet. Bake for 15 to 16 minutes, or until the almonds are golden brown. Let cool completely on a rack. The almonds will continue to darken slightly and become crisper as they cool.

When cool, lift the parchment and invert it onto the baking sheet. Slowly peel away the paper, leaving the almonds on the sheet. Some parchment may stick to the almonds; just continue to peel them off carefully. Break up any large clumps of nuts with your fingers. Don't worry if some of the almond slices crumble. (The candied almonds may be made up to 2 weeks ahead. Store them in an airtight container at room temperature until ready to use.)

To assemble the cake, first whip the whipping cream, sugar, and rum, following the directions for the vanilla-flavored whipped cream on page 258, except substitute the rum for the vanilla.

Using a long, serrated knife, level the cake, then cut it into 2 even layers. Next, cut each layer into 2 even layers. Place a layer of cake that has been cut on both sides on a 9-inch cake cardboard. Brush it lightly with Soaking Solution, being careful not to oversoak it.

Using a metal icing spatula, spread a heaping cup of the whipped cream on the cake. The whipped cream layer should be about $3/8$ inch thick. Place the layer of cake that has the top crust cut side down over the whipped cream. Brush it with Soaking Solution and then spread it with one-half of the Pastry Cream. Place the other layer of cake that has been cut on both sides over the Pastry Cream. Brush it with Soaking Solution, then spread it with a $3/8$-inch layer of the whipped cream. Place the remaining layer of cake cut side down over the whipped cream. Brush the top with Soaking Solution. Ice the cake with the remaining whipped cream. The top should be perfectly level and form a right angle with the sides of the cake.

Slide the icing spatula under the cake cardboard and tilt the cake up enough to get the palm of your other hand underneath to lift it without touching the sides. Using the icing spatula, scrape off any whipping cream hanging over the edge of the cardboard.

To cover the sides of the cake with the candied nuts, continue to hold the cake up with one hand under the cake cardboard. Pick up a handful of nuts with your other hand and, with your palm slightly cupped, gently press the nuts into the whipped cream on the sides of the cake, working from the bottom to the top.

Once the sides are evenly covered, sprinkle the remaining nuts over the top of the cake. The candied nuts will not completely cover the cake; the whipped cream should peek through in places. Place the cake on a serving platter and refrigerate for at least 30 minutes before serving in order to allow the flavors to marry. This cake is best served the day it is made, but it may be refrigerated overnight in an airtight plastic cake container.

FRESH BERRY GENOISE

This is our version of strawberry shortcake. At Gayle's we are lucky to be located within ten miles of one of the premier berry-growing regions in the country. During the peak season, we make many versions of this cake, using strawberries, raspberries, olallieberries, blackberries, and blueberries, or any combination thereof. For the Fourth of July, we make it in the shape of the U.S. flag and use red and blue berries to make stars and stripes. The cake is so popular even our bakers choose it more often than any other for their own celebrations.

BAKER'S BASICS TO REVIEW
Assembling, Soaking, Filling, and Icing Cakes, page 192
Filling and Using a Nylon Pastry Bag, page 20
Piping Borders and Other Decorations, page 215
Using Fruit Glazes, page 123

———

24 to 30 strawberries, or 2 ($1/2$-pint) baskets of raspberries
1 Vanilla Genoise Layer Cake (page 195)
1 recipe Soaking Solution (page 257)
$1/3$ recipe (1 cup) Pastry Cream (page 127)
4 cups prepared whipped cream (page 258)
$1/2$ cup red currant jelly (if using strawberries),
    or $1/4$ cup (if using raspberries)

If using strawberries, place them in a colander and rinse them with cold water. Spread the strawberries out on a clean towel to dry. If using raspberries, gently wipe with a damp cloth to clean; do not wash with water.

Using a small paring knife, stem, hull, and trim any "white shoulders" from the strawberries. Set the strawberries cut side down on the towel. Select 12 of the nicest, most uniformly sized berries for the top of the cake and set aside. If using raspberries, set aside 36 of the nicest ones for the top.

Using a long, serrated knife, level the top of the vanilla genoise, then cut it into 2 even layers. Place the top layer cut side down on a 10-inch cake cardboard or serving platter. Brush it lightly with Soaking Solution.

Using a metal icing spatula, spread the Pastry Cream on the cake. Cut the strawberries into $1/4$-inch-thick slices. Place the slices on the Pastry Cream in tight concentric circles. If using raspberries, sprinkle the berries close to each other in one layer over the Pastry Cream.

Place the second layer of cake cut side down over the berries. Brush the top with Soaking Solution. Using about one-third of the whipped cream, ice the top and sides of the cake. The whipped cream layer on the top should be about $1/2$ inch thick, smooth, and level. The whipped cream on the sides should only be about $1/4$ inch thick (just enough to hold any crumbs and cover any exposed cake).

Fill a pastry bag fitted with a #1 or #2 star tip with the remaining whipped cream. Pipe 8 horizontal "S" shaped scrolls about 3 to 4 inches wide and 2 to 3 inches tall around the sides of the cake. Pipe with enough pressure to make large, full scrolls.

Next, pipe 12 large open rosettes right next to each other around the top of the cake, about $3/8$ inch in from the outside edge. Again it is easiest to space them evenly apart if you first pipe 4 equally spaced rosettes around the cake and then fill in the space between each one with 2 more equally spaced rosettes.

In a small heavy saucepan over medium heat, heat the currant jelly. Using a small whisk, stir frequently until the jelly is melted and smooth. If using strawberries, hold the berry by the very bottom in one hand. With a 1-inch pastry brush in the other hand, gently brush the berry with glaze, leaving $1/2$ inch unglazed at the base. Place the glazed berry cut side down in the center of a rosette and gently press it in about $1/2$ inch. Repeat until all berries are glazed and placed on cake. Reheat the jelly if it thickens and becomes hard to apply smoothly. As you put the remaining berries on the cake, try to place them so that they face in the same direction. Also, for stability, lean the berries just slightly toward the center. If using raspberries, place three unglazed berries in a triangular shape on each of the rosettes. Once all the raspberries are on the cake, dot each one with a dab of the red currant jelly, using just enough to look like morning dew.

This cake should be served the day it is made. If not serving immediately, store uncovered or in an airtight container in the refrigerator. Remove 30 minutes before serving.

GÂTEAU CITRON

Citron means "lemon" in French. With its rich pastry cream and tart lemon curd moistening and flavoring the vanilla genoise, this delicate and subtle cake is perfect for lemon lovers.

BAKER'S BASICS TO REVIEW

Toasting Nuts, page 23
Folding, page 20
Leveling and Cutting Cakes into Layers, page 191
Assembling, Soaking, Filling, and Icing Cakes, page 192
Filling and Using a Nylon Pastry Bag, page 20
Piping Borders and Other Decorations, page 215
Garnishing Cakes, page 214

$1/2$ recipe ($1 1/2$ cups) Pastry Cream (page 127)
1 recipe English Lemon Curd (page 173)
4 cups prepared whipped cream (page 258)
1 Vanilla Genoise Layer Cake (page 195)
1 recipe Soaking Solution (page 257)
$1/2$ cup ground toasted, skinned hazelnuts (page 23; see also Note)
12 crystallized violets or organic pansies,
    or 1 tablespoon minced lemon zest (optional)
12 small mint leaves (optional)

In a small bowl, combine the Pastry Cream and $1/4$ cup of the lemon curd. Set aside.

In a separate bowl, gently fold $1/2$ cup of the lemon curd into the whipped cream. Set aside.

Using a long, serrated knife, level the vanilla genoise, then cut the cake into 3 even layers. Place the top layer of the vanilla genoise cut side down on a 9-inch cake cardboard. Brush it very lightly with Soaking Solution. Using a metal icing spatula, spread half of the remaining lemon curd over the top of the cake in a very thin layer.

Fill a pastry bag fitted with a large #1 or #2 star tip with a heaping cup of the whipped cream. Pipe a border of the whipped cream around the out–side edge of the cake to hold in the filling. Spread half of the pastry cream–lemon curd mixture inside the border.

Place the layer of cake that has been cut on both sides over the filling. Brush it with Soaking Solution. Spread the cake with the remaining lemon curd. Pipe another border of whipped cream around the top and spread the remaining pastry cream-lemon curd mixture inside the border.

Place the remaining cake layer cut side down over the filling. Brush the top with Soaking Solution. Ice the top and sides with the whipped cream. The top should be perfectly level and form a right angle with the sides.

Slide the icing spatula under the cake cardboard and tilt the cake up enough to get the palm of your other hand underneath to lift it without touching the sides. Using the icing spatula, scrape off any whipped cream hanging over the edge of the cardboard.

To make a 1-inch border of the ground hazelnuts around the base of the entire cake, continue to hold up the cake with one hand under the cake cardboard. Pick up a handful of nuts in your other hand and, with your palm slightly cupped, gently press the nuts into the whipped cream as you work around the cake. When finished, tap the cake cardboard to remove any excess nuts. Set the cake on a serving platter.

Fill a pastry bag fitted with a #1 or #2 star tip with the remaining whipped cream. Pipe 12 evenly spaced 3/4-inch rosettes around the top of the cake. It is easiest to space them evenly apart if you first pipe 4 equally spaced rosettes around the cake and then fill in the space between each one with 2 more equally spaced rosettes.

Garnish the top of each rosette with a crystalized violet or a pansy (or strip of zest) and mint leaf.

This cake is best served the day it is made, although it may be refrigerated overnight in an airtight plastic cake container. Remove the cake from the refrigerator 30 minutes before serving.

NOTE: Grind the toasted, skinned hazelnuts in a food processor by pulsing several times, stopping when they are finely ground but not pastelike.

TIRAMISU

MAKES ONE 9-INCH 3-LAYER CAKE

Tiramisu is an Italian specialty. Translated, *tiramisu* means "pick me up." Several years ago, while traveling in Tuscany, we stopped at Fattoria di Barbi near Montepulciano for lunch. Their tiramisu was incredible, and the owner gladly gave us the recipe, which we've been using for seven years.

Tiramisu deserves its recently won popularity. This moist, luscious cake is the perfect finish to almost any meal, combining the traditional European dessert courses—cheese, sweet, coffee, and liqueur. Mascarpone is a mild and light Italian cream cheese. Its consistency varies considerably: sometimes it is stiff and firm, other times quite soft. Don't worry if your icing is a little different each time you make this cake.

Separating Eggs, page 22

Whipping Cream, page 258

Folding, page 20

Leveling and Cutting Cakes into Layers, page 191

Assembling, Soaking, Filling, and Icing Cakes, page 192

ICING

1 cup heavy whipping cream

3 large egg yolks

3 tablespoons sugar

1 pound imported or domestic mascarpone cheese

_____

1 Vanilla Genoise Layer Cake (page 195)

COFFEE-RUM SOAKING SOLUTION

1¹/4 cups very strong brewed coffee or espresso, cooled

¹/4 cup dark rum

_____

¹/4 cup unsweetened cocoa

To make the icing, whip the cream to soft peaks in the bowl of a table-top mixer fitted with the whip attachment. Transfer the whipped cream to another bowl and set aside.

In the same mixer bowl, again using the whip attachment, whip the egg yolks and sugar on high speed until thick and lemon-colored, about 2 minutes.

Pour off any liquid that has collected on the mascarpone. Add the cheese to the egg yolks and whip on low speed just until blended. The mixture will look slightly separated or grainy. Using a rubber spatula, fold the whipped cream into the mascarpone mixture. Set aside.

In a small bowl, combine the coffee and rum to make the soaking solution. Using a long, serrated knife, level the vanilla genoise, then cut it into 3 even layers. Place the top layer cut side down on a 9-inch cake cardboard. Brush it with ¹/3 cup of the Soaking Solution. Using a metal icing spatula, spread a ¹/4-inch-thick layer of the icing on the cake. Place the layer of cake that has been cut on both sides over the icing. Brush this layer with one-half of the remaining Soaking Solution, then spread it with a ¹/4-inch-thick layer of icing. Place the remaining cake layer cut side down over the icing. Brush it with the remaining Soaking Solution.

Ice the cake with the remaining icing. Although the icing will be very thin and the cake may almost show through in places, try to get the top perfectly level so that it forms a right angle with the sides. Place the cocoa in a fine-mesh sifter and set aside.

Slide the icing spatula under the cake cardboard and tilt the cake up enough to get the palm of your other hand underneath to lift it without touching the sides. Using the icing spatula, scrape off any icing hanging over the edge of the cardboard. Sift a light dusting of cocoa over the top and sides of the cake. Set the cake on a serving platter. Immediately refrigerate the cake, uncovered or in an airtight cake container. This Tiramisu is best refrigerated at least 4 hours or overnight before serving to allow the flavors to marry. It may be stored in an airtight cake container in the refrigerator for up to 2 days.

RICH CHOCOLATE CAKE

MAKES ONE 9-INCH 2-LAYER CAKE

This is one of the two cakes we made when the bakery first opened its doors. It's truly a chocolate lover's dream—moist devil's food, tart jam, and rich ganache icing. The smoothness of the chocolate icing never fails to impress and astound. Many of our customers ask how we get the icing so smooth the first time they see the cake. Most people don't believe that the icing is simply poured on.

BAKER'S BASICS TO REVIEW
  Leveling and Cutting Cakes into Layers, page 191
  Assembling, Soaking, Filling, and Icing Cakes, page 192
  Filling and Using a Nylon Pastry Bag, page 20

———

  1 Devil's Food Cake (page 199)
  1 recipe Soaking Solution (page 257)
  1/3 cup apricot or raspberry jam (see Note)
  Double recipe (6 cups) Chocolate Ganache,
      made 1 day in advance (page 262)

Using a long, serrated knife, level the top of both cake layers. Place one cake layer leveled side up on a 9-inch cake cardboard circle. Brush the top of the cake thoroughly with Soaking Solution. Spread the jam on the cake in a thin layer, being careful not to let it drip over the edge. Place the other cake layer cut side down over the jam. Brush the top layer thoroughly with Soaking Solution.

To skim coat the cake, the ganache should be the consistency of whipped cream cheese. If it is too soft, it will be difficult to get the desired sharp edges. Using an icing spatula, apply a very thin skim coat of ganache (some of the cake should show through). Refrigerate the cake for 15 minutes so the skim coat will set up. Once the first skim coat is set, apply a second skim coat,

RICH CHOCOLATE CAKE VARIATIONS

This cake may be filled with any flavor of butter-cream or whipped cream instead of jam. However, these fillings are softer than jam and may cause the cake to shift during skim coating. To prevent this, using a pastry bag fitted with a large #1 or #2 star tip, pipe a 1/2-inch-border of ganache around the top outside edge of the bottom cake layer before you spread it with the filling. This will hold the filling in and stabilize the cake.

Skim coat and glaze the cake as directed. When filled with buttercream or whipped cream, the cake should be refrigerated (which dulls the sheen of the icing a bit) about 15 minutes after it is glazed, then removed from the refrigerator to soften 1 hour before serving. Refrigerate leftover cake in an airtight cake container.

We even make this cake, layered with various fillings, into huge 4- or 5-tiered wedding cakes decorated with handmade chocolate roses or colorful fresh flowers. It's a dramatic change from the ubiquitous all-white cake.

working quickly so the chilled cake doesn't cause the ganache to set up. The final skim coat must be extra smooth. The top of the cake should be perfectly level and form a right angle with the sides. (This makes the final icing more sleek and professional looking.)

Slide the icing spatula under the cake cardboard and tilt the cake up enough to get the palm of your other hand underneath to lift it without touching the sides. Using the icing spatula, scrape off any ganache hanging over the edge of the cardboard. Set a wire rack on a baking sheet and place the cake on the rack.

To glaze the cake, reheat and cool the remaining ganache as directed on page 263. The ganache is ready for glazing when it is still slightly warm and is the consistency of unwhipped heavy cream. Hold the bowl of ganache about 4 inches over the cake and quickly pour it in a circular motion over the top. Start in the center and work out to the edges, letting the ganache flow over the sides until they are completely covered.

Pouring the glaze should only take a few seconds, so work quickly. Any large air bubbles may be popped with the point of a sharp knife if done immediately after pouring. Let the cake sit undisturbed for 15 minutes after glazing. Remove the cake from the rack without touching the sides and use the icing spatula to scrape off any ganache that has dripped over the edge of the cardboard. Transfer the cake to a serving platter.

Let the cake set up at room temperature at least 1 hour before serving. This cake should not be refrigerated or it will lose its shine. It keeps at room temperature for 2 days, but is best served the day it is made. Store in a cool location out of direct sunlight in an airtight plastic cake container.

NOTE: If you prefer a smooth filling, process the jam in a food processor or blender.

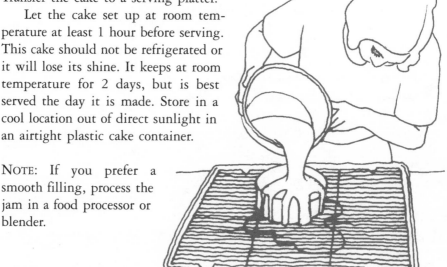

GERMAN CHOCOLATE CAKE

MAKES ONE 9-INCH 3-LAYER CAKE

The only problem with making our German Chocolate Cake is that you'll want to eat the icing by the spoonful before you assemble the cake. For this cake, a gooey, caramely, nutty, coconut-laced icing is layered between moist devil's food, which is then iced with ganache. It's a Father's Day favorite at the bakery, but it's also great for picnics because it can be left out of the refrigerator for quite a while.

BAKER'S BASICS TO REVIEW

Separating Eggs, page 22

Toasting Nuts, page 23

Leveling and Cutting Cakes into Layers, page 191

Assembling, Soaking, Filling, and Icing Cakes, page 192

Filling and Using a Nylon Pastry Bag, page 20

Piping Borders and Other Decorations, page 215

Garnishing Cakes, page 214

GERMAN CHOCOLATE ICING

1 cup heavy whipping cream

1 cup sugar

4 large egg yolks

$1/2$ cup (4 ounces) butter, cut into 4 pieces

1 tablespoon pure vanilla extract

$2^2/3$ cups (one 7-ounce package) sweetened shredded coconut

2 cups coarsely chopped pecans, lightly toasted (page 23)

1 Devil's Food Cake, baked in three pans (page 199)

1 recipe Soaking Solution (page 257)

1 recipe Chocolate Ganache, made 1 day in advance (page 262)

1 cup pecan pieces, lightly toasted and finely ground
  (page 23; see also Note)

To make the German Chocolate Icing, with a whisk mix together the cream, sugar, and egg yolks in the top of a double boiler off the heat. Add the butter and heat the mixture over boiling water. Once the butter has melted, cook for 10 minutes, whisking occasionally, until slightly thickened. Remove from the heat and pour the mixture into a medium mixing bowl. Whisk in the vanilla. Let cool completely, stirring occasionally, about 2 hours.

When the sugar-egg mixture is cool, stir in the coconut and pecans. Let sit for 15 minutes. Use as directed or store tightly covered in the refrigerator for up to 1 week. If refrigerated, let come to room temperature and stir to remix before using.

Using a long, serrated knife, level the tops of the cake layers. Place one cake layer leveled side up on a 9-inch cake cardboard. Brush the cake with Soaking Solution. Using a metal icing spatula, spread one-third of the German Chocolate Icing onto the cake, being careful to spread it to the edges but not onto the sides. Place another cake layer leveled side up over the icing. Brush it with Soaking Solution and then spread it with one-third of the German Chocolate Icing. Place the last layer of cake leveled side down over the icing. Lightly brush with Soaking Solution. Let the cake sit for a minute or two to absorb the soaking solution.

Ice the sides of the cake with a thin coat of the ganache, using just enough to form straight sides. Fill a pastry bag fitted with a #1 or #2 star tip with ganache. Pipe a $1/2$-inch border of ganache around the top outside edge of the cake. With the icing spatula, spread the remaining German Chocolate Icing on top of the cake inside the ganache border.

Slide the icing spatula under the cake cardboard and tilt the cake up enough to get the palm of your other hand underneath to lift it without touching the sides. Using the icing spatula, scrape off any ganache hanging over the edge of the cardboard.

To cover the sides of the cake with the nuts, continue to hold up the cake with one hand under the cake cardboard. Pick up a handful of the nuts in your other hand and, with your palm slightly cupped, gently press the nuts into the ganache, working from the bottom to the top. When the sides of the cake are completely covered, tap the cake cardboard to remove any excess nuts.

Transfer the cake to a serving platter and serve at room temperature. The German Chocolate Cake may be stored at room temperature for 1 day or refrigerated in an airtight cake container for 3 days. Let the cake return to room temperature before serving.

NOTE: Grind the pecans in a food processor by pulsing several times, stopping when they are finely ground but not pastelike.

OPERA CAKE

MAKES ONE 9-INCH 4-LAYER CAKE

In France, you'll find *L'Opera* in almost every pâtisserie. Thin layers of vanilla and hazelnut cake are combined to create this classic, elegant cake. Beautiful when cut, one of our recipe testers thought it might be named Opera Cake because the many layers look like stacks of sheet music.

BAKER'S BASICS TO REVIEW
Leveling and Cutting Cakes into Layers, page 191
Assembling, Soaking, Filling, and Icing Cakes, page 192

———

3 tablespoons instant espresso powder
1 1/2 teaspoons hot water
1/2 recipe (3 cups) Buttercream (page 259)
1 Hazelnut Sponge Cake (page 201)
1 Vanilla Genoise Layer Cake (page 195)
1/2 recipe (6 tablespoons) Soaking Solution (page 257)
Double recipe (6 cups) Chocolate Ganache, made 1 day in advance
    (page 262)

In a small bowl, dissolve the espresso powder in the water. Using a whisk, stir the espresso mixture into the buttercream until well blended. Set aside.

Using a long, serrated knife, level and trim each hazelnut layer to about 3/8 inch thick or no thicker than 1/2 inch thick. Set aside.

Using the serrated knife, level the genoise, then cut it into 2 layers the same height as the hazelnut layers. Cover the layers tightly with plastic wrap and freeze any remaining genoise for another use.

Place one of the layers of the genoise cut side down on a 9-inch cake cardboard. Brush it lightly with Soaking Solution. Using a metal icing spatula, spread the cake with 1/3 cup of the ganache. Because the ganache layer is so thin, it may pick up some cake crumbs as it is spread, which is okay; just blend them in. Spread 1 cup of buttercream over the ganache. Place a layer of hazelnut cake over the buttercream. Don't worry that the hazelnut cake is slightly smaller in diameter than the genoise. The skim coat will hide any difference in size. Do not brush the hazelnut cake with soaking solution. Spread the hazelnut cake with 1/3 cup of the ganache. Spread 1 cup of buttercream over the ganache. Place the other layer of genoise over the buttercream. Brush it with Soaking Solution. Spread it with 1/3 cup of the ganache. Spread another cup of buttercream over the ganache. Place the other layer of hazelnut cake leveled side down on the buttercream.

To skim coat the cake, the ganache should be the consistency of whipped cream cheese. If it is too soft, it will be difficult to get the desired sharp edges. Using an icing spatula, apply a very thin skim coat of ganache (some of the cake should show through). Refrigerate the cake for 30 minutes so the skim coat will set up. Once the first skim coat is set, apply a second skim coat, working quickly so the chilled cake doesn't cause the ganache to set up. The final skim coat must be extra smooth. The top of the cake should be perfectly level and form a right angle with the sides. (This makes the final icing more sleek and professional looking.)

Slide the icing spatula under the cake cardboard and tilt it up enough to get the palm of your other hand underneath the cake to lift it without touching the sides. Scrape off any ganache hanging over the edge of the cardboard. Set a wire rack on a baking sheet and place the cake on the rack.

To glaze the cake, reheat and cool the ganache as directed on page 263. The ganache is ready for glazing when it is still slightly warm and is the consistency of unwhipped heavy cream. Hold the bowl of ganache about 4 inches over the cake and quickly pour it in a circular motion over the cake. Start in the center and work out to the edges, letting the ganache flow over the sides until they are completely covered.

Pouring the glaze should only take a few seconds, so work quickly. Any large air bubbles may be popped with the point of a sharp knife if done immediately after pouring. Let the cake sit undisturbed for 15 minutes after glazing. Remove the cake from the rack without touching the sides and use the icing spatula to scrape off any ganache that has dripped over the bottom edge of the cardboard. Transfer the cake to a serving platter.

Let the cake set up at room temperature at least 1 hour before serving. The cake should be served at room temperature, but should be stored in the refrigerator if it is not served within 4 hours after it is made. It may be stored in the refrigerator uncovered for 1 day or in an airtight container for 3 days. Once refrigerated, the cake should be returned to room temperature at least 2 hours and up to 6 hours before serving.

RASPBERRY-POPPY SEED CAKE

MAKES ONE 9-INCH 3-LAYER CAKE

We like the way the fruity, sweet raspberries complement the earthy poppy seeds, as well as the wonderful color they give the whipped cream icing.

BAKER'S BASICS TO REVIEW

Leveling and Cutting Cakes into Layers, page 191
Whipping Cream, page 258
Folding, page 20
Assembling, Soaking, Filling, and Icing Cakes, page 192
Filling and Using a Nylon Pastry Bag, page 20
Piping Borders and Other Decorations, page 215

———

1 Poppy Seed Cake (page 202)
3/4 cup raspberry jam
4 cups prepared whipped cream (page 258)
1 recipe Soaking Solution (page 257)

Using a long, serrated knife, level the top of one of the cake layers, cutting off just enough so that none of the brown crust remains. Flip over the layer and again cut off any brown crust on the bottom. This will become the middle layer. Level the tops of the two other layers, cutting off just enough so that they are the same height as the middle layer.

In a small bowl, stir the jam with a whisk to break up any large lumps. Using a rubber spatula, fold the jam into the whipped cream.

Place one of the cake layers that has been leveled on only one side cut side up on a 10-inch cake cardboard or serving platter. Brush it with Soaking Solution.

Using a metal icing spatula, spread 1 heaping cup of the whipped cream on the cake; the icing should be about 3/8 inch thick. Place the middle layer over the whipped cream. Brush it with Soaking Solution. Spread it with another cup of the whipped cream. Place the remaining layer cut side down on the whipped cream. Brush the top with Soaking Solution. Ice the cake with a final coat of whipped cream. The top should be perfectly level and form a right angle with the sides.

Fill a pastry bag fitted with a #1 or #2 star tip with the remaining whipped cream, and pipe an "S" border around both the top edge and base of the cake.

This cake is best served the day it is made, but it may be stored overnight in an airtight cake container in the refrigerator.

Norman Love: A Master Craftsman

Norman Love is a self-described "pastry animal." You can see his playfulness as he strides around the pastry kitchen, perpetually searching for the next task to attack. At age thirty-seven, Norman is the executive pastry chef at the Ritz-Carlton in Naples, Florida. Part of his job is the formidable task of overseeing the pastry production for thirty-one Ritz-Carlton hotels worldwide. A typical month of travel for Norman might include flying to Seoul to set up the pastry kitchen for a new Ritz-Carlton hotel, then on to Washington, DC, to make a cake for the Smithsonian Institute's 150-year celebration, and, finally, to Chicago to help orchestrate a New Year's Eve banquet for two thousand people.

When Joe and I met Norman, he was working in a climatized pastry room in the basement of the Ritz-Carlton in Kapalua, Maui, teaching the pastry staff how to make chocolate filigree lattices to decorate the tops of cakes. When we exchanged business cards, we thought we'd just made another contact with a friendly, creative chef, whose busy work schedule might prevent us from ever having the opportunity to get to know him. Several months later, we got a call from Norman. He said he wanted to study with our bread bakers to learn hearth breads, and in exchange he would conduct several classes on chocolate and pastry making for our staff and customers. The deal was set.

On the appointed day of his arrival, Norman showed up with two black duffel bags—one bag for his clothes and another containing all of the tools, implements, and contraptions he uses to make original, architectural pastries.

Armed with his spray gun, offset metal spatula, set of pastry combs, and expanded aluminum screens, he descended on our pastry kitchen and, in two days of hands-on instruction, showed our pastry bakers creative ways to update, and revitalize our desserts. Using a spray gun actually designed for spraying oil- or latex-based paints (but adapted by Love to spray melted chocolate), he sprayed a textured coating onto a sculpture he made out of couverture chocolate so it looked like velvet. After laying down coats of milk, dark, and white chocolate on a piece of clear plastic, he dragged and scraped the chocolate with a pastry comb (normally used for spreading tile mastic), creating a design that looked like tree bark or the skin of an alligator. With the offset spatula he spread chocolate over the metal screens (originally manufactured to serve as the bottom panels for screen doors) onto a clear plastic sheet. When the metal was lifted away, a patterned design was left on the plastic sheet below; when the chocolate dried, small pieces of it were cut and used to decorate cakes or petits fours. For tempering chocolate, he uses a wide-blade metal spackle knife.

Norman explains that you can buy this equipment in a pastry supply shop in Paris, but you'll pay a fortune for it. Instead, he scours his local hardware store for items that can be adapted.

We learned a lot from Norman's ingenuity and creativity. Perhaps most important, we learned to look at simple "tools" from a new perspective. As you dabble in your pastry kitchen, be sure to follow Norman's lead and use your imagination.

❧ ❧ ❧

LEMON–POPPY SEED CAKE

MAKES ONE 9-INCH 3-LAYER CAKE

A classic combination, the tangy lemon curd and rich buttercream are the perfect partners for moist poppy seed cake. This is one of our most popular wedding cakes.

BAKER'S BASICS TO REVIEW
Leveling and Cutting Cakes into Layers, page 191
Assembling, Soaking, Filling, and Icing Cakes, page 192
Filling and Using a Nylon Pastry Bag, page 20
Piping Borders and Other Decorations, page 215
Making and Filling a Paper Pastry Bag, page 208
Zesting Citrus, page 24

———

1 Poppy Seed Cake (page 202)
Double recipe (2½ cups) English Lemon Curd (page 173)
1 recipe Buttercream (page 259)
1 recipe Soaking Solution (page 257)
1 lemon, for zesting
1 teaspoon poppy seeds

Using a long, serrated knife, level the top of one of the layers of the cake, cutting off just enough so that none of the brown crust remains. Flip over the layer and again cut off any brown crust on the bottom. This will become the middle layer. Level the tops of the two other layers, cutting off just enough so that they are the same height as the middle layer.

Using a whisk, blend 1¼ cups of the lemon curd into the buttercream. It may look slightly separated or grainy. Set aside.

Place one of the cake layers that has been leveled on only one side cut side up, on a 10-inch cake cardboard or serving platter. Brush it with Soaking Solution. Using a metal icing spatula, spread about 3 tablespoons of lemon curd over the top of the cake. (The coat of lemon curd will almost be thin enough to see through.) Spread a heaping cup of the buttercream over the lemon curd. (Don't worry if some of the lemon curd gets pushed over the edge of the cake.) The buttercream layer should be about ¼ inch thick. Place the middle layer over the buttercream. Brush it with Soaking Solution. Spread the remaining lemon curd and another heaping cup of buttercream on top of the middle layer. Place the remaining layer leveled side down on the buttercream. Brush the top with Soaking Solution. Using the spatula, blend together and spread any lemon curd or buttercream that has dripped out from between the layers onto the sides of the cake.

Skim coat the cake with a thin layer of buttercream, using the icing to smooth out the sides and make the top level. Refrigerate the cake for at least 30 minutes.

Ice the cake with a final coat of buttercream, heating the spatula to help smooth the buttercream if necessary. The top should be perfectly level and form a right angle with the sides.

Fill a pastry bag fitted with a #1 or #2 star tip with the remaining buttercream. Pipe sixteen to twenty 1/2-inch rosettes in a tight ring around both the top and base of the cake.

Fill a paper pastry bag with the remaining lemon curd. Cut a small hole in the tip and pipe a dot of lemon curd on each rosette.

Remove 1 teaspoon zest from the lemon and mince. Sprinkle both the poppy seeds and zest over both the borders.

The cake should be served at room temperature, but should be stored in the refrigerator if it is not served within 4 hours after it is made. It may be stored uncovered in the refrigerator for 1 day or in an airtight plastic cake container for 3 days. Once refrigerated, the cake should be returned to room temperature to soften at least 2 and up to 6 hours before serving.

BANANA SPLIT CAKE

MAKES ONE 9-INCH 2-LAYER CAKE

As you might imagine, this banana cake, which is filled with a thin layer of ganache and strawberry whipped cream, is very popular with kids and teenagers. The outside is iced with vanilla-flavored whipped cream and decorated with a border that resembles miniature banana splits: scoops of vanilla whipped cream are drizzled with a ganache, then topped with a dab of strawberry jam.

BAKER'S BASICS TO REVIEW
Toasting Nuts, page 23
Leveling and Cutting Cakes into Layers, page 191
Assembling, Soaking, Filling, and Icing Cakes, page 192
Garnishing Cakes, page 214
Making and Filling a Paper Pastry Bag, page 208
Piping Borders and Other Decorations, page 215

1 Banana Cake (page 205)
1 recipe Soaking Solution (page 257)
1/4 recipe (3/4 cup) Chocolate Ganache, cooled (page 262)
4 cups prepared whipped cream (page 258)
1/2 cup strawberry jam
1/2 cup toasted almonds, finely chopped (page 23)

Using a long, serrated knife, level the cake layers. Place one of the layers leveled side up on a 9-inch cake cardboard. Brush it with Soaking Solution. Using a metal icing spatula, spread the cake with one-half of the ganache.

Combine 1 cup of the whipped cream with 1/4 cup of the jam. Spread the whipped cream mixture over the ganache on the bottom cake layer. Place the other cake layer leveled side down on the whipped cream. Brush it with Soaking Solution.

Ice the cake, using most of the remaining whipped cream. The top should be perfectly level and form a right angle with the sides.

Slide the icing spatula under the cake cardboard and tilt the cake up enough to get the palm of your other hand underneath to lift it without touching the sides. Using the icing spatula, scrape off any whipped cream hanging over the edge of the cardboard.

To make a 1-inch border of the chopped almonds around the base of the entire cake, continue to hold up the cake with one hand under the cardboard. Pick up a handful of the nuts in your other hand and, with your palm slightly cupped, gently press the nuts into the whipped cream, as you work around the cake. When finished, tap the cake cardboard to remove any excess nuts. Set the cake on a serving platter.

Using a melon baller, place 10 evenly spaced scoops of the whipped cream around the outside edge of the cake, dipping the melon baller in water between each scoop.

Place the remaining ganache in a paper pastry bag. Pipe it loosely over each scoop to resemble hot fudge. Place the remaining jam in a paper pastry bag and dot each scoop with a dab of jam.

This cake is best served the day it is made, but it may be refrigerated overnight in an airtight plastic cake container.

CHOCOLATE MOUSSE CAKE

MAKES ONE 9-INCH 4-LAYER CAKE

CHOCOLATE MOUSSE CAKE ADVANCE PREPARATION SCHEDULE

Although the recipe looks challenging because of its many steps, it is actually easy to master and very versatile. Temperature and timing are especially important when making the mousse layer; be sure to have all the ingredients measured and at room temperature and all the equipment ready. In order to make this recipe a little less daunting, we have provided the following advance preparation schedule:

Step 1: The Devil's Food Cake can be made and frozen up to 2 weeks in advance. If made the same day the cake is assembled, bake and cool it at least 2 hours before starting the mousse layer.

Step 2: The mousse layer can be made and frozen up to 2 weeks in advance. If made the same day the cake is assembled, prepare and freeze it at least 3 hours before making the whipped cream layer.

Step 3: The ganache should be made the day before the whipped cream layer is prepared. If the cake isn't going to be glazed the day after making the whipped cream layer is made, refrigerate the ganache until ready to use it again.

This is another recipe that we learned at Le Feyeaux in Paris. After seventeen years, it's still our best-selling cake. With four layers of chocolate—devil's food cake, chocolate mousse, whipped cream, and ganache—this the ultimate chocolate dessert. We bake it once or twice a week in a batch that requires 224 eggs—all separated by hand.

You can create your own variations by substituting Hazelnut Sponge Cake (page 201) for the devil's food or by using different toppings, such as Mocha Whipped Cream (page 2580). The mousse itself can also be used as a cake filling.

BAKER'S BASICS TO REVIEW

Leveling and Cutting Cakes into Layers, page 191
Separating Eggs, page 22
Melting Chocolate, page 21
Whipping Egg Whites and Making Meringues, page 198
Creaming, page 20
Folding, page 20
Whipping Cream, page 258
Garnishing Cakes, page 214

———

1 layer Devil's Food Cake, leveled and cut $1/4$ inch thick (page 199)

MOUSSE LAYER

$3 1/2$ ounces unsweetened chocolate, coarsely chopped
1 ounce semisweet chocolate, coarsely chopped
6 large eggs, separated
$1 1/2$ cups sugar
$1/3$ cup water
1 cup (8 ounces) unsalted butter
$1/2$ cup twice-sifted unsweetened cocoa

WHIPPED CREAM LAYER

1 cup heavy whipping cream
1 tablespoon sugar
$1/6$ recipe ($1/2$ cup) Chocolate Ganache, cooled (page 262)

———

$1/3$ recipe (1 cup) Chocolate Ganache (page 262)
1 cup ground toasted hazelnuts (page 23; see also Note),
    or 1 cup finely grated semisweet chocolate

Place the cake in the bottom of a 9-inch-diameter x 2-inch-deep spring-form pan or cake pan with a removable bottom. Set aside.

To make the mousse, in the top of a double boiler over low heat, combine and melt the chocolates. Remove from heat and set aside.

Place the egg whites in the bowl of a tabletop mixer fitted with the whip attachment. Set a glass of water, a small pastry brush, and a candy thermometer next to the stove.

Combine 1 cup and 2 tablespoons of the sugar and the ⅓ cup water in a small heavy saucepan (ideally one with a pouring spout), then place the candy thermometer in the saucepan. Cook the mixture, without stirring, over medium-high heat for approximately 4 minutes. While cooking, use the pastry brush dipped in water to brush down the sides of the pan two or three times to prevent sugar crystals from forming. When the syrup reaches 220°, decrease the heat to medium and start whipping the egg whites on medium speed. When the whites are foamy, add the remaining ¼ cup and 2 tablespoons sugar and continue whipping. Immediately remove the syrup from the heat. At this point the egg whites should form soft peaks, not stiff or dry, and the syrup should be at approximately 230°. With the mixer running, add the syrup in a steady stream to the egg whites. As soon as the syrup is incorporated, turn off the mixer. Transfer the meringue to a large wide-mouthed bowl, leaving any of the syrup that is stuck to the sides of the bowl. Let cool.

In the bowl of the mixer refitted with the flat beater, cream the butter, scraping the bowl often, until it is very fluffy, about 2 minutes. Add the melted chocolate to the butter. The chocolate should now be just cool, but not thick or chunky. Beat until very fluffy, scraping the bowl often, about 2 minutes. With the mixer on low speed, add the egg yolks one at a time, waiting until each is incorporated before adding the next. Beat until fluffy, scraping the bowl often.

With the mixer off, add the cocoa. Start mixing on very low speed. Once the cocoa is incorporated, scrape down the bowl and beater. Beat on high speed until fluffy, scraping the bowl often. At this point the meringue should be cool and at approximately the same temperature as the butter mixture.

Fold one-quarter of the meringue into the butter mixture to lighten it, then fold in the remainder. Return the mousse to the mixer bowl and, using the whip attachment, mix on the lowest speed just until smooth, about 30 seconds. Spread the mousse evenly over the cake layer in the pan, covering it completely and smoothing it to deflate any air pockets. It will come to about ¾ inch from the rim of the pan. Freeze for at least 2 hours before continuing.

To make the whipped cream layer, whip the cream and sugar on high speed until very soft peaks form. Do not overwhip; the cream will thicken when you add the ganache. Add the ganache, whipping on low speed just

Step 4: The whipped cream layer can be made and frozen up to 2 weeks in advance. If made the same day the cake is assembled, prepare and freeze it at least 2 hours before glazing the cake.

Step 5: The cake may be glazed up to 24 hours before serving.

Step 6: Thaw the cake in the refrigerator at least 4 hours before serving.

Cakes, Icings, and Decorations

until blended. Spread the mixture evenly over the frozen mousse cake. Freeze for at least 2 hours before continuing.

To glaze the mousse cake, reheat and cool the ganache as directed on page 263. The ganache is ready for glazing when it is still slightly warm and is the consistency of unwhipped heavy cream. Remove the pan from the freezer. Pour a 5-inch pool of ganache onto the center of the mousse cake. Pick up the pan and quickly tilt it in a circular motion to spread the ganache out to the edges while keeping the ganache below the lip of the pan. Let the ganache set up for 5 minutes.

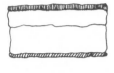

To depan the mousse cake, dampen two or three kitchen towels with hot water and wring out well. Wrap the sides of the pan with the towels, being careful not to get any drops of water on the ganache, and let it sit for about 2 minutes. Test to see if the mousse cake is loose enough to depan by barely releasing the tension of the sides of the springform pan or, if using a removable-bottom pan, by slightly pushing up on the bottom of the pan while holding the side of the pan with your other hand. If the mousse cake yields to gentle pressure, continue to depan by releasing the sides or pushing up on the removable bottom and letting the ring fall onto your arm. If it isn't quite ready, repeat the hot towel procedure.

The cake may be left on the base of the pan or transfered to a 9-inch cake cardboard. To transfer the cake, work the spatula underneath the cake in a gentle sawing motion. Using the spatula, tilt the cake up and place the palm of your other hand under it. Supporting the cake with your open palm, set the back edge of the cake on the cardboard or platter. Support the front edge of the cake with the spatula as you slowly remove your hand and lower the cake onto the cardboard. Gently pull the spatula out from underneath the cake.

To cover the sides of the mousse cake with the nuts, slide the icing spatula under the cake cardboard and tilt the cake up enough to get the palm of your other hand underneath to lift it without touching the sides. While continuing to hold up the mousse cake with one hand under the cake cardboard, pick up a handful of the nuts (or grated chocolate) in your other hand and, with your palm slightly cupped, gently press the nuts into the side of the mousse cake, working from the bottom to the top. When the sides are completely covered, tap the cake cardboard to remove any excess nuts. Set the cake on a serving platter.

Let the mousse cake thaw uncovered in the refrigerator for 4 to 24 hours before serving. If it is not being served until the next day, store in an airtight plastic cake container for up to 3 days, but the whipped cream layer may soften slightly after the second day.

NOTE: Grind the toasted, skinned hazelnuts in a food processor by pulsing several times, stopping when they are finely ground but not pastelike.

CHOCOLATE SOUFFLÉ ROLL

MAKES ONE 15-INCH-LONG CAKE ROLL

This cake is as much of a pleasure to make as it is to eat. It doesn't require a lot of complicated ingredients or techniques, and it shows off the soft, subtle side of chocolate not often seen. After it is rolled, the soufflé absorbs a little moisture from the whipped cream, creating a wonderful texture that is fudgy but light and airy at the same time. Flourless and without any leavening, it's a great cake for Passover or for anyone allergic to flour.

BAKER'S BASICS TO REVIEW

Melting Chocolate, page 21
Separating Eggs, page 22
Whipping Egg Whites and Making Meringues, page 258
Folding, page 20
Mixing Cake Batters and Filling Pans, page 189
Whipping Cream, page 258
Cooling and Depanning Cakes, page 190

SOUFFLÉ

6 ounces semisweet chocolate, coarsely chopped
6 large eggs
Pinch of salt
3/4 cup sugar
1 1/2 teaspoons pure vanilla extract
2 tablespoons brewed coffee, cooled

FILLING

1 cup heavy whipping cream
1 tablespoon sugar
1 teaspoon Grand Marnier

Preheat the oven to 350°. Line the bottom and ends of a 15 x 10-inch jelly roll pan with parchment paper, making sure it is snugly fitted into the corners. Hold the paper in place with tiny dabs of butter underneath each corner.

In a medium mixing bowl set over a medium saucepan of barely simmering water, melt the chocolate. Remove the pan from the heat and let cool about 5 minutes.

Separate the eggs. Place the egg whites in the bowl of a tabletop mixer fitted with the whip attachment or in a large mixing bowl. Place the egg yolks in a small mixing bowl and set aside. Whip the egg whites until foamy and, while whipping, add the pinch of salt and then gradually add the sugar. Whip until the meringue is glossy and forms stiff peaks. Set aside.

With a whisk, stir together the egg yolks and the vanilla, then whisk into

Cakes, Icings, and Decorations

the cooled chocolate mixture. The mixture will thicken slightly. Whisk the cooled coffee into the chocolate mixture.

Using a rubber spatula, fold one-quarter of the meringue into the chocolate mixture to lighten it, then thoroughly but gently fold in the rest of the meringue. Make sure there are no white pockets of meringue or dark streaks of chocolate remaining.

Spread the batter in the prepared pan, making it as level as possible with a plastic bowl scraper or offset spatula. Place the soufflé on the center rack in the oven and bake for 18 minutes. To check for doneness, lift a small section of the top crust with a paring knife. The soufflé underneath should look very moist and airy, not wet. Let cool in the pan on a wire rack for 1 hour. Do not roll the soufflé in a towel as is customarily done for jelly roll cakes.

To make the filling, whip the cream, sugar, and Grand Marnier.

To assemble the soufflé, lay a 22 x 12-inch piece of plastic wrap perpendicular to the edge of the work surface. Gently flip the soufflé onto the plastic wrap. Carefully peel away the parchment paper.

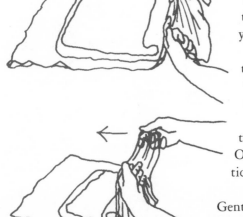

Using a metal icing spatula, spread the whipped cream evenly over the entire soufflé. Start the roll by lifting up on the edge of the plastic wrap closest to you and letting about 1 inch of the soufflé fold over onto itself. The tighter this first roll is the better. You may need to guide it with your index fingers through the plastic wrap.

Once the first roll is established, you won't need to touch the soufflé again; the plastic wrap will do all the work. Pick up the edge of the wrap again and in one motion pull it up and away from you, rolling up the soufflé.

Keep rolling until the seam is in the middle of the bottom. The soufflé will crack on the outside as it is rolled. Once the soufflé is rolled, it will still be sitting on the plastic wrap.

Wrap the remaining plastic wrap snugly over the soufflé. Gently tilt the bottom up just enough to slide the plastic wrap underneath the soufflé. Transfer the soufflé to a baking sheet, supporting the bottom with your open palms while touching the sides and top of the soufflé as little as possible. Wrap another sheet of plastic lengthwise over the soufflé so the ends are completely sealed. Chill overnight before serving. The soufflé may be stored in the refrigerator for up to 4 days.

CHOCOLATE TRUFFLE CAKE

MAKES ONE 9-INCH CAKE

This dense fudgy cake is easy to make and will delight any chocolate lover. You may create your own variation by substituting another flavor of whipped cream. For Saint Patrick's Day, we top our truffle cakes with green crème de menthe–flavored whipped cream and decorate each rosette with chocolate shamrocks.

BAKER'S BASICS TO REVIEW

> Melting Chocolate, page 21
> Separating Eggs, page 22
> Whipping Egg Whites and Making Meringues, page 198
> Folding, page 20
> Cooling and Depanning Cakes, page 190
> Whipping Cream, page 258
> Filling and Using a Nylon Pastry Bag, page 20
> Piping Borders and Other Decorations, page 215
> Garnishing Cakes, page 214

CAKE

> 1/2 cup (4 ounces) unsalted butter
> 1 pound semisweet chocolate, coarsely chopped
> 4 large eggs
> 1 1/2 teaspoons sugar

> ———

> 4 cups prepared whipped cream (page 258)

> ———

> 1/2 cup finely grated semisweet chocolate

Preheat the oven to 300°. Lightly butter the sides and line the bottom of a 9-inch removable-bottom or springform pan with parchment paper.

In the top of a double boiler over boiling water, melt the butter. When the butter is melted, decrease the heat so that the water is barely simmering. Add the chocolate and stir until the butter and the chocolate are combined and the chocolate is melted. Remove from the heat and let cool about 10 minutes.

Separate the eggs. Place the egg whites in the bowl of a tabletop mixer fitted with the whip attachment. Place the egg yolks in a small mixing bowl. Whip the egg whites on high speed until foamy and, with the mixer still running, gradually add the sugar. Whip until the egg whites are stiff but not dry. Set aside.

With a whisk, beat the egg yolks until they are fluffy. Quickly whisk the egg yolks into the cooled chocolate. The mixture will thicken slightly.

Gently, but thoroughly, fold the egg whites into the chocolate mixture. Pour the chocolate mixture into the prepared pan. Set the pan on a baking sheet and place it on the center rack in the oven. Bake for 7 to 8 minutes, or until the edges (about $1/2$ inch in from the sides of the pan) are just barely beginning to set. Do not overbake. The cake will be very soft.

Let the cake cool completely in the pan on a wire rack. When cool, cover the the pan with plastic wrap, being careful not to let it touch the cake. Refrigerate at least 8 hours and up to 3 days before icing.

When you are ready to ice the cake, depan it by holding it 4 to 6 inches over a heated stovetop burner. Slightly warming the bottom and sides will allow the cake to be easily released from the pan. Do not let the cake start to melt. If using a removable-bottom pan, push up on the bottom and let the sides of the pan fall onto your arm. If using a springform pan, unbuckle the sides of the pan and remove.

Slide a metal icing spatula between the cake and the base of the pan and lift it off. Peel off the paper and place the cake on a 9-inch cake cardboard.

Using the icing spatula, ice the top and sides of the cake with the whipped cream. The icing should be about 1 inch thick on the top and $1/4$ inch thick on the sides. The top of the cake should be perfectly level and form a right angle with the sides.

Fill a pastry bag fitted with a #1 or #2 star tip with the remaining whipped cream and pipe 12 to 16 rosettes, about 1 inch wide and 1 inch high, next to each other around the edge of the cake.

To cover the sides of the cake with the chocolate, slide the icing spatula under the cake cardboard and tilt the cake up enough to get the palm of your other hand underneath to lift it without touching the sides. Pick up a handful of the chocolate in your other hand and, with your palm slightly cupped, gently press the chocolate into the whipped cream, working from the bottom to the top. When the sides of the cake are completely covered, tap the cake cardboard to remove any excess chocolate. Set the cake on a serving platter. Sprinkle the rosettes lightly with grated chocolate.

The cake is best served the day it is iced, but it may be stored overnight in an airtight cake container in the refrigerator.

PETITS FOURS

Petits fours are traditional wedding and baby shower treats, but at Gayle's we make them for every holiday and occasion. We start the year with pale pink hearts decorated with red rose buds. In spring, pastel green petits fours with Kelly green shamrocks pop up. Pastel yellow petits fours are topped with cute chicks and bunnies for Easter. Cool white petits fours explode with red, white, and blue firecrackers for the Fourth of July. In the fall, fat pumpkins sit on our Halloween petits fours. Probably most popular are the icy green Christmas petits fours topped with three-dimensional, handmade buttercream trees, Santas, and snowmen. We end the year with dark chocolate petits fours sprinkled with candy confetti and a clock striking midnight, or for the light-hearted, petit fours topped with pink elephants.

BAKER'S BASICS TO REVIEW

Separating Eggs, page 22

Assembling, Soaking, Filling, and Icing Cakes, page 192

Making and Filling a Paper Pastry Bag, page 208

Piping Borders and Other Decorations, page 215

———

^{1}/4 recipe (about 7 ounces) Marzipan, made at least 1 day
    in advance (page 261)

Flour, for dusting

Confectioners' sugar, for dusting

1 Vanilla Genoise Sheet Cake (page 195)

1 recipe Soaking Solution (page 257)

^{1}/2 cup raspberry jam

^{1}/4 recipe (1^1/2 cups) Buttercream (page 259)

FONDANT ICING

1^1/2 cups light corn syrup

5 cups sifted confectioners' sugar

1 large egg white, at room temperature

1 tablespoon melted butter

Green or pink food coloring
    (use the same color as the marzipan)

———

20 to 30 paper petit four cups

Pink and green food coloring

About 30 minutes before assembling the petits fours, remove the marzipan from the refrigerator and let it come to room temperature. Dust the work surface with flour, then invert the cake onto the floured area. Gently peel off the parchment or waxed paper, then flip the cake over so the top side is facing up. Dust off any excess flour on the top of the cake. Cut the cake in half widthwise to form two 7^1/$_2$ x 10-inch rectangles.

Invert a baking sheet to use as a work surface. (This makes it easier to move the cake as it is filled and iced.) Place one of the rectangles top side up on the baking sheet. Brush it with Soaking Solution. Spread the cake with ^{1}/$_4$ cup of the jam. The jam layer will be very thin.

Set aside ^{1}/$_2$ cup of the buttercream to use for decorating the petits fours. Combine the remaining buttercream with the remaining jam. Using a metal icing spatula, spread half of the raspberry buttercream over the jam. Place the other rectangle of cake top side down over the buttercream. Brush the top of the cake with Soaking Solution, then spread the top with a smooth coat of the remaining buttercream. Don't worry if a little falls over the edges.

Dust the work surface with confectioners' sugar. Using a rolling pin, roll out the marzipan into an 8 x 11 x ^{1}/$_8$-inch rectangle. Frequently dust the marzipan with confectioners' sugar and turn it often to prevent it from sticking to the work surface.

Set the cake, still on the baking sheet, alongside the marzipan. Loosely roll the marzipan onto the rolling pin, starting at the back and rolling toward you. Lift the rolling pin with the marzipan wrapped around it. Unroll the marzipan over the cake, starting at the front and unrolling toward the back while making sure to cover the entire cake. If necessary, gently smooth the top with the palm of your hand. It is all right if the sides look messy or uneven, as they will be trimmed later. To make it easier to cut the petits fours, cover the cake with plastic wrap and freeze for at least 1 hour or up to 2 weeks.

To complete the petits fours, remove the cake from the freezer. While the cake is still frozen, with a serrated knife trim ^{1}/$_2$ inch from the sides so they are clean and straight. To cut the cake into sections, measure the long side of the cake and score the edge about every 1^1/$_2$ inches (to make 6 sections). Then measure and score the short side about every 1^1/$_2$ inches (to make 4 sections). With the serrated knife, cut the cake into squares with a gentle sawing motion, using the score marks as guides. Wipe off the knife with a wet kitchen towel after each cut. If the cake seems too soft, refreeze it for a few minutes. The more uniform and straight the squares are, the better the finished petits fours will look, so score and cut with care.

Once all the cuts are made, slide the knife or an icing spatula under the cake to loosen it from the pan. Return the cake to the freezer while you prepare the icing. (The cold cake will help the icing set up more quickly.)

To make the Fondant Icing, place the corn syrup in the top of a double boiler off the heat. With a wooden spoon, stir in the confectioners' sugar to form a thick paste. It is okay if there is a little undissolved sugar on the sides of the bowl.

Place the double boiler over barely simmering water, stirring frequently, until the mixture is smooth and just lukewarm to the touch. Turn off the heat. Beat in the egg white with a wooden spoon and then the melted butter. Tint the icing by stirring in 1 drop of the food coloring; the icing should be the same color as the marzipan, but a paler, more delicate shade. If necessary, add 1 more drop of food coloring to achieve the right tint. Leave the icing over the warm water until ready to pour over the petits fours. (The icing may be stored in an airtight container in the refrigerator for up to 1 month. Bring it to room temperature and stir to remix before using.)

Set a large wire rack on a baking sheet. Place the petits fours about 2 inches apart on the rack. Slowly pour the icing over each petit four, making sure to cover the corners. (This takes a little practice, so try a couple and then inspect the results. You'll find that it takes a lot more icing than you expected to cover each one.) Cover as many petits fours as the icing allows, then remove the rack from the baking sheet and scrape the icing on the sheet back into the bowl. Gently reheat the icing as directed. Repeat this procedure as many times as necessary until all the petits fours are covered.

Let the petits fours sit on the racks at room temperature for 1 hour to firm up. Using a metal icing spatula, transfer each one from the rack to a paper petit four cup.

To decorate the petits fours, tint half of the reserved buttercream pale green and the other half light pink. Place the green buttercream in a paper pastry bag and cut a tiny hole in the tip. Place the pink buttercream in a pastry bag fitted with a #104 rose tip. With the green buttercream, pipe 3 thin flower stems and a few tiny dots on all of the petits fours. With the pink buttercream, pipe a rosebud at the end of each stem by holding the bag at a 45-degree angle to the petit four with the wide end just touching the surface. Pipe while lifting the tip slightly up and to the right, then release as you move it back toward the center. To make a larger rosebud, make another petal in the opposite direction (to the left, then center) that slightly overlaps the first petal. To pipe leaves, flatten about 1/2 inch of the tip end of the bag filled

with green buttercream, then make small cuts on either side of the flattened end to form a "V." Pipe a leaf at the base of each rosebud.

The petits fours may be stored in an airtight container in the refrigerator for up to 3 days.

FLATTEN END   **THIS CUT CREATES LEAF SHAPE**

NEW YORK CHEESECAKE

MAKES ONE 9-INCH CHEESECAKE

Perhaps this should be called California-style New York cheesecake. Not too creamy and not too dry, it's delicious by either name.

BAKER'S BASICS TO REVIEW
Measuring Dry Ingredients, page 21
Zesting Citrus, page 24

CRUST
1/4 cup (2 ounces) unsalted butter
1 cup graham cracker crumbs
2 tablespoons sugar

CHEESECAKE
2 1/2 pounds cream cheese, at room temperature
    at least 4 hours in advance
1 1/2 cups sugar
1/4 cup flour
2 teaspoons minced lemon zest
1/2 teaspoon salt
1 tablespoon pure vanilla extract
5 large eggs
1/2 cup heavy whipping cream

TOPPING
1 1/2 cups sour cream
1/3 cup sugar
1 teaspoon pure vanilla extract

Preheat the oven to 375°.

Melt the butter in a small saucepan over medium heat. Combine the graham cracker crumbs and the sugar in a small mixing bowl. Pour the melted butter into the crumb mixture. Stir until combined. Pat the crumbs into the bottom of a 9-inch-diameter x 3-inch-deep removable-bottom or springform pan. Place on the center rack in the oven and bake for 5 minutes. Let cool while you prepare the cheesecake.

Lower the oven temperature to 350°.

Place the cream cheese in the bowl of a tabletop mixer fitted with the flat beater and beat on medium speed until well combined and fluffy, about 2 minutes. Scrape down the bowl and beater well. Add the sugar and mix on medium-high speed for 2 minutes. Again scrape down the bowl and beater. Add the flour, lemon zest, and salt and beat on medium-high speed for 1 minute. Scrape down again and beat in the vanilla. With the mixer on medium speed, add the eggs one at a time, waiting until each is incorporated before adding the next. Again scrape down the bowl and beater. With the mixer on medium speed, slowly add the cream. Scrape again and mix for about 1 more minute. The batter will be somewhat thin, about the consistency of heavy cream. Pour the batter into the prepared pan.

Set the pan on a baking sheet and place on the center rack in the oven. Bake for 45 minutes. When the cake has baked for 45 minutes, turn off the oven. Let the cheesecake sit in the oven with the door closed for 15 minutes, then open the door and let the cheesecake cool in the oven for $1^{1}/2$ hours. After $1^{1}/2$ hours, remove the cheesecake from the oven. Don't worry if it has cracked a little.

To make the topping, again preheat the oven to 350°.

Whisk together the sour cream, sugar, and vanilla in a small mixing bowl until smooth. Pour the topping over the cheesecake and bake on the center rack in the oven for 6 minutes. Remove the cheesecake from the oven and let it cool competely on a wire rack before refrigerating.

Refrigerate the cheesecake in an airtight cake container overnight or up to 3 days before serving. Do not cover with plastic wrap because it will stick to the topping.

When ready to serve the cheesecake, depan it by holding it 4 to 6 inches over a heated stovetop burner. Slightly warming the bottom and sides will allow the cheesecake to be easily released from the pan. Do not let the cheesecake start to melt. If using a removable-bottom pan, push up on the bottom and let the sides of the pan fall onto your arm. If using a springform pan, unbuckle the sides of the pan and remove. The cheesecake may be left on the base of either pan or may be transferred to a 9-inch cake cardboard or a serving platter.

To transfer the cheesecake to a cake cardboard or serving platter, slide a metal icing spatula between the bottom crust of the cheesecake and the base of the pan. Work the spatula underneath the cake in a gentle sawing motion until the spatula can slide freely under the whole cake. Using the spatula, tilt the cake up enough to get the palm of your other hand underneath to lift it off the base of the pan and transfer it to the cardboard or platter, supporting the cake with your open palm. Set the back edge of the cheesecake on the cardboard or platter. Support the front edge of the cheesecake with the spatula as you slowly remove your hand and lower the cake onto the cardboard or platter. Gently pull the spatula out from underneath the cheesecake.

PRALINE CHEESECAKE

MAKES ONE 9-INCH CHEESECAKE

Pecans, brown sugar, and butter add just the right amount of sweetness and crunch to this cheesecake. It's a nice fall or winter dessert and good alternative to Thanksgiving pumpkin pie.

CRUST

1/4 cup (2 ounces) unsalted butter

1 cup graham cracker crumbs

2 tablespoons granulated sugar

CHEESECAKE

2 pounds cream cheese, at room temperature at least 4 hours
    in advance

1 1/4 cups granulated sugar

1 tablespoon freshly squeezed lemon juice

2 teaspoons pure vanilla extract

4 large eggs

PRALINE

3 cups pecan pieces

3/4 cup firmly packed light brown sugar

2 tablespoons cold unsalted butter

Preheat the oven to 375°.

Melt the butter in a small saucepan over medium heat. Combine the graham cracker crumbs and the sugar in a small mixing bowl. Pour the melted butter into the crumb mixture. Stir until combined. Pat the crumbs into the bottom of a 9-inch-diameter x 3-inch-deep removable-bottom or springform pan. Place on the center rack in the oven and bake for 5 minutes. Let cool while you prepare the cheesecake.

Lower the oven temperature to 350°.

Place the cream cheese in the bowl of a tabletop mixer fitted with the flat beater and beat on medium speed until well combined and fluffy, about 2 minutes. Scrape down the bowl and beater well. Add the sugar and mix on medium-high speed for 2 minutes. Again scrape down the bowl and beater. Beat in the lemon juice and vanilla. With the mixer on medium speed, add the eggs one at a time, waiting until each is incorporated before adding the next. Again scrape down the bowl and beater. Beat on medium-high speed for 1 minute. Set aside.

In a small mixing bowl, combine the pecan pieces and brown sugar. Set aside.

Pour about two-thirds of the cheesecake batter into the prepared pan. Sprinkle the batter with half of the pecan-sugar mixture. Dot the top with half of the butter. The dots of butter should be thin, small, and placed evenly over the cake.

Pour the remaining cheesecake batter over the pecan-sugar mixture. Top the cheesecake with the remaining nuts, sugar, and butter.

Set the cheesecake on a baking sheet and place on the center rack in the oven. Bake for 45 minutes. When the cake has baked for 45 minutes, turn off the oven. Let the cheesecake sit in the oven with the door closed for 10 minutes, then open the door and let the cheesecake cool in the oven for $1^1/_2$ hours. After $1^1/_2$ hours, remove the cheesecake from the oven. Cover with plastic wrap or place in an airtight cake container and refrigerate overnight before serving. The cheesecake may be stored in the airtight cake container in the refrigerator for up to 5 days.

When ready to serve the cheesecake, depan it by holding it 4 to 6 inches over a heated stovetop burner. Slightly warming the bottom and sides will allow the cheesecake to be easily released from the pan. Do not let the cheesecake start to melt. If using a removable-bottom pan, push up on the bottom and let the sides of the pan fall onto your arm. If using a springform pan, unbuckle the sides of the pan and remove. The cheesecake may be left on the base of either pan or may be transferred to a 9-inch cake cardboard or a serving platter.

To transfer the cheesecake to a cake cardboard or serving platter, slide a metal icing spatula between the bottom crust of the cheesecake and the base of the pan. Work the spatula underneath the cake in a gentle sawing motion until the spatula can slide freely under the whole cake. Using the spatula, tilt the cake up enough to get the palm of your other hand underneath to lift it off the base of the pan and transfer it to the cardboard or platter, supporting the cake with your open palm. Set the back edge of the cheesecake on the cardboard or platter. Support the front edge of the cheesecake with the spatula as you slowly remove your hand and lower the cake onto the cardboard or platter. Gently pull the spatula out from underneath the cheesecake.

PUMPKIN CHEESECAKE

MAKES ONE 9-INCH CHEESECAKE

Like clockwork, the requests for this cheesecake start coming each October. By Thanksgiving, we can't keep up. We think you'll agree it's the perfect alternative to pumpkin pie.

BAKER'S BASICS TO REVIEW

Measuring Dry Ingredients, page 21

Toasting Nuts, page 23

Whipping Cream, page 258

Filling and Using a Nylon Pastry Bag, page 20

Piping Borders and Other Decorations, page 215

Garnishing Cakes, page 214

CRUST

1/4 recipe (8 ounces) Ginger-Molasses Cookie dough (page 150)

CHEESCAKE

1 1/4 pounds cream cheese, at room temperature for at least 4 hours

1 1/4 cups sugar

1 tablespoon plus 1 teaspoon all-purpose or cake flour

1 teaspoon ground cinnamon

1/2 teaspoon ground cloves

1 teaspoon pure vanilla extract

1/2 cup heavy whipping cream

4 large eggs

1 cup canned pumpkin

ICING

2 cups heavy whipping cream

2 tablespoons sugar

2 teaspoons brandy

1/2 cup almond pieces, toasted and finely chopped (page 23)

Ground cinnamon (optional)

Place the cookie dough on a sheet of plastic wrap. Cover it loosely in the plastic wrap and form it into a 7- or 8-inch round disc. Wrap the dough tightly and refrigerate it for 30 minutes.

Preheat the oven to 325°.

On a lightly floured surface, roll the dough out to about 1/8 inch thick.

Using the bottom of a 9-inch removable-bottom or springform pan as a template, cut a 9-inch circle out of the dough. With a cookie cutter or knife, cut the remaining dough into cookies and place around the perimeter of a large baking sheet, leaving room for the cheesecake pan to be placed in the middle.

Slide the bottom of the pan under the circle of dough, then place it in the removable-bottom pan or buckle on the sides of the springform pan.

Set the pan on a baking sheet in the middle of the cookies and place on the center rack in the oven. Bake for 15 minutes, or until the dough puffs slightly, starts to brown around the edges, and becomes slightly firm to the touch. Let the crust cool completely on a rack and snack on the cookies while you prepare the filling.

Increase the temperature of the oven to 350°.

Place the cream cheese in the bowl of a tabletop mixer fitted with the flat beater and beat on medium speed until fluffy, about 1 minute. Scrape down the bowl and beater well.

Add the sugar and mix on medium-high speed for 1 minute. Again scrape down the bowl and beater. Add the flour and spices and beat on medium-high speed for 1 minute. Again scrape down the bowl and beater. With the mixer on medium speed, add the vanilla and cream, mixing until incorporated. In a medium bowl, lightly beat the eggs with a fork, then blend in the pumpkin. With the mixer on medium speed, slowly add the pumpkin mixture. Again scrape down the bowl and beater, then mix on medium speed for about 1 more minute. Pour the batter into the prepared pan.

Again set the pan on the baking sheet and place on the center rack in the oven. Bake for about 45 minutes. When the cake has baked for 45 minutes, turn off the oven and crack open the door. The cheesecake will probably have cracked a little and continue to crack further as it cools, which is all right. Let the cheesecake sit in the oven with the door ajar for 15 minutes, then open the door completely and let the cheesecake cool in the oven for 1 hour. After 1 hour, remove the cheesecake from the oven and let cool completely on a rack before refrigerating.

Cover with plastic wrap or place in an airtight cake container and refrigerate overnight or for up to 3 days before icing and serving.

When ready to serve the cheesecake, depan it by holding it 4 to 6 inches over a heated stovetop burner. Slightly warming the bottom and sides will allow the cheesecake to be easily released from the pan. Do not let the cheesecake start to melt. If using a removable-bottom pan, push up on the bottom and let the sides of the pan fall onto your arm. If using a springform pan, unbuckle the sides of the pan and remove. The cheesecake may be left on the base of either pan or may be transferred to a 9-inch cake cardboard.

To transfer the cheesecake to a cake cardboard, slide a metal icing spatula between the bottom crust of the cheesecake and the base of the pan. Work the spatula underneath the cake in a gentle sawing motion until the spatula can slide freely under the whole cake. Using the spatula, tilt the cake up enough

**PUMPKIN
CHEESECAKE
VARIATION**

*Substitute the Graham
Cracker Crust (page 116) for
the Ginger-Molasses Cookie
Dough crust.*

to get the palm of your other hand underneath to lift it off the base of the pan and transfer it to the cardboard, supporting the cake with your open palm. Set the back edge of the cheesecake on the cardboard. Support the front edge of the cheesecake with the spatula as you slowly remove your hand and lower the cake onto the cardboard. Gently pull the spatula out from underneath the cheesecake.

To make the icing, whip the cream, sugar, and brandy. Using a metal icing spatula, spread a 1-inch thick layer of the whipped cream on top and a $1/4$-inch-thick layer on the sides of the cheesecake. Fill in any depressions or cracks in the cheesecake with the icing, smoothing the top and sides. The top should be perfectly level and form a right angle with the sides.

Fill a pastry bag fitted with a #1 or #2 star with the remaining whipped cream. Pipe twelve to sixteen 1-inch-wide, 1-inch high rosettes around the top of the cheesecake.

Slide the icing spatula under the base of the cake pan or cake cardboard and tilt the cake up enough to get the palm of your other hand underneath to lift it without touching the sides. Using the icing spatula, scrape off any whipping cream hanging over the edge of the base of the pan or cardboard.

To cover the sides of the cake with the nuts, continue to hold up the cake with one hand under the base of the pan or cake cardboard. Pick up a handful of the nuts in your other hand and, with your palm slightly cupped, gently press the nuts into the whipped cream, working from the bottom to the top. When the sides of the cake are completely covered, tap the cake cardboard to remove any excess nuts. Lightly sprinkle each rosette with the cinnamon. Set the cheesecake on a serving platter.

Store the cheesecake in an airtight cake container in the refrigerator until 30 minutes before serving. The cheesecake is best served the day it is iced, but it may be stored in an airtight cake container in the refrigerator overnight.

DAIQUIRI CHEESECAKE

MAKES ONE 9-INCH CHEESECAKE

This light, creamy, refreshing no-bake cheesecake is perfect after Mexican food and a great summer dessert.

BAKER'S BASICS TO REVIEW
    Separating Eggs, page 22
    Zesting Citrus, page 24
    Whipping Egg Whites and Making Meringues, page 198
    Folding, page 20
    Whipping Cream, page 258

CRUST
    $1/4$ cup (2 ounces) unsalted butter
    1 cup graham cracker crumbs
    2 tablespoons granulated sugar

CHEESECAKE
    1 package unflavored gelatin
    $1/2$ cup granulated sugar
    $1/3$ cup light rum
    $1/2$ cup freshly squeezed lemon juice
    4 large eggs, separated
    1 pound cream cheese, at room temperature
    1 tablespoon minced lemon zest
    $1/2$ cup sifted confectioners' sugar
    1 cup heavy whipping cream

Thin slices lemon or lime
Superfine sugar, for dusting
Fresh mint leaves

Preheat the oven to 375°.

Melt the butter in small saucepan over medium heat. Set aside. Combine the graham cracker crumbs and the sugar in a small mixing bowl. Pour the melted butter into the crumb mixture. Stir until combined. Pat the crumbs into the bottom of a 9-inch-diameter x 2-inch-deep removable-bottom or springform pan. Bake for 5 minutes. Let cool while preparing the cheesecake.

In a medium saucepan, combine the gelatin and the granulated sugar. Using a whisk, stir in the rum and lemon juice. Cook and stir over low heat just until the gelatin is dissolved, about 3 minutes. Remove from the heat. Whisk in the egg yolks. Let cool for 30 minutes, stirring occasionally.

Cakes, Icings, and Decorations

Before depanning, the
cheesecake can be topped
with a very thin layer of
English Lemon Curd (page
173) or with 1 cup of vanilla-
flavored whipped cream
(page 258), then garnished
as directed. Or, use a pastry
bag fitted with a #1 or #2
large open star tip to pipe 12
evenly spaced 1-inch rosettes
(for directions, see "Piping
Borders and Other Decora-
tions," page 215) around the
top of the cake. Sprinkle the
rosettes with freshly grated
lemon zest.

In the bowl of a tabletop mixer fitted with the flat beater, beat the cream cheese and lemon zest on high speed until fluffy, scraping the bowl and beater twice, about 1 minute.

With the mixer running on medium-low speed, slowly add the cooled gelatin mixture. As soon as it is incorporated, scrape the bowl and beater, then beat on medium-high speed until well blended, about 2 minutes. The batter will be thin. Set aside.

In a separate mixer bowl, whip the egg whites on high speed until they form soft peaks. Reduce the speed to medium-high and slowly add the confectioners' sugar. Whip until the meringue forms stiff peaks. Fold the meringue into the cream cheese mixture.

Using the same bowl the egg whites were whipped in, whip the heavy cream until stiff. Fold the whipped cream into the cream cheese mixture. Pour the batter into the prepared pan and level the top with a metal icing spatula.

Place the cheesecake in an airtight cake container and refrigerate overnight or up to 3 days before serving. Do not cover with plastic wrap because it will stick to the cheesecake.

When ready to serve the cheesecake, depan it by holding it 4 to 6 inches over a heated stovetop burner. Slightly warming the bottom and sides will allow the cheesecake to be easily released from the pan. Do not let the cheesecake start to melt. If using a removable-bottom pan, push up on the bottom and let the sides of the pan fall onto your arm. If using a springform pan, unbuckle the sides of the pan and remove. The cheesecake may be left on the base of either pan or may be transferred to a 9-inch cake cardboard or a serving platter.

To transfer the cheesecake to a cake cardboard or serving platter, slide a metal icing spatula between the bottom crust of the cheesecake and the base of the pan. Work the spatula underneath the cake in a gentle sawing motion until the spatula can slide freely under the whole cake. Using the spatula, tilt the cake up enough to get the palm of your other hand underneath to lift it off the base of the pan and transfer it to the cardboard or platter, supporting the cake with your open palm. Set the back edge of the cheesecake on the cardboard or platter. Support the front edge of the cheesecake with the spatula as you slowly remove your hand and lower the cake onto the cardboard or platter. Gently pull the spatula out from underneath the cheesecake.

Lay the citrus slices on waxed paper and dust with the superfine sugar. Make a straight cut from the center to the rind of each slice. Twist open the slices and place on the top outside edge of the cheesecake along with the mint leaves.

SOAKING SOLUTION

MAKES ¾ CUP
(ENOUGH FOR A 9-INCH 3-LAYER CAKE)

This recipe may be multiplied in any amount and kept on hand if you do a lot of cake baking. It makes a little too much for a 9-inch 2-layer cake, so don't feel you have to use it all.

> ½ cup water
> ¼ cup sugar
> 1 teaspoon Myers's dark rum

In a small saucepan, combine the water and sugar and bring just to a boil over medium heat. Remove from the heat and let cool. Add the rum. Let cool completely before using or refrigerating.

Store the solution in an airtight container in the refrigerator for up to 1 month.

SOAKING SOLUTION VARIATIONS

Any liqueur that complements the flavors in the cake you are assembling can be substituted for the rum. For example, use Kahlua for Opera Cake (page 231), or use Framboise for Raspberry–Poppy Seed Cake (page 233). Or, if you prefer, omit the liqueur entirely.

Whipping Cream

As explained in Part One (see "About Ingredients," page 12), two types of cream are readily available to the home baker: ultra-pasteurized and heavy whipping cream. Ultra-pasteurized cream has been heat-processed to increase its shelf life, allowing it to keep for up to 6 weeks. To reintroduce some of the characteristics lost during processing, additives and stabilizers are added to the cream. Use ultra-pasteurized cream only if heavy whipping cream is not available. It takes longer to whip, tends to weep water, and breaks down faster than heavy whipping cream. Heavy whipping cream is preferable because it is a more natural product and contains more butterfat than ultra-pasteurized cream. Try to find a brand without any preservatives—the only ingredient listed should be cream. Do not use a brand that has vanilla and sugar already added; it will be too sweet.

Whipping cream is one of the easiest pastry techniques. Just follow these simple guidelines:

- Whip the cream in a bowl that can hold roughly four times the amount of cream you are going to whip, so that the cream has enough room to reach full volume. This means 4 cups of cream can be comfortably whipped in the bowl of a $4^1/_2$- or 5-quart tabletop mixer.

- Chill the bowl and whip attachment for 10 minutes before whipping the cream.

- Shake the cartons of cream before pouring them into the bowl, then add the sugar and vanilla.

- Begin whipping with the mixer on medium speed so that the cream doesn't spatter. As soon as it has thickened slightly, increase the speed to high. A 3-cup recipe takes only 2 or 3 minutes to whip, so don't leave the whipping cream unattended or you may make butter!

- The cream is done whipping when it just holds soft peaks and the cream around the inside edge of the bowl still looks more thick than whipped.

- Be careful not to overwhip cream. The cream continues to stiffen as you handle it. To prevent this from happening, stop the mixer a little before you think the cream is ready and finish whipping by hand with a whisk. This is especially important if you will be adding other flavorings, such as ganache, to the cream. Overwhipped cream will look cottage cheesy and dry. If the cream is slightly overwhipped, you can salvage it by very gently folding in a little unwhipped cream to loosen it.

- You may reuse cream that has been whipped by adding it to another batch of unwhipped cream, as long as the amount of whipped cream isn't greater than the amount of unwhipped cream.

USING WHIPPED CREAM FOR CAKES

When whipped, 3 cups of cream makes 6 cups, which is enough to generously fill, ice, and trim a 9-inch 2-layer cake. The recipe can be increased or reduced as follows:

CREAM	SUGAR	VANILLA	YIELD
1 cup	1 tablespoon	1 teaspoon	2 cups
2 cups	2 tablespoons	2 teaspoons	4 cups
3 cups	3 tablespoons	1 tablespoon	6 cups
4 cups	$1/_4$ cup	1 tablespoon plus 1 teaspoon	8 cups

In the prechilled bowl of a tabletop mixer fitted with a prechilled whisk attachment, whip the cream, sugar, and vanilla just until the mixture holds soft peaks and the cream around the outside edge of the bowl still looks more thick than whipped. Use as recipe directs, or cover with plastic wrap and refrigerate until ready to use.

- Refrigerate cakes iced with whipped cream immediately after icing. Remove the cake from the refrigerator 30 minutes to 1 hour before serving, depending on how cool the weather is.

- Any cake iced with whipped cream should be served the day it is made because whipped cream absorbs refrigerator odors. If the cake is not served the day it is iced, store the whipped cream in an airtight cake container in the refrigerator.

BUTTERCREAM

MAKES 6 CUPS

A friend of ours named Jean Pierre, whose family owned a bakery in Lyons, France, for generations, gave us this recipe. It's the best buttercream we have ever tasted. Instead of using an Italian meringue, which can be too sweet and cloying, it uses pastry cream, which gives it a pleasing texture and taste.

BAKER'S BASICS TO REVIEW
Separating Eggs, page 22

_____

2 cups (1 pound) unsalted butter, at room temperature for
    at least 2 and as much as 6 hours in advance (depending
    on how warm the weather is)

PASTRY CREAM
3 cups milk
1 cup sugar
3 large egg yolks
1/2 cup cornstarch
1 tablespoon pure vanilla extract

Note: The butter and the pastry cream must be at the same temperature, about 75°, when they are combined. You can adjust the timing as needed to bring the butter and pastry to the same temperature before they are combined. The butter may be cut into small pieces to hasten softening as long as it still has body and hasn't started to melt. The pastry cream can be cooled as quickly as necessary as long as you don't allow a skin to form. If the pastry cream is warmer than the butter, it will melt the butter and you will have soup.

Before assembling the buttercream, take the butter out of the refrigerator and allow it to come to room temperature for at least 2 and up to 6 hours, depending on the weather.

To make the pastry cream, place 1 cup of the milk in a small mixing bowl and set aside. Measure the remaining 2 cups of the milk into the top of a double boiler. Add the sugar to the milk in the double boiler and stir until dissolved. Heat the mixture over boiling water, stirring once or twice, until hot and steaming, about 6 minutes.

While the milk mixture is heating, whisk the egg yolks into the reserved milk, then whisk in the cornstarch until the mixture is smooth and the cornstarch is well incorporated.

When the milk-sugar mixture is hot, slowly add about half of it to the cornstarch mixture, whisking continuously. Whisk this back into the mixture in the double boiler and continue whisking vigorously until the pastry cream thickens, about 5 to 6 minutes. Once it has thickened, remove from the heat, whisk in the vanilla, and transfer the pastry cream to another bowl to speed cooling. To keep the cream from forming a skin while cooling, leave the bowl uncovered and whisk every 5 minutes or so until cool, about 1 hour. Using a larger bowl with more surface area can speed up the cooling process, but it is crucial that you don't allow the cream to develop a skin. To cool without stirring, cover the bowl immediately with plastic wrap and let it sit for about 3 hours before making the buttercream.

When both the butter and pastry cream are at about 75°, complete the buttercream. In the bowl of a tabletop mixer fitted with the flat beater, beat the butter, scraping the bowl and beater twice, until very fluffy, at least 2 minutes. With the mixer running on medium speed, add the pastry cream steadily, about 2 tablespoons at a time, just barely incorporating each addition. As soon as all the pastry cream is incorporated, stop the mixer and again scrape down the bowl and beater well. Mix on medium-high speed for 15 seconds.

Use the buttercream as recipe directs or store in an odor-free airtight container in the refrigerater for up to 3 days. Another easy way to store buttercream is to divide it between 2 or 3 sheets of plastic wrap, then tightly wrapping and refrigerating the pats. The buttercream may also be frozen for up to 2 weeks, but tends to become a little watery after freezing. Buttercream that has been refrigerated or frozen must be reheated to achieve its original smooth consistency. If buttercream has been frozen, thaw it overnight in the refrigerator and let it come to room temperature before reheating.

To reheat, place the buttercream in a large wide-mouthed metal mixing bowl. Break the buttercream apart into chunks with a spoon or a whisk. Place the bowl directly on a burner over medium-low heat and whisk continuously. When the buttercream in the bottom of the bowl starts to melt, remove it from the heat and, using a whisk, incorporate the melted portion into the rest of the icing. Continue to warm while whisking, always removing the buttercream from the heat as it starts to melt.

As the buttercream heats up, it will start to look separated and resemble cottage cheese, which is all right. Just keep whisking, and just as your arm gets tired, after about 3 minutes, the buttercream will begin to come together and look like it did when it was first made. The reheated buttercream can be refrigerated and reheated several times without damaging its consistency.

FLAVORING BUTTERCREAM AND WHIPPED CREAM

Different flavors of icing can be created with ingredients commonly found in the pantry. To flavor icing, first whisk your choice of flavoring into about 1 cup of icing to make it easier to incorporate. Blend or fold the mixture into the remaining icing. Experiment with the following flavors, using the amounts given to flavor 1 cup of buttercream or whipped cream:

- *Caramel: add 1/4 cup caramel ice cream topping.*
- *Chocolate: add 1/2 cup Chocolate Ganache (page 262). The ganache should be completely cool, but not stiff or hard.*
- *Hazelnut: add 1/4 cup Nutella hazelnut spread (usually shelved with the ice cream toppings at the supermarket).*
- *Lemon: add 1/4 cup English Lemon Curd (page 173).*
- *Mocha: dissolve 1 teaspoon instant espresso powder in 1/2 teaspoon of hot water or coffee to make a paste. Let cool before using.*
- *Raspberry, apricot, or strawberry: add 1/4 cup good-quality jam.*
- *Praline: add 1/3 cup Hazelnut Nougat (page 185).*
- *Grand Marnier, Framboise, Frangelico, or any liqueur: substitute for the vanilla.*

MARZIPAN

MAKES ONE 9 X 9 X ½-INCH PAT
(29 OUNCES)

At Gayle's, marzipan is used to cover the Princess Cake (page 217) as well as many whimsical creations. Our decorators turn red marzipan into lady bugs, strawberries, and firecrackers. Uncolored marzipan becomes baseballs and soccer balls. Two of our favorites have been a large green jumping frog and a smiling pink pig. At Easter, pastel yellow and lavender eggs rival Faberge's. At Halloween, the marzipan is shaped into pumpkins. In January, dark rust–colored footballs fly out the door.

3 cups sifted confectioners' sugar
1 pound almond paste
3 tablespoons light corn syrup
2 to 3 tablespoons water
⅛ to ¼ teaspoon green, pink, or other food color

Place the confectioners' sugar in the bowl of a tabletop mixer fitted with the flat beater. With the mixer running on medium-low speed, add the almond paste about 1 teaspoon at a time. This will take about 5 minutes. Once you have added all of the almond paste, the mixture will be crumbly. Scrape down the bowl and beater. Add the corn syrup and mix on low speed until incorporated. The mixture will still be crumbly. Again scrape down the bowl and beater.

In a small bowl, combine the water and food color. With the mixer on medium-low speed, add about half of the food coloring mixture and beat until incorporated. Continue gradually adding the food coloring until the marzipan just comes together and reaches the consistency of sugar cookie dough. It should be smooth but not crumbly or overly sticky.

If more color is desired, knead it in by hand after removing the marzipan from the mixer. (Remember it is easier to add a little more color at the end than to make a new batch!) Different colors have different intensities and will require different amounts.

Place the marzipan on a sheet of plastic wrap and form it into a 9-inch round disc about ½ inch thick. Wrap and refrigerate overnight before using. The marzipan may be stored in an airtight container or covered in plastic wrap in the refrigerator for up to 1 month.

CHOCOLATE GANACHE

MAKES 3 CUPS

Ganache is a creamy chocolate mixture made by melting chopped chocolate with hot whipping cream. There are many formulas, techniques, and variations for ganache. At Gayle's we use the most basic recipe, with equal parts chocolate and cream. The beauty of ganache is that with one recipe, you can make a variety of desserts just by manipulating the temperature.

At Gayle's, ganache is made fresh early in the morning. While still fluid and warm, it is poured over our Rich Chocolate Cake and becomes a gorgeous glaze. Next, when it is a little cooler and thicker, we dip the tops of our éclairs in it. Throughout the day the cake decorators use the room temperature ganache, which at this point has the consistency of very soft butter, as a filling in cakes or to flavor buttercream and whipped cream. At the end of their shift the decorators combine any remaining ganache, stirring until smooth, wrap it, and leave it out overnight at room temperature. The next morning, this ganache will have firmed up to about the consistency of whipped cream cheese. Completing the cycle, this firm, spreadable ganache is then used to skim coat the day's Rich Chocolate Cakes before they can be glazed with that morning's fresh ganache.

12 ounces semisweet chocolate, coarsely chopped
1½ cups ultra-pasteurized whipping cream (see Note)

Place the chocolate in a medium mixing bowl. In a large saucepan over medium-high, heat the cream, stirring once or twice, until it begins to boil. Don't worry about any skin that forms on the surface of the cream; it will dissolve later. Remove the saucepan from the heat and immediately pour one-half of the cream into the chocolate. Let the mixture sit a few seconds, then gently stir with a rubber spatula until smooth, being careful not to incorporate air into the ganache. It's all right if a few chunks of unmelted chocolate remain.

Add the remaining cream to the chocolate in two parts, each time reheating the cream and stirring the mixture until smooth. If the ganache is still not perfectly smooth after all the cream has been stirred in, strain it through a medium-mesh sieve. Straining the ganache will produce a lot of small air bubbles, but air bubbles are preferable to hard bits of chocolate. Gently tap the bowl on the work surface to remove as many of the bubbles as possible.

Let the mixture cool, uncovered, at room temperature, stirring about every 5 minutes for the first 30 minutes, then stirring about every 15 minutes for the first hour. Ganache thickens as it cools, so the longer it cools, the thicker it will become. Do not refrigerate. Ganache that is refrigerated at any stage will permanently lose its shine.

The ganache is ready to be used in its different cooling stages as follows:

- As a cake glaze: Let cool for about 1 hour. It should be just barely warm and have the consistency of unwhipped cream.

- As an éclair glaze: Let cool for 1 hour.

- As a flavoring for whipped cream and buttercream: Cool for at least 2 hours, or overnight.

- As a skim coat or cake filling: Cool overnight.

If you are not using the ganache until the following day, continue to cool to room temperature, stirring occasionally. Cover the bowl with plastic wrap when the ganache has cooled completely and set in a cool place.

Cooled or firm ganache may be reheated to be used as a glaze by warming over a pan of water that has been brought to a boil and then turned off. Stir frequently, again being careful not to incorporate air. Remove from the heat and let cool as directed.

Ganache can be covered and stored at room temperature for up to 2 days in warm weather and 2 to 3 days in cool weather. After that it may be refrigerated for up to 5 days.

NOTE: This is the only recipe we recommend using ultra-pasteurized whipping cream. It makes a smoother ganache with fewer air bubbles than the non-pasteurized variety.

THE MANY USES FOR CHOCOLATE GANACHE

Here are a few of Gayle's recipes that use Chocolate Ganache:

- *Baci di Dama (page 154)*
- *Bûche de Noël (page 306)*
- *Chocolate Mousse Cake (page 238)*
- *Cream Puffs (page 180)*
- *Chocolate Éclairs (page 182)*
- *Opera Cake (page 231)*
- *Raspberry-Almond-Chocolate Danish (page 73)*
- *Rich Chocolate Cake (page 227)*
- *German Chocolate Cake (page 229)*

In addition to using ganache for dipping, filling, coating, writing, glazing, and flavoring, there are many uses for ganache, including:

- *Flavoring buttercream and whipped cream.*
- *Whipped and flavored with liqueur or ground nuts, then scooped into small balls and rolled in cocoa to make simple truffles*
- *Reheated until soft and poured over vanilla ice cream*

CREAM CHEESE ICING

MAKES 3¼ CUPS

BAKER'S BASICS TO REVIEW
Creaming, page 20

---

8 ounces cream cheese, at room temperature
½ cup (4 ounces) unsalted butter, at room temperature
4 cups sifted confectioners' sugar
1 teaspoon pure vanilla extract
Milk

CREAM CHEESE ICING VARIATION

To make Chocolate Cream Cheese Icing, after adding the vanilla, add 4 ounces of melted, cooled unsweetened chocolate. This icing is great on brownies (pages 131 and 132), Devil's Food Cake (page 199), and Banana Cake (page 205).

In the bowl of a tabletop mixer fitted with the flat beater, cream together the cream cheese and butter, scraping down the bowl and beater twice, until fluffy. Add the confectioners' sugar, first mixing on low speed, then increasing the speed to high. Beat until light and fluffy, again scraping down the bowl and beater twice. Blend in the vanilla.

The icing should be a smooth, spreadable consistency, just a little firmer than soft butter. If it is too stiff, add milk, 1 tablespoon at a time, while mixing on medium speed, until the icing is the desired consistency.

It is best to use this icing immediately, but it may be covered and stored in the refrigerator for up to 2 days, if necessary. If refrigerated, let the icing come to room temperature before using.

Flo Braker: The Ultimate Baker

When professional chefs and bakers can't find the answer to a baking question or need to know how to make a difficult cake, they often call Flo Braker. Take James Beard for example. Flo was a student at Mr. Beard's cooking school in Oregon back in the early 1970s, when he tried making a new cake and had disastrous results. Perplexed at the failure, he asked Flo to try it. The cake turned out perfectly, and Flo taught the class that day.

Julia Child also called when Flo's first book, *The Simple Art of Perfect Baking,* was published. Julia thought the book was so terrific, she asked Flo to come out to her home in Cambridge, Massachusetts, to teach her a few things. Julia gathered several cooking teachers, writers, and chefs for five days of classes. And some years ago, Flo was even invited to train Ted Danson to look like a professional pastry chef in the movie *Getting Even with Dad.*

More recently, Flo impressed everyone at a Baker's Dozen meeting. The Baker's Dozen is a California-based organization of professional bakers who meet every two months to discuss different baking issues. Everyone was asked to make an angel food cake that was reputed to be divine. The recipe was a generic one with nonspecific instructions like "Whip egg whites until barely stiff enough to hold a peak." Each one of the thirty-five members had the exact same instructions.

When all of the thirty or so cakes were gathered onto a table, not one of them looked a thing like the others. Some were as flat as pancakes, some were a dark brown, some were just plain ugly. But Flo's cake was pristine white, towered above the rest, and was lighter than a goose feather.

Marion Cunningham asked Flo to teach the rest of the bakers how she had done it. So right there in the middle of the meeting, they gathered the necessary supplies and Flo taught her fellow professionals how to make the perfect angel food cake. Marion later said that Flo's knowledge of baking was astounding. That's something I've known for twenty years.

I first met Flo at Jack Lirio's San Francisco cooking school back in 1975, when I took a six-week French pastry course she taught. I loved it so much I took another six weeks. I would sit on my stool watching this diminutive woman make pastries that were not only technically correct but the best-tasting desserts I had ever eaten. It was then that I realized that Flo is a perfectionist whose knowledge is only exceeded by her grace and kindness.

These days, Flo is on the road teaching quite a bit. Loaded down with hatboxes full of baking equipment, she's always boarding a plane to places like the Greenbriar Cooking School, where she teaches lucky students the simple art of perfect baking. ❀ ❀ ❀

Gayle at Home

People always ask if I still bake at home. When I say I do, they are often surprised. I guess they think that I have no incentive to bake as long as I can trot down to the bakery (it's only three blocks from our home) for whatever I want. Or maybe they figure I must be so sick of baking that I wouldn't dream of doing it on my time off. The truth is I still love to get my hands in the flour, but Gayle's has gotten so big it's impossible for me to really bake there anymore. And, some of my favorite desserts and pastries don't hold up or sell well for me to make at the bakery. So this chapter includes all the goodies I make in my own kitchen for every occasion from casual get-togethers to fancy dinner parties. It's an eclectic bunch, ranging from a messy cobbler to an ethereal Chocolat Pot de Crème, which is the only chocolate dessert in my home repertoire. My family and friends usually show their approval by managing to save room for dessert (and sometimes even seconds!).

In this chapter, you'll also find a few recipes that Joe makes and one from our friend Christie Carlson. We hope you and your guests enjoy them as much as we do.

My baking pal, Buddy

GREEN TOMATO PIE

When our friend Tory Wilson made a green tomato pie for us, we didn't know what to think. But when we took our first bites, we were hooked. There is no true taste of tomatoes in this pie, just the combination of sweet, tart, and spice.

BAKER'S BASICS TO REVIEW
Measuring Dry Ingredients, page 21
Baking Fruit Pies, page 109
Rolling Out Pie Crusts, page 98
Fluting Pie Crusts, page 98
Making a Lattice Crust, page 105

5 cups green tomato slices (1/8 inch thick)
1 recipe Pie Dough (page 99)
1 1/2 cups sugar
6 tablespoons flour
1/2 teaspoon salt
1/2 teaspoon ground nutmeg
1/2 teaspoon ground cinnamon
1/8 teaspoon ground ginger
1 tablespoon cider vinegar
1 tablespoon (1/2 ounce) butter

Preheat the oven to 425°.

Place the sliced tomatoes in a sieve to drain. (Draining off the excess juice keeps the pie from becoming soggy.)

Roll out one disc of the pie dough and fit it into a 10-inch pie plate. Flute the edge of the crust. To make the lattice crust, roll out the second disc of pie dough and cut into 12 strips; set aside.

In a large bowl, combine the sugar, flour, salt, and spices. Place the drained tomatoes in another bowl and stir in the cider vinegar. Spoon 3 tablespoons of the sugar mixture over the pie shell. Toss the remaining sugar mixture with the tomatoes. Place the tomatoes in the shell and dot the top with the butter.

Assemble the lattice crust over the filling. Trim the ends of the lattice strips and press to seal well with the bottom crust.

Place the pie on the lower rack in the oven. Bake for 15 minutes, then decrease the temperature to 325°, move the pie to the center rack, and continue baking for 40 to 60 minutes, or until the crust is golden brown and the center of the filling is bubbling.

Set the pie on a wire rack to cool. This pie is best the day it is baked. Warm leftover pie in a 350° oven for 15 to 20 minutes before serving.

APRICOT PIE

MAKES ONE 10-INCH PIE

My family has been buying apricots from Mr. and Mrs. Young in Saratoga, California, for over 15 years. Norma and Jack grow some of the best apricots in the state; their fruit has the true essence of apricot flavor. We always buy cases of apricots around the Fourth of July and make jams, cobblers, and pies. What I don't use up right away, I freeze in cobbler and pie quantities for the winter months. Apricot pie in January has a way of bringing the sun out.

BAKER'S BASICS TO REVIEW
Measuring Dry Ingredients, page 21
Baking Fruit Pies, page 109
Rolling Out Pie Crusts, page 98
Fluting Pie Crusts, page 98

1 recipe Pie Dough (page 99)
6 cups pitted and quartered fresh
    or home-frozen apricots (see Note)
1/2 to 2/3 cup sugar
4 to 6 tablespoons all-purpose flour

Preheat the oven to 425°.

Roll out one disc of the pie dough and fit it into a 10-inch pie plate. Roll out the other disc and leave it on the work surface.

Place the apricots in a large bowl and taste several quarters to determine how much sugar to use. In a separate bowl, combine the sugar and flour. Sprinkle the flour mixture over the apricots and mix gently to coat.

Pour the mixture into the pie shell. Arrange the top crust over the filling and flute the edges, sealing them very well to prevent the juices from bubbling over as the pie bakes. Cut four to six 1 1/2-inch-long vents in the top crust.

Place the pie on the lower rack in the oven. Bake for 15 minutes, then decrease the temperature to 325°, move the pie to the center rack, and continue baking for 40 to 60 minutes, or until the top crust is golden brown and the filling is bubbling in the center.

Set the pie on a wire rack to cool. This pie is best the day it is baked. Warm leftover pie in a 350° oven for 15 to 20 minutes before serving.

NOTE: If using home-frozen apricots, remove them from the freezer serveral hours before you start baking. Set the fruit in a bowl to defrost at room temperature. When fully defrosted, transfer the fruit to a strainer set over a bowl and drain for 30 minutes.

APRICOT COBBLER

I'm known for my apricot cobblers, primarily because that's what I almost always want for dessert. I've tried several cobbler dough recipes, but could never find one that was rich and buttery enough. I finally found one in Lindsey Shere's book, *Chez Panisse Desserts,* that I adapted slightly.

BAKER'S BASICS TO REVIEW
Measuring Dry Ingredients, page 21

DOUGH
1 1/2 cups all-purpose flour
1 1/2 tablespoons sugar
2 1/2 teaspoons baking powder
6 tablespoons (3 ounces) cold butter, cut into 1/2-inch pieces
3/4 cup heavy whipping cream, buttermilk, or whole milk

FILLING
7 cups fresh or home-frozen apricots (see Note, page 268)
3 to 5 tablespoons all-purpose flour
1/4 to 1/2 cup sugar

Preheat the oven to 375°.

To make the dough, combine the flour, sugar, and baking powder in a bowl and mix well. Toss the pieces of butter in the flour mixture, then cut them into the flour with a pastry blender or two knives until the butter pieces are the size of peas. The butter may also be cut in using a food processor; pulse several times to create a coarse meal. Or work in the butter with your hands, using the sheeting method described on page 99.

Measure out the whipping cream. Place the cream and flour-butter mixture in the refrigerator to chill.

To make the filling, place the prepared fruit in a large bowl. In a small bowl, combine the flour and sugar and mix well. Pour the flour mixture over the fruit and toss well to coat. Pour the filling into a 13 x 10-inch baking pan.

Remove the dough ingredients from the refrigerator and add the cream to the flour-butter mixture. With a fork, stir just until the cream is barely incorporated. Do not overmix; the dough should have dry spots and barely hold together. Arrange 1/4-cup pieces of dough over the filling and slightly flatten the small islands of crust.

Place the cobbler on the center rack in the oven and bake for 35 to 40 minutes, or until the crust is golden brown and the filling is bubbling. Place the baking pan on a wire rack to cool. Serve the cobbler warm or at room temperature the day it is baked.

APPLE CRISP

MAKES ONE 15 X 10-INCH CRISP

We are fortunate enough to live in one of the best apple-growing regions in the United States. Watsonville, California, is home to dozens of apple growers who ship Golden Delicious, Jonagold, Gravenstein, Pippin, Granny Smith, and many other varieties all over the world. During the season, which is in the fall, we try to find the crispest, tastiest apples we can. We like Pippin and Granny Smith apples for baking, but your area may offer other good varieties. Different apples give this crisp very different flavors. Experiment—it's fun and can teach you a lot about apple flavors.

At home, we've planted a Belgian fence, which is a 13-foot-long line of eight different varieties of apple trees that are espaliered into a diamond pattern. In years to come, we will have different varieties of apples to bake as each tree's fruit matures.

BAKER'S BASICS TO REVIEW
  Zesting Citrus, page 24
  Measuring Dry Ingredients, page 21

FILLING
  5 cups peeled, cored, and sliced (¹/4 inch thick) baking apples
  ¹/2 teaspoon ground cinnamon
  1 teaspoon lemon zest
  1 teaspoon orange zest
  4 tablespoons Grand Marnier
  3 tablespoons apricot jam

TOPPING
  ³/4 cup all-purpose flour
  ¹/4 teaspoon salt
  ³/4 cup granulated sugar
  ¹/4 cup firmly packed dark brown sugar
  ¹/2 cup (4 ounces) cold butter

Preheat the oven to 350° .

Butter a 15 x 10-inch baking pan and arrange the apples in it. Sprinkle the cinnamon, lemon and orange zests, Grand Marnier, and apricot jam over the apples.

To make the topping, combine the flour, salt, granulated sugar, and brown sugar in a mixing bowl. Cut the butter into ¹/2-inch pieces. Add to the bowl and toss with the dry ingredients. With a pastry cutter or two knives, cut in the butter until it resembles coarse meal. Alternatively, combine the dry ingredients in the bowl of a food processor fitted with the metal blade. Add the butter pieces and toss to coat, then process just until the mixture is crumbly. Spread the topping over the apples.

Place the pan on the center rack in the oven and bake for about 1 hour, or until the top is slightly brown and the apples are tender when pierced with a knife. The crisp is best about 30 minutes after baking. Store at room temperature. Warm leftover crisp in a 350° oven for 10 minutes.

JOHANNE'S CROSTATA DOUGH

MAKES 18 TO 20 OUNCES (ENOUGH FOR 2 CROSTATAS)

Whenever we're within three hundred miles of Providence, Rhode Island, we visit what we think is the best restaurant on the eastern seaboard, Al Forno. It is owned by Johanne Killeen and George Germon (for more about them, see page 273). They are famous not only for their savory food but also for their desserts, which Johanne presides over. She uses this wonderful dough for her Fig Crostata, but it is marvelous with any fruit tart. The dough freezes well and is great to have on hand.

BAKER'S BASICS TO REVIEW
Measuring Dry Ingredients, page 21

———

1 cup (8 ounces) cold unsalted butter
2 cups all-purpose flour
$^1/_4$ cup superfine sugar
$^1/_2$ teaspoon salt
$^1/_4$ cup ice water

Cut the butter into $^1/_2$-inch pieces and return it to the refrigerator.

Place the flour, sugar, and salt in the bowl of a food processor fitted with the metal blade. Pulse several times to combine.

Add the butter and toss once or twice with your hands to coat it with flour. Pulse 15 times, or until the butter pieces are the size of small peas. With the processor running, add the ice water all at once through the feed tube. Process for about 10 seconds, stopping the machine before the dough becomes a solid mass.

Divide the dough in half and place each half on plastic wrap, pressing any loose particles into the mass of dough. Gently form it into a 7-inch disk.

Seal the dough with the plastic wrap and refrigerate for at least 1 hour. The dough may be refrigerated for up to 2 days or frozen for up to 2 weeks. To use frozen dough, thaw overnight in the refrigerator.

JOHANNE'S FIG CROSTATA

This fig tart is an adaptation of a recipe from Johanne Killeen and George Germon's wonderful cookbook, *Cucina Simpatica: Robust Trattoria Cooking from Al Forno.* It is very simple to make and astoundingly good. It proves that fruit can taste extra ethereal when prepared simply. Johanne uses Mission figs, but we use figs from our tree at home.

2 tablespoons superfine sugar
1/4 teaspoon ground cinnamon
12 fresh figs (about 12 ounces), stemmed
1/2 recipe (9 to 10 ounces) Johanne's Crostata Dough (page 271)
Confectioners' sugar, for dusting

Preheat the oven to 450°.

In a small bowl, combine the sugar and cinnamon. Cut the figs in half vertically.

Place the dough on a lightly floured work surface and roll it out into an 11-inch free-form circle. Transfer the dough to a 13 x 9-inch baking sheet and sprinkle with 1 tablespoon of the cinnamon-sugar mixture.

Starting in the center, cover the dough with a starburst of figs placed skin side down, leaving a 1 1/2-inch border around the edge. Sprinkle the remaining sugar and cinnamon over the figs.

In a casual fashion, bring the edges of the dough up, letting it slightly drape over the outer edge of the fruit. Press down on the dough where the sides form a corner at the bottom, being careful not to mash the fruit.

Place the tart on the center rack in the oven and bake for 20 to 25 minutes, or until the crust is golden and the figs are soft and slightly caramelized. Place the baking sheet on a wire rack and let cool for about 10 minutes. Dust with confectioners' sugar and serve warm.

George Germon and Johanne Killeen:
Only Made to Order Will Do

We've known George Germon and Johanne Killeen, owners of Al Forno restaurant in Providence, Rhode Island, for over a dozen years. Johanne and George have a big appetite for life, food, and entertaining. They were voted two of the top ten best new chefs by *Food and Wine* magazine in 1988, but unlike the other award winners, both have taken a circuitous path to get where they are today. Both graduated from the Rhode Island School of Design with art degrees—George's in sculpture, Johanne's in photography. After graduation, George got involved in restaurant design and construction and eventually went to work as a cook in the first restaurant he built. Johanne teamed up with two friends to open a bakery called Smart Cookie in Providence. A few years later they opened their own place, Al Forno, and have been dishing out robust, flavorful food ever since.

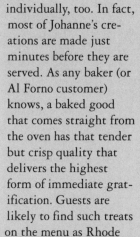

The restaurant immediately became their artistic medium. They spent as much time creating and designing the dining rooms as they now spend shaping the menu and cooking. And critics nationwide agree that Al Forno's food lifts their artistry to even grander heights. The primary reason for this is George and Johanne's obsession with making foods to order. Everything—even the croutons on the salads—is made to order. When George got a new ice machine, the staff joked that the premade ice went against George's made-to-order mandate because the ice was often ready up to an hour in advance.

It's only natural in a restaurant that makes everything to order that the desserts be made individually, too. In fact, most of Johanne's creations are made just minutes before they are served. As any baker (or Al Forno customer) knows, a baked good that comes straight from the oven has that tender but crisp quality that delivers the highest form of immediate gratification. Guests are likely to find such treats on the menu as Rhode Island Shortcakes, made with Johnnycake meal (from Gray's Grist Mill in nearby Adamsville) and garnished with locally grown strawberries and whipped cream; Mission Fig Crostata, in a tart dough baked in one of the restaurant's wood-burning ovens; a caramelized pumpkin crostata with crème anglaise, dusted with confectioners' sugar; and even fresh-churned ice cream.

In the introduction to the dessert section of their book, *Cucina Simpatic: Robust Trattoria Cooking from Al Forno,* Johanne says, "There's nothing worse than a soggy piece of pastry, or one that tastes of the refrigerator. And there is nothing more satisfying than a warm crostata, or tart...hot from the oven....The ingredients need not be complex or exotic to create a fabulous dessert." We couldn't agree more.

CHOCOLAT POT DE CRÈME

MAKES EIGHT ¹/₂-CUP CUSTARDS

I got this recipe from *Baking with the American Harvest,* a quarterly newsletter for home and professional bakers (for more information, see page 318). I love the newsletter because its topics and recipes are timely, seasonal, and always well done. I highly recommend it for anyone who loves to bake. I like to make these rich custards in the assorted ramekins I have found in antique stores, but they can also be made in Pyrex custard cups.

> 1¹/₂ cups milk
>
> 3 cups heavy whipping cream
>
> ¹/₂ cup sugar
>
> 11 ounces bittersweet chocolate, finely chopped
>
> 13 large egg yolks

Preheat the oven to 325°.

Place the milk, cream, and sugar in a saucepan and heat just until ingredients begin to simmer. Remove from the heat, add the chocolate, and let sit for several minutes. Stir the mixture until it is well blended.

Add the yolks and whisk until incorporated. Pour the mixture through a fine sieve. (This step is necessary to achieve the custard's velvety smooth texture.)

Divide the custard among eight ¹/₂-cup ramekins. Place the ramekins in a baking pan and fill the pan with enough water to reach halfway up the outside of the ramekins (to make a water bath). Place the pan on the center rack in the oven and cover it with foil. Bake for 30 to 40 minutes, or until the edges of the custards are set and an area the size of a quarter in the center is not fully set. Test by gently shaking one of the ramekins. Remove from the water bath and cool. Serve while still slightly warm.

NOTE: I usually put the custards in the oven when we sit down to dinner.

CHRISTIE'S TRIFLE

MAKES ONE 2-QUART TRIFLE

Our friend Christie Carlson is one of the best cooks we know. She is inventive and makes everything look easy. Because of our long-standing friendship, Christie knows everyone at the bakery. One day, she finagled some Pastry Cream and other ingredients out of our head cake decorator, Linda Younger, and transformed them into this fabulous trifle, which she served us that night.

BAKER'S BASICS TO REVIEW

> Whipping Cream, page 258
> Filling and Using a Nylon Pastry Bag, page 20
> Piping Borders and Other Decorations, page 215

> 1/2 loaf Lemon Bread (page 169)
> 1/4 cup crème de cassis, Grand Marnier, brandy, Armagnac, Myers's
>   rum, or your own favorite liqueur
> 1/4 cup raspberry jam
> 3 cups heavy whipping cream
> 3 tablespoons sugar
> 1 tablespoon pure vanilla extract
> 2 cups Pastry Cream (page 127)
> 3 cups berries, hulled and sliced strawberries,
>   or peeled and sliced nectarines or peaches

Cut the Lemon Bread into 1/2-inch-wide slices. Using a pastry brush, lightly coat both sides of the slices with the liqueur and then spread one side with the jam.

Whip the cream, sugar, and vanilla to medium peaks.

Layer the ingredients in a 2-quart trifle dish, beginning with one-third of the bread (cut the pieces to fit the shape of the bowl). Spread half of the Pastry Cream and one-third of the whipped cream on the layer of bread. Place a single layer of fruit on top of the whipped cream. Repeat the layering process one more time, finishing with a layer of bread. Reserve the remaining one-third whipped cream, covered, in the refrigerator. Cover the trifle with plastic wrap and store in the refrigerator for 2 to 5 hours.

To serve, refresh the remaining whipped cream by whipping slightly. Place the whipped cream in a pastry bag fitted with a star tip and pipe rosettes around the top edge of the trifle. Alternately, spread the whipped cream over the trifle.

NOTE: If I am able to get perfect berries, I often place one well-dried berry on top of each rosette.

Boris and the Tarte Tatin

When we travel, it's our habit to return repeatedly to some restaurants, squeezing every drop of inspiration out of the great meals we enjoy there. We always hope we'll be able to get into the kitchen to peel the onion, so to speak, and have a look at the heart of the food. If that's not possible, we figure maybe one more taste will help us decipher how a favorite pastry (or bread or entrée) was made. The Bistro des Alpilles, in St. Remy de Provence, France, is one such restaurant we've frequented as often as opportunity has allowed.

We had eaten at the Bistro des Alpilles half a dozen times when, on our third trip to St. Remy, we met Boris. He had such a carefree manner and magnetic charm, we thought he was the owner's son; at the very least, we thought he was our waiter. Because we immediately got on so well with Boris, we asked him about the restaurant's Tarte Tatin, a magical upside-down apple tart, for which we were eager to get the recipe. We indicated we'd like to watch how it was made. He led us to believe it was his grandmother's recipe, then told us that the Moroccan cook who controlled the kitchen would never permit customers to observe him at work. So we had to satisfy ourselves with quizzing Boris, who proved to be a willing accomplice.

The second day we visited the restaurant, as Boris seated us, he began to explain how the tart was made. "Any firm green apples will work," he said. We glanced at each other. "You're sure?" I asked. "We thought Golden Delicious were best." Boris disappeared before answering, running off to fill someone's water glass. The next night at dinner, he leaned over our table and clandestinely said, "Golden Delicious. You were right."

The next day, Boris invited us home to meet his parents, an experience that confirmed our suspicions that he was actually a busboy (albeit an enterprising and outgoing envoy for the restaurant) and not the insider we had initially thought. We learned he was planning a trip to California and, in order to escape his aunt who lived in San Francisco, he hoped to rent a car and drive the ninety miles to visit us. This was how Boris became our spy. We would entertain him in California in exchange for information about the tart.

The next day, when our friends from Rogne, Jerome and Kathleen, asked to meet for dinner, the logical choice was Bistro des Alpilles. When we arrived, Boris was standing at the door wearing his long white apron and perky smile, waiting to show us to our table. After the first course, Boris whispered in my ear, "You have to remember to drain the liquid off of the apples after they're cooked." When I asked him why, he shrugged. It went on like this all night. Between each course, another tip, another layer of the tart explained.

Looking back on the experience, we're glad we figured out how to make the tart one piece at a time (literally!), because it reinforced that invaluable lesson every skilled baker must learn and relearn: to make great desserts, one must consider all the aspects of how a recipe goes together, not just study the formula.

❀ ❀ ❀

TARTE TATIN

MAKES ONE 7½-INCH TART

Although the Tarte Tatin is an informal dessert, it requires some skill and practice. This recipe is as simple as it gets.

6 tablespoons (3 ounces) unsalted butter

⅓ cup sugar

4 Golden Delicious apples, peeled, cored, and cut in half

5 ounces Basic Puff Pastry Dough (page 85)

Preheat the oven to 400°.

Over medium heat, melt the butter in a 7½-inch noncorrosive, ovenproof skillet (a cast-iron skillet will work, if you don't leave the tart in the pan overnight) with 2-inch-high sides. Add the sugar and stir continuously for 15 to 20 minutes, or until a medium-brown caramel forms.

After the caramel has attained its color, place the apple halves on edge in the caramel and continue cooking. Using metal tongs, turn the apples about every 5 minutes so that they cook evenly and all sides are coated with the sauce. Cook for 20 to 25 minutes, or until all sides of the apples are coated and nearly cooked through. To test for doneness, pierce an apple half with a paring knife; the apple should be tender but slightly resist the knife blade. Remove the pan from the heat and let cool for 15 minutes.

Roll the dough out into an 8½-inch circle about ⅛ inch thick. Place the pastry over the cooked apples in the pan and tuck the edges into the pan. Cut three 1-inch-long, equally spaced slits (vents) in the pastry dough.

Place the skillet on the center rack in the oven and bake for 25 to 30 minutes, or until the puff pastry is golden brown. Let the tart cool in the skillet for 10 to 15 minutes. Place a 10-inch (or larger) platter on top of the skillet. Place one hand on the bottom of the platter, and quickly invert the skillet so the tart is on the platter. The tart can remain in the pan for several hours or even in the refrigerator before it is inverted. When ready to serve, place the skillet over medium heat for 5 or 6 minutes to lightly melt the caramel, then invert as directed.

START SMALL

The easiest way to learn to make big, beautiful Tarte Tatins is to start out making smaller (4- to 6-inch) ones. Once you have perfected the method making small tarts (which might take 3 or 4 tries), you can make larger ones by increasing the recipe proportionally, according to the pan size you're using. Just keep in mind that for an 11-inch pan, you'll need twice the amount of butter and sugar and three times as many apples.

KOUIGN AMMAN

Kouign amman literally means "bread and butter" in the Breton dialect. These caramelized, flaky pastries are traditionally made in a larger size, but legendary baker Pierre Hermé makes miniature ones because he discovered they have more crunch. Everyone who has tasted them says they're irresistible.

BAKER'S BASICS TO REVIEW
Measuring Dry Ingredients, page 21
Doing the Roll-In and Turns, page 34

———

1½ cups warm water
½ package (⅛ ounce) active dry yeast
3½ cups bread flour
4 teaspoons coarse sea salt
1½ cups (12 ounces) unsalted butter
1¾ cups sugar
1½ tablespoons unsalted butter, melted

Place the water in a small bowl and sprinkle the yeast over it. Stir to dissolve. In a large bowl, combine the flour and salt. Add the yeast mixture and stir rapidly to blend. Turn the dough out onto a well floured work surface and knead until smooth and not too sticky, about 2 to 3 minutes. Place the dough in a lightly oiled bowl and cover with plastic wrap or a moist kitchen towel. Set aside in a warm place to rise slightly, about 30 minutes.

Turn the dough out onto a lightly floured surface. Join and shape the butter into a flat square. Spread the dough out into a 12 x 10-inch oval, place the square of butter in the center, and fold the sides of the dough over the butter to form an envelope. Let the dough rest in the refrigerator for 20 minutes. Roll the dough out into a 22 x 10-inch rectangle. Do a three-fold turn, folding the bottom third up and the top third down. Cover with plastic wrap and let the dough rest in the refrigerator for 1 hour.

Sprinkle ⅔ cup of the sugar on the work surface and set the dough on top, seam side down. Roll the dough out into a 14 x 7½-inch rectangle. Sprinkle some of the sugar over the dough and do another three-fold turn. Let the dough rest in the refrigerator for 30 minutes. Again sprinkle ⅔ cup of the sugar on the work surface and set the dough on top. Re-roll into a 14 x 7½-inch rectangle. Sprinkle sugar over the dough, reserving a few tablespoons to sprinkle over the formed pastries, and do a final three-fold turn. Cover and refrigerate again for 30 minutes.

Roll the dough out to ¹/₄ inch thick and cut it into 3¹/₄-inch squares if using circle molds, 2¹/₄-inch squares if using muffin tins, or 1¹/₄-inch squares if using tassie pans.

Lightly butter and sugar the molds (place circle molds on a nonstick baking sheet tray), muffin tins, or tassie pans. Place the dough squares in the molds, tins, or pans. Using a pastry brush, lightly coat them with the melted butter and sprinkle with the remaining sugar. Fold the corners of each square to meet in the center. Let rise at room temperature for 1¹/₂ hours. Preheat the oven to 350°.

Place the pastries on the center rack in the oven and bake for 40 minutes for the circle molds or about 35 minutes for the muffin tins and tassie pans. Serve at room temperature.

Pierre Hermé: Pâtissier, Sculptor, Avant-Gardist

Serious food lovers who visit Paris often find themselves with their noses pressed up against the window of the famous food shop Fauchon, mesmerized by pastries that look like whimsical, colorful sculptures; cakes covered by a red, violet, and fuchsia tapestry of assorted berries; tarts like miniature boats with thin chocolate wafers for sails; individual desserts shaped like music boxes with white chocolate filigree and lace; and cakes sheathed in a shiny mahogany-like coating decorated with rose petals.

The sculptor in residence is Pierre Hermé, pastry chef at Fauchon for more than ten years. Recognized as an avant-gardist for his ingenious techniques for giving traditional French pastry a new-age look and infusing it with a new spirit, Hermé is intimately familiar with the classical elements of his craft. An unlikely combination of sleeping giant and joyous child, he has spent well over half of his thirty-three years making pastries. Descended from four generations of bakers in the Alsatian town of Colmar, Hermé started apprenticing at age fourteen with Gaston Lenôtre and quickly climbed up through the ranks. By age nineteen he had taken over the reins of the Lenôtre Boutique on Avenue Victor Hugo. After a stint in the military and several years opening bakeries in Brussels and Luxembourg, he returned to Paris and Fauchon. When he started at Fauchon, Fauchon president Martine Prémat asked him not only to reorganize the pastry department, but also to create a new lineup of pastries twice each year.

Today, in a basement pâtisserie that's more like a labyrinthine cave than the high-tech laboratory one might expect, Hermé oversees a staff of thirty-five, which turns out nine hundred different desserts. Among these are the 150 original creations from his collection and many more that are revisions of old classics, most of which are featured in his book *Pierre Hermé, Pâtissier: Secrets Gourmands.* Hermé works his magic by recombining the classic pâtisserie elements (puff pastry, sponge cake, almond paste, chocolate) the way a Parisian architect might remodel a palace. For example, when he makes *pâte feuilletée inversée,* which is a puff pastry, he places the butter on the outside of the dough, which is the exact opposite of the traditional method.

(continued)

Hermé has also reinvented the traditional Paris-Brest, a circle of choux pastry filled with whipped cream, by adding caramelized almonds on top and praline (crispy bits of burnt sugar and almonds) to a mousse filling.

And there's no better example of Hermé's gift for reconstruction than his triangular palace of milk chocolate with a glazed cherry on top—*la cerise sur la gâteau.* It exemplifies one of Hermé's dictums: "A good cake depends on proportion, texture." The interior of this cake is made up of many alternating creamy and crispy layers of hazelnut sponge cake, thin milk chocolate wafers, thin praline sheets, creamy chocolate ganache, and milk chocolate–flavored whipped cream, all repeated so that each piece offers the same pattern of flavors and textures.

But it is more than just the interplay of combined textures and the visual appeal that sets Hermé's work apart from the run-of-the-mill pastry we find in France, or anywhere else for that matter. Hermé is also finicky, even obsessive, about ingredients. He knows that slight adjustments in ingredients play a subtle but important role in how a pastry comes off. "A caramel made with salted butter helps create a balance," he insists. "It's not too sweet." He uses *fleur de sel,* a brand of coarse sea salt that gives all of his doughs a unique taste. The butter he uses—a golden, creamy product—comes from Charentes and is often less than a week old. Whether it's vanilla beans from Tahiti or rose extract from Ceylon, these specially picked ingredients all create an extraordinary taste and feel when his finished desserts dance on the palate.

Hermé often gets ideas and inspiration from the decorative arts. He walks the streets of Paris, visiting art galleries, sculpture exhibitions, and flea markets, absorbing the shapes of things. He loves objects, furniture, paintings. All of these influences show up in his pastries. His *canellés* are ebony-colored domes with a caramelized patina like the artifacts one might find in an antique shop; his *Kouign Amann* are golden medallions of crystallized butter and sugar reminiscent of amulets one might uncover at a *marché aux puces;* his roasted pineapple, *ananas rôti,* is an amber dome of light that certainly may have been inspired by one of Monet's haystack paintings.

When Hermé visualizes a new creation, he approaches its construction from an architectural perspective: "With *la cerise sur le gâteau,* I told my friend Yan Pennor (who also designed Hermé's book) what I wanted to have on the inside and he did a drawing, a model of what the cake would look like." The first time *la cerise sur la gâteau* appeared in the showcase in July 1993, it became an instant success. But Hermé doesn't always hit the mark on the first shot. He's always tinkering, trying to find the perfect combination of texture, flavor, and appearance. "Sometimes I have an idea to build a cake," he says. "But not the decoration. Sometimes the decoration changes. Each recipe has an evolution. Although the design may be different, the spirit is the same."

So that we don't get lost in the spirit or the spectacle, we have to remember that, like most dedicated pastry chefs, Hermé demands that purity of ingredient and complexity of flavor are far more important than physical beauty. "When you eat cake, it's for pleasure," he insists. And yet, a pastry's initial task is to tantalize us to take a bite. Pierre Hermé calls this *"susciter d'envie"*— an arousal of desire. Those who have tasted Hermé's creations agree that his pastries satisfy as thoroughly as they arouse.

Holiday and Other Festive Desserts

Holidays at Gayle's are time to gear up, quadruple production, make new friends and customers, and thank the loyal customers who support us throughout the year. We make dozens of desserts for the various holidays and special events, including at least half a dozen special ones for each of the major—and many of the minor—holidays. On Father's Day, we make pretzels that spell "Dad," and at graduation time we make cakes with scrolls and mortarboards on top. For Halloween, we fill the showcase with truffles that look like eyeballs; every Easter, we construct intricate Faberge-type cakes. For Super Bowls when our beloved '49ers are playing, we've even made cakes that look so much like pigskins our customers are tempted to send a friend out toward the end zone on a post pattern.

It would take another book the size of this one to hold all the festive goodies we make for every holiday, so we've included only our most popular items here. We're sure you'll find something to make your next holiday celebration especially sweet (or savory!).

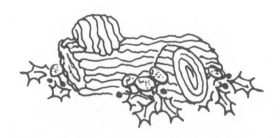

BRIOCHE DOUGH

MAKES ABOUT 4 POUNDS

Brioche is a rich, buttery bread that goes well with caviar or foie gras. It is wonderful toasted and makes great French toast.

BAKER'S BASICS TO REVIEW
Measuring Dry Ingredients, page 21

1/2 cup warm water
3 packages (3/4 ounce) active dry yeast
6 1/2 cups flour
3 1/2 teaspoons salt
1/2 cup sugar
1 1/2 cups (12 ounces) unsalted butter, at room temperature
6 large eggs, lightly beaten
1/4 cup cold milk

Place the water in a small bowl and sprinkle the yeast over it. Stir to dissolve. Set aside until creamy, 5 to 10 minutes.

Place the flour, salt, and sugar in the bowl of a tabletop mixer fitted with the dough hook. Add the butter, yeast mixture, and two-thirds of the eggs. Mix on the lowest speed for 4 to 5 minutes, or until all the ingredients are incorporated and the dough is smooth but firm. While the mixer is running, slowly add the rest of the eggs in 3 or 4 additions, waiting until each is fully incorporated before adding the next, about 4 to 5 minutes more. Increase the speed to medium and mix for 2 to 3 minutes. Slowly add the milk to the side of the bowl, allowing the very wet dough to pull away from the sides of the mixing bowl. The final dough will be elastic, satiny, and very wet.

Cover the dough with plastic wrap and let it rise for 1 hour. After the dough has nearly doubled, remove it from the bowl and place it on a lightly floured work surface. Punch the dough down and round it into a ball using a little of the flour on the work surface. Place the dough in a clean bowl, cover with plastic wrap, and refrigerate overnight.

The next morning, remove the dough from the refrigerator and use as directed.

BRIOCHES DE MOUSSELINES

MAKES FOUR 14-OUNCE LOAVES

For this recipe you'll need 4 small coffee cans, each measuring 5 inches tall by 4 inches in diameter. The molds create a handy, festive-shaped bread; the cylindrical loaves can be sliced in rounds and used for canapés or toasted for eggs Benedict.

1 recipe Brioche Dough (page 282)

EGG GLAZE
2 eggs
2 tablespoons milk

Clean four small 5-inch-diameter x 4-inch-deep coffee cans, then coat them with softened butter. Divide the dough into 4 equal pieces. Shape each piece into a tight ball. Place one ball of dough in each can.

In a small bowl, whisk together the eggs and milk to make the glaze. Using a pastry brush, coat the top of the loaves with the glaze. Cover the cans with plastic wrap and place in a warm, draft-free spot to rise for 2 to 2^1/$_2$ hours. When the loaves have been rising for 1^1/$_2$ hours, preheat the oven to 375°.

When the loaves have risen to just below the rim of the cans, remove the plastic wrap and again brush them with glaze. With a razor blade or very sharp knife, make a small cross on top of each loaf.

Set the cans on a baking sheet and place on the lower rack in the oven. Bake for 25 to 30 minutes, or until the loaves are golden brown and sound hollow when removed from their cans and gently thumped on the bottom. Remove from molds and let cool on wire racks.

BRIOCHES DE NANTERRE

For this recipe, you'll need four small loaf pans measuring 6 x 3 x 2 inches. Because fluted brioche molds are hard to come by, instructions for shaping Brioche à Tête (brioche with nobs on top) have been omitted here. Instructions for shaping them may be found in *The Village Baker*.

    1 recipe Brioche Dough (page 282)

EGG GLAZE
    2 eggs
    2 tablespoons milk

Lightly coat four 6 x 3 x 2-inch loaf pans with butter. Divide the dough into 4 equal pieces, then divide each piece into 3 equal pieces. Shape each piece into a tight ball. Place 3 balls of dough side by side in each loaf pan.

In a small bowl, whisk together the eggs and milk to make the glaze. Using a pastry brush, coat the tops of the loaves with the glaze. Cover the pans with plastic wrap and place in a warm, draft-free spot to rise for 2 to 2½ hours. When the loaves have been rising for 1½ hours, preheat the oven to 375°.

When the loaves have risen slightly higher than the rim of the pans, remove the plastic wrap and again brush them with glaze. With scissors, snip small crosses in the top of each ball of dough.

Place the pans on the center rack in the oven. Bake for 20 minutes, or until the loaves are golden brown and sound hollow when removed from their pans and gently thumped on the bottom. Remove the loaves from pans and let cool on wire racks.

BRIOCHE FEUILLETÉ

MAKES TWO 7 X 3¹/₂ X 2¹/₄-INCH LOAVES

This is a recipe we learned at Le Feyeux in Paris. It's a fun project for the advanced baker who likes roll-in doughs and lots of butter. If you've tried the croissant, Danish, or puff pastry recipe, this one will be a snap.

BAKER'S BASICS TO REVIEW
Doing the Roll-In and Turns, page 34

---

¹/₄ recipe (1 pound) Brioche Dough, risen overnight in refrigerator
  (page 282)
¹/₂ cup (4 ounces) cold butter

EGG GLAZE
1 egg
2 tablespoons milk

Place the dough on a lightly floured work surface. Roll it out into a 10 x 8-inch rectangle. Take the butter out of the refrigerator and, while still in the wrapper, pound it with a rolling pin on all four sides to soften. Unwrap the butter and shape it into a 4-inch square about ¹/₂ inch thick.

Place the butter on one half of the dough and spread to within ¹/₂ inch of the edge, then fold the unbuttered half over the top. Seal the edges. Roll the dough into an 18 x 9-inch rectangle. Fold the dough in thirds. Cover it with plastic wrap and place in the refrigerator for 30 minutes. Repeat the process two more times.

To shape, roll the dough out to 18 x 7 inches. Cut it in half. Roll each piece into a log. Place each log in a loaf pan.

In a small bowl, whisk together the egg and milk to make the glaze. Using a pastry brush, coat the top of the loaves with the glaze. Cover the pans with plastic wrap and place in a warm, draft-free spot to rise for 2 to 2¹/₂ hours. When the loaves have been rising for 1¹/₂ hours, preheat the oven to 375°. When the loaves have risen 1 inch above the rim of the pans, remove the plastic wrap and again brush them with glaze.

Place the pans on the lower rack in the oven. Bake for 40 minutes, or until the loaves are dark golden brown and sound hollow when removed from the pans and gently thumped on the bottom. Let cool in the pans on wire racks for 5 minutes, then depan and let cool completely on the racks.

SAUSAGE ROLLS

These are tasty appetizers. Use your favorite bulk sausage—any moderately lean breakfast or Italian sausage will work.

1/4 recipe (1 pound) Brioche Dough, risen overnight in the
    refrigerator (page 282)
1/2 pound bulk sausage

GLAZE
1 egg
2 tablespoons milk

Line two baking sheets with parchment paper.

Place the dough on a lightly floured work surface. Roll out into a 14 x 9 x 1/8-inch rectangle. Cut the dough in half lengthwise to make two long strips 4 1/2 inches wide.

Divide the sausage in half and roll each half into a 14-inch-long, 3/4-inch-thick log. Place one sausage log in the center of each strip of dough. Fold the top edge of the dough over the sausage log, then fold the bottom section over the top edge to seal the sausage inside.

With your palms, gently roll each dough log to even it out and gradually stretch to measure 18 inches long. Cut the sausage rolls into 2-inch sections.

In a small bowl, whisk together the egg and milk to make the glaze. Place the rolls on the prepared baking sheets. Brush with the glaze.

Preheat the oven to 375°.

Place the sausage rolls in the refrigerator to chill for at least 30 minutes. Remove from the refrigerator and let rise at room temperature for 30 to 45 minutes.

Place the baking sheet on the lower rack in the oven and bake for 20 to 25 minutes, or until the pastry is light brown. (Some of the sausage fat may have dripped out.) To test for doneness, remove one of the sausage rolls and cut it in half. When the sausage is done to your liking, remove from the oven and serve. The rolls may also be served at room temperature for up to 1 hour after baking.

ROSA SALVA VENETIAN PARTY SANDWICH

MAKES 10 TO 12 APPETIZER SERVINGS
(UP TO 64 INDIVIDUAL PIECES)

At Rosa Salva bakery in Venice, Italy, this sandwich is made with a simple white bread. We've found that substituting brioche adds a special touch of color and flavor. These small sandwiches make great appetizers.

This recipe uses a No. 10 tin can for a mold. You can get one of these cans from a local restaurant or bakery. If you can't find one, a mold can be made out of a piece of parchment paper. Cut a 19 x 14-inch piece. Fold it in half so that it is double thickness and measures 19 x 7 inches. Then, make a cylinder 6 inches in diameter and 7 inches high and secure the cylinder on the outside with two pieces of tape or string.

> ¹/₂ recipe (2 pounds) Brioche Dough, risen overnight in the
>   refrigerator (page 282)
> Assorted sandwich fillings (page 288)

Let the dough come to room temperature for at least 1 hour. On a lightly floured work surface, shape the dough into a tight round ball. Butter a clean No. 10 tin can and place the dough inside. Alternatively, stand the paper mold on a parchment-lined baking sheet and place the ball of dough inside the paper mold.

Let the dough rise for 4 to 5 hours, or until doubled in bulk. About 1 hour before the brioche is ready to bake, preheat the oven to 375°.

Place the No. 10 can or baking sheet on the lower rack in the oven and bake for 40 to 50 minutes, or until the loaf is golden brown and sounds hollow when gently thumped on the bottom. Let the loaf cool on a wire rack. When cool, after about 50 minutes, place the loaf in the freezer to set up for 1 hour.

When the loaf is very cold and firm, remove it from the freezer and, using a serrated bread knife or sharp meat knife, slice into twenty to twenty-two ³/₈-inch-thick slices, beginning at the bottom. The last slice, which will be the loaf's domed top, should be reserved to top the panettone.

Lay one slice of bread on the work surface and spread with a thin coat of one of the fillings. Top with a second slice of bread. Cut the sandwich into 6 equal triangles and transfer, still in a round shape, to a platter. Repeat the process, using a different filling each time, first layering bread, then filling, then bread. Slice into triangles, and stack the sandwich rounds on the platter.

Cap the whole thing with the domed piece from the original loaf and serve.

The following are just some of the spreads you might use in the Rosa Salva Party Sandwich. You'll need three to four of them.

Deviled Ham Spread

Combine 4 ounces ham, chopped into a paste in food processor; 1 tablespoon grated yellow onion; 2 teaspoons Dijon mustard; 3 tablespoons mayonnaise; and 2 tablespoons cream cheese. *Makes about 1¹/₄ cups.*

Smoked Salmon and Cream Cheese Spread

Combine 4 ounces smoked salmon; ¹/₄ cup (2 ounces) unsalted butter, at room temperature; 1 teaspoon Worcestershire sauce; 1 teaspoon freshly squeezed lemon juice; and 1 teaspoon chopped fresh dill. *Makes about 1 cup.*

Cucumber and Herb Cheese Spread

Combine 6 ounces cream cheese, 3 tablespoons chopped fresh dill, 2 teaspoons freshly squeezed lemon juice, and a pinch of salt. Peel and cut 1 cucumber into paper-thin slices. When filling the sandwiches, spread filling on the bread, cover with the cucumber slices, and then top with another piece of bread. *Makes about 1 cup.*

Egg Salad with Curry

Hard-boil 5 eggs. Chop 3 of the eggs and thinly slice the other 2. In a separate bowl, combine the chopped eggs, ¹/₄ cup mayonnaise, 1 teaspoon Dijon mustard, 1 tablespoon minced capers, 1 teaspoon curry powder, and salt and pepper to taste. When filling the sandwiches, spread filling on the bread, cover with the egg slices, and then top with another piece of bread.

CHRISTMAS STOLLEN

MAKES 1 LARGE STOLLEN

This is a Dresden stollen that we learned many years ago from Linde Martin, a local artist. It is a buttery, flavorful cake to serve with coffee or liqueur.

BAKER'S BASICS TO REVIEW
Measuring Dry Ingredients, page 21
Zesting Citrus, page 24

3³/4 cups all-purpose flour
1 cup warm milk
1 drop bitter almond oil (see Note)
¹/2 cup sugar
4 packages (1 ounce) active dry yeast
1¹/4 cups sliced almonds
2 cups raisins
¹/3 cup Candied Orange Peel (page 111)
Zest of 1 lemon, grated
¹/2 teaspoon cardamom
¹/4 cup rum
1 cup (8 ounces) unsalted butter, at room temperature
¹/2 teaspoon salt
¹/4 cup butter, melted
¹/4 cup confectioners' sugar

Place the flour in a mound on the work surface. Make a well in the flour and add the warm milk, bitter almond oil, and sugar. Sprinkle the yeast on top. With the fingers of one hand, swirl the yeast mixture, incorporating the sugar and some of the flour until you have a thick paste. Let this sponge rise, supported by the flour around the well, for 1 hour.

Meanwhile, in a small bowl, combine the almonds, raisins, orange peel, lemon zest, and cardamom. Add the rum. Set aside.

After the sponge has risen for 1 hour, add the softened butter and the salt to the mixture in the middle of the well, then mix all ingredients until smooth and no dry spots remain, about 5 to 6 minutes. The dough will be moist and satiny but not wet. Cover with a damp kitchen towel and let rise 1 hour.

When the dough has risen, incorporate the almond and raisin mixture. Shape into a ball and let rise 30 to 45 minutes.

Preheat the oven to 350°. Line a baking sheet with parchment paper.

To shape the dough into a loaf, place it on the work surface without deflating it. Place a rolling pin in the middle of the dough, then roll the pin back

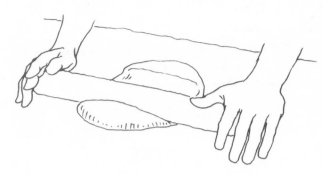

and forth to make a flat area about 5 inches wide, bordered by two logs of dough. Fold in half so the log on the left side is now resting on the log on the other side. Place the rolling pin on top of the part you just folded over and roll the pin back and forth. Tuck the upper (middle) flap into the newly created indentation, so you have what looks like three log-shaped mounds. The middle one symbolizes the "babe in the manger."

 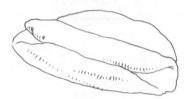

Place on the center rack in the oven and bake for 30 to 35 minutes, or until golden brown. When done, gently lift the parchment paper and place the loaf on a cooling rack, being careful not to let the stollen deflate. Immediately brush the loaf with the melted butter. Once the stollen has cooled, about 45 minutes, brush it again. Dust with the confectioners' sugar and serve. When completely cooled, the stollen may be covered in plastic wrap and stored at room temperature for up to 1 week.

NOTE: Bitter almond oil is difficult to find, but worth the effort. If you can't find it at your local specialty food shop, try the King Arthur Flour catalog (page 317). If you can't find it at all, you may substitute almond extract.

PANETTONE

This moist, flavorful panettone is much simpler to make than the sourdough version. As for the Rosa Salva Venetian Party Sandwich, you will need two No. 10 tin cans or parchment paper molds to bake the bread in. See page 287 for more about this. The following sample schedule is given simply as a guideline.

BAKER'S BASICS TO REVIEW
Measuring Dry Ingredients, page 21
Zesting Citrus, page 24
Separating Eggs, page 22

TIMETABLE

Day One, noon: mix starter, prepare fruit mixture and aroma mixture

Day Two, 8 A.M.:	**3 P.M.:**	**4 P.M.:**	**10 P.M.:**
mix first dough	mix second dough, combine with first	shape the loaf	bake the loaf

---

STARTER
$1/2$ cup warm water
$1/2$ teaspoon active dry yeast
1 cup all-purpose flour

FRUIT MIXTURE
2 cups raisins
1 cup Candied Orange Peel (page 111)
$1/4$ cup dark rum

AROMA
1 tablespoon pure vanilla extract
$1/2$ teaspoon almond extract
1 tablespoon grated lemon zest
4 teaspoons grated orange zest

FIRST DOUGH
$3/4$ cup warm water
1 teaspoon active dry yeast
$4^1/2$ cups all-purpose flour
$1/2$ cup sugar
1 cup starter (see above)
5 large egg yolks, lightly beaten, at room temperature
$1/2$ cup (4 ounces) unsalted butter, at room temperature

Unable to sleep our first night in that ancient town in northern Italy, I quietly slipped out of our hotel room in search of an espresso. The town was still, and dawn was slowly beginning to define the stone buildings and narrow cobblestone streets. I found a small cafe around the corner from two of Orvieto's most extraordinary features: a medieval cathedral covered with mosaics in brilliant hues of gold, turquoise, and ocher, and the other, a salumeria (an Italian sausage and salami shop) that features salami made with cinghiale, or wild boar.

The cafe I ended up at was sparklingly new, with marble floor, oak trim, chrome appointments, and the obligatory espresso machine. Italian pastries, piled high in trays and baskets, were displayed in a spotless glass showcase. When I arrived, the owner, Mario Polleggioni, offered me an espresso, and every time I took a sip, he tried to whisk the cup away, thinking I had knocked it down in one gulp as is the custom in Italy.

When he found out that I was a baker from California, he told me his story. He, too,

(continued)

SECOND DOUGH

2 teaspoons active dry yeast

¹/₄ cup warm water

2 cups all-purpose flour

2 teaspoons salt

¹/₄ cup sugar

2 large egg yolks, lightly beaten

¹/₄ cup (2 ounces) unsalted butter, at room temperature

———

2 pats butter

To make the starter, place the warm water in a medium ceramic bowl and sprinkle the yeast over it. When creamy, add the flour. Stir until a thick batter with no dry spots forms. Cover the batter with a damp kitchen towel and let rise in a warm place for at least 10 hours or overnight.

To prepare the fruit mixture, combine the raisins, orange peel, and rum and set aside, uncovered, to soak.

For the aroma, mix all of the ingredients together in a small bowl and set aside uncovered.

To make the first dough, place the warm water in a small bowl and sprinkle the yeast on top. Stir briefly. In a large bowl, combine the flour and sugar. Pour the dry ingredients onto the work surface in a mound and make a well in the center. Pour the starter, yeast mixture, and egg yolks into the well. With the fingers of one hand, stir the liquid mixture in the well, gradually pulling in some of the flour to make a sticky paste. As the flour is incorporated into the paste, it will become elastic and should be stretched and pulled vigorously. When all except 1 cup of the flour has been incorporated, add the butter in small pieces. Coat your hands with flour and work the butter bits into the dough. The dough will be moist and sticky. Incorporate the remaining 1 cup flour, kneading for 8 to 10 more minutes, or until the dough is smooth and moist. Cover the dough with a damp kitchen towel and let rise in a warm place for 5 to 6 hours, or until doubled. The dough is ready when it does not immediately spring back when gently pressed with a fingertip.

To make the second dough, stir the yeast into the warm water as described for the first dough. In a large bowl, combine the flour, salt, and sugar. Measure out and set aside ¹/₂ cup of the flour mixture. Place the remaining flour mixture in a mound on the work surface. Make a well in the mound. Place the beaten egg yolks, yeast mixture, and aroma mixture in the well. With the fingers of one hand, stir the liquid while incorporating the flour a little at a time until a moist, satiny dough forms, about 10 to 12 minutes. (Incorporating the flour too quickly may cause lumps or dry spots to form.)

When the dough is smooth, add the softened butter in small pieces, working it in by stretching and folding the dough back onto itself. When all of the butter is incorporated and the dough is very soft and shiny, add the fruit mixture and knead to incorporate. Knead in the remaining $1/2$ cup of flour. The dough will have a thick batterlike consistency.

On a lightly floured work surface, combine the soft second dough with the fully risen first dough by kneading them together with wide sweeping strokes for 20 to 25 minutes. The dough will be moist and sticky; incorporate any dough pieces that cling to your hands and the work surface as you knead. If the dough is too moist and sticky to handle, gradually work in an extra $1/2$ cup or so of flour during the last 5 minutes of kneading. Cover with a damp kitchen towel and let the final dough rise in a warm place for 1 hour.

Butter the No. 10 cans or parchment molds. If using parchment molds, place them on a baking sheet lined with parchment paper. Divide the dough in half and shape each half into a ball. Place one ball in each prepared No. 10 can or parchment mold. Cover the loaves with a damp kitchen towel and let rise for 6 to 7 hours, checking them every 2 hours to make sure they are not drying out. If they are drying out, spray them with a fine mist of water. When the loaves have been rising for 5 hours, preheat the oven to 375°. When properly risen, the loaves will have doubled in size and will fill two-thirds of the cans.

To bake the loaves, cut a 2-inch cross in the top of each one with a sharp knife or razor blade. Place 1 pat of butter in each cut. Place the cans or baking sheet on the lower rack in the oven. Bake the loaves for 1 hour to 1 hour and 15 minutes, or until they are well browned and sound hollow when removed from the cans or molds and thumped on the bottom. (If the tops start to get too dark while baking, cover them loosely with a piece of aluminum foil.) Remove the panettone from the cans or molds and let cool on wire racks.

had been a baker, but was now an entrepreneur and developer of sorts. He said he designed, built, furnished, stocked, opened, and sold many a cafe-pasticceria similar to the one in which we were standing. Many years ago in Milan, he had been a baker for Motta, the immense wholesale bakery that has supplied mass-produced pastries to all of Italy and many other countries in the world.

When I mentioned the panettone, an Italian sweet bread traditionally made at Christmas and an item for which Motta is famous, Mario's face lit up. He explained the intricate process in baker's terms, cupping his hands to describe kilos, pinching his fingers to denote grams, swirling his hands to simulate mixing. He gave me no exact measurements, just ratios. Although I understood the concept, I had nothing specific to follow. He could tell I wanted to know more, so he told me to come back in a few hours. In the meantime, his wife would bring his recipe book to the store, so he'd be able to share the recipe with me, down to the smallest detail.

I was surprised to learn that the best panettone is made using sourdough starter. Odd to think that something so sweet and aromatic could be made with an intensely sour dough. But as it turns out, the sourdough is what gives panettone its voluptuous texture. And that same sourdough culture also helps keep the crumb of the panettone fresh (what we bakers call shelf life) for up to 3 months when packaged correctly.

SOURDOUGH PANETTONE

MAKES TWO 2-POUND LOAVES

This panettone, adapted from a recipe we learned in Orvieto, Italy, uses a soupy refrigerator sourdough starter. Again, you'll need two No. 10 tin cans or parchment paper molds to bake the loaves in. For more about this, see page 287.

BAKER'S BASICS TO REVIEW
Measuring Dry Ingredients, page 21
Zesting Citrus, page 24
Making a Liquid Sourdough Starter (Refrigerator Sour)
from a Firm Levain, page 49
Separating Eggs, page 22

TIMETABLE

Day One, noon: mix starter, prepare fruit mixture and aroma mixture

Day Two, 8 A.M.:	**3 P.M.:**	**4 P.M.:**	**10 P.M.:**
mix first dough	mix second dough, combine with first	shape the loaf	bake the loaf

---

STARTER
¼ cup warm water
¼ cup refrigerator sourdough starter (page 49)
½ cup all-purpose flour

FRUIT MIXTURE
2 cups raisins
1 cup Candied Orange Peel (page 111)
¼ cup dark rum

AROMA
1 tablespoon pure vanilla extract
½ teaspoon almond extract
1 tablespoon grated lemon zest
4 teaspoons grated orange zest

FIRST DOUGH
¾ cup warm water
½ teaspoon active dry yeast
4½ cups all-purpose flour
½ cup sugar
1 cup starter (see above)
5 egg yolks, at room temperature
½ cup (4 ounces) unsalted butter, at room temperature

SECOND DOUGH

1 teaspoon active dry yeast

¹/₄ cup warm water

2 cups all-purpose flour

2 teaspoons salt

¹/₄ cup sugar

2 large egg yolks, lightly beaten

¹/₄ cup (2 ounces) unsalted butter, at room temperature

———

2 pats butter

To make the starter, place the ingredients in a medium ceramic bowl and stir to combine. Cover with a damp kitchen towel and let the soupy mixture rise in a warm place overnight or for up to 24 hours.

To prepare the fruit mixture, combine the raisins, orange peel, and rum and set aside, uncovered, to soak.

For the aroma, mix all of the ingredients together in a small bowl. Cover with plastic wrap and place in the refrigerator overnight.

To make the first dough, place the water in a small bowl. Sprinkle the yeast on top and stir in. Let sit until creamy, about 5 minutes. In a separate bowl, combine the flour and sugar and place the mixture in a mound on the work surface. Make a well in the mound. Place all of the starter, the yeast mixture, and the egg yolks in the well. With the fingers of one hand, stir the liquid mixture in the well, gradually pulling in some of the flour to make a sticky paste. As the flour is incorporated into the mixture in the well, the paste will become elastic and should be stretched and pulled vigorously. When all but 1 cup of the flour has been incorporated, add the butter in small pieces. Coat your hands with flour and work the butter bits into the dough. The dough will be moist and sticky. Incorporate the remaining 1 cup flour, kneading for 8 to 10 more minutes, or until the dough is smooth and moist. Cover the dough with a damp kitchen towel and let rise in a warm place for 5 to 6 hours, or until doubled. The dough is ready when it does not immediately spring back when gently pressed with a fingertip.

To mix the second dough, stir the yeast into the warm water as described for the first dough. In a separate mixing bowl, combine the flour, salt, and sugar. Measure out and set aside ¹/₂ cup of the flour mixture. Place the remaining flour mixture in a mound on the work surface. Make a well in the mound. Place the beaten egg yolks, yeast mixture, and aroma mixture in the well. With the fingers of one hand, stir the liquid while incorporating a little flour at a time until a moist, satiny, batterlike dough forms, about 10 to 12 minutes. (Incorporating the flour too quickly may cause lumps or dry spots to form.)

When the dough is smooth, add the softened butter in small pieces, working it in by stretching and folding the dough back onto itself. When all of the butter is incorporated and the dough is very soft and shiny, add the fruit mixture and knead to incorporate. Knead in the remaining 1/2 cup of flour. The dough will have a thick batterlike consistency.

On a lightly floured work surface, combine the soft second dough with the fully risen first dough by kneading them together with wide sweeping strokes for 20 to 25 minutes. The dough will be moist and sticky; incorporate any dough pieces that cling to your hands and the work surface as you knead. If the dough is too moist and sticky to handle, an extra 1/2 cup or so of flour can be gradually worked in during the last 5 minutes of kneading. Cover with a damp kitchen towel and let the final dough rise in a warm place for 1 hour.

Butter the No. 10 cans or parchment molds. If using parchment molds, place them on a baking sheet lined with parchment paper. Divide the dough in half and shape each half into a tight ball. Place one ball in each prepared No. 10 can or parchment mold.

Cover the loaves with a damp kitchen towel and let rise for 5 to 6 hours, checking them every 2 hours to make sure they are not drying out. If they are drying out any time during rising, spray them with a fine mist of water. When the loaves have been rising for 4 hours, preheat the oven to 375°. When properly risen, the loaves will have doubled in size and will fill two-thirds of the cans.

To bake the loaves, cut a 2-inch cross in the top of each one with a sharp knife or razor blade. Place 1 pat of butter in each cut. Place the cans or baking sheet on the center rack in the oven. Bake the loaves for 1 hour to 1 hour and 15 minutes, or until they are well browned and sound hollow when removed from the cans or molds and thumped on the bottom. Remove the panettone from the cans or molds and let cool on wire racks.

BOB HIRSCH'S
SOURDOUGH WAFFLES

MAKES 6 TO 8 WAFFLES

This recipe, which comes from Louisa's father, makes delicious, foolproof waffles that are perfect for holiday breakfasts. If you don't already have a refrigerator sour, see page 49 for instructions on starting one.

BAKER'S BASICS TO REVIEW

Making a Liquid Sourdough Starter (Refrigerator Sour) from
 a Firm Levain, page 49
Measuring Dry Ingredients, page 21
Folding, page 20

SPONGE

1 cup sourdough starter
1 1/2 cups flour
1 cup water

---

1 to 2 beaten eggs
1/4 cup powdered milk
5 tablespoons (2 1/2 ounces) butter, melted
2 tablespoons sugar
1 scant teaspoon salt
1 scant teaspoon baking soda

Preheat a waffle iron.

In a large mixing bowl, combine the sponge ingredients. Cover and let stand at room temperature overnight. The next morning, remove 1 cup of the sponge mixture and stir it into your starter to replenish it. Add the beaten eggs, powdered milk, and butter to the sponge remaining in the bowl and stir gently to combine well.

In a separate mixing bowl, combine the sugar, salt, and baking soda. Sprinkle this mixture over the sourdough batter. Gently fold in the dry ingredients, then let the batter rest for 1 to 2 minutes. Spoon batter into hot waffle iron and cook until waffle is golden brown on both sides. Repeat until all batter is cooked.

CARDINALS

MAKES 30 PASTRIES

LEVAINS FOR JULIA

Joe was one of twenty-six bakers who taped segments with Julia Child for her PBS series, "Baking with Julia." It was an honor as well as a logistical feat to transport live starter all the way from Capitola, California, to Cambridge, Massachusetts, and then to make it perform within the producers' time frame. Here he tells how the adventure unfolded:

Julia called a few weeks before I was scheduled to tape the show to say she wanted me to do something other than demonstrate elementary bread sculptures, regional bread shapes, and simple loaf decorations. She wanted me to make sourdough. I was pleased but knew it would be a challenge. She said no one had done sourdough.

I suppose many other bakers, anticipating the risks, would have been more careful. Not me. Shortly after I hung up the phone, the thought crossed my mind that my fellow bakers had wisely avoided disaster. But it was too late for me. I would have to negotiate airport security with my starters and carry them on the airplane, make a culture grow in an unfamiliar environment, allow for differences in climate during rising, and bake in a strange oven. It's one thing to keep a levain happy, healthy, and well exercised at home, where it can be coddled and

(continued)

Cardinals are extra crunchy, decadent bar cookies with a glistening amber color and a pungent cinnamon flavor, so named because they were originally made by the priests who baked for a Portuguese cardinal many years ago. We learned it from a Parisian baker who was originally from Portugal. It is a tantalizing way to use day-old croissants, brioche, panettone—any yeasted and enriched dough.

BAKER'S BASICS TO REVIEW

Separating Eggs, page 22

Whipping Egg Whites and Making Meringues, page 198

Folding, page 20

TOPPING

1/3 cup sliced almonds

1/4 cup granulated sugar

2/3 cup confectioners' sugar

1 1/2 teaspoons ground cinnamon

FILLING

8 to 10 day-old croissants or brioche or panettone slices (see Note)

1/2 cup whole almonds

2/3 cup whole hazelnuts

1/4 cup Candied Orange Peel (page 111)

1 tablespoon ground cinnamon

2 cups coarse or regular granulated sugar

2/3 cup raisins

1 cup walnut pieces

2 tablespoons brandy

1/2 recipe (1 pound) Basic Puff Pastry Dough (page 85)

6 egg whites (about 1 cup)

1/2 cup water (optional)

To make the topping, combine all the ingredients in a small bowl; set aside.

To make the filling, place half of the day-old pastries in a food processor fitted with the metal blade and process 20 to 30 seconds, or until fine crumbs form. Transfer to a large mixing bowl and repeat with the remaining pastries. Measure out 8 cups into a large mixing bowl. Add the almonds, hazelnuts, orange peel, cinnamon, sugar, raisins, and walnuts to the crumbs. Using both hands, mix the ingredients with a gentle folding motion until well combined. Drizzle the brandy over the mixture and mix once more. Set aside.

Remove the puff pastry dough from the refrigerator and place it on a lightly floured work surface. Roll the dough out into a 16 x 12 x ⅛-inch rectangle. Prick the dough all over with a fork, then place it on a baking sheet and return it to the refrigerator.

Preheat the oven to 275°.

In a tabletop mixer fitted with the whisk, whip the egg whites until soft peaks form, about 3 to 4 minutes. Immediately fold the whites into the crumb mixture and combine using both hands. Squeeze some of the mixture firmly in one hand. If it sticks together easily, it's done. If it crumbles and falls apart, add 1 or 2 tablespoons of water, mix, and retest. Repeat until the proper consistency is reached. (Mixing with your hands allows you to fluff the mixture and test the consistency of the dough.)

Remove the puff pastry dough from the refrigerator and place it on a work surface. Spread the filling mixture in the center of the dough in a rectangular shape measuring 14 x 9 inches and 1 inch thick. Square off the sides of the filling and make sure it is relatively flat on top. Push on the filling lightly to even it out, but not hard enough to compact it. Sprinkle the topping mixture evenly over the filling. Cut off the excess puff pastry dough to make a perfect rectangle. Line two baking sheets with parchment paper.

Cut the sheet lengthwise into three 3-inch-wide strips. Cut each strip into 1¼-inch pieces. (Each strip will yield about 10 pieces.) With a chef's knife or icing spatula, lift each piece onto one of the prepared baking sheets, spacing them at least 1 inch apart.

Place the baking sheets on the center rack in the oven and bake for 1½ to 2 hours, making sure the temperature of the oven stays at 275° or lower. When done, the pastries will be a caramelized amber brown color and crunchy outside, but slightly soft inside when gently squeezed. Let cool on the baking sheets, then store in airtight containers for up to 1 week.

NOTE: If using frozen day-old pastries, allow them to come to room temperature before processing into crumbs. The pastries, once placed on the lined baking sheets, can be covered with plastic wrap and stored in the freezer for up to 1 week. To bake, transfer the frozen pastries directly from the freezer to the preheated oven.

nurtured; it's another to know how to handle it on the road. Levains like to be used on a regular basis. They have to be refreshed with flour and water so they don't get too sour. This feeding is a form of exercise. It gives the starter what the sourdough scientists call genetic memory. This is why our housesitters must sign an affidavit affirming their love for sourdough waffles and swear to eat them once a week.

Traditionally, levains have been seasoned travelers. For centuries they have gone to war, been carried on religious crusades, crossed the ocean on passenger ships, and bounced along the trail in miners' saddlebags. But I'd never heard of one jetting to Julia's.

Before I left for the airport, I took one precaution: I put the five starters I brought in the freezer for a couple of hours. Keeping them cool makes them take a nap.

After I checked in, I headed toward the gates with my carry-on bag clutched close to my chest. I heard an ominous voice over the loud speaker: "Proceed past security." My heart sank. Would they seize the starters? Would they subject my little micro-chums to x-rays? Would that rob them of their strength? We made it onto the plane without incident, but when I nodded off during the movie, I dreamed a white foam was oozing out of the overhead compartment. Would I have to tame the unruly levains by

(continued)

HOT CROSS BUNS

MAKES 12 BUNS

These are very popular at Easter and are surprisingly easy to make at home.

BAKER'S BASICS TO REVIEW

Measuring Dry Ingredients, page 21
Separating Eggs, page 22
Filling and Using a Nylon Pastry Bag, page 20
Making and Filling a Paper Pastry Bag, page 208

FRUIT SOAK

1/2 cup Candied Orange Peel (page 111)
1 cup raisins

SPONGE

2/3 cup milk, warmed to 100°
3 packages (3/4 ounce) active dry yeast
1/4 cup all-purpose flour
2 teaspoons granulated sugar

DOUGH

2 1/4 cups all-purpose flour
4 1/2 tablespoons granulated sugar
1 teaspoon salt
1/4 teaspoon ground cinnamon
1/4 teaspoon ground nutmeg
1/4 teaspoon ground mace
3 tablespoons butter, at room temperature
1 large egg, lightly beaten

EGG GLAZE

1 large egg
2 tablespoons cold milk

ROYAL ICING

1 cup confectioners' sugar
1 teaspoon egg white
1 tablespoon freshly squeezed lemon juice
1 teaspoon corn syrup
1 teaspoon water

To make the fruit soak, place the orange peel and raisins in a small bowl and pour hot tap water over them. Set aside.

To make the sponge, pour the warm milk in a medium mixing bowl.

stuffing them back into their containers? When I awoke and checked the starters, they were well behaved, not yet over the tops of their containers, probably because the bag was still cool from the earlier freezing.

When I reached the hotel, I checked the starters again. They were about to collapse. Looking for a solution, I ran around the room opening cabinets. Right under the television, I found what I needed: I've never been happier to see a mini-bar in my life. Four out of the five levains would be okay if kept cool. The fifth starter, the liquid one, would have to undergo a little repair via feeding. It would not be the first time I had ever refreshed my sourdough starter in a hotel room. It was, however, the first time I used Evian as the mixing water.

Everything went well until we started taping, when I truly began to realize what I had gotten myself into. What if they didn't perform on command? It was too late to worry. Everything was set in motion. There were twenty people on the set in Julia's kitchen. Every time the director said, "Standby," I would look down at my micro-pals and pray. When he finally said, "Action," it was as if drums rolled and music started to play. I was as proud as the father of a valedictorian on graduation day. The bread came out great. Julia was happy, and so was I.

Sprinkle the yeast over the milk and stir it in. Let rest until creamy, about 5 minutes, then add the flour and sugar and mix to incorporate. Let rise 30 minutes, stirring with a wooden spoon every 10 minutes. At the end of the time, the mixture will be frothy.

To make the dough, place the flour in the bowl of a tabletop mixer fitted with the dough hook. Pour the sponge into the bowl, then sprinkle the sugar, salt, and spices over the top. Add the butter in small pieces, then add the egg. Mix on low speed for 5 to 6 minutes, or until the ingredients are evenly distributed and a moist and elastic yet slightly firm dough has formed.

Drain the fruit mixture and squeeze out as much moisture as possible. Flatten the dough on the work surface and place the fruit on top. Incorporate the fruit into the dough by folding the dough over the fruit and kneading several times. When incorporating the wet ingredients, it may be necessary to dust the work surface with flour to counteract the extra moisture the fruit adds. Try to use as little flour as possible so the finished dough will be moist and smooth.

When the fruit is fully incorporated, shape the dough into a ball, cover with a damp kitchen towel and let rise for 30 minutes.

Roll the dough into an 18-inch log. Divide the log into 12 equal pieces. Shape each piece into a tight ball. Line an 11 x 9-inch baking sheet with parchment paper. Place the buns in rows of three across and four down on the baking sheet. They will be about 1 inch apart (after rising, they will be touching). This placement gives the buns their classic pull-apart look.

In a small bowl, crack open the egg and remove 1 teaspoon of 1 egg white for later use. Whisk together the remaining egg and the milk to make the glaze. Brush the buns with a light coat of glaze. Set buns aside to rise uncovered for 1^1/$_2$ to 2 hours, or until they are touching and have doubled in size. Preheat the oven to 375°.

Place the baking sheet on the center rack in the oven and bake for 16 to 18 minutes, or until very brown. Let cool on the baking sheet.

To make the icing, place the confectioners' sugar in a small bowl and add the reserved 1 tablespoon of egg white. Mix with a whisk. The mixture will be crumbly. Add the lemon juice and corn syrup and mix until smooth. If the mixture does not run off of the whisk in a slow but steady stream, add water and mix again. The frosting should be thick, but liquid enough to run off of a spoon. Place the frosting in a pastry bag fitted with a ^{1}/$_4$-inch tip. When the buns are cool, pipe a crisscross on top of each. Allow the frosting to set up, then serve.

IRISH SODA BREAD

MAKES TWO 7-INCH ROUNDS

This is popular for Saint Patrick's Day. Many of our customers have told us this is a very authentic version. It has a texture somewhat like scones, but it is easier to make.

BAKER'S BASICS TO REVIEW
Measuring Dry Ingredients, page 21
Preparing Cake Pans, page 189

1¹/₄ cups raisins
1 cup Candied Orange Peel, finely chopped (page 111)
¹/₄ cup Myers's rum
2 cups whole-wheat flour
2¹/₄ cups all-purpose flour
1¹/₂ teaspoons salt
1¹/₂ teaspoons baking soda
2 tablespoons firmly packed brown sugar
¹/₂ cup (4 ounces) butter, at room temperature
2 cups buttermilk

Preheat the oven to 350°. Butter, flour, and line two 7-inch cake pans.

In a small bowl, soak raisins and orange peel in the rum. Set aside.

Combine the flours in the bowl of a tabletop mixer fitted with the flat beater. Add the salt and baking soda and mix just to incorporate. Add the brown sugar and mix 30 seconds or so to make sure all the dry ingredients are well incorporated. Add the butter and mix on low speed until the butter is broken up into small pieces. Add the fruit mixture, then the buttermilk ¹/₂ cup at a time. Mix gently on low speed just until the mixture resembles biscuit dough, making sure to scrape down the bowl and beater as necessary. This should be a moist dough; don't overmix it.

Divide the dough in half and place one half in each prepared pan. Spread the dough with a spatula or wooden spoon. Place the pans on the center rack in the oven and bake for 45 to 50 minutes, or until medium dark brown and the rounds sound hollow when thumped on the bottom. Remove the loaves from the pans and let cool on a wire rack. The bread keeps for several days covered in plastic wrap.

CHOCOLATE-APRICOT FRUITCAKE

**MAKES TWO 9 X 5¹/₂-INCH LOAVES
OR SIX 5¹/₂ X 2¹/₂-INCH MINI-LOAVES**

We've been making fruitcake at Gayle's since the beginning. Fruitcake is often a maligned dessert, but in 1989 we developed this version, which has proven to be popular. The secrets are using dried apricots and chocolate, along with plenty of rum and brandy, and nothing green or red! We make 450 fruitcakes the day after Thanksgiving and we're sold out by Christmas every year.

BAKER'S BASICS TO REVIEW
Measuring Dry Ingredients, page 21
Creaming, page 20

---

³/₄ cup golden raisins
²/₃ cup currants
1¹/₄ cups coarsely chopped dried apricots
¹/₂ cup Candied Orange Peel (page 111)
1 cup brandy
¹/₄ cup Myers's rum
1¹/₄ cups (10 ounces) butter, at room temperature
1¹/₂ cups firmly packed dark brown sugar
4 large eggs
2¹/₂ cups all-purpose flour
1¹/₂ teaspoons ground mace
1 tablespoon plus 1 teaspoon ground cinnamon
1 teaspoon ground cloves
¹/₂ teaspoon ground ginger
¹/₂ cup strong black coffee
1 cup walnuts, coarsely chopped
¹/₂ pound bittersweet chocolate

The day before you plan to bake the fruitcakes, combine the raisins, currants, apricots, orange peel, ¹/₂ cup of the brandy, and the rum in a small bowl. Stir, cover, and let soak overnight, stirring occasionally.

When you are ready to bake the fruitcakes, preheat the oven to 300°. Butter two 9 x 5¹/₂-inch loaf pans or six 5¹/₂ x 2¹/₂-inch mini-loaf pans.

In the bowl of a tabletop mixer, cream the butter and sugar. Add the eggs, one at a time, waiting until each is incorporated before adding the next.

In a separate bowl, combine the flour and spices. Add the flour mixture to the batter in two additions, blending well after each addition. Fold in the fruit and liquor. Add the coffee and mix thoroughly. Add the walnuts and chocolate and mix until incorporated.

Pour the batter into the prepared loaf pans. Place the pans on the center rack in the oven and bake 50 minutes for large loaves or 35 minutes for small ones. The cakes should be just set up; a toothpick inserted in the center will come out with a few crumbs on it. (Do not overbake this cake—there's nothing worse than a dry fruitcake.)

Let the fruitcakes cool in their pans on a wire rack. When almost cool, depan and brush them with the remaining $^1/_2$ cup brandy. Double wrap the loaves in plastic wrap and store until ready to serve. These cakes may be eaten at this time or left to mature.

GAYLE'S BUTTERFLAKE ROLLS

MAKES 12 ROLLS

For year's, Gayle's bread bakers have been trying to come up with a recipe that could be reproduced in a large batch size that would still achieve the flavor of the handmade Parker House rolls we made for Thanksgiving back in the '80s. Not until last year, when bread department head Chris Rominger came up with the following recipe, have we been able to offer a light, buttery roll that could easily be made several thousand at a time. This is a great recipe, whether you're making 12 or 1,200.

BAKER'S BASICS TO REVIEW
Measuring Dry Ingredients, page 21
Separating Eggs, page 22
Doing the Roll-In and Turns, page 34

DOUGH
$^1/_2$ cup warm water
2 packages ($^1/_2$ ounce) active dry yeast
$3^1/_2$ cups all-purpose flour
3 tablespoons sugar
1 teaspoon salt
$^1/_2$ cup milk
$^1/_4$ cup (2 ounces) butter, at room temperature
1 large egg yolk

———

6 tablespoons (3 ounces) butter, at room temperature
$^1/_2$ teaspoon salt

Place the warm water in a small bowl. Sprinkle the yeast on top and mix. Let stand until creamy, about 5 minutes.

Place the flour, sugar, and salt in a medium bowl. Make a small well in the center of the flour. Place the milk, butter, and egg yolk in the well. With a wooden spoon, mix all of the ingredients together until well combined. Place the dough on a lightly floured work surface and knead 3 to 5 minutes, or until all dry spots have disappeared and the dough is smooth and satiny. Flatten dough, transfer to a baking sheet, cover with plastic wrap, and refrigerate for 2 to 3 hours.

Roll out the dough on the lightly floured work surface until it measures 15 x 10 inches. Spread the softened butter over two-thirds of the dough. Sprinkle the salt over the butter. Fold the uncoated piece of dough toward the middle over one-third of the butter-coated dough. Fold the remaining one-third butter-coated dough over the two folded thirds, so that you have 3 layers of dough, 2 of which are butter coated. Pinch the ends to seal the dough.

With one of the folded edges on your right, roll the dough out vertically to measure 15 x 8 inches. Fold the top third of the dough over the middle third and the bottom third over the two folded sections. Rotate the dough one-quarter turn to the right, so that the long seam side is on the right. Repeat the rolling out and three-fold turns twice more. The dough will measure 8 x 5^1/$_4$ inches and will be 1^1/$_2$ inches thick. Place the dough on a baking sheet, cover with plastic wrap, and freeze for at least 1 hour or overnight.

Remove the dough from the freezer and cut it lengthwise into 3 strips, each measuring 1^3/$_4$ inches. Cut each strip into 2-inch pieces. Stand the pieces with the 2-inch sides upright, in a 12-cup nonstick muffin pan (if pan is not nonstick, coat with butter).

Let the rolls rise for 2^1/$_2$ hours, or until they almost fill the mold and begin to fan out. (Dough that has been frozen for 8 hours or overnight may take 3^1/$_2$ hours or more for the final rise.) After the dough has been rising for 2 hours, preheat the oven to 375°.

Place the muffin pan on the center rack in the oven. Bake the rolls for 17 to 20 minutes, or until golden brown. Let the rolls cool in the pan.

BÛCHE DE NOËL (YULE LOG)

Bûche de Noël is a traditional French Christmas cake that symbolizes the Yule log that's often burned in fireplaces on Christmas Eve. This festive cake will delight young and old and is the perfect way to finish a holiday meal.

The rustic appearance of the log is created with a pastry bag, and impressive results are possible even if you haven't had much practice icing cakes. The Bûche de Noël recipe looks a bit complicated, but it is easily assembled a little bit at a time over as long as 2 weeks, which makes it possible to find the time in a busy holiday schedule to make this beautiful dessert. However, holiday orders don't allow us this luxury at the bakery. Two days before Christmas, our cake room is a flurry of activity. In addition to everything else being produced during that crazy time, we make about 200 Bûche de Noël. This requires a special shift of cake decorators working late into the night. Nieces, nephews, sisters, and brothers have often been enlisted to help with the finishing touches.

Because of its unusual size, this cake requires a 14 x 10-inch flat serving platter or a quarter sheet cake cardboard covered in foil. When using a cake cardboard, we like to wrap it in gold foil, which is available from a florist, but regular aluminum foil works just fine.

BAKER'S BASICS TO REVIEW

Assembling, Soaking, Filling, and Icing Cakes, page 192

Filling and Using a Nylon Pastry Bag, page 20

Making and Filling a Paper Pastry Bag, page 208

Piping Borders and Other Decorations, page 215

CAKE

1 recipe Chocolate Ganache, made 1 day in advance (page 262)

1 Vanilla Genoise Sheet Cake (page 197)

$1/2$ recipe (6 tablespoons) Soaking Solution (page 257)

2 cups prepared whipped cream (page 258)

$1/3$ recipe (about 2 cups) Buttercream (page 259)

$1/3$ cup Nutella hazelnut spread

DECORATIONS

Red food color

6 to 7 Meringue Mushrooms (page 310)

9 small holly leaves or pine sprigs

3 small pine cones (optional)

Confectioners' sugar

Set aside ¹/₄ cup of the ganache for the mushrooms. Lightly flour an area on the work surface about the same size as the cake. Invert the cooled cake onto the floured area. Gently peel off the parchment or waxed paper, then flip the cake over so the top is up. Dust off any excess flour from the top of the cake. Position the cake so that the long side is parallel to the edge of the work surface.

Brush the cake with the Soaking Solution and let rest for about 1 minute. Then, using a metal icing spatula, spread 1 cup of the ganache on the cake. (The layer of ganache will be fairly thin.)

Spread the whipped cream evenly over the ganache. Roll the cake into a log by lifting the edge closest to you with your fingers and tucking it under while rolling it, gently pushing the cake away from you with your palms. (Don't worry if the cake cracks a little.) Finish the roll with the seam down in the middle underneath the roll.

At this point, the log may be well wrapped and refrigerated overnight or frozen for up to 2 weeks. To wrap, lay a 30-inch length of plastic wrap parallel to the log. Gently lift the log up, supporting the bottom with your palm, and place it, seam down, on the plastic wrap. Some of the filling may spill out on the work surface. Wrap the log well with plastic wrap and seal the ends securely.

To complete the log, place it parallel to the edge of the work surface. (If the log has been frozen, it is not necessary to thaw it before proceeding.) To create the knots, trim ¹/₂ inch off both ends and discard (or eat!), then make angled cuts on the ends, starting with the right side. Starting ¹/₂ inch from the top right edge, cut with the knife blade slanted toward the middle of the log, completing the slice 1¹/₄ inches from the bottom right edge. Set the slice on the work surface to the right of the log; this piece will become the top knot on the log. Repeat on the left side, starting 1¹/₄ inches from the top left and cutting down to ¹/₂ inch from the bottom left edge. This piece will become the front knot.

To ice the log, place it on a serving platter or foil-covered cake cardboard. Set aside ¹/₄ cup of buttercream for the holly berry decorations. Using a whisk, blend the Nutella and ¹/₄ cup of the ganache into the remaining buttercream until smooth.

Fit a pastry bag with a #1 or #2 star tip. Check the ganache to be sure it is about the same consistency as the buttercream. If it is too stiff, reheat it gently over warm water. To simulate the mottled look of tree bark, fill the pastry bag with ganache and the buttercream mixture by using the icing spatula to spread a stripe of ganache about 1¹/₂ inches wide and ¹/₄ inch thick around the inside of the bag. Once the bag is striped with ganache, fill the bag with the buttercream mixture. Each time it is necessary to refill the bag, remember to first stripe the inside with ganache.

Starting at the bottom of the log, pipe rows of icing on top of each other until you reach the top of the log. Rotate the log and repeat until both sides are covered. Don't worry that the amount of ganache is different in each row; it should look rustic and natural. To ice the ends, start in the center and pipe a continuous spiral out to the edge.

Check to make sure no cake is exposed and pipe on additional icing to fill in any holes. Turn the cake so the overhanging edge is on the top right. Center the knot cut from the right side of the log angled side down with the widest side facing toward the front on top of the log about 2 inches from the right end.

Place the knot cut from the left side wide side down at the base of the log about 2 inches from the left end on the platter or cardboard with the angled side facing out. The knot should rest snugly against the log.

Ice the edge of the knot on the top of the log by starting at the base and piping 2 to 3 rows of icing on top of each other until you reach the top edge. Cover the top of the knot by starting at the center and spiraling out to the edge. Ice the second knot by starting at the bottom where it meets the log and piping 2 to 3 rows of icing over the arch to cover the cake. Cover the front of the knot by starting in the center and spiraling out to the edge. Wipe off any icing that has dropped onto the platter or cake cardboard. At this point, you can finish decorating the Bûche de Noël and serve it or refrigerate it overnight (uncovered), complete the decorating the next day, and serve it then.

To decorate the cake, tint the remaining ¹/₄ cup of buttercream bright red with the food coloring. Place the buttercream in a paper pastry bag and cut about ¹/₈ inch off the tip. Set aside.

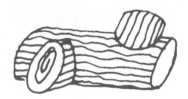

THE RECIPES

Place 2 Meringue Mushrooms on the front of the cake so they appear to be growing where the left knot meets the log. Repeat on the right knot, placing the mushrooms to the left of the top knot and leaning them against the knot for stability. Place a grouping of 2 to 3 mushrooms near the back of the cake.

About 4 inches to the right of the mushrooms on the front of the cake, press 3 of the holly leaves or pine sprigs into the icing. Pipe three $^1/_4$-inch red dots in the center of the greenery to resemble holly berries. **(Never use real holly berries, which are poisonous.)** Place another grouping of leaves and berries to the right of the top knot and at the back of the cake. Press the pine cones into the icing near the greenery.

Dust the Bûche de Noël and platter or cake cardboard with confectioners' sugar to simulate snow. Refrigerate the cake, uncovered, until 1 to 2 hours before serving, then remove from the refrigerator and let soften at room temperature.

MERINGUE MUSHROOMS

This recipe makes more than enough mushrooms for the Bûche de Noël (page 306). Select the nicest ones for the cake, then give away the rest in holiday cookie tins.

BAKER'S BASICS TO REVIEW
Separating Eggs, page 22
Whipping Egg Whites and Making Meringues, page 198
Filling and Using a Nylon Pastry Bag, page 20
Making and Filling a Paper Pastry Bag, page 208

—————

3 large egg whites
3/4 cup sugar
1/4 teaspoon cream of tartar
Unsweetened cocoa
1/4 cup Chocolate Ganache (reserved from the Bûche de Noël)

Preheat the oven to 200°. Line two baking sheets with parchment paper. Fit a nylon pastry bag with a #5 or #6 plain tip or make a paper pastry bag. Set aside.

Using a whisk, combine the egg whites, sugar, and cream of tartar in the bowl of a tabletop mixer. Bring 1 inch of water to a gentle simmer in the bottom on a double boiler. Place the bowl over the simmering water. Stir the mixture continuously with the whisk until it is just warm to the touch.

Place the bowl on the mixer fitted with the whip attachment and whip at high speed until the meringue holds soft peaks, about 2 minutes. The meringue should be smooth and glossy, not chunky. Fill the pastry bag with the meringue. If using a paper bag, fill it with meringue, then cut a 1/2-inch opening at the end.

Holding the bag perpendicular to the tray, use half the meringue to pipe the mushroom stems, lifting up and releasing pressure when each stem is 1 1/2 inches tall. The stems should be about 1/2 inch at the base and taper to a small point at the tip

To pipe the mushroom caps, again hold the bag perpendicular to the tray and make 1 1/2-inch-wide domed caps. While piping, lift the bag slightly so that the center of the cap is about 1/2 to 3/4 inch tall. If the caps are pointy instead of smooth, wet your finger with cold water and gently press the tips. The sizes and shapes should be inconsistent; it makes the mushrooms look more natural. Sift a fine sprinkling of the cocoa over the caps.

Place the baking sheet on the center rack in the oven and bake for 2 hours or until completely dry. Test for dryness by breaking 1 cap in half. Let cool completely on the baking sheet on a wire rack. Mushroom pieces may be stored at room temperature in an airtight container for up to 2 weeks.

To assemble the mushrooms, be sure the ganache is the consistency of soft butter. If it is not, gently reheat it in the top of a double boiler over warm water. Using the point of a paring knife, hollow out a 1/4-inch-deep hole on the underside of each cap. Spread the underside of one cap with a very thin layer of ganache. Insert the pointed end of a stem into the hole and stand the mushroom on the baking sheet to set. Repeat until all mushrooms are assembled. Assembled mushrooms will keep for 3 days at room temperature in an airtight container.

George Touzet, Pâtisserie Bechard

In the summer of 1995, Joe and I invited Louisa and her husband Brian (who is one of Gayle's best bread bakers and our production manager) to go to Europe to savor some of the inspiration—and food—that has influenced us through the years.

On previous trips to Aix-en-Provence, we would stop to ogle the pastries in the colorful shop window of Pâtisserie Bechard on Cour Mirabeau, the town's main street, which is punctuated by fountains on each end, lined with plane trees, and always overflowing with browsers and students who lounge in cafes or race by on noisy Vespas. There were times when we would buy five or six pastries and stand right on the street stuffing them into our mouths. There were also the times we cruised through for a more modest fix while on antique-hunting trips. Our trips there were always, as I like to say, in the name of research, but one year, our friends the Costas, who own a bread bakery in Aix-en-Provence, were kind enough to introduce us to the owner, so we could really study the operation.

If there were ever a pastry shop that looked like Christmas, Pâtisserie Bechard was it. I'll never forget how Louisa's eyes lit up when she first saw the window display of jewel-like pastries. Fortunately, it is one of the few pâtisseries where the pastries taste as good as they look. Inside, the shop is lined with glass cases that literally hold hundreds of colorfully decorated pastries in every imaginable size and shape: there are *friantines,* sweet fan-shaped puff pastry sandwiches filled with whipped cream or raspberry jam; music box–shaped cakes decorated with pink marzipan roses and chartreuse leaves; upside-down tarts topped with perfectly fanned slices of fresh apples; small lemon custard cakes, encircled by lady fingers, tied with a red ribbon, decorated with paper-thin chocolate fans, and dusted with confectioners' sugar; a rich clafouti made with pears arranged in a star pattern surrounded with the caramelized cream filling; and miniature nougat cones filled with mocha buttercream and sprinkled with shaved chocolate.

After exchanging a few pleasantries—some

(continued)

in French and some in English—Monsieur Touzet, Pâtisserie Bechard's owner, he led us down to the basement to watch the bakers at work. As we've seen in scores of bakeries throughout Europe, pastry makers in sparkling chefs' whites worked at benches assembling assorted pastries. Such visits usually begin with a brief tour, but instead Touzet left us with the baker who makes the *calissons,* small, leaf-shaped marzipan cookies coated with various pastel-colored icings. The petite cookies are the region's specialty and a product the bakery sells throughout the world. The baker, a short, bespectacled man who chattered as fast as he worked, explained every step of the process: first he mixed the marzipan in a special mixer, then he placed small wafers in the bottom of each leaf-shaped mold, scraped the marzipan into the molds with a large stainless-steel spatula, and pushed them from below with another tool until they popped out like regimented soldiers. Then, with long tongs, he dipped them in the pastel icing.

Next, M. Touzet asked one of the pastry chefs to pull several prepared cakes out of a special refrigerator. He sliced small pieces off the edges and started tasting them, inviting us to do the same. The pastries were filled with many layers of pastry cream, fruit, and cake. Each was delicious in its own way. One of the more fascinating ones, and a shop specialty, was made with pistachio buttercream and topped with a pistachio brittle.

Our next stop was the ice cream room, where we saw two bakers cranking out ice cream sculptures shaped like baskets of bouquets. The sculptures were made with assorted scoops of sorbet and *glace Francaise* (French ice cream) separated by meringues, fruits, and dots of whipped cream and scattered with blueberries, cherries, and miniature strawberries.

At the end of our visit, Monsieur Touzet invited us back to do an *étage* (a structured study session), saying we could stay for a couple of weeks. Louisa and I looked at each other and I could tell that Joe immediately knew what I had in mind—studying pastries in the early mornings and shopping for antiques in the afternoons.

VANILLA SHORTBREAD

MAKES ABOUT FORTY 2-INCH COOKIES

We use this shortbread dough for all our holiday cut-out cookies. It simplifies holiday cookie baking because it's easily colored, it keeps well in the refrigerator, it's sturdy enough to be dipped, and, best of all, it's delicious. Although we call it Vanilla Shortbread, it has a subtle almond flavor that adds richness. By adding food coloring to the dough or dipping baked cookies in Fondant Icing (page 314), you can make red valentine hearts, green shamrocks, yellow chicks, pink bunnies, purple dinosaurs, orange pumpkins, black bats, red- and yellow-tailed turkeys, and green Christmas trees.

Separating Eggs, page 22
Measuring Dry Ingredients, page 21
Creaming, page 20

------

¹/₂ cup (4 ounces) almond paste
4 large eggs yolks
2 cups (1 pound) butter
1³/₄ cups sugar
1 to 2 teaspoons liquid or paste food color (optional)
3¹/₂ cups all-purpose flour
1 recipe Fondant Icing (page 314; optional)

In the bowl of a tabletop mixer fitted with the flat beater, beat the almond paste on medium speed for about 5 minutes. The almond paste will look slightly grainy and oily. With the mixer off, add 1 of the egg yolks. Mix on medium speed for 1 minute, then scrape down the bowl and beater. Add another yolk, increase the speed to medium-high, and mix another minute. Repeat, adding the remaining 2 yolks, one at a time, beating well and scraping down the bowl beater before adding the second yolk. Increase the speed to high and continue to mix and scrape down the bowl and beater until the mixture is completely smooth and creamy, about 1 minute.

In a separate bowl, using the flat beater, cream the butter on medium speed for 1 minute. Add the sugar and beat on medium-high for 2 to 3 minutes, scraping the bowl and beater once.

Add the almond paste mixture to the butter mixture and beat on medium speed for 1 to 2 minutes, or until well blended, scraping the bowl twice. With the mixer running on low speed, add the food coloring 1 teaspoon at a time until the desired color is achieved. (Remember that the color will become slightly lighter when the flour is added.)

With the mixer off, add the flour. Slowly turn the mixer on and off on low speed to incorporate the flour without spilling. Once all the flour is incorporated, mix on slow speed just until blended, about 1 minute. Scrape the bowl and beater, then mix for another 10 seconds. Do not overmix.

Turn the dough out onto plastic wrap. Pat the dough into a disc about ¹/₂ inch thick and seal well in the plastic wrap. Refrigerate overnight. (The dough will keep, well wrapped, in the refrigerator for up to 1 month.)

The next day, remove the dough from the refrigerator and let it sit at room temperature for about 45 minutes. The dough should still be slightly cool, not warm or soft. Meanwhile, preheat the oven to 375°.

On a lightly floured surface, roll the dough out to ³/₈ to ¹/₂ inch thick. Cut out cookies and place about 1 inch apart on an unbuttered, unlined baking sheet. Bake on the center rack in the oven for 10 minutes, or until the cookies start to brown slightly around the edges and the bottoms are light golden. Transfer cookies to a wire rack to cool. When completely cool, dip the cookies in the icing. To dip cookies, hold each one face down and press into icing until it comes one-quarter of the way up the sides. Scrape off the excess icing on the side of the bowl as you lift the cookies out of the icing. Turn the cookies icing side up and, holding your other index finger at a 45-degree angle to the cookie, scrape off any excess icing that remains. (Holding your finger at an angle allows you to scrape off the icing just in from the outside edge, giving the icing room to spread as it sets. Let the cookies rest until the icing is set, about 1 hour. Store undipped cookies in an airtight container for 3 days. Store dipped cookies in a single layer in an airtight container. Do not stack dipped cookies.

FONDANT ICING

MAKES 3¹/₃ CUPS
(ENOUGH TO DIP FORTY 2-INCH COOKIES)

1¹/₂ cups light corn syrup
5 cups sifted confectioners' sugar
1 large egg white, at room temperature
1 tablespoon butter, melted
¹/₃ cup warm water
Food coloring

Place the corn syrup in the top of a double boiler. Using a wooden spoon, stir in the confectioners' sugar to make a thick paste. (There may be a little undissolved confectioners' sugar on the side of the bowl.) Over barely simmering water, stir the mixture frequently until it is smooth and just lukewarm.

Turn off the heat. Beat in the egg white, then the melted butter, and then the water. The icing should be the consistency of unwhipped cream. If it is thicker than that, thin with warm water. Stir in 1 to 2 drops of food coloring to tint the icing the desired color. Use immediately or cover with plastic wrap and store overnight at room temperature. Thin with more warm water as needed before using. When icing cookies, stir the icing frequently to prevent a crust from forming.

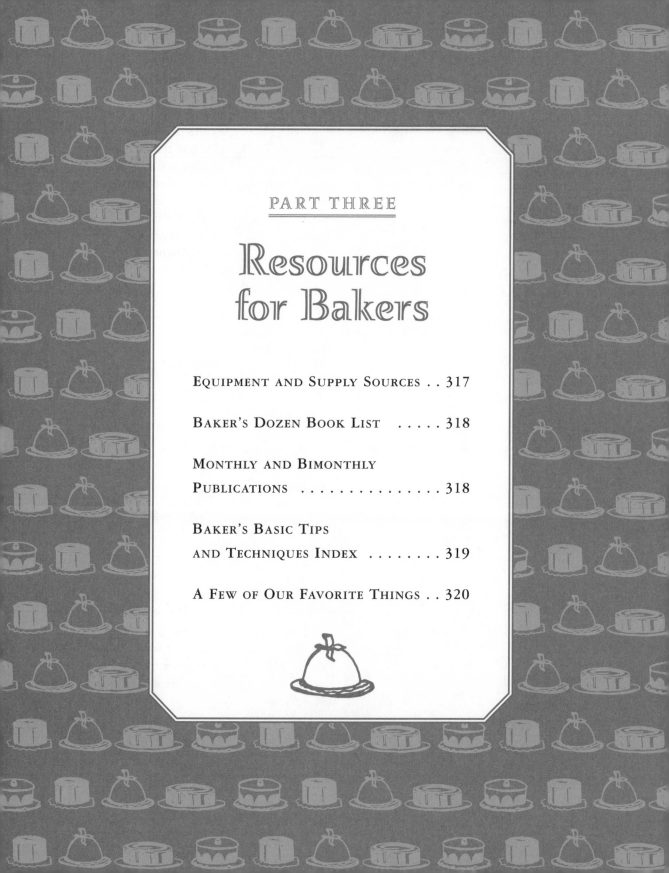

PART THREE

Resources for Bakers

Like other craftspeople, bakers amass a collection of resources and knowledge—our tools, so to speak—that we use on a daily basis. It takes a lot of experimentation and experience to figure out what goes in the toolbox, so we're delighted to share what we've found.

Throughout this book, you'll find the insights of various professional bakers whose tips and ideas are invaluable tools. The actual equipment and ingredients we use are outlined in Part One (pages 7–17), and in every chapter we've included instructional essays explaining what we think are the best ways to perform basic baking steps, such as how to roll in butter and make a lattice crust. (For your reference, in this section you'll find a list of all these techniques and the pages they appear on.) In addition to these resources, we've come to rely on a collection of publications and retailers. Each of the books we list takes a slightly different approach to baking and has special value for home bakers. We use all of these resources in our home kitchens as well as at the bakery—we wouldn't think of baking without them and recommend that you don't either.

EQUIPMENT AND SUPPLY SOURCES

King Arthur Flour
The Baker's Catalogue
P.O. Box 876
Norwich, VT 05055-0876
(800) 827-6836

This catalog is the best thing that ever happened to the home baker. We order out of it all the time for home and professional use. It has everything from baking equipment to ingredients. They also have an advice hotline for bakers: (802) 649-371. Hours of operation are 9 to 5 (eastern time), Monday through Friday.

Sur la Table
(800) 243-0852

You'll find top-of-the-line baking equipment at Sur la Table's two stores, which are at 84 Pine Street in Seattle, 77 Maiden Lane in San Francisco, and 1806 4th Street in Berkeley, California. Their wares are also available through their catalog.

Williams-Sonoma
(800) 541-2233

This company sells fine baking equipment and supplies. Call for their list of stores and a catalog.

Maid of Scandinavia
3244 Raleigh Ave.
Minneapolis, MN 55416
(800) 328-6722

This company offers an especially good selection of cake decorating supplies, all available through their catalog.

Nellie and Joe's
(800) LIME-PIE

Call to find a retailer in your area that stocks their Famous Key Lime Juice, which we use in our Key lime pies (page 116).

Parrish's Cake Decorating Supplies, Inc.
225 West 146th St.
Gardena, CA 90248
(800) 736-8443

Another source for all types of decorating supplies and equipment, all offered through their catalog.

BAKER'S DOZEN BOOK LIST

1. *The Art of Fine Baking,* by Paula Peck. (Simon and Schuster, 1961)

2. *Chez Panisse Desserts,* by Lindsey R. Shere. (Random House, 1985)

3. *Cucina Simpatica: Robust Trattoria Cooking from Al Forno,* by Johanne Killeen and George Germon. (HarperCollins, 1991)

4. *Baking with Jim Dodge: Simple & Tempting Delights from the American Baker,* by Jim Dodge with Elaine Ratner. (Simon and Schuster, 1991)

5. *Baking with Julia: Sift, Knead, Flute, Flour & Savor the Joys of Baking with America's Best Bakers,* by Dorie Greenspan. (William Morrow, 1996)

6. *Death by Chocolate: The Last Word on a Consuming Passion,* by Marcel Desaulniers. (Rizzoli, 1993)

7. *The Fannie Farmer Baking Book,* by Marion Cunningham. (Knopf, 1984)

8. *The French Cookie Book: Classic and Contemporary Recipes for Easy & Elegant Cookies,* by Bruce Healy and Paul Bugat. (William Morrow, 1994)

9. *How to Bake: The Complete Guide to Perfect Cakes, Cookies, Pies, Tarts, Muffins, Sweet and Savory,* by Nick Malgieri. (HarperCollins, 1995)

10. *Joy of Cooking,* by Irma S. Rombauer and Marion R. Becker. (New American Library, 1973)

11. *Martha Stewart's Pies & Tarts,* by Martha Stewart. (Clarkson N. Potter, 1985)

12. *The Simple Art of Perfect Baking,* by Flo Braker. (Chapters Publishing Ltd., 1992)

13. *Stars' Desserts,* by Emily Luchetti. (HarperCollins, 1991)

MONTHLY AND BIMONTHLY PUBLICATIONS

"The Baking Sheet" is a bimonthly newsletter published by King Arthur Flour. Call (800) 827-6836 for subscription details.

"Baking with the American Harvest" is a quarterly newsletter edited and published by Cindy Mushet. Write the newsletter at 626 Santa Monica Blvd., #526, Santa Monica, CA 90401 for subscription information.

Cooks Illustrated is a bimonthly magazine, that features detailed articles on cooking and baking techniques; it's required reading for serious cooks. Write the magazine at Box 7446, Red Oak, IA 51591-2446 for subscription information.

BAKER'S BASIC
TIPS AND TECHNIQUES INDEX

A FEW OF OUR FAVORITE THINGS

(PLEASE REFER TO THE INDEX FOR PAGE NUMBERS)

Baker's Dozen Best Goodies for Picnics and Hikes

1. Lemon Lust
2. Chocolate Chip Cookies
3. Healthy Lowfat Bran Bars
4. Raspberry-Walnut Brownies
5. Garlic-Cheese Pretzels
6. Pecan Tassies
7. Ham and Cheese Croissants
8. Parmesan Cheese Sticks
9. Jalapeño-Corn Muffins
10. Lemon Bread
11. Ginger-Molasses Cookies
12. Orange Chiffon Cake
13. Fresh Fruit Tartlets

Baker's Dozen Favorites from Gayle's Staff

1. Fresh Berry Genoise
2. Pumpkin Cheesecake
3. Florentines
4. Tiramisu
5. Napoleons
6. Chocolate Éclairs
7. Christopher's Buns
8. Opera Cake
9. Downtowners
10. Clafouti
11. Mushroom Turnovers
12. Chocolate Mousse Cake
13. Princess Cake

Baker's Dozen Best Treats for Kids' Parties

1. Carrot Cake with Cream Cheese Icing
2. Spritz Cookies
3. Princess Cake
4. Vanilla Shortbread
5. Bear Claws
6. Gayle's Croissants
7. Fresh Berry Genoise
8. German Chocolate Cake
9. Raspberry-Walnut Brownies
10. Chocolate Chip Cookies
11. Carrot Cupcakes
12. Christopher's Buns
13. Bread Pudding

Gayle's Baker's Dozen Best-Selling Sweets

1. Raspberry–Poppy Seed Cake
2. Princess Cake
3. All of our cookies
4. Crocodile
5. Chocolate Éclairs
6. Chocolate Mousse Cake
7. Tiramisu
8. Pecan Tassies
9. Fresh Fruit Tartlets
10. Napoleons
11. Florentines
12. Bear Claws
13. Key Lime Pie

Baker's Dozen Best Desserts for Chocoholics

1. Chocolate Macaroons
2. Chocolate Truffle Cake
3. Opera Cake
4. Rich Chocolate Cake
5. Raspberry-Walnut Brownies
6. Rocky Road Brownies
7. Chocolate Éclairs
8. Chocolate Mousse Cake
9. Chocolate Pot de Creme
10. Triple Chocolate Chunk Cookies
11. Florentines
12. Chocolate Soufflé Roll
13. Chocolatines

Gayle's Baker's Dozen Most Decadent Goodies

1. Key Lime Pie
2. Chocolate Truffle Cake
3. Princess Cake
4. Christie's Trifle
5. Raspberry-Walnut Brownies
6. Crocodile
7. Napoleons
8. Chocolate Mousse Cake
9. Rocky Road Brownies
10. Praline Cheesecake
11. Choclate Éclairs
12. Christopher's Buns
13. Raspberry–Poppy Seed Cake

Index

ALSO BY JOE ORTIZ

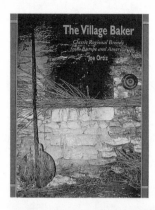

Nominated for a Julia Child award and regarded as the definitive guide to baking classic artisanal breads, *The Village Baker* includes anecdotes, tips, and nearly 100 recipes from the village bakers of France, Italy, Germany, and regional America.

7 3/8 x 9 1/4 inches, 192 pages, 24 color photos, **available in hardcover and paperback**

Another framing-quality, full-color poster showing nearly 20 classic bread shapes and styles from the ovens of Europe's village bakers.
24 x 36 inches

This framing-quality, full-color poster shows more than 25 bread shapes and styles inspired by Europe's village bakers.
24 x 36 inches